QUARRELS THAT HAVE
SHAPED THE CONSTITUTION

JOHN MARSHALL.
Portrait by James Reid Lambdin after 1831 oil by Henry Inman.

REVISED EDITION

QUARRELS THAT HAVE SHAPED THE CONSTITUTION

Edited by
JOHN A. GARRATY

 HarperPerennial
A Division of HarperCollinsPublishers

QUARRELS THAT HAVE SHAPED THE CONSTITUTION *(Revised Edition)*. Copyright © 1987 by
Harper & Row, Publishers, Inc. All rights reserved. Printed in the United States of
America. No part of this book may be used or reproduced in any manner whatsoever
without written permission except in the case of brief quotations embodied in critical
articles and reviews. For information address Harper & Row, Publishers, Inc., 10 East
53rd Street, New York, N.Y. 10022.

First hardcover edition published 1962 by Harper & Row, Publishers.
Harper Torchbooks edition published 1975. Reissued 1988.

Copyeditor: Karen McDermott

Indexer: Auralie Logan

Library of Congress Cataloging-in-Publication Data

Quarrels that have shaped the Constitution.

    "Harper Torchbooks."
    1. United States. Supreme Court—History.
2. United States—Constitutional history.
I. Garraty, John Arthur, 1920–
KF8742.A5Q37   1988   342.73   86-46066
ISBN 0-06-132084-6 (pbk.)   347.302

06 07 08 09 RRD-H 20

Contents

Illustrations

Introduction

"The judicial power of the United States shall be vested in one Supreme Court, and in such inferior courts as the Congress may from time to time ordain and establish." So begins Article III of the United States Constitution. This simple sentence provides the authorization for the entire structure of the federal judiciary. The Supreme Court, unique, prestigious, but controversial, is the crown of the system. Beyond question it is the best-known and most powerful judicial body in the world. Designed chiefly as a court to settle arguments between the states, matters involving foreign ambassadors, and other quarrels beyond the scope of state courts, it has from the time of John Marshall to that of William Rehnquist added to its power by slow accretion, until today its influence affects every aspect of American life. Troops deploy, great corporations dissolve because nine black-robed justices in Washington have discovered new meanings in an old and hallowed document.

The Constitution has endured because of its flexibility. The Founding Fathers knew better than to pin down their descendants too closely. Principles rather than details were what they sought to establish at the Philadelphia Convention in 1787. Even so, anticipating future growth, they provided (Article V) an orderly process for amending the Constitution, and, of course, this process has been put to use on a number of occasions.

In 1791 the ten amendments that make up the Bill of Rights were added, and over the years other changes and additions have been made, such as the Thirteenth Amendment abolishing slavery, the Sixteenth giving Congress the right to levy taxes on incomes, the

1

Nineteenth providing for women's suffrage, and the Twenty-second limiting Presidents to two terms in office.

The amendment process was made complicated and time-consuming in order to discourage ill-considered changes and petty alterations of the nation's fundamental law. To allow for necessary minor adjustments, the Founding Fathers counted upon the Supreme Court, which, they reasoned, could interpret the Constitution and thus clarify doubtful points when important cases came before it.

However, the Fathers really expected the Supreme Court to preserve, rather than to change, the Constitution. For partisan or other reasons, Congress might be tempted to exceed the powers granted it, but the Court, magisterial, conservative, and aloof, could be counted upon to cleave to first principles. Although nowhere does the Constitution state explicitly that the Court has the right to void unconstitutional laws, this power was clearly understood to exist. Alexander Hamilton put it plainly in the 78th *Federalist:*

> The courts were designed to be an intermediate body between the people and the legislature, in order, among other things, to keep the latter within the limits assigned to their authority. . . . Whenever a particular statute contravenes the Constitution, it will be the duty of the judicial tribunals to adhere to the latter and disregard the former.

In practice it has not worked out entirely as the Constitution-makers expected. The Court has many times protected the Constitution against the illegal acts of Congress and the state legislatures, but it has also repeatedly altered the document itself by its decisions. It has modified the fundamental frame of government more extensively in this manner than have all the amendments taken together. The very broadness and generality of the Constitution have permitted—indeed required—that the justices expand, explain, and elaborate upon its terse phraseology. The famous "necessary and proper" clause, the due process of law provision of the Fourteenth Amendment, and many other parts of the Constitution have been time and again explicated in decisions of immense importance. To try to understand the modern Constitution without a knowledge of these judicial landmarks would be like trying to comprehend Christianity without reading the Bible.

The elaboration of the Constitution by judicial interpretation has added to its flexibility and durability, but it has left its evolution partly in the hands of chance. Amendments have always been carefully considered and debated before passage. The nature of the process, requiring, in addition to initial approval by either two-thirds of both houses of Congress or of two-thirds of the states, final ratification by three-quarters of the states, has made this inevitable. Only one amendment, the Eighteenth, prohibiting the manufacture and sale of alcoholic beverages, has ever been repealed, and few of the others have been seriously criticized after ratification by thoughtful students of government.

However, constitutional changes resulting from judicial interpretation have come about in far more casual and unplanned fashion. The Supreme Court can only explain what the Constitution means when specific cases are brought to it for settlement. The Constitution gives Congress the power to "regulate Commerce . . . among the several States," but only when Aaron Ogden sued Thomas Gibbons because he was operating a ferry between New York and New Jersey did Chief Justice John Marshall have the opportunity to declare that this phrase means every kind of "intercourse" and not merely the movement of goods across state lines. Even legislative acts plainly in violation of the Constitution remain in force until some actual suit comes before the courts for decision. If Congress should abolish trial by jury, for example, nothing could be done about it until someone convicted without a jury trial appealed to the judiciary to obtain his rights.

Thus, constitutional questions of tremendous significance often depend upon the actions of individuals unconcerned with large legal issues. In the hypothetical case just mentioned, the person convicted without a jury trial might be a great reformer unjustly persecuted or a tramp convicted of stealing a chicken. Constitutionally, it would not matter.

In the following pages, twenty historians examine the personal conflicts, many of them trivial, that led the Supreme Court to hand down some of its most important decisions. In each instance, attention has been focused on the actual controversies and the people whose antagonisms gave the justices the opportunity to act. The cast of characters in these dramas includes smugglers and black slaves, bankers and butchers, ferryboat captains, rebels, sweated workers, and great tycoons. Yet in every case the authors have also pointed out the significance of the controversy.

William Marbury wanted his commission as a justice of the peace for the District of Columbia, snatched almost literally from his hand by Thomas Jefferson, but by making the effort he established once and for all the right of the Supreme Court to declare acts of Congress unconstitutional. The trustees of Dartmouth College were trying to prevent New Hampshire from turning their college into a state university, but their suit resulted in the Court severely restricting the power of all the states to control corporations. When William McCulloch refused to pay a state tax, he was hoping to save his bank from destruction, but in effect he was broadly expanding the power of the federal government vis-à-vis that of the states. Such trivial arguments begun by people concerned only with their own interests have often resulted in decisions that have shaken the foundations of American society. No doubt this is illogical and perhaps even against the national interest. Nevertheless, it is part of American history, and a particularly absorbing part because its basic elements are conflict, surprise, and human passions.

I wish to thank the authors of the following chapters for their cooperation and understanding in dealing with their subjects from the particular point of view required by the approach outlined above. With minor editing the pieces in this book by John A. Garraty, Richard N. Current, George Dangerfield, C. Peter Magrath, Alan F. Westin, and C. Vann Woodward first appeared in *American Heritage,* The Magazine of History. *Heritage* editors Oliver Jensen and Robert L. Reynolds were especially helpful both in working out the general scheme of this book and in editing some of the chapters. Margaret Butterfield of Harper & Row also made many important editorial suggestions, and my son, John A. Garraty, Jr., provided valuable assistance in preparing the manuscript for publication.

The continuing interpretation of the Constitution by the Court during the years that have passed since this book was published in 1964 and the interest occasioned by the celebration of the 200th anniversary of the Constitution have encouraged me to offer this expanded edition. In addition to a new essay on the Dred Scott case, four cases have been added: these deal with controversies affecting freedom of expression, the rights of persons accused of crimes, minimum wage laws, and the legality of abortion. Some of the earlier essays have been revised by their authors to take into account new data and new views of the significance of the cases discussed.

I wish to thank the staff at American Heritage, particularly James Long, for help in obtaining the illustrations used in this edition.

J. A. G.

Columbia University
May 1986

WILLIAM MARBURY.

The Case of the Missing Commissions

I

BY JOHN A. GARRATY

(*Marbury* v. *Madison*, 1 Cranch 137)

Paradoxically, the first of our controversies and in some respects the most important rose from by far the least significant of causes and the meanest of motives. It is a tale of narrow partisanship, clashing ambitions, and a man seeking the humble office of justice of the peace for the District of Columbia.

It was the evening of March 3, 1801, his last day in office, and President John Adams was in a black and bitter mood. Assailed by his enemies, betrayed by some of his most trusted friends, he and his Federalist party had gone down to defeat the previous November before the forces of Thomas Jefferson. His world seemed to have crumbled about his doughty shoulders.

Conservatives of Adams's persuasion were convinced that Thomas Jefferson was a dangerous radical. He would, they thought, in the name of individual liberty and states' rights import the worst excesses of the French Revolution, undermine the very foundations of American society, and bring the proud edifice of the national government, so laboriously erected under Washington and Adams, tumbling to the ground. Jefferson was a "visionary," Chief Justice Oliver Ellsworth had said. With him as President, "there would be no national energy." Secretary of State John Marshall, an ardent believer in a powerful central government, feared that Jefferson would "sap the fundamental principles of government." Others went so far as to call Jefferson a "howling atheist."

Adams himself was not quite so disturbed as some, but he was deeply troubled. "What course is it we steer?" he had written to an old friend after the election. "To what harbor are we bound?" Now on the morrow Jefferson was to be inaugurated, and Adams was so disgruntled that he was unwilling to remain for the ceremonies, the first to be held in the new capital on the Potomac. At the moment, however, John Adams was still President of the United States, and not about to abandon what he called "all virtuous exertion" in the pursuit of his duty. Sitting at his desk in the damp, drafty, still unfinished sandstone "palace" soon to be known as the White House, he was writing his name on official papers in his large, quavering hand.

The documents he was signing were mostly commissions appointing various staunch Federalists to positions in the national judiciary, but the President did not consider his actions routine. On the contrary: he believed he was saving the Republic itself. Jefferson was to be President and his Democratic Republicans would control Congress, but the courts, thank goodness, would be beyond his control. As soon as the extent of Jefferson's triumph was known, Adams had determined to make the judiciary a stronghold of Federalism. Responding enthusiastically to his request, the lame-duck Congress had established sixteen new circuit judgeships (and a host of marshals, attorneys, and clerks as well). It had also given the President authority to create as many justices of the peace for the new District of Columbia as he saw fit, and—to postpone the evil day when Jefferson would be able to put one of his sympathizers on the Supreme Court—it provided that when the next vacancy occurred it should not be filled, thus reducing the Court from six justices to five.[1]

In this same period between the election and Jefferson's inauguration, Chief Justice Ellsworth, who was old and feeble, had resigned, and Adams had replaced him with Secretary of State Marshall. John Marshall was primarily a soldier and politician; he knew relatively little of the law. But he had a powerful mind, and, as Adams reflected, his "reading of the science" was "fresh in his head." He was also but forty-five years of age, and vigorous. A more forceful opponent of Jeffersonian principles would have been hard to find.

Marshall had been confirmed by the Senate on January 27, and

[1]The Constitution says nothing about the number of justices on the Court; its size is left to Congress. Originally six, the membership was enlarged to seven in 1807, and to nine in 1837. Briefly during the Civil War the bench held ten; the number was set at seven again in 1867 and in 1869 returned to nine, where it has remained.

without resigning as secretary of state he had begun at once to help Adams strengthen the judicial branch of the government. Perforce they had worked rapidly, for time was short. The new courts were authorized by Congress on February 13; within two weeks Adams had submitted a full slate of officials for confirmation by the Senate. The new justices of the peace for the District of Columbia were authorized on February 27; within three days Adams had submitted for confirmation the names of no less than forty-two justices for that sparsely populated region. The Federalist Senate had done its part nobly too, pushing through the necessary confirmations with dispatch. Now, in the lamplight of his last night in Washington, John Adams was affixing his signature to the commissions appointing these "midnight justices" to office.

Working with his customary diligence, Adams completed his work by nine o'clock, and went off to bed for the last time as President of the United States, presumably with a clear conscience. The papers were carried to the State Department, where Secretary Marshall was to affix to each the Great Seal of the United States and see to it that the documents were then dispatched to the new appointees. But Marshall, a Virginian with something of the easygoing carelessness about detail that is said to be characteristic of Southerners, failed to complete this routine task. All the important new circuit judgeships were taken care of, and most of the other appointments as well. But in the bustle of last-minute arrangements, the commissions of the new District of Columbia justices of the peace went astray. As a result of this slipup, and entirely without anyone's having planned it, a fundamental principle of the Constitution—affecting the lives of countless millions of future Americans—was to be forever established. Because *Secretary of State* Marshall made his last mistake, *Chief Justice* Marshall was soon to make the first—and in some respects the greatest—of his decisions.

It is still not entirely clear what happened to the missing commissions on the night of March 3. To help with the rush of work, Adams had borrowed two State Department clerks, Jacob Wagner and Daniel Brent. Among his other tasks that fateful night, Brent prepared a list of the forty-two new justices and gave it to another clerk, who "filled up" the appropriate blank commissions. As fast as batches of these were made ready, Brent took them to Adams's office, where he turned them over to William Smith Shaw, the President's private secretary. After Adams had signed them, Brent brought them back to the State Department, where Marshall was supposed to attach the Great Seal. Evidently Marshall did seal these documents, but he did not trouble to make sure that they were delivered to the appointees. As he later said: "I did not send out the commissions because I apprehended such . . . to be completed when signed & sealed." He admitted that he would have sent them out in any case "but for the extreme hurry of the time & the absence of Mr. Wagner who had been called on by the President to act as his private secretary."

March 4 dawned and Jefferson, who does not seem to have digested the significance of Adams's partisan appointments at this time, prepared to take the oath of office and deliver his brilliant inaugural address. His mood, as the speech indicated, was friendly and conciliatory. He even asked Chief Justice Marshall, who administered the inaugural oath, to stay on briefly as secretary of state while the new administration was getting established.

That morning it would still have been possible to deliver the commissions. As a matter of fact, a few actually were delivered, although quite by chance. Marshall's brother James (whom Adams had just made circuit judge for the District of Columbia) was disturbed by rumors that there was going to be a riot in Alexandria in connection with the inaugural festivities. Feeling the need of some justices of the peace in case trouble developed, he went to the State Department and picked up a batch of the commissions. He signed a receipt for them, but "finding that he could not conveniently carry the whole," he returned several, crossing out the names of these from the receipt. Among the ones returned were those appointing William Harper and Robert Townshend Hooe. By failing to deliver these commissions, Judge James M. Marshall unknowingly enabled Harper and Hooe, obscure men, to win for themselves a small claim to legal immortality.

The new President was eager to mollify the Federalists, but when he realized the extent to which they had packed the judiciary with his "most ardent political enemies," he was indignant. Adams's behavior, he said at the time, was an "outrage on decency," and some years later, when passions had cooled a little, he wrote sorrowfully: "I can say with truth that one act of Mr. Adams' life, and only one, ever gave me a moment's personal displeasure. I did consider his last appointments to office as personally unkind." When he discovered the J.P. commissions in the State Department, he decided at once not to allow them to be delivered.

James Madison, the new secretary of state, was not yet in Washington. So Jefferson called in his attorney general, a Massachusetts lawyer named Levi Lincoln, whom he had designated acting secretary. Giving Lincoln a new list of justices of the peace, he told him to put them "into a general commission" and notify the men of their selection.

In truth, Jefferson acted with remarkable forbearance. He reduced the number of justices to thirty, fifteen each for Washington and Alexandria counties. But only seven of his appointees were new men; the rest he chose from among the forty-two names originally submitted by Adams. (One of Jefferson's choices was Thomas Corcoran, father of W. W. Corcoran, the banker and philanthropist who founded the Corcoran Gallery of Art.) Lincoln prepared the general commissions, one for each county, and notified the appointees. Then, almost certainly, he destroyed the original commissions signed by Adams.

For some time thereafter Jefferson did very little about the way Adams had packed the judiciary. Indeed, despite his famous remark that officeholders seldom die and never resign, he dismissed relatively few persons from the government service. For example, the State Department clerks, Wagner and Brent, were permitted to keep their jobs. The new President learned quickly how hard it was to institute basic changes in a going organization. "The great machine of society" could not easily be moved, he admitted, adding that it was impossible "to advance the notions of a whole people suddenly to ideal right." Soon some of his more impatient supporters, like John Randolph of Roanoke, were grumbling about the President's moderation.

But Jefferson was merely biding his time. Within a month of the inauguration he conferred with Madison at Monticello and made the basic decision to try to abolish the new system of circuit courts. Aside from removing the newly appointed marshals and attorneys, who served at the pleasure of the chief executive, little could be done until the new Congress met in December. Then, however, he struck. In his annual message he urged the "contemplation" by Congress of the Judiciary Act of 1801. To direct the lawmakers' thinking, he submitted a statistical report showing how few cases the federal courts had been called upon to deal with since 1789. In January, 1802, a repeal bill was introduced; after long debate it passed early in March, thus abolishing the jobs of the new circuit judges.

Some of the deposed jurists petitioned Congress for "relief," but their plea was coldly rejected. Since these men had been appointed for life, the Federalists claimed that the Repeal Act was unconstitutional, but to prevent the Supreme Court from quickly so declaring, Congress passed another bill abolishing the June term of the Court and setting the second Monday of February, 1803, for its next session. By that time, the Jeffersonians reasoned, the old system would be dead beyond resurrection.

This assault on the courts thoroughly alarmed the conservative Federalists; to them the foundations of stable government seemed threatened if the "independence" of the judiciary could be thus destroyed. No one was more disturbed than the new chief justice, John Marshall, nor was anyone better equipped by temperament and intellect to resist it. Headstrong but shrewd, contemptuous of detail and of abstractions but a powerful logician, he detested Jefferson, to whom he was distantly related, and the President fully returned his dislike.

In the developing conflict Marshall operated at a disadvantage that a modern chief justice would not have to face. The Supreme Court had none of the prestige and little of the accepted authority it now possesses. Few cases had come before it, and none of much importance. A prominent newspaper of the day referred to the chief justiceship, with considerable truth, as a "sinecure." Before appointing Marshall, Adams had offered the chief justiceship to John Jay, the first man to hold the post. Jay had resigned from the Court in 1795 to become governor of New York. He refused reappointment, saying the Court lacked "energy, weight, and dignity." One of the reasons Marshall had accepted the post was his belief that it would afford him ample leisure for writing the biography of his hero, George Washington. Indeed, in the grandiose plans for the new capital, no thought had been given to housing the Supreme Court, so that when Marshall took office in 1801 the judges had to meet in the office of the clerk of the Senate, a small room on the first floor of what is now the North Wing of the Capitol.

Nevertheless, Marshall struck out at every opportunity against the power and authority of the new President. But the opportunities were few. In one case, he refused to allow a presidential message to be read into the record on the ground that this would bring the President into the Court in violation of the principle of separation of powers. In another, he ruled that Jefferson's action in a ship seizure case was illegal. But these were matters of small importance. When he tried to move more boldly, his colleagues would not sustain him. He was ready to declare the Judicial Repeal Act unconstitutional, but none of the deposed circuit court judges would bring a case to court. Marshall also tried to persuade his associates that it was unconstitutional for Supreme Court justices to ride the circuit, as they must again do since the lower courts had been abolished. But although they agreed with his legal reasoning, they refused to go along because, they said, years of acquiescence in the practice lent sanction to the law requiring it. Thus frustrated, Marshall was eager for any chance to attack his enemy, and when a case that was to be known as *Marbury* v. *Madison* came before the Court in December 1801, he took it up with gusto.

William Marbury, a forty-one-year-old Washingtonian, was one of the justices of the peace for the District of Columbia whose commissions Jefferson had held up. Originally from Annapolis, he had moved to Washington to work as an aide to the first secretary of the navy, Benjamin Stoddert. It was probably his service to this staunch Federalist that earned him the appointment by Adams. Together with one Dennis Ramsay and Messrs. Harper and Hooe, whose commissions James Marshall had *almost* delivered, Marbury was asking the Court to issue an order (a writ of mandamus) requiring Secretary of State Madison to hand over their "missing" commissions. Marshall willingly assumed jurisdiction and issued a rule calling upon Madison to show cause at the next term of the Supreme Court why such a writ should not be drawn. Clearly here was an opportunity to get at the President through one of his chief agents, to assert the authority of the Court over the executive branch of the government.

This small controversy quickly became a matter of great moment both to the administration and to Marshall. The decision to do away with the June term of the Court was made in part to give Madison more time before having to deal with Marshall's order. The abolition of the circuit courts and the postponement of the next Supreme

Court session to February 1803 made Marshall even more determined to use the Marbury case to attack Jefferson. Of course, Marshall was embarrassingly involved in this case, since his carelessness
was the cause of its very existence. He ought to have disqualified
himself, but his fighting spirit was aroused, and he was in no mood
to back out.

On the other hand, the Jeffersonians, eager to block any judicial
investigation of executive affairs, used every conceivable mode of
obstruction to prevent the case from being decided. Madison ignored Marshall's order. When Marbury and Ramsay called on the
secretary to inquire whether their commissions had been duly
signed (Hooe and Harper could count on the testimony of James
Marshall to prove that theirs had been attended to), he gave them
no satisfactory answer. When they asked to *see* the documents, Madison referred them to the clerk, Jacob Wagner. He, in turn, would
only say that the commissions were not then in the State Department files.

Unless the plaintiffs could prove that Adams had appointed them
their case would collapse. Frustrated at the State Department, they
turned to the Senate for help. A friendly senator introduced a motion calling upon the secretary of the Senate to produce the record
of the action in an executive session on their nominations. But the
motion was defeated after an angry debate on January 31, 1803.
Thus tempers were hot when the Court finally met on February 9
to deal with the case.

In addition to Marshall, only Justices Bushrod Washington and
Samuel Chase were on the bench, and the chief justice dominated
the proceedings. The almost childishly obstructive tactics of the
administration witnesses were no match for his fair but forthright
management of the hearing. The plaintiffs' lawyer was Charles Lee,
an able advocate and brother of "Light-Horse Harry" Lee; he had
served as attorney general under both Washington and Adams. He
was a close friend of Marshall, and his dislike of Jefferson had been
magnified by the repeal of the Judiciary Act of 1801, for he was
another of the circuit court judges whose "midnight" appointments
repeal had canceled.

Lee's task was to prove that the commissions had been completed
by Adams and Marshall, and to demonstrate that the Court had
authority to compel Madison to issue them. He summoned Wagner

and Brent, and when they objected to being sworn in because "they were clerks in the Department of State, and not bound to disclose any facts relating to the business or transactions in the office," he argued that in addition to their "confidential" duties as agents of the President, the secretary and his deputies had duties "of a public nature" delegated to them by Congress. They must testify about these public matters, just as, in a suit involving property, a clerk in the land office could be compelled to state whether or not a particular land patent was on file.

Marshall agreed and ordered the clerks to testify. They then disclosed many of the details of what had gone on in the President's "palace" and in the State Department on the evening of March 3, 1801. But they claimed to be unsure of the fate of the particular commissions of the plaintiffs.

Next Lee called Attorney General Levi Lincoln. He too objected strenuously to testifying. He demanded that Lee submit his questions in writing so that he might consider carefully his obligations both to the Court and to the President before making up his mind. He also suggested that it might be necessary for him to exercise his constitutional right (under the Fifth Amendment) to refuse to give evidence that might "criminate" him. Lee then wrote out four questions. After studying them, Lincoln asked to be excused from answering, but the justices ruled against him. Still hesitant, the attorney general asked for time to consider his position further, and Marshall agreed to an overnight adjournment.

The next day, the tenth of February, Lincoln offered to answer all of Lee's questions but the last: What had he done with the commissions? He had seen "a considerable number of commissions" signed and sealed, but could not remember—he claimed—whether the plaintiffs' were among them. He did not know if Madison had ever seen these documents, but was certain that *he* had not given them to the secretary. On the basis of this last statement, Marshall ruled that the embarrassing question as to what Lincoln had done with the commissions was irrelevant; he excused Lincoln from answering it.

Despite these reluctant witnesses, Lee was able to show conclusively through affidavits submitted by another clerk and by James Marshall that the commissions had been signed and sealed. In his closing argument he stressed the significance of the case as a test of the principle of judicial independence. "The emoluments or the dignity of the office," he said, "are no objects with the applicants." This was undoubtedly true; the positions were unimportant and two years of the five-year terms had already expired. As Jefferson later pointed out, the controversy itself had become "a moot case" by 1803. But Marshall saw it as a last-ditch fight against an administration campaign to make lackeys of all federal judges, while Jefferson looked at it as an attempt by the Federalist-dominated judiciary to usurp the power of the executive.

In this controversy over principle, Marshall and the Federalists were of necessity the aggressors. The administration boycotted the hearings. After Lee's summation, no government spokesman came forward to argue the other side, Attorney General Lincoln coldly announcing that he "had received no instructions to appear." With his control over Congress, Jefferson was content to wait for Marshall to act. If he overreached himself, the chief justice could be impeached. If he backed down, the already trifling prestige of his court would be further reduced.

Marshall had acted throughout with characteristic boldness; quite possibly it was he who had persuaded the four aggrieved justices of the peace to press their suit in the first place. But now his combative temperament seemed to have driven him too far. As he considered the Marbury case after the close of the hearings, he must have realized this himself, for he was indeed in a fearful predicament. However sound his logic and just his cause, he was on dangerous ground. Both political partisanship and his sense of justice prompted him to issue the writ sought by Marbury and his fellows, but what effect would the mandamus produce? Madison almost certainly would ignore it and Jefferson would back him up. No power but public opinion could make the Executive Department obey an order of the Court. Since Jefferson was riding the crest of a wave of popularity, to issue the writ would be an act of futile defiance; it might even trigger impeachment proceedings against Marshall that, if successful, would destroy him and reduce the Court to servility.

Yet what was the alternative? To find against the petitioners would be to abandon principle and surrender abjectly to Jefferson. This a man of Marshall's character simply could not consider. Either horn of the dilemma threatened disaster; that it was disaster of his own making could only make the chief justice's discomfiture the more complete.

But at some point between the close of the hearings on February 11 and the announcement of his decision on the twenty-fourth, Marshall found a way out. It was an inspired solution, surely the cleverest of his long career. It provided a perfect escape from the dilemma, which probably explains why he was able to persuade the associate justices to agree to it despite the fact that it was based on questionable legal logic. The issue, Marshall saw, involved a conflict between the Court and the President, the problem being how to check the President without exposing the Court to his might. Marshall's solution was to state vigorously the justice of the plaintiffs' cause and to condemn the action of the Executive, but to deny the Court's power to provide the plaintiffs with relief.

Marbury and his associates were legally entitled to their commissions, Marshall announced. In withholding them Madison was acting "in plain violation" of the law of the land. But the Supreme Court could not issue a writ of mandamus because the provision of the Judiciary Act of 1789 authorizing the Court to issue such writs was unconstitutional. In other words, Congress did not have the legal right to give that power to the Court!

So far as it concerned the Judiciary Act, modern commentators agree that Marshall's decision was based on a very weak argument. The Act of 1789 stated (section 13) that the Supreme Court could issue the writ to "persons holding office under the authority of the United States." This law had been framed by experts thoroughly familiar with the Constitution, including William Paterson, who now sat by Marshall's side on the Supreme Bench. The justices had issued the writ in earlier cases without questioning section 13 for a moment. But Marshall now claimed that the Court could not issue a mandamus except in cases that came to it *on appeal* from a lower court, since, under the Constitution, the Court was specifically granted original jurisdiction only over "cases affecting ambassadors, other public ministers and consuls, and those in which a state shall be a party." The Marbury case had *originated* in the Supreme Court; since it did not involve a diplomat or a state, any law that gave the Court the right to decide it was unauthorized.

This was shaky reasoning because the Constitution does not say the Court may exercise original jurisdiction *only* in such cases. But

Marshall was on solid ground when he went on to argue that "the constitution controls any legislative act repugnant to it," which he called "one of the fundamental principles of our society." The Constitution is "the *supreme* law of the land," he emphasized. Since it is "the duty of the judicial department to say what the law is," the Supreme Court must overturn any law of Congress that violates the Constitution. "A law repugnant to the constitution," he concluded, "is void." By this reasoning section 13 of the Act of 1789 simply ceased to exist and without it the Court could not issue the writ of mandamus. By thus denying himself authority, Marshall found the means to flay his enemies without exposing himself to their wrath.

Although this was the first time the Court had declared an act of Congress unconstitutional, its right to do so had not been seriously challenged by most authorities. Even Jefferson accepted the principle, claiming only that the executive as well as the judiciary could decide questions of constitutionality. Jefferson was furious over what he called the "twistifications" of Marshall's gratuitous opinion in *Marbury* v. *Madison*, but his anger was directed at the chief justice's stinging criticisms of his behavior, not at the constitutional doctrine Marshall had enunciated.

Even in 1803, the idea of judicial review had had a long history in America. The concept of natural law (the belief that certain principles of right and justice transcend the laws of mere men) was thoroughly established in American thinking. It is seen, for example, in Jefferson's statement in the Declaration of Independence that men "are endowed by their Creator" with "unalienable" rights. Although not a direct precedent for Marshall's decision, the colonial practice of "disallowance," whereby laws had been ruled void on the ground that local legislatures had exceeded their powers in passing them, illustrates the belief that there is a limit to legislative power and that courts may determine when it has been overstepped.

More specifically, Lord Coke had declared early in the seventeenth century that "the common law will controul acts of Parliament." One of the chief legal apologists of the American Revolution, James Otis, had drawn upon this argument a century and a half later in his famous denunciation of the Writs of Assistance. In the 1780s courts in New Jersey, New York, Rhode Island, and North Carolina had exercised judicial review over the acts of state legislatures. The debates at the Constitutional Convention and some of the *Federalist Papers* (especially No. 78) indicated that most of the Founding Fathers accepted the idea of judicial review as already established. The Supreme Court, in fact, had considered the constitutionality of an act of Congress before—when it upheld a federal tax law in 1796—and it had encountered little questioning of its right to do so. All these precedents, when taken together with the fact that the section of the Act of 1789 nullified by Marshall's decision was of minor importance, explain why no one paid much attention to this part of the decision.

Thus the "case of the missing commissions" passed into history, seemingly a fracas of slight significance. When it was over, Marbury and his frustrated colleagues disappeared into the obscurity whence they had arisen.[2] In the partisan struggle for power between Marshall and Jefferson, the incident was of secondary importance. The real showdown came later in the impeachment proceedings against Justice Chase and the treason trial of Aaron Burr. In the long run, Marshall won his fight to preserve the independence and integrity of the federal judiciary, but generally speaking, the Courts have not been able to exert much influence over the appointive and dismissal powers of the President. Even the enunciation of the Court's power to void acts of Congress wrought no immediate change in American life. Indeed, more than half a century passed before another federal law was overturned.

Nevertheless, this squabble over some small political plums was of vital importance. For with the expansion of the federal government into new areas of activity in more recent times, the power of the Supreme Court to nullify acts of Congress has been repeatedly employed, with profound effects upon our social, economic, and political life. At various times income tax, child labor, wage and hours laws, and many other types of legislation have been thrown out by the Court, and always, in the last analysis, its right to do so has depended upon the decision John Marshall made to escape from a dilemma of his own making. The irony is that in 1803 no one— not even the great chief justice himself—realized how tremendously significant the case of the missing commissions would one day become.

[2]Marbury became president of a Georgetown bank in 1814 and died in 1835.

WILLIAM HENRY WOODWARD.
Portrait by M. S. Doyle

JOHN WHEELOCK.
Portrait by Ulysses Dow Tenney.

The Dartmouth College Case

II

BY RICHARD N. CURRENT

(*Trustees of Dartmouth College* v. *Woodward*, 4 Wheaton 518)

John Marshall's brilliant handling of Marbury v. Madison *marked the opening of his long service as chief justice, a period of thirty-four years during which he dominated the Court as no other justice has in its history. In more than a thousand decisions rendered during his reign, he found himself in the minority only eight times, and this despite the fact that Jefferson and his Republican successors were gradually able to replace all the Federalist justices with men of their own choosing. Repeatedly he enunciated decisions strengthening the national government at the expense of the states and buttressing the position of the property interests of the country. In* Fletcher v. Peck *(1810), his Court threw out a Georgia law rescinding large land grants even though it was proved that many members of the legislature that had made the original grants had been bribed by speculators. A contract, once agreed to, could not be summarily broken, Marshall decreed. Even more momentous was his handling of a controversy involving the clash of federal and state authority which was settled in 1819. This quarrel concerned the charter of Dartmouth College. Richard N. Current has written a biography of Daniel Webster, who figured prominently in the case, and many other books.*

Spring had found its way to the valley of the upper Merrimack, and petals were falling from the apple trees, lately in full bloom. The streets of Concord, New Hampshire, were no longer full of soldiers, the three years of war with Great Britain and Canada having ended that winter. Instead, the capital was beginning to bustle with the usual June crowd of men from out of town. Lawmakers and their hangers-on were arriving, to meet from day to day in the long, low, cupolaed wooden building that doubled as a town house and a state house.

This year—1815—they came together in an atmosphere that was unusually tense, despite the return of both spring and peace. State politics were beginning to be stirred by a campus quarrel brought over from the village of Hanover. Before long, this quarrel was to attract attention far beyond the boundaries of New Hampshire, and after dragging on for nearly four years, it was to leave its mark indelibly upon the Constitution of the United States.

The trouble arose from the sinister scheming of a few men—if a certain anonymous pamphlet, going the rounds in Concord that June, was to be believed. This pamphlet made more exciting reading than was suggested by the wordy title: *Sketches of the History of Dartmouth College . . . with a Particular Account of Some Late Remarkable Proceedings of the Board of Trustees from the Year 1779 to the Year 1815.* From these eighty-eight pages, pedantically yet vigorously written, it appeared that the wicked trustees were interfering with the work of the virtuous president. Worse, they were misapplying college funds. Worse still, they were plotting somehow to extend their tyranny to the entire state.

The anonymous author of the *Sketches* was present in Concord, among the legislators and lobbyists. Over sixty but still very erect, he walked with slow and measured steps and with exaggerated dignity. He wore the old-fashioned outfit of dun-colored coat, knee breeches with buckles, white stockings, and three-cornered beaver hat. From time to time he lifted his hat and bowed and smiled. He could be gracious enough, in his way, but he was not here for a social visit. John Wheelock, president of Dartmouth, was here to launch a fight to the finish against his rebellious professors and trustees.

Wheelock expected to need legal as well as legislative aid. To help him in court, he counted on the services of a young man of growing reputation, a thirty-three-year-old congressman and lawyer named Daniel Webster, now living in Portsmouth. Wheelock had sounded him out, and Webster had promised to be in Concord. Wheelock kept an eye out for his prospective attorney.

Wheelock and other older people of Dartmouth and Hanover could recall Webster from the day of his arrival, back in 1797, to enroll as a student at the college. He was dressed in homespun which his mother had made and dyed; he had ridden through a hard rain, and the color had run. As he dismounted at the Hanover Inn, the bystanders smiled at his streaked and mottled appearance. They also wondered at his swarthy complexion. Surely this boy, Black Dan, must be an Indian whom Wheelock, after a lapse of several years during which the college enrolled none of the aborigines for whom it presumably had been founded, had finally brought in!

To Webster, as to the townspeople and to other students, Wheelock himself was a figure no less memorable. Often enough they had observed him as he made his way, slowly, stiffly, across the college green. The boys would snicker and repeat their stock joke: Wheelock's profile, with that tremendous nose, they said, made a perfect quadrant.

In the chapel, when he officiated, they found additional cause for amusement. He possessed no training as a minister, and he prayed in unconventional ways. One day, after having attended a chemistry experiment, he fervently addressed the ceiling: "We thank thee, O Lord, for the oxygen gas; we thank thee, O Lord, for the hydrogen gas; we thank thee, O Lord, for the nitrogen gas and for all the gases." (He spoke in a sanctimonious falsetto, which young Webster learned to mimic perfectly.)

Wheelock taught history and theology to the seniors. In the classroom he would ask, textbook in hand, "What does the author say on such and such a page?" If a curious boy raised questions of his own, Wheelock would shut him up with sarcasm. In his office, students invariably discovered him with a tome he had been poring over; he was the most indefatigable reader that Webster ever saw. Covetous of his time, Wheelock would dispose of the student's business as quickly as possible, then inquire: "Will you sit longer, or will you go now?" It is not recorded that any boy ever sat longer.

This caricature of a college president had inherited his job. His father, Eleazar Wheelock, was Dartmouth's founder and first president. By the terms of the charter he had gotten from King George III in 1769, Eleazar could name his own successor, who was to hold office "until such appointment" should be "disapproved by the trustees." He chose his son John.

When Eleazar died, the trustees hesitated to approve John's appointment. John was only twenty-five, a devil-may-care army officer. Though a Dartmouth graduate, he hardly seemed to qualify as a Dartmouth president. But the trustees could not very well pick and choose. They had not the wherewithal to provide a salary, and the younger Wheelock, like the elder, was willing to serve (at least for the time being) without pay.

At the time he took over, in 1779, John Wheelock apparently had, deep inside, a feeling of inadequacy and insecurity. He was scarcely older or more distinguished than the college boys themselves. Desperately eager to command the respect that his new office required, he went too far. He introduced rules compelling the students to remove their hats in his presence and to remain standing until he told them to sit. He took to reading, or at least to looking at printed pages, at all hours of the day and night, so as to give the appearance of diligent scholarship. And he put on a stiff formality of speech and manner.

Wheelock came to act as if he owned the college—and the village too. Well, he did own them, practically. From his father he had inherited, along with his job, a sizable estate. Through marriage to the well-to-do Maria Suhm he had acquired additional property. By lending money at steep rates, and foreclosing without mercy, he got still more. He could, and did, contribute much to the material support of the college.

Dartmouth continued to be pretty much a one-man show for nearly thirty years, until 1809. Then, after the passing, one by one, of older trustees who deferred to Wheelock, the board acquired a majority of newer members who chose to defy him. These men were disgusted by, among other things, the president's pertinacity in quarreling with the parishioners of the Hanover church, who resisted his efforts to impose an unwanted minister upon them. By vetoing his nominations to the college faculty, the newer trustees soon had most of the professors and tutors on their side.

After several years of forced retreat, Wheelock took the offensive. At the board meeting in November, 1814, he made a proposal which he thought would put his opponents in a dilemma. A part of his back salary, amounting to about $8,000 with interest, had never been paid. He now offered this sum as a gift to endow two professorships —but only on the condition that he be allowed to appoint the two professors. In case the trustees should reject his offer, he would have to demand immediate payment of the $8,000.

His opponents were infuriated. Their first impulse was to demand his resignation. Still, with the college owing him so much money, they hesitated to do that. Perhaps, by humiliating him, they could obtain his resignation without coming out and demanding it. Accordingly, they passed a resolution that, "to relieve the President of some portion of the burdens" weighing heavily upon him, he hereby "be excused from hearing the recitations of the Senior Class" in the theology course. This was considerately worded, yet well calculated to sting the Wheelock pride. The day before, he had met the seniors, as usual, to query them on such matters as the freedom of the will; the day after, he was absent, and another man was in his place.

Humiliated though he was, Wheelock had no intention of resigning. He prepared to strike back, put down the trustees, and regain control of the college, and when spring came he was ready. Whether he sued the trustees or not, Wheelock was determined to appeal to the sovereign people and to their representatives in the legislature. So he wrote his *Sketches of the History of Dartmouth College,* got the pamphlet printed, and sent bundles of copies to Isaac Hill, editor of the Concord *New Hampshire Patriot,* with instructions in an unsigned letter to see that each member of the legislature received a copy. Then, in plenty of time for the 1815 session, Wheelock set out for Concord.

A majority of the legislators, though a very small majority, belonged to the Federalist party, and so did Governor John T. Gilman. The Federalists sponsored theocracy and aristocracy, if one was to believe their rivals, the Jeffersonian Republicans. These men itched to overthrow the Federalist rule and, along with it, the arrangement by which public taxes went to the support of the Congregational Church.

The Jeffersonians had a shrill but effective journalist in the youthful hunchback Isaac Hill (who in years to come was to devote his invective talents to the service of Andrew Jackson). With Hill and the *Patriot* in the forefront, they took up the cause of Wheelock. In it they saw, or pretended to see, the cause of religious and political liberty. Now Wheelock was in fact no libertarian of any kind. He was a good Calvinist and a conservative Federalist. With Hill and the rest of his newfound friends he really had nothing in common— except to the extent that they, for whatever reason, were willing to help him recover his authority at Dartmouth.

When the legislature met, Wheelock got at least a part of what he had come for. He had stolen a march on the trustees: they were not prepared to launch organized opposition to him. Before a sympathetic committee, with no one to refute him, he stated his case, charging the trustees with misusing college funds, overpaying professors, infringing on the president's prerogatives, and conspiring to subvert popular liberties! He asked the legislature to look into Dartmouth's affairs. The legislators agreed, meanwhile endorsing neither Wheelock nor his opponents.

While in Concord, Wheelock also succeeded in finding Webster, who said he would be happy to provide professional assistance.

Several weeks later, at home in Hanover, Wheelock received notice that the investigating committee of the legislature would meet in Hanover on August 16. He could not be sure what tack the committee might take. Promptly he wrote to Webster, enclosing twenty dollars and requesting him to come at once. Wheelock waited, with growing impatience. By August 16 Webster had not appeared and had not answered. So Wheelock faced the committee without him. The committee only tried to patch up a truce. Failing in that, the members withdrew and composed a report—which turned out to be more critical of Wheelock than of his foes.

About a week after the committee hearing, the board of trustees held its annual meeting in Hanover. The eight majority members, "the Octagon," were in no mood to temporize. They voted to remove Wheelock immediately from his positions as president, professor, and trustee. Then they named as the new president the Reverend Francis Brown, thirty-one years old, of Yarmouth, Maine.

Having regained the initiative, the men of the Octagon pressed on to confirm and justify what they had done, publishing a *Reply* to Wheelock's *Sketches* and collecting affidavits to show that he had been incompetent as Dartmouth's head. None of the eight was more active than William W. Thompson, of Concord. Thompson, a United States senator, was a friend of Representative Webster, and during congressional terms the two roomed in the same Washington house.

Before Wheelock could recover from the trustees' blow, he received another shock when he saw what Trustee Thompson had written to one of the Dartmouth professors. Thompson's letter must have been opened and copied in the Hanover post office; apparently Wheelock had an ally there. Thompson had written: "I have had a long conversation with Mr. D. W., by which it appears that a strong desire prevails that the *Reply,* with the *Committee's Report,* should effectually put down a certain man." From this and other sentences, Wheelock could not mistake the unhappy fact. Instead of helping *him,* Mr. D. W. obviously was taking a big part in the strategy talks of the opposing camp!

A friend of Wheelock's wrote to Webster to protest. Back came the reply that Webster had heard from Wheelock too late to go to Hanover and aid him at the legislative committee's hearing. Anyhow, Webster now said, "I regard that as no professional call." Coldly, if disingenuously, he explained: "On the subject of the dispute between the president and the trustees, I am as little informed as any reading individual in society; and I have not the least inclination to espouse either side, except in proceedings in which my services may be professional." Webster's meaning in this bit of double-talk and his motivation in changing sides in the battle are as obscure today as they must have been to Wheelock himself.

Throughout the ensuing autumn and winter the New Hampshire papers argued the Dartmouth question back and forth. The Jeffersonian Republicans made Wheelock a martyr and Dartmouth a leading issue in the state elections of March 1816. In that year, for the first time in history, the voters chose a Republican governor, William Plumer, and a predominantly Republican legislature. The trustees and their friends, including Webster, expected a strong counterattack from the now strategically placed Wheelock forces. It was not long in coming.

This was a year without a summer. In June 1816, while the legislature was meeting, snow fell in Concord, the ground froze, and the young corn was killed. Addressing the legislators in the chill state house, Governor Plumer condemned the Dartmouth charter as one that "emanated from royalty" and contained, as was to be expected, "principles congenial to monarchy." It had no reason for existence in a republic like the United States.

Proud of his message, Plumer sent a copy to his party's founder and patron saint, then in retirement at Monticello. "It is replete with sound principles, and truly republican," Thomas Jefferson replied. He went on to condemn those "lawyers and priests" who believed that "the earth belongs to the dead, and not to the living."

The Republicans in Concord were as much impressed as Jefferson. In response to the governor's message, they passed a law to lift the dead hand of the past and supersede the royal charter—and give control back to old John Wheelock. The law changed the name of Dartmouth College to Dartmouth University, increased the number of trustees from twelve to twenty-one, and provided for a board of overseers with a veto over the decisions of the trustees. The law gave the governor and his council the power to appoint the additional trustees and the overseers. In effect, it transformed Dartmouth from a private college into a state university.

Governor Plumer called the enlarged board of trustees, the university board, together at Hanover, in August. It was still cold, and morning after morning there was frost on the ground. The Hanover reception for the new Plumer trustees was as chilly as the weather. Somehow no one could find the key to the library room where the board customarily met, and when the meeting was called to order in a college office, none of the eight anti-Wheelock trustees was there. Without a quorum present, the Plumer men could do nothing.

The men of the Octagon could not do much either. They had lost the college charter, seal, records, and account books. These were in the hands of the treasurer of the board, and he was an old crony of Wheelock's named William H. Woodward. He was, of course, on the side of the new university.

With this deadlock the first phase of the public controversy, the strictly political one, came to an end. The second, the legal and constitutional (as well as political), phase was to begin after a lull of several months.

In February 1817, Governor Plumer renewed his attack. He called a second meeting of the university board, this time in Concord, not in Hanover. No longer could the anti-Wheelock trustees frustrate the proceedings by staying away. The legislature had reduced the quorum so that the new Plumer appointees would suffice. At its Concord meeting the university board removed President Brown, two professors, and three of the Octagon trustees. The board then restored Wheelock to the presidency and named his son-in-law William Allen to a professorship.

To Wheelock, who had remained in Hanover, all this was gratifying, though it had come a little late. He now lay in bed, propped up on pillows, coughing his life away. He took some consolation, however, from writing his last will and testament. In it he bequeathed property worth $20,000 to Dartmouth University and made clear that the bequest would be void if, in place of the university, the old college should ever be restored. Too weak to perform the duties of his office, he let his son-in-law serve as acting president.

That same February the college trustees, refusing to accept the new state of affairs, took the advice of Webster and other friends and resorted to a lawsuit. They undertook an action in trover, an action based upon the common-law principle (the opposite of "finders keepers") that one who finds goods must return them to the owner on demand. In this case the trustees called upon their deserting treasurer, William H. Woodward, to return to them the college charter, seal, records, and account books, and to pay $50,-000 damages besides. Woodward himself was judge of the Court of Common Pleas of Grafton County, before which the action was brought, and so the case was transferred directly to the New Hampshire Superior Court at Exeter.

While the college trustees were trying to recover the items that Woodward had "found," they lost another big one: the Dartmouth plant itself. The spring term of the college—or was it the university? —was scheduled to begin on March 3. A few days ahead of time three "superintendents of buildings," representing the university, called upon President Brown of the college and asked for a set of keys. He refused to give them up. So the university men enlisted a mason and a carpenter and went the rounds of Dartmouth Hall, the chapel, and the rest of the buildings, forcing the doors and installing new locks.

"There were several boys with them, and among others," the waggish *Dartmouth Gazette* reported, "some or all of the aborigines who are in this place for the purpose of acquiring civilized habits."

When the term opened, the university had the buildings, but the college had the students, all but one of them! These stalwarts met in borrowed rooms in the village. They were summoned to classes by a cow horn instead of a bell, since the university forces commanded the belfry.

The term passed quietly enough. When Wheelock finally died, in April, he was duly mourned by a large crowd, including many of his old opponents, at the funeral in the meetinghouse. But the controversy did not die with him; he was merely replaced by his son-in-law as university president. When, in July, President James Monroe arrived in Hanover on the way from Boston, where even the Federalists had hailed him for bringing an "Era of Good Feelings," he was awarded *two* honorary degrees, one from the college and another from the university.

At the beginning of the fall term, in September, the college numbered ninety-five students, the university fourteen. The campus calm continued until November, when news came that the state Superior Court had decided in favor of Woodward and against the college trustees. Only one student now shifted from the college to the university, but the university students, few though they were, dared to attempt a coup.

Earlier the university had taken over the college library, with its approximately four thousand volumes. The college boys had managed, however, to hold on to the quarters of the two literary societies, the Social Friends and the United Fraternity, on the second floor of Dartmouth Hall. Together, these societies owned as many books as the library, and new and better ones.

On the night of November 11, after bedtime, a band of university students and villagers, along with university professor Nathaniel H. Carter, sneaked into Dartmouth Hall. At the entrance to the room of the Social Friends, they bunched together and crashed into the door. They could not move it. So one of them took an ax to the door and cut a hole big enough to crawl through.

The noise awakened some of the college boys. They arrived in time to arm themselves with sticks of firewood from the hallway and to trap the enemy inside the Social Friends' room. "It appears to me we are in a cursed poor scrape," the village shoemaker, one of those inside, was heard to say. "I had rather be in a nest of hornets than among the college boys when they get mad and roused up."

Finally the university forces capitulated. In token of their abject surrender, they were made to file out beneath the crossed clubs of the college boys, lined up in two rows. From this indignity, Professor Carter was excused. He was shaking with fright and was complaining that he had lost his cane; besides, he had once given the Social Friends fifteen dollars for books, which he now wanted back. Two of the college boys led him home.

Saving the society's books did not save the college. The college trustees could appeal from the Superior Court of New Hampshire to the Supreme Court of the United States, but if they did so, the prospects were most uncertain. Writing contemptuously of "Brown & Co.," Governor Plumer said: "I think they can have no rational grounds to hope for success in the National Court."

The trustees needed money to resume legal action. As they pointed out in a circular soliciting contributions, the annual income from the Dartmouth endowments amounted to barely more than $1,500—only about half the endowment income of Phillips Exeter Academy. Even this $1,500 was not available to the college, since Treasurer Woodward controlled the funds. The college managed to keep going only because loyal parents continued to pay tuition fees and generous alumni and friends rallied with gifts.

Daniel Webster, Dartmouth '01, was not moved to contribute. If an appeal should be carried to the Supreme Court, he was expected, for a fee, to represent the college, and Joseph Hopkinson—famous as a Baltimore lawyer and even more famous as the author of "Hail, Columbia!"—was being mentioned as a suitable associate. On November 15, Webster, now living in Boston, wrote to President Brown to inquire about the college's plans. "I am aware that there must be great difficulty in obtaining funds on this occasion," he said. "I think that I would undertake, for a thousand dollars, to go to Washington and argue the case, and get Mr. Hopkinson's assistance also. I doubt whether I could do it for a much less sum." A thousand-dollar gift to the college made it possible for the trustees to hire Webster and Hopkinson.

Already Webster was thoroughly familiar with the case. He had followed it from the beginning, and he had joined with Jeremiah Mason and Jeremiah Smith to present the college's argument before the New Hampshire court at Exeter. Their brief contended that the legislators, in reorganizing the college as a university, had gone beyond their rightful powers in these three respects:

1. They had violated an accepted legal principle: only the courts, not the legislature, could take away a vested right.

2. They had violated the constitution of New Hampshire, which provided that no person should be deprived of his property except by the "law of the land," meaning the common law and not a legislative act.

3. They had violated the Constitution of the United States, which provided that no state should pass any law "impairing the obligation of contracts."

Only on the third of these contentions, as Webster knew, could the case properly be reargued before the Supreme Court, and he thought the point weak and unconvincing. To hedge the case, and to bring in the whole range of arguments, he persuaded the trustees to lease Dartmouth properties to Vermont residents and then arrange for the lessees to sue. These suits, involving citizens of two states, would go directly to the federal courts.

Before any of these synthetic cases reached the Supreme Court, however, the case of the *Trustees of Dartmouth College* v. *Woodward* was taken up, on appeal. Webster opened for the trustees on the morning of March 10, 1818. The courtroom was small, and it was jammed.

Among those who had crowded in were representatives of other colleges, which might lose their independence if Dartmouth lost its. Chauncey A. Goodrich, professor of oratory at Yale, was present on Yale's behalf. It was a good thing he was there; otherwise, his colorful account of Webster's performance would never have been recorded for posterity.

For more than four hours, on past noon, Webster spoke in a calm and conversational tone, as if dealing with propositions everyone knew and accepted. For more than three of the hours he dealt in irrelevancies, cleverly bringing in all the arguments that had been used before the New Hampshire court. He also hinted strongly, for the benefit of Chief Justice Marshall, the arch-Federalist, that the college was a victim of political machinations by the Jeffersonians.

Webster took plenty of time, however, to elaborate upon the one relevant point. What, he asked, was the full meaning of the clause in the United States Constitution prohibiting the states from "impairing the obligation of contracts"? The Supreme Court itself, he answered, had decided in the case of *Fletcher* v. *Peck,* involving land grants by the State of Georgia, that "a *grant* is a contract." The Dartmouth charter, he went on, "is embraced within the very terms of that decision," for "a grant of corporate powers and privileges is as much a *contract* as a grant of land."

At the end of his formal argument, as Professor Goodrich afterward recalled, Webster stood silent for a time. Then, addressing Chief Justice John Marshall, he said:

"This, sir, is my case. It is the case not merely of that humble institution; it is the case of every college in our land. . . . It is more. It is, in some sense, the case of every man who has property of which he may be stripped, for the question is simply this: Shall our state legislature be allowed to take that which is not their own, to turn it from its original use, and apply it to such ends or purposes as they, in their discretion, shall see fit?"

Webster pulled out the stops and continued: "Sir, you may destroy this little institution. It is weak. It is in your hands. I know it is one of the lesser lights in the literary horizon of the country. You may put it out. But if you do so, you must carry through your work. You must extinguish, one after another, all those great lights of science which, for more than a century, have thrown their radiance over our land. It is, sir, as I have said, a small college, and yet *there are those that love it.*"

Here Webster, the consummate actor, pretended to break down. His lips quivered, his voice choked, his eyes filled with tears. From this spectacle Professor Goodrich turned to observe the judges. Marshall bent his tall, gaunt figure forward as if straining to catch every word. His eyes seemed wet. Joseph Story still sat, pen in hand, as if to take notes, which he never took. The rest of the justices, too, appeared to be transfixed.

But the show had to go on. Other attorneys had to be heard— the two for Woodward that afternoon and the next day, and Hopkinson for the trustees on the third day. After Hopkinson had concluded, Marshall announced that some of the justices could not make up their minds and that the case therefore would be continued to the next term. This meant postponing the decision for a year or so.

Webster and other advocates of the college cause put the interim to good use. On the day after the postponement he guessed that, of the seven judges then on the Court, two sided with the college, two were opposed, and three were wavering. The trustees and their counsel faced the delicate task of bringing over to their side at least two of the doubtful three.

"Public sentiment has a great deal to do in affairs of this sort, and it ought to be well founded," the chief justice of Massachusetts wrote to Webster in April 1818. "That sentiment may even reach and affect a court; at least, if there be any members who wish to do right, but are a little afraid, it will be a great help to know that all the world expects they will do right." The Massachusetts judge was responding to a gift from Webster—a printed copy of Webster's argument in Washington. The judge urged that it be "extensively circulated." It was.

Of all the various state judges, much the most influential was James Kent, chancellor (the highest judicial officer) of New York. In July, while on a tour by chaise with his wife, Kent stopped in Hanover and in neighboring Windsor, Vermont. He visited with university but not with college officials, and in conversation he casually implied approval of the New Hampshire decision in favor of Woodward.

This worried the college officials, especially President Brown. They quickly sent a copy of Webster's brief to Kent. In September Brown went to Albany and called on him. Kent now came out unequivocally for the college. He agreed to talk with William Johnson, one of the wavering federal justices. Johnson, a dissenter in the case of *Fletcher* v. *Peck,* had held that a grant of land was *not* a contract, and so he found it hard to believe that a grant of corporate powers could be one. But Kent convinced him and drafted an opinion for him.

That summer, while the struggle for judicial minds was going on, the defendant in the case, William H. Woodward, quietly died in Hanover, at the age of forty-three.

By the time the Supreme Court reconvened, in February 1819, five of the justices favored the college, one was still opposed, and one was absent. The university officials, having hired the impressive William Pinkney of Baltimore as their new attorney, hoped to have the case reopened and reargued, but Marshall ignored Pinkney and calmly read his magisterial opinion. A grant of corporate powers, Marshall opined, was indeed a contract within the meaning of the Constitution; a state legislature had no power to void it.

This was to be one of the most often cited of Marshall's opinions. As the nation's leading magazine, the *North American Review,* remarked about a year afterward: "Perhaps no judicial proceedings in this country ever involved more important consequences." The Dartmouth case enhanced the prestige of John Marshall and the

Supreme Court. It extended the national power at the expense of state power. It confirmed the charter rights not only of Dartmouth College but of all private colleges. It protected and encouraged business corporations as well as nonprofit corporations. And, incidentally, it brought Daniel Webster to the top of the legal profession.

Poor old John Wheelock! He could have had no idea what he was starting, back in 1815, when he took his problems into politics.

DANIEL WEBSTER.   *Portrait by Francis Alexander.*

The Bank Cases III

By Bray Hammond

(*McCulloch* v. *Maryland,* 4 Wheaton 316; *Osborn* v. *Bank of the United States,* Wheaton 738)

Although the Dartmouth College case was very important, it did not finally lay to rest the knotty problem of federal versus state power. Equally epoch-making and even more bitterly contested were two cases rising out of the efforts of Maryland and Ohio to drive a federal corporation, the Bank of the United States, from their territories. Bray Hammond, a former assistant secretary of the Federal Reserve Board, wrote, among other books, Banks and Politics in America from the Revolution to the Civil War, *which was awarded the 1958 Pulitzer Prize in History.*

I

In Baltimore on a day early in May 1818, an informer named John James mounted the stairs to the floor above the Union Bank where the local office of the Bank of the United States was maintained. His call was formal. He had come for legal evidence that the Bank and James W. McCulloch, its local cashier, were violating the law.

Back in February, the Maryland Assembly had enacted a statute which gave the Baltimore office of the Bank the hard choice of buying stamped paper from the state, on which notes issued by the office were to be printed, of paying the state $15,000 a year, or of going out of business. The law was to come into effect the first day of May. That day had now passed, with no sign that the law was to be obeyed. So Maryland, whose motto, roughly translated from the Italian, is that deeds are for men and words are for women, was taking prompt action. There was a penalty of $100 for each note issued on unstamped paper since the effective date of the law, one-half for the state and one-half for the informer; but if John James expected to leave the Bank richer than he came he was certainly stupid, for the tax was prohibitive, as he must have known, and not intended to provide revenue but to force the office to close. Maryland chartered banks for its people, and the state wanted the Bank of the United States, chartered by the federal government, to leave its sovereign soil and stay off it.

McCulloch, the cashier, could not have been surprised by his visitor. He acknowledged that notes were being issued by him in defiance of Maryland's law. He refused to pay the penalty demanded by John James. And he presumably let the latter depart with the impression that the Bank considered Maryland's law nugatory and that it intended to remain in business in Baltimore without either buying stamped paper or paying the $15,000 tax.

The state at once brought suit, and judgment against McCulloch —that is, against the Bank—was given by the Baltimore County Court. The Bank took the case to the Maryland Court of Appeals, which affirmed the lower court's judgment, and thence by writ of error to the United States Supreme Court. In the appeals to both the higher Maryland court and the Supreme Court the two parties to the case agreed upon the facts, so that the only questions to be decided were whether the federal law chartering the Bank and the state law taxing it were in conflict and if so which was constitutional and overrode the other.

Maryland's action was the first which several states in the Southern and Western parts of the country were taking against the bank. Tennessee, Georgia, North Carolina, Kentucky, and Ohio authorized measures to the same end, the Bank having one or two offices in each of these states; the tax was $50,000 for each of the two offices in Ohio and $60,000 for each of the two in Kentucky. Similar measures were being advocated elsewhere. Illinois and Indiana, where the Bank had no offices, forbade the establishment of any.

II

There were three things that in general counted most heavily with the public against the Bank. One was a strong traditional hatred of all banks and especially of the biggest one. Banks were enemies of the farmer and of all other common folk. This was an orthodox principle of the Republicans, as the Jeffersonians then called themselves, and though there was a split over it within the party, what was probably a majority maintained an agrarian fear of banking and a passionate will to curb or forbid it. Years later, in 1852, there were no incorporated banks in seven of the thirty-one states—Arkansas, California, Florida, Illinois, Iowa, Texas, and Wisconsin—none in the two organized territories shortly to become states—Minnesota and Oregon—and none in the District of Columbia. They were kept out either by bans in the states' constitutions or by steadfast legislative refusal to enact charters. In Indiana and Missouri banking was a state-controlled monopoly; in still other states banks undoubtedly would have been prohibited but for the fear that prohibition would aggravate the evil. The effort to stamp out banking resembled in some respects the attempt a century later to stamp out the consumption of alcoholic beverages.

The second force working against the Bank of the United States in 1818, also political and an orthodox Republican tenet dating back thirty years to the formation of the Union, was the idea that the federal Constitution was a compact by which the states had created a collective government and delegated certain powers to it but reserved to themselves (or to the people) the powers not delegated. Since the power to issue corporate charters had not been delegated, the corporate charter of the Bank of the United States was considered unconstitutional and the Bank had no legal standing.

The third force inimical to the Bank was the self-interest of the banks which the individual states had chartered. These state institutions found the federal Bank oppressive and monopolistic, and they got the ready sympathy of their customers, to whom they explained that if it were not for the big Bank, lending would be much easier. Times were hard and bankers, like other debtors, were trying to avoid paying what they owed their depositors and note holders. The federal Bank had been set up for the direct purpose of making the state banks resume payments in specie. This the state banks called oppression.

The difference between those persons who hated all banks and those—the state bankers with their borrowers—who hated merely the federal Bank was readily compounded: each party thought that it could destroy the other once the big Bank was done for.

III

The Bank, paradoxically, owed its charter to the Republicans, who as a party had from the first opposed banking in principle and denied that the federal government was permitted by the Constitution to share with the states the power to grant corporate charters. For these reasons the Republicans had denounced the present Bank's predecessor, established in 1791 at Alexander Hamilton's instance and over Thomas Jefferson's sharp protests. But between 1791 and 1818 the two parties had altered greatly. The Federalists had lost power with the election of Jefferson in 1800 and were plaintively approaching their extinction. The Republicans had flourished, holding their original agrarian core but also gaining the major part of the business community, which, thanks to the industrial revolution, now comprised many entrepreneurs, engaged in manufacturing as well as commerce, in transportation by turnpike and canal, in banking and brokerage, and in feverish speculation. Being recruited mostly from farm families, retaining agrarian dislike of the old mercantile aristocracy—which equally disliked them as smelly, freckled upstarts—they found the principles of the Declaration of Independence as congenial to enterprise as to farming. This change gave the Republican party two wings, which, years later when it adopted the name Democratic, were distinguished within the party as "Democrats in principle" and "Democrats by trade."

In 1811, early in James Madison's administration, the two had joined in letting the federal Bank expire, the agrarians for orthodox reasons, the enterprisers and state bankers because the Federalist management of the old relic, stubbornly conservative, was interfering with easy money. But five years later, still in Madison's administration, the party leadership decided after all that a government bank was necessary. The Treasury was in a desperate situation in consequence of monetary disorder, weak fiscal policy, and the general peace which in 1815 ended a long period of wars. In its legal and proper aspect the Bank was fiscal agency of the government, public depository, and regulator of the currency and of the commercial banks' lending powers. It was what is now called a central bank. It had a capital of $35 million—a foolishly large sum for its purposes —and was by far the largest corporation in America and one of the largest anywhere. It was inspected by the Treasury, to which it reported. One-fifth of its shares were owned by the federal government, and one-fifth of its directors were appointed by the President of the United States with the approval of the Senate. Its home office was in Philadelphia. When it came before the Supreme Court in 1819, the Bank had eighteen branch offices in as many cities, ranging from Portsmouth and Boston in the Northeast to Savannah and New Orleans in the South and to Louisville and Cincinnati in the West. Louisiana, Mississippi, and Illinois were then the westernmost states of the Union. The Bank's various offices were located where business was considerable and the federal Treasury's receipts and expenditures could be most conveniently handled.

IV

The Bank had its good angels and its bad.

Among its better angels was the Madison administration itself, including particularly the secretary of the Treasury, William Crawford of Georgia. As a senator years before, he had been, with Albert Gallatin, one of the few Republicans actively advocating renewal of the first Bank's charter. Another Republican was the cast-iron John C. Calhoun of South Carolina, under whose strenuous and inexorable leadership the new charter had been enacted in 1816.

Prominent among the Bank's darker angels was General Samuel Smith of Baltimore, long a member of Congress, a former Federalist but now a Republican, a rich trader, and the senior partner in the Baltimore firm of S. Smith and Buchanan, which John Quincy Adams called "one of the greatest commercial establishments in the United States." The firm was especially active in the export of silver to India and to that extent obstructed the return of the banks to a specie basis. General Smith had been a tireless, aggressive enemy of the old Bank and a prominent sponsor of the new one. His partner, James Buchanan, was president of the new Bank's Baltimore office, which, it came out a year later, he and another director, with the help of the cashier, James McCulloch, had been busy looting for a year or more. The General, who was to be distracted and put to bed by the disclosure, had his rank from military service in the Revolution, the Whiskey Rebellion, and his more recent defense of Baltimore from the British. He was active in public life, a man of distinguished appearance, an uncle by marriage to that forsaken beauty, Betsy Patterson of Baltimore, whose star-crossed marriage to Prince Jerome Bonaparte, brother of the Emperor, had been imperiously annulled. "The moral, political, and commercial character" of Baltimore, wrote John Quincy Adams, then secretary of state, "has for twenty-five years been formed, controlled, and modified almost entirely by this house of Smith and Buchanan. . . . It may be added that there is not a city in the Union which has had so much apparent prosperity or within which there has been such complication of profligacy."

The Bank's directors were in two camps paralleling its sponsors. Stephen Girard of Philadelphia and John Jacob Astor of New York were both Republicans, but conservative. Girard had early complained of several directors whom he plainly considered fly-by-nights. He intended, he said, to use all his "activity, means, and influence to change and replace the majority of directors with honest independent men." Instead, he had given up and resigned. The majority had chosen for president of the Bank a former merchant of Philadelphia, William Jones, who, having gone through bankruptcy, became a Republican politician. He had served as secretary of the navy and acting secretary of the Treasury. Jones informed Secretary Crawford that he was not disposed to follow the conservative example of the former Bank of the United States, whose policy he thought "less enlarged, liberal, and useful" than it should have been. Men like him filled positions throughout the Bank.

McCulloch, the Baltimore cashier, also thought the "timid and faltering course" of the former Bank should not be emulated. Neither did George Williams, a director both of the Baltimore branch and of the home office in Philadelphia. How "enlarged and liberal" his ideas were is illustrated by his ingenuity in getting around a complex restriction in the Bank's charter which limited to thirty the number of shares that any shareholder might vote, no matter how many he owned. He, McCulloch, and the Smith and Buchanan partnership purchased among themselves over four thousand of the Bank's shares, using money "borrowed" from the Baltimore office, and had each share registered in a different name, with themselves, severally, designated to vote all the shares as attorneys. So together they were able to vote four thousand shares or more instead of the mere 120 that was the maximum any four shareholders might vote otherwise. Williams later explained that he had gone into the mar-

ket and bought names "at eleven pence each." This practice became
so common in Baltimore and Philadelphia that according to R.C.H.
Catterall, the Bank's historian, a clique of speculators in the two
cities "controlled the Bank as soon as it was organized," those from
Baltimore alone casting close to a majority of all the votes at the first
election of directors.

The directors so chosen favored speculation and encouraged
lending on the Bank's own shares. This was done on such loose
terms that the Bank was supplying the money for much of its own
capital and financing a rash speculative advance in the market price
of the shares. But finding even this "enlarged and liberal" policy
insufficiently enlarged and liberal for their ambitions, Williams,
Smith and Buchanan, and McCulloch lent themselves still more,
McCulloch as cashier arranging advances through discounts and
overdrafts without adequate security and without reporting them
honestly. The net loss sustained by the Bank as a result of these
shenanigans in the end was estimated to be in excess of $1.4 million,
which in those days was a fairly large sum. Though McCulloch
achieved legal immortality from his byplay with the informer John
James, he seems to have been a mere clerk to his partners, useful
because he controlled the office records and could lend them money
freely without letting it be known—or so they fancied.

Though all this was slow in coming to light, enough had got
about to whet existing antagonism to the Bank and to make Congress order an investigation in October 1818. Maryland's demand
through John James had by then been refused, the suit had gone
successfully through two state courts, and the Bank's appeal was on
the Supreme Court's docket. There was already much talk of the
Bank's surrendering its charter, but Secretary Crawford would not
listen to it. He rallied the Madison administration to help the Bank
in its plea to the Supreme Court and encouraged the Bank's directors to speed their housecleaning. Attorney General William Wirt
joined the Bank's counsel in preparing for the Supreme Court hearing. The congressional committee's report, though severe on the
Bank, recommended it be continued minus its abuses. In January,
Jones was forced out of the presidency and an able lawyer from
Charleston, Langdon Cheves, was engaged to replace him. Resigna-
tions were obtained from incompetent directors and officers, and
suits were filed against defaulters. Half the branch office directors,

it was estimated, resigned. It was pretty late to be resorting to soap and water, but the Bank was going to come before the Court with its hands as clean as possible.

V

The hearing opened on February 22, 1819, and continued till March 3. The Bank was represented by Daniel Webster, who as a Federalist congressman three years before had opposed the bill chartering it, by William Pinkney of Baltimore, and by Attorney General Wirt. Maryland was also represented by distinguished counsel, Joseph Hopkinson and Walter Jones, of Philadelphia and Washington respectively, and Luther Martin, who had been an active dissident in the Constitutional Convention of 1787. In the battle over ratification of the Constitution, Martin had cried out against the chains being forged for "his country," meaning Maryland, and its subjection to the new federal authority. Now, thirty years later, Martin was protesting for "his country" against the reality that he had foreseen.

But the argument that most impressed the Court was that of Pinkney, who spoke for three days, attaining heights of eloquence and persuasiveness that Justice Joseph Story found brilliant and overwhelming. The decision was given by Chief Justice Marshall March 6. It affirmed the constitutionality of the Bank's charter, and it was unanimous—a circumstance galling to Thomas Jefferson and other orthodox Republicans, for of the seven justices only two were Federalists. The other five were appointees of Jefferson and Madison. Marshall's opinion followed the same line of reasoning as Pinkney's in his argument and as Alexander Hamilton's in his exposition of the problem in 1791.

Hamilton, while secretary of the Treasury in that early period following organization of the federal government under the Constitution, had recommended measures to Congress of which one was the chartering of a government bank. The proposal had immediately aroused sharp differences of opinion in Congress about the nature of the federal government and its relation to the individual states, but it had been adopted. President Washington, who was so far uncommitted, had then faced the question of if he should approve or veto the charter Congress had enacted. He had consulted

Thomas Jefferson, the secretary of state, and Edmund Randolph, the attorney general, both of whom roundly condemned the measure as unconstitutional. Jefferson had argued that the federal government had not been given the power to grant charters of incorporation. Washington had then consulted Hamilton, who had held that the federal government, though not endowed with all powers, was supreme and sovereign with respect to those it did possess. He had contended that every power vested in the federal government "is in its nature sovereign and includes, by force of the term, a right to employ all the means requisite" to make the power effective, unless the means were specifically forbidden by the Constitution, were immoral, or were inexpedient. Congress had decided the services of a bank were requisite to the government's discharge of its services, and Congress was competent to make that decision. Therefore the act was constitutional. Washington had sided with Hamilton and approved the charter on February 25, 1791.

His choice was not the popular one. The Republicans, becoming the political majority, rested their case against the Bank on the Ninth and Tenth Amendments to the Constitution, and on the Kentucky and Virginia resolutions of 1798. In the two amendments it was declared in effect, as contended by Jefferson, that the federal government had only those powers delegated to it by the Constitution and that those not delegated remained with the states and the people. The resolutions, though only a statement of political principle, affirmed the sovereignty of the states and the limitation on the powers of the federal government.

By 1819 these affirmations had gained in popular support, especially in the West. The government in Washington through the federal judiciary had tentacles penetrating every state, and through the federal Bank it had still others penetrating half of them. Popular resentment was intensified by hard times, which made both the federal courts and the local offices of the Bank instruments of oppression. For the Bank, following the "enlarged and liberal" policy of William Jones, had led men into debt by offering easy credit, and now, under the conservative Cheves and with the federal courts' assistance, it was taking their property from them. It seemed to people as Thomas Jefferson had said: a strong, consolidated government was crushing them and their liberties.

So in *McCulloch* v. *Maryland*, in 1819, when the controversy of

1791, never dead, flared up violently, the Supreme Court defied a strong drift toward a weak Union. Marshall, reverting to the argument of Hamilton, affirmed the implied powers of the federal government—and by further implication the subordination to them of the powers of the individual states—in words pregnant with significance for subsequent American history. "Let the end be legitimate," he said, "let it be within the scope of the Constitution, and all means which are appropriate, which are plainly adapted to that end, which are not prohibited, but consist with the letter and spirit of the Constitution, are constitutional."

A loud popular outcry arose. Congress could establish a bank and the bank could spread its branches into the individual states without leave. The states, it seemed, could only submit. For perhaps most of the public, the Court's decision appeared revolutionary. The masses could understand the Tenth Amendment but not the subtleties of Hamilton and Marshall, according to whom the Constitution meant yes when it said no. A week after the decision was announced, Hezekiah Niles wrote in his popular *Weekly Register* that "every person must see" in the courts' validation of the Bank's charter "a total prostration of the states' rights and the loss of the liberties of the nation." Niles was convinced "that the welfare of the union has received a more dangerous wound than fifty Hartford conventions, hateful as that assemblage was, could inflict." Still deeper than this dismay, which was rational, whether right or wrong, lay the unsophisticated conviction that the Court should not ignore moral considerations and blandly imply, in silence, an unquestioning approval of the Bank, whose reputation was already bad and was soon to grow still worse.

VI

Anger at the Court's decision was especially strong in Ohio, where the ravage produced by speculation and aggravated by the federal Bank was sensational. After a burst of lending, the Bank had had to turn to a rigorous contraction which through foreclosures drew an immense amount of Cincinnati property into its hands. The bitterness of the public was intense. In February 1819, the month before *McCulloch* v. *Maryland* was decided, the legislature enacted the law levying prohibitive taxes—$50,000 each—on the local offices in Cincinnati and Chillicothe. The legislature declared it "just and necessary that such unlawful banking while continued should be subject to the payment of a tax." It authorized the state auditor to demand payment, to ransack the premises for cash if refused, and when the money was found to take it and deliver it to the state treasury. The tax was to be due in September.

Early in March the Ohio officials concerned were made uneasy by the Supreme Court's decision in *McCulloch* v. *Maryland*. They hesitated to carry out the legislature's authorization, for they might find themselves landed in prison by federal court action no matter what the Ohio legislature said. But in May it was disclosed that funds of the Bank's Baltimore office had been embezzled by McCulloch and his two associates, George Williams and James Buchanan.

Langdon Cheves, the new president, who had taken office back in March the day before the announcement of the decision for the Bank in *McCulloch* v. *Maryland,* had got on the trail of the Baltimore speculators within a week. By the end of May the investigation was complete; McCulloch was dismissed and his two associates had to resign. All three were brought to court—but not General Smith, who apparently was left unmolested on the ground that he was but a sleeping partner, a hero absorbed in public affairs and unaware of what his junior was doing.

Ohio's excuse for holding firm despite the Supreme Court's decision had been that the case was collusive and not managed by Maryland in a way that fairly presented Ohio's interest. Maryland had been too polite; by agreeing with the Bank as to the facts, it had tamely laid the case in the Court's lap to be decided. This dissatisfied Ohio; now, after the Baltimore disclosures, the state had still greater reason to act. The Baltimore affair did not show the Bank to be a victim of thieves but a den of them. Resolute politicians urged resort to the crowbar law to ensure collection of the taxes due in September.

The Bank, apprehending what would be attempted, obtained a federal court order to prevent it. However, the state auditor, Ralph Osborn, was informed by legal counsel that the order was defective and lacked the force of an injunction. So he instructed his deputy, John L. Harper, with assistants, to enter the Chillicothe office and get the money. They arrived just before closing time on September 17, 1819. According to the report of the Chillicothe cashier to

Secretary Crawford, Harper and his party "suddenly entered the office and in a ruffian-like manner jumped over the counter," and took possession of the vault. Harper asked the cashier if he was going to pay the tax. The cashier said no; he tried to force the intruders from the vault, warned them not to touch the Bank's property, and waved the court order at them. In spite of his efforts, they gathered up specie and banknotes amounting to $120,425 and moved it over to the Bank of Chillicothe with the wagon and horses they had left hitched outside. The state allowed Harper to keep $2,000 as his fee, returned $20,425 to the Bank as overpayment, and retained $98,000 as the net tax in the hands of H. M. Curry, the state treasurer.

There ensued a long period of abortive struggle to clear up the conflict of duty and jurisdiction. Harper and an assistant were sued for having taken the Bank's money, were kept in prison four months for want of bail, and were then released on a technicality. Osborn the auditor and Curry the treasurer were sued for recovery of the money, which, however, the treasurer could not give up without a warrant, which the auditor could not issue without legislative appropriation, which, of course, the legislature would not authorize.

Meanwhile a joint committee of the legislature reviewed the whole problem of state and federal sovereignties, the Ninth and Tenth Amendments, the Kentucky and Virginia resolutions of 1798, and the question of federal court jurisdiction in matters involving a state. The report of the committee was prepared by Charles Hammond, one of Ohio's foremost lawyers, who thought the principles of the McCulloch decision "not worth refutation." The report vigorously denounced the pretensions of the federal judiciary. Ohio's sovereignty, it declared, should not be sacrificed by the "inadvertence or connivance" of Maryland in its suit against the Bank. "This case dignified with the important and high-sounding title of 'McCulloch v. the State of Maryland,' when looked into, is found to be an ordinary *qui tam* action of debt, brought by a common informer of the name of John James. . . ." It was "throughout an agreed case," the report said, "manufactured in the summer of the year 1818 and passed through the county court of Baltimore county and the court of appeals of the state of Maryland in the same season, so as to be got upon the docket of the Supreme Court of the United States for adjudication at their February term, 1819. It is only by the management and concurrence of the parties that causes can be thus expeditiously brought to a final hearing in the Supreme Court." The report recommended that an agreement be negotiated whereby Ohio would return to the Bank the $100,000 taken from it and the Bank would withdraw from the state. As an inducement for the Bank to leave, Ohio should outlaw it, forbidding the state's courts, judges, jailors, notaries, and other agencies to serve or protect it. The report, which also recommended that Ohio formally approve the Kentucky and Virginia resolutions, was adopted by the legislature in December 1820, and its recommendations were enacted.

The proposal for negotiations leading to return of the $100,000 upon the Bank's closing its local offices came to naught. Instead, in September 1821, after continued skirmishing, the Bank obtained a federal court order for return of the money outright. The state's treasurer, a new incumbent named Sullivan, disregarded the order; he was arrested by federal officers, lodged in prison, and deprived of his keys, with which the state's vault was opened, and the money, which had lain there intact for two years, was put back in the Bank.

Ohio was in an uproar. Whose state was this? When would the encroachments of the federal courts on state sovereignty be curbed? These encroachments had been growing from the organization of the federal government. Ohio was now the victim; it had "to complain of the imprisonment of the treasurer, the taking from his pockets the keys of the treasury whilst so imprisoned, and the entry into the treasury and violent seizure of monies therein contained, the property of the state!!! If our sister states patiently look on and permit scenes of this kind to be acted in broad daylight, we may well despair of the Republic." Largely on questions of jurisdiction, Ohio took its complaint to the Supreme Court, against the will of the state's more ardent citizens, who wished to snub that presumptuous body.

VII

The sister states to whom Ohio had appealed differed in opinion. Several were sympathetic but hesitant. They denounced the federal courts but stopped short of flouting them. Kentucky had started to assert its liberties and then deferred to a federal court injunction, as Ohio had not. But in South Carolina, where nullification was to be attempted ten years later, and in New England, where five years before, the Hartford convention had advocated defense by the individual states of their sovereignties and the liberties of their people, Ohio's action was condemned. No state followed its example.

Least of all Maryland. Ohio had already denounced *McCulloch* v. *Maryland* as a collusive case, "manufactured" for a quick decision favorable to the Bank. Now, cheek by jowl with the Bank it had pretended to sue for not paying its tax, Maryland was helping the Bank to prosecute, in its courts, three victims of the Bank's wrath.

But fortunately for the three, Maryland, still in the main an agrarian community, had as yet no statute against embezzlement, and though the Bank's charter authorized punishment for counterfeiting the Bank's notes, it too was mute about embezzlement. There was doubt if the accused had committed an indictable offense. Maryland had a law against larceny, a simple crime as obvious as murder, and had the three men robbed a bank other than their own, they could have been dealt with readily. But how could one steal something of which he had lawful possession? The three, after considerable delay, were charged with conspiracy, an ancient form of wrongdoing well known to the law, and indicated "for being evil disposed and dishonest persons and wickedly devising, contriving, and intending, falsely, unlawfully, fraudulently, craftily, and unjustly, and by indirect means to cheat and impoverish" the stockholders of the Bank. William Pinkney, who had represented the Bank before the Supreme Court in *McCulloch* v. *Maryland,* was now counsel for the "traversers" (as the accused were styled "in criminal cases less than felony"); William Wirt, the attorney general, was counsel for the Bank throughout.

At their first trial, in April 1821, judgment was given for the traversers, thanks to the county court's conclusion, on the basis of a statute of King Edward I enacted nearly two centuries before Columbus discovered America, that the offense charged was not punishable in Maryland. The case was carried to the state court of appeals, which held to the contrary. In an opinion ranging over precedents from the reign of Edward I to that, just closed, of George III, it held that under the common law inherited by Maryland from the mother country the offense charged was a punishable one. Accordingly, in December 1821, it returned the case to the county court for retrial. But to no purpose. Though the traversers were charged with an offense that the higher court said was indictable and punishable, they were again found not guilty by the lower court.

They had in their favor the rising sympathy for men of enterprise. They were exemplars of what was already recognized in America as the "almost universal ambition to get forward." The entrepreneur was crowding up alongside the farmer as an ideal American figure. He too was in his origins typically humble, born on a farm, but by hard work, ingenuity, ambition, and force of character he was advancing himself, rising in the world, developing his country's resources, arousing emulation in his fellows, and making America great.

The defense for the traversers made much of this new trend. What they had done was not denied but was said to have turned out badly through the mistakes of others. They had "relied too strongly upon the hopes and calculations in which the whole community indulged," and "the failure of their stock speculations was rather to be pitied as a misfortune than condemned as a crime." England was to blame for it because its investors had lent money to France that they might have bought Bank stock with instead; France was to blame because it had borrowed the money which the English might have invested in Bank stock; and the Bank itself was to blame because it had been poorly managed. These things had depressed the value of the Bank's shares and ruined the traversers' projects. If, instead, the Bank's shares had risen in value, then the traversers "would have been looked upon as nobles, as the architects of their fortunes . . . and lauded to the skies as possessing spirits fraught with enterprise."

This attitude toward success in business, as achieved notably by "self-made men," was to become popular later in the century with a host of Americans and unpopular with another host of them. Already in 1823 it helped the Baltimore conspirators, though it is impossible to measure its influence besides that of animosity toward the Bank and of technical deficiencies in the law. The men being again acquitted, the prosecution ceased, though the dissenting judge averred that the traversers had in fact "taken from the funds of the office a large sum of money, which they converted to their own use," and that they had "failed to return to the Bank a cent of their spoil."

VIII

Meanwhile, the Ohio case, *Osborn* v. *the Bank of the United States,* was pending on the Supreme Court docket; it was heard in March 1824. The court may well have indulged in delay in order to let Ohio calm down, which it did when business began to improve and its citizens could become preoccupied with returning prosperity. The Court was sensitive about popular charges of "encroachment" by the federal judiciary, and in hearing the Ohio case it had the question of jurisdiction reargued. Ohio's counsel was Charles Hammond and the Bank's was Henry Clay. In the reargument Daniel Webster and John Sergeant joined Clay, and Hammond was joined by Ethan Allen Brown, a former governor of Ohio. The Court reaffirmed its decision in *McCulloch* v. *Maryland* summarily but gave lengthy consideration to the federal circuit court's jurisdiction, which it affirmed. The case died quietly, with none of the excitement of its beginning. Time, prosperity, and federal firmness had quieted things, for a while.

A generation later, though, the quarrel of Ohio and other states with the federal government broke out again, in different circumstances which nevertheless involved the same constitutional issue as in the Bank cases. The Fugitive Slave Act of 1850 authorized infamous procedure, in free states, against blacks alleged to be escaped slaves and against their protectors. Ohio revolted and, citing its measure of 1820 outlawing the Bank as a precedent, refused the use of state jails and the aid of state officers and agencies in the enforcement of the hated federal statute. Its courts checkmated the federal courts, and its people, in the Oberlin-Wellington rescue, in the attempt to save Margaret Garner, and in other similar actions defied the federal government and the slave catchers with every extreme of violence, ruse, and litigation. Members of the new Republican party, out of repugnance to the South's "peculiar institution" and the behavior of Southern politicians, accepted the example of the South Carolina nullifiers less than thirty years before, finding it "the only sound, logical, and tenable position, unless we give up everything to the sweep of centralization." It was much the same in other states, east and west. In 1855 the Massachusetts legislature had declared the Fugitive Slave Act "a direct violation of the Xth amendment," as the charter of the Bank of the United States had been called in 1819. In 1859 the Wisconsin supreme court pronounced the same act unconstitutional, and the state legislature supported the court, denouncing the act as a federal usurpation, violating both the Tenth Amendment and "the compact" between the states.

IX

In the North, emotions over slavery and the South's success in Washington during the 1850s certainly helped to weaken the force of John Marshall's opinions, but it is doubtful if the principles affirmed in *McCulloch* v. *Maryland* and reiterated in *Osborn* v. *the Bank of the United States* had ever been heartily accepted by most people. The popular aversion to a Hamiltonian or strong central government grew rather than diminished in the following decades. It had been nourished on agrarianism; it now throve on business enterprise democratized, as described so admiringly in 1823 in the Baltimore conspiracy cases. By the time of Andrew Jackson's election in 1828 there had evolved a business class very different in size and character from the merchant class which had constituted the entire business community in early Federalist days. The industrial revolution had diversified business enterprise, had made it dynamic and democratic. For other than tariff matters, these new businessmen turned more readily to their familiar state authorities than to Washington. It was the states that taxed, regulated, and promoted enterprise. So, except to maintain the Bank of the United States for a few years, the McCulloch decision had little force until the Civil War.

When the Bank's charter was renewed by Congress in 1832, Jackson vetoed it, saying among other things that it was unconstitutional. He believed the President had as much right to decide what was constitutional as the Supreme Court had. *His* decision, in 1832, was greeted with popular enthusiasm, and the Jeffersonian and Jacksonian doctrine of a strictly limited federal sovereignty preponderated till the Civil War. It purposed and achieved a limitation of federal powers that is amazing in contrast with what those powers have since become.

Yet this implied no corresponding disrespect for the national government. Quite the contrary. No one was more devoted to the Union than Andrew Jackson. The Americans, in a world that had been shaken by revolutionary menaces and torn by Napoleonic wars from the time they formed their Union till long after, had sense enough to recognize that a federation afforded better military protection than could a growing number of small, separate sovereignties, that it was acquiring for them more and more continental territory, and that it enabled them to boast of citizenship in no small nation. Otherwise the federal Union was held in esteem much the way contemporary women were—revered affectionately so long as it kept within its sphere, which was important but modest.

The Civil War brought about a revolutionary change. Besides forcing the federal government to assume powers "to the very verge of the Constitution" and even beyond, it made the Union, in the eyes of the North, a beneficent power fighting slavery and secession and eventually worthy of all sorts of responsibilities: economic, paternal, conservatory, corrective, educational. First the farmers, its original enemies, and then labor became its suppliants. By their votes they have multiplied its powers. It taxes, it regulates, and it affords security to a degree unpracticed and undreamt in 1819. Its spirit is not Hamiltonian, but its structure and its operations are.

There is no older issue in American politics than that of the relation between the federal government's powers and those of the individual states, each side of which got its classic statement in 1791, by Hamilton and Jefferson respectively. The differences of opinion then expressed as to means have never been reconciled, though sides have changed. Seventy years after the issue arose and despite Marshall's opinion in 1819, it produced a ghastly civil war; seventy-five years after that the welfare state arose—an innovation as far from Hamilton's purpose as from Jefferson's—yet involving the same constitutional questions that separated them.

At no time have the differences subsided into more than uneasy sleep. The issue is one bound to beset confederations of groups unwilling on the one hand to lose their individual sovereignties and on the other to forgo the incontestable advantages of union. It has troubled Canada. It troubles Western Europe. It is an issue tempting to interests—economic, political, social, religious—which see advantages now from one side, now from the other. And these characteristics give it a history, in the United States at least, in which motives become curiously mixed.

The conventional contrast between Hamilton and Jefferson, for example, is that Hamilton was materialistic and a spokesman for wealth and privilege, and that Jefferson was humane and a champion of the neglected interests of the common man and the lowly. But the weapons, like those of Hamlet and Laertes, have somehow got exchanged. With respect to responsibility for employment, security, and welfare in general, it is the posterity of Jefferson's party who thankfully acclaim a strong federal government and the posterity of Hamilton's who shrink away from its alleged hypertrophy.

Thomas Gibbons.

Aaron Ogden.

The Steamboat Case   IV

BY GEORGE DANGERFIELD

(*Gibbons* v. *Ogden,* 9 Wheaton 1)

As the country expanded in the early nineteenth century, efficient transportation become increasingly necessary, for unless people and goods could circulate freely from section to section the United States could scarcely hope to remain a single nation. Once again, however, uncertainties over the extent of federal and state authority caused quarrels that hampered development. These could only be settled by the Supreme Court. The great landmark in this area rose out of a fight between rival steamboat operators in New York Harbor. George Dangerfield is the author of the Pulitzer Prize winning Era of Good Feelings *and of a biography of Robert R. Livingston, a pioneer in the development of the steamboat.*

The famous case of *Gibbons* v. *Ogden,* decided on March 2, 1824, was, with its preceding litigation, ultimately concerned with a single question: the power of Congress to regulate interstate as well as foreign commerce. It produced a triumph for nationalism, in the most generous and constructive sense of that term, and its influence has been immense. Its immediate effect, however, was to release from monopoly, like a genie from a bottle, a sooty, romantic, and useful servant to the American people—the steamboat.

One cannot altogether understand this aspect of *Gibbons* v. *Ogden* without considering the origins and consequences of the Livingston-Fulton steamboat monopoly, and the personalities involved in them: personalities of considerable determination and marked eccentricity, one of them brushed with genius, and all displaying a strong desire to move to some location more favorable to themselves that neighborly landmark which lies between *meum* and *tuum.*

The actual inaugurators of the American steamboat—John Fitch,

James Rumsey, perhaps Oliver Evans—were also its innocent victims: they could make it run, but they could not make it run economically, nor could they raise sufficient funds to enable them, by research and experiment, to overcome this problem. One still sees them, nobly (and in Fitch's case somewhat drunkenly) silhouetted against the pale dawn of the Age of Steam, gesticulating in vain to the inattentive financier, the jocose and sceptical public. From their valiant dust springs *Gibbons* v. *Ogden.*

The great case may be taken back to March 27, 1798, when the New York legislature repealed an exclusive privilege to run steamboats on state waters, which it had conferred on John Fitch, and bestowed it instead upon Robert R. Livingston, chancellor of the state. Livingston had what Fitch conspicuously lacked—social status, political influence, wealth, credit. He resembled Fitch only in one respect: he was an enthusiast. An amateur scientist, he believed that nature might at any moment yield one of her tremendous secrets to some chance experiment or happy flash of insight. The building of grist mills on a novel principle which should eliminate friction between the stones, the crossing of cows with the elk in his park at Clermont on the Hudson, the manufacture of paper out of river weed locally known as frog's spit—such schemes occupied his leisure hours. His spirit, one might almost say, dwelt more and more apart on the farthest and most airy borders of rational speculation; almost but not quite. He was a progressive farmer, for example, whose work was of the first importance. And there was a hard, practical element in his singular composition—he was, after all, of Scottish and Dutch descent—which made it unlikely that he would throw good money after bad. To his great credit, he had perceived that the steamboat had a future: and although steamboat legislation, like Vulcan among the gods, excited the immortal laughter of the New York legislature, Livingston was quite impervious to mockery of this sort.

His experiments with John Stevens (one of the fathers of the railroad) and Nicholas J. Roosevelt proved abortive, and when he left for France in 1801, where as American minister he plunged into those complex and exasperating negotiations which ultimately led to the purchase of Louisiana, it was presumed that no more would be heard of the steamboat. But in Paris he met the one man who could give his schemes what they needed—precision, economy, practicability.

Robert Fulton, darkly handsome, supremely self-confident, the very embodiment of energy, had been raised as an artisan in Lancaster, Pennsylvania. He had been a locksmith, a gunsmith, a draftsman, a portrait painter; he had gone to England to study under Benjamin West; and in England he had first conceived what was to become a permanent preoccupation with submarines and submarine torpedoes. Of Fulton it might indeed be doubted whether his lifelong purpose was to put boats upon the water or to blow them out of it. One thing, however, was certain. He had, supremely, the faculty of coordination. Other men's original ideas, in the realm of steamboats, existed only to be borrowed: "All these things," he said airily, "being governed by the laws of nature, the real invention is to find [such laws]." To him, it was all a matter of exact proportions, of nicely calculated relations. Where the steamboat was concerned, it was Fulton's destiny, and his genius, to find a commotion and to turn it into a revolution.

Fulton and Livingston put an experimental steamboat upon the Seine; its performance satisfied them, and Fulton left for England, to cajole out of the British government a Boulton & Watt engine built to his own specifications. The engine was claimed by Fulton from the New York customs house on April 23, 1807, it was placed in a boat built at the Charles Brownne shipyards at Paulus Hook, and on August 17, 1807, *The Steamboat* (she seems never to have been called the *Clermont*)[1] made her triumphant voyage from New York to Albany.

On her maiden night, as she passed through the darkling Highlands of the Hudson, a plangent volcano, *The Steamboat* excited great terror among the pious dwellers beside the banks of that river. One rustic is said to have raced home, barred the doors, and shouted that the Devil himself was going up to Albany in a sawmill.

Here he was, perhaps understandably, wrong. It was not a demon, it was a most useful spirit, which had been released by

[1]Fulton variously referred to the vessel as the *North River Steamboat of Clermont*—after Livingston's Hudson estate—the *North River Steamboat,* or the *North River.* On her first voyage, she seems simply to have been *The Steamboat.* But the public came to call her the *Clermont,* and the name stuck.

Fulton and Livingston; the trouble was that, having released it, they at once imprisoned it again. Fulton did indeed take out two United States patents—perhaps more interesting as essays than valid as claims—but it was not upon these that he and Livingston relied; their great support was restrictive state legislation.

On April 6, 1808, the New York legislature extended their privilege up to a limit of thirty years and imposed thumping penalties upon anyone who should dare, without a license from the monopoly, to navigate upon any of the waters of New York. In 1809, a sister to *The Steamboat,* the *Car of Neptune,* was built; in 1810, the *Paragon* appeared; on April 9, 1811, the New York legislature passed a monopoly act even more stringent in its penalties than the one enacted in 1808. And in April 1811, the legislature of the territory of Orleans conferred upon Livingston and Fulton privileges fully as extensive as those granted by New York. Thus they controlled two of the greatest commercial waterways in the United States.

Although they had shown true vision in their estimate of the steamboat's future, Livingston and Fulton had been somewhat less perceptive in gauging the reaction of their countrymen. They had not supposed that their monopoly would be unpopular, still less that it would be seriously resisted. From the outset, however, obloquy and litigation became their portion. The litigation reached its climax in 1811, when twenty-one enterprising gentlemen of Albany started a rival steamboat, the *Hope,* upon the Albany–New York run, and threatened to follow her up with a sister ship, not inaptly to be called the *Perseverance.*

The monopolists, of course, fought back in the courts, and in March 1812 New York chief justice James Kent issued a permanent injunction against the *Hope.* Kent's very learned opinion may be reduced to this simple proposition: either the New York steamboat acts violated the federal Constitution or they did not. Obviously, he said, where a national and a state law are aimed against each other, the state law must yield. But this was not the case here, since all commerce within a state was exclusively within the power of that state. Supported by Kent, one of the most respected jurists in the nation, the monopoly had certainly become respectable. When Robert R. Livingston, full of years and honors, died in 1813, when Robert Fulton followed him into the shades in 1815, they left to their heirs and assigns an inheritance as rich and safe as state laws could make it.

Nonetheless, the contentious atmosphere which had clouded the monopoly from the beginning seems to have been increased rather than diminished by Kent's decision. New Jersey had already passed a retaliatory act in 1811; in the course of time its example was followed by Connecticut and by Ohio. Massachusetts, Georgia, New Hampshire, Vermont, and Pennsylvania bestowed exclusive rights upon their own favored monopolists. Elsewhere, unlicensed steamboats blew their lonely, defiant whistles upon remote lakes and waterways, and pale denizens of the uncharted wilderness crept down to watch and wonder. The development of the steamboat was a great adventure, but it was threatening to turn into that gravest of evils, a commercial civil war—unless, indeed, someone could break the Livingston-Fulton grip upon Louisiana and New York. In the former state, by 1819, there were distinct signs of rebellion; but the latter, the cradle of the whole restrictive movement, would undoubtedly prove to be the more dramatic and decisive scene for some abrupt reversal of this ominous trend. . . .

In May 1819, John R. Livingston of New York brought suit in the chancery court of that state against Aaron Ogden and Thomas Gibbons of New Jersey. Mr. Livingston, a younger brother of Robert R. Livington, was a wealthy merchant who had dedicated his youth to making what he called "something clever" out of the Revolution, and who had thereafter devoted his energies to the single-minded pursuit of material advantage. In 1808, for the extremely stiff price of one-sixth of his gross proceeds, he had purchased from his brother's monopoly the exclusive right to navigate steamboats "from any place within the city of New York lying south of the State Prison, to the Jersey shore and Staten Island, viz: Staten Island, Elizabethtown Point, Amboy and the Raritan up to Brunswick, but to no place or point north of Powles Hook." (The location of Powles or Paulus Hook may be determined by drawing a line from the southernmost tip of Manhattan Island due west to the Jersey shore.) He was certain to extract from this hard-bought concession whatever there was to be extracted—and thus arose his suit against Ogden and Gibbons.

Aaron Ogden, finding his own legislature unwilling to support him in his claim to run steamboats on his own, had reluctantly yielded to the monopoly in 1815 and had purchased from Mr. Livingston, its assignee, the right to run a steamboat ferry from Elizabethtown Point to New York. A Revolutionary soldier who had fought at Yorktown, a former governor of New Jersey, and one of the state's leading lawyers and most prominent Federalists, Ogden was a man of impressive physique, a craggy and truculent countenance, and a character to match. He bore the monopoly no goodwill, and in the course of time he acquired in Thomas Gibbons a partner even more truculent than himself.

Gibbons was a wealthy lawyer from Georgia who had been a Loyalist during the Revolution, thereby (since his brother and father were both patriots) saving the Gibbons plantation from both British vandalism and anti-Loyalist revenge. His was not exactly a happy record, but he survived it, to acquire at length a reputation, notable even in Georgia, for some of the more opprobrious and quarrelsome forms of political intermeddling. "His soul," said one enemy, "is faction and his life has been a scene of political corruption." In 1811 he acquired a home in Elizabethtown, New Jersey.

The partnership between Ogden and Gibbons, instituted in 1817, was no doubt doomed from the start. In October 1818, Ogden obtained an injunction against Gibbons in the New York chancery court, presumably because that oblique personage could not resist the temptation to cheat his partner by running a steamboat on his own account from Powles Hook to New York. Nonetheless, when John R. Livingston brought suit against the pair in 1819, their partnership was still uneasily alive and upon the following terms: Ogden ran passengers from New York to Elizabethtown Point in his steamboat *Atalanta.* At Elizabethtown Point, the passengers changed into Gibbons's *Bellona,* for which (as for his smaller steamboat the *Stoudinger*) Gibbons had taken out a United States coasting license. The passengers were then carried to New Brunswick, whence they proceeded overland to Trenton and Philadelphia.

John R. Livingston, whose steamboat *Olive Branch* ran regularly from New York to New Brunswick, claimed that the Ogden-Gibbons partnership constituted a single voyage, in defiance of his exclusive right. He also showed that the partners had a common booking agent in New York, by the name of William B. Jaques. Livingston petitioned for an injunction restraining them from navigating their two boats, except from New York to Elizabethtown Point. Since Ogden had already enjoined Gibbons from doing any such thing, this meant that in future the *Atalanta* would have to transfer her passengers not into Gibbons's *Bellona* but into Livingston's *Olive Branch.*

Both Gibbons and Ogden disclaimed any partnership or any knowledge of Mr. Jaques. Both insisted that the ports and harbors of Elizabethtown Point and New Brunswick were within the jurisdiction of New Jersey, as were the waters lying between them, and both asserted that the agreement between the monopoly and John R. Livingston gave the latter no right whatsoever to navigate between a port in New York and one in New Jersey. Gibbons had other arguments, but the chief of them—and this in time became the crux of the whole matter—was that under his national coasting license he had a perfect right to navigate between one point in New Jersey and another.

The reigning chancellor of New York was now none other than James Kent, who, as chief justice, had delivered the decisive opinion in the case of the *Hope* in 1812. That he would reverse in the Court of Chancery a decision he had delivered in the Court of Errors was not to be expected. In a complicated decision that adds nothing to his fame as a jurist, he held that Ogden could continue to steam between New York and Elizabethtown Point in the *Atalanta,* but that Gibbons's *Bellona* could not operate between the Point and New Brunswick.

If the temperaments of Ogden and Gibbons had been more compatible, they might have continued the fight together. The New York law, claiming jurisdiction all the way to the Jersey shore, was clearly preposterous, and simple justice should have compelled the partners to stand together for their common rights. But Ogden decided to content himself with Kent's decision. No doubt he contemplated the discomfiture of Gibbons with a certain amount of ill-concealed complacency.

The result was the final break between Gibbons and Ogden. Gibbons was justifiably angry and full of fight. Since Kent had ignored his federal coasting license argument, he planned to bring the case to the United States Supreme Court. Meanwhile he hoped to stir up trouble in the New Jersey legislature, and he proposed to be a thorn in the side of the monopoly by breaking the New York statute wherever and whenever he could.

For this latter project he had ready, in the rude person of Cornelius Vanderbilt, master of the *Bellona* (who feared no man, and in whom one may detect even in this early stage of his memorable career a characteristic admixture of talent, forthrightness, and low cunning), precisely the instrument he needed. Together they invented many ingenious ways of outwitting the monopoly. One of the finest of these was to run passengers in the *Bellona* out of Elizabethtown Point and transship them, in Jersey waters, to the *Nautilus* of Daniel D. Tompkins, who had acquired from the monopoly the ferry rights between Staten Island and New York. Tompkins was an old opponent of the Livingston faction in the New York Republican party and was not unwilling to make a little mischief. The physical risks of transshipment were far from negligible, but Americans were made of stern stuff in those days, the fare of fifty cents a head was undeniably attractive, and all was going beautifully—one might say swimmingly, except that no one fell overboard—until brought to a halt by the decision of Chancellor Kent in *Ogden* v. *Gibbons* of December 4, 1819.

The web of litigation was already tangled. Ogden had earlier sued Gibbons before Kent on October 6, 1819, on the grounds that Gibbons was running his two steamboats between New Jersey and New York, in open defiance of the monopoly rights that Ogden had purchased from Livingston, and on this occasion Gibbons had at least wrung from Kent what he most needed, and that was a ruling upon the scope of national coasting licenses. Nobody could deny that an act of Congress of February 18, 1793, permitted vessels of over twenty tons' burden to be enrolled and licensed. The question was: Did this national license permit a vessel to trade not only between port and port of one state but between the port of one state and the port of another? If it did, it was clear that there would be little comfort thereafter for the Livingston-Fulton monopoly.

Chancellor Kent, however, was now ready with an ingenious reply. A national license, he said, merely conferred upon any given vessel a national character, freeing it from those burdensome duties which were imposed upon foreign vessels if they attempted to engage in the coasting trade. That it was a license to trade, still less to trade in waters restricted by a state law, he steadfastly denied.

Was it likely, he asked, that the New York steamboat acts, every one of which had been written and passed subsequent to the act of Congress, would have been written and passed at all if it could have been held that the act of Congress had annihilated them all in advance?

This argument was certainly forcible, but whether it cast more darkness upon New York legislation than light upon the act of Congress must remain in some doubt. Gibbons, of course, appealed Kent's ruling to the New York Court of Errors; the appeal was heard in January 1820; and Gibbons's counsel now contended that the licensing act was derived from the eighth section of the first article of the federal Constitution—from the power of Congress, that is, to regulate commerce among the several states. Thus in *Gibbons* v. *Ogden* in the New York Court of Errors there dawned what was afterward to become the high nationalist noonday of *Gibbons* v. *Ogden* in the Supreme Court of the United States. Justice Jonas Platt, pronouncing the decision of the Court of Errors, upheld Chancellor Kent, and against this decision Gibbons appealed to the Supreme Court.

The times, if not necessarily the law, were now certainly on Gibbons's side. With the passing of the War of 1812, a new light seemed to fall upon the map of the United States. The nation, now figuratively facing westward, began to think of its lamentable roads, its lack of canals, the primitive counterclockwise motion of its exchange of staples for manufactures as that exchange moved down the Ohio and the Mississippi, up the Atlantic coast, and back across the Appalachians. That the steamboat might do much to reverse this process, nobody now doubted; but the steamboat, a strange but sufficient symbol of nationalism, was struggling in the grip of a monopoly, dubiously bottomed upon the doctrine of states rights.

Nor was this all. The contest between state-conferred steamboat monopolies, the clash of state retaliatory laws, threatened to reduce the nation's commerce to that particularist chaos which the Constitution itself had been providentially designed to avert. And here the indefatigable Thomas Gibbons was not backward. He persuaded the New Jersey legislature to pass a new retaliatory act, and on February 20, 1820, it did so. By this act, any nonresident of New Jersey who enjoined a New Jersey citizen, in the chancery court of New York, from navigating by steamboat any of the waters between

the "ancient" shores of New Jersey could in turn be enjoined by the
chancery court of New Jersey from navigating between those "ancient" shores. Moreover—and this was the sting—he could be made
liable for all damages, *with triple costs,* in any action for trespass or
writ of attachment which he had obtained against a New Jersey
citizen in the New York court.

Thus John R. Livingston, to his dismay, discovered that his *Olive
Branch* had been detained and attached in New Brunswick to answer
for damages alleged to have arisen from the injunction he had won
against Gibbons in May 1819. Threatened with successive attach-
ments and prohibitive costs, he had at one time withdrawn the *Olive
Branch* from service. In *Livingston* v. *D. D. Tompkins* (June 1, 1820),
Livingston v. *Gibbons* (August 26, 1820), and *Livingston* v. *Gibbons,
impleaded with Ogden* (May 8, 1821), one may trace his efforts, on
behalf of Ogden as well as himself, to wriggle out of this predicament. But, alas, there was in Livingston's character just a touch of
Sir Giles Overreach; he succeeded only in arousing the wrath
of Chancellor Kent, a high-minded gentleman, who cared little for
the stratagems of entrepreneurs, but much for the dignity of the
law.

Actually, Chancellor Kent had now thrown in the sponge. He had
done his best for the rights and dignity of his state and his court;
he might talk about state reprisals and jurisdictions until the very
walls of his courtroom reverberated with his declamations, but he
was, after all, one of the first jurists in the nation, and there had been
growing upon his shuddering inner vision, feature by feature, like
some Cheshire cat's, the implacably smiling visage of the commerce
clause of the Constitution. In the meantime, he had left the quarrel
between Ogden and Gibbons in a state of armed neutrality, and
Gibbons and Vanderbilt continued, by one device or another, to
keep the *Bellona* steaming between New Jersey and New York until
such time as the Supreme Court should rule upon Gibbons's appeal
from the New York Court of Errors.

This appeal had been docketed with the Supreme Court in 1820,
dismissed for technical reasons in 1821, docketed again in 1822,
and continued from term to term until February 1824. By that time
and in that political climate, with nationalism and states' rights
opposed on many fronts, it was already a famous case. Eminent
counsel had been briefed on both sides: Daniel Webster and Attor-

ney General William Wirt for Gibbons; Thomas J. Oakley and
Thomas Adis Emmet for the monopoly.

One might have supposed, since the nationalist John Marshall
was chief justice and the Court was supposedly "Marshall's Court,"
that a decision in favor of Gibbons was a foregone conclusion. But
the assertion that Congress could actually regulate interstate trade
was in those days a very daring one, and although John Marshall was
a bold man, many people doubted if he would be as bold as all that.
Nor could one be sure that, in this instance, he would be supported
by a majority of his brethren.

The legal questions were extremely complicated and Gibbons's
able lawyers exploited every possible argument. Wirt, for example,
reasoned that the monopoly laws conflicted with certain acts of
Congress, and were therefore void. Webster, however, who opened
for Gibbons, went boldly to the heart of the matter by claiming that
it was of no moment whether or not the New York statutes were in
conflict with an act of Congress. The constitutional authority of
Congress was such that it had the power exclusively to regulate
commerce in all its forms upon all the navigable waters of the
United States. Afterward he said—whatever Webster's faults, self-
depreciation was not among them—that Marshall took in his words
"as a baby takes in his mother's milk." This was not quite the case.
The truth seems to be that the two men thought very much alike on
the question, but that it required all Marshall's gifts to weave into
a more prudent form the arguments so vehemently presented by
Webster.

The pleadings consumed four and a half days, and it was generally conceded that every one of the counsel had surpassed himself
—in learning, in subtlety, in eloquence. Nearly a month passed
before Marshall delivered the Court's opinion. It was one of the
most statesmanlike he had ever penned, and, from a legal point of
view, one of his soundest. (There was only one dissent, Justice
William Johnson's, and that uttered doctrine more extreme than
Marshall's.) And one should always remember, as Justice Frankfurter said, that when Marshall applied the commerce clause in
Gibbons v. *Ogden* "he had available no fund of mature or coherent
speculation regarding its implications." Like the steamboat itself,
the decision which freed the steamboat was a pioneer.

Marshall began by defining "commerce," not in the strict sense of "buying and selling" (as Ogden's counsel had urged), but (this was Wirt's definition) as "intercourse," and this of course included navigation. It comprehended also the power to prescribe rules for carrying on that intercourse. ("I shall soon expect to learn," wrote Henry Seawall to Thomas Ruffin, "that our fornication laws are unconstitutional.")

This being the case, one had then to ask whether the power of Congress, under the commerce clause, invalidated the monopoly statutes of the state of New York. Here Marshall ruled that the coasting license act of 1793, dealing with the subject matter of that clause, was superior to a state law dealing with the same subject matter. Thus Gibbons's license did not merely confer upon his vessel an American character; it also permitted that vessel to trade between the port of one state and the port of another; nor did the fact that it was a *steamboat* have any relevance. Marshall's majestic reasoning struck down the monopoly in twenty words: "The laws of Congress, for the regulation of commerce, do not look to the principle by which vessels are moved."

Congress, in short, has power over navigation "within the limits of every State" so far as navigation may be, in any way, connected with foreign or interstate trade. (It should be remarked, in passing, that it took two more suits in the New York courts to determine whether or not the Livingston-Fulton monopoly was valid for purely *intrastate* commerce, and that when Chief Justice Savage in the Court of Errors—*North River Steamboat Co.* v. *John R. Livingston,* February 1825—declared that it was not, both Justice Woodworth and a handful of state senators felt obliged to dissent.)

The subtleties, the complexities, the mass of subsequent legal glossing, the vexed questions of state taxing and state police powers —all these are irrelevant to this bare narrative; the point is that Marshall's great decision, which has been called "the emancipation proclamation of American commerce," has substantially survived the erosions of time and of change. Its immediate effect was to set the steamboat free on all the waters of the United States. Its more distant effects were beyond the scrutiny of Marshall and his contemporaries: the railroad, the telegraph, the telephone, the oil and gas pipelines, the airplane, as they moved across state borders, all came under the protection of *Gibbons* v. *Ogden.*

The decision was one of the few popular ones which Marshall

ever rendered. And yet there were many dissidents. Slaveowners, for example, were deeply alarmed for the future of the interstate slave trade. Others, more selfless and high-minded—and of these Thomas Jefferson was the first and greatest—saw in *Gibbons* v. *Ogden* only a despotic extension of the powers of the federal government. What Gibbons and Ogden had to say has not been recorded for the instruction of posterity. One might add, however, by way of postscript, that Ogden died a bankrupt and Gibbons a millionaire. Since Ogden was undoubtedly the more estimable of the two, one must leave it to the reader to decide whether the tendency of this essay is on the whole to emphasize the injudiciousness of yielding to a monopoly or the advantage of breaking the law.

THE CHARLES RIVER BRIDGE DEPICTED IN A POPULAR MAGAZINE A FEW
YEARS AFTER THE SPAN'S COMPLETION.

The Charles River Bridge Case

BY HENRY F. GRAFF

(*Charles River Bridge* v. *Warren Bridge*, 11 Peters 420)

The safeguarding of property rights, one of John Marshall's major objectives, was a necessary condition for rapid economic growth. By making property too sacrosanct, however, some of Marshall's decisions threatened to slow up progress by hindering the development of new enterprises. The Charles River Bridge case, which came to a climax only after Marshall's death in 1835, involved the claims and counterclaims of rival bridge builders in Boston, Massachusetts. It produced a decision as epochal as many of Marshall's greatest. Professor Graff of the Columbia University history department has written many works in the field of American history and is coauthor of The Modern Researcher.

       Bridges and the rivers they span have long been the subject of romancers as well as the business of engineers. And whether at San Luis Rey or over the Kwai or where Horatius stood alone, the drama inevitably revolves about the tension a bridge creates between, on the one hand, its own brave existence and, on the other, the magical changes it brings in the lives of the people who use it. Every bridge, real no less than fictional, is one of a kind —in design, in impact, in significance.

    At least one American span lives in assured immortality. It is the one that the descendants of the Massachusetts Puritans put across the Charles River at Boston in 1786. An ordinary bridge by some standards, its draw swayed in the strong winter wind and its broad planks froze over badly when the weather was cold and the spray from the river high. But it became in time the symbol of a clash between two conceptions of government's role in the economy, and gave rise ultimately to a case enshrined in the nation's constitutional history. The impress of the dispute on the development of the country's transportation, on the course of antitrust actions, and on American free capitalism itself has been abiding.

The Charles River Bridge case began on October 17, 1640, when the General Court of the Massachusetts Bay Colony, then only seventeen years old, bestowed on Harvard College the right to operate a ferryboat across the Charles River between Boston and Charlestown. Over the years the tolls from this enterprise fluctuated, but the profits were never large. After 1701 the ferry franchise was sublet, but returns still remained modest because the cost of maintaining the ferry and the ferry slip was high. Not until after the War of Independence, when the river traffic had increased markedly, did the promise of higher profits seem close to fulfillment —a significant fact in the life of an impecunious liberal arts college, as Harvard was.

In the year 1785, though, the Commonwealth of Massachusetts took a bold step that its leaders believed would keep Massachusetts abreast of the times. It incorporated as the "Proprietors of the Charles River Bridge" a group of entrepreneurs which included, among other well-known figures, that old friend of enterprise and progress, the merchant John Hancock. The proprietors were empowered to replace the Boston-Charlestown ferry with a bridge. For the "income of the ferry which they might have received had not said bridge been erected," Harvard College was to be reimbursed during the next forty years in the amount of £200 annually, equivalent to about $670. At the end of that time a reasonable sum would be paid to Harvard College as final compensation.

The new bridge, a remarkable example of the engineering skill of the day, was opened on June 17, 1786—a glorious way to mark the eleventh anniversary of the Battle of Bunker Hill. Standing 1,470 feet long and 42 feet wide, it would defy the lugubrious predictions that the tidal currents or the breaking up of the ice on the Charles would smash its footings and bring it down. The designer of this masterpiece was Major Samuel Sewall; the supervisor of construction was the gifted artisan Lemuel Cox, who earned something of an international reputation for his labors. At the jubilant celebration of the opening, fellow citizens paid Cox tribute in a poem containing the lines:

> Now Boston, Charlestown, nobly join,
> And roast a fatted Ox;
> On noted Bunker Hill combine,
> To toast our patriot, Cox.

Among the twenty thousand people who were present on that bright occasion, no one could have foreseen the long legislative and legal battles that would make the name of the bridge legendary. In 1786 there was simply rejoicing. Such a splendid example of American technology must surely be only a foretaste of other marvels to come. At the time the span was completed, 150 shares of capital stock were outstanding; representing the cost of the bridge—$50,000—they were worth at par $333.33 each.

Within a few years, as the prosperity that accompanied the establishment of the Constitution continued, a petition was offered in the state legislature to build another bridge—this one to cross the Charles River between Boston and Cambridge. The proprietors of the Charles River Bridge and the spokesmen for Harvard College (often difficult to tell apart) were understandably distressed. They argued vehemently that the loss of revenue on the Charles River Bridge in consequence of a new span would be substantial. But the committee of the legislature before which the matter had come took the position that the proprietors had never been granted a monopoly on the crossing of the river. This stand carried the day, and authorization to build the new bridge was approved by the General Court. The grantees, nevertheless, were obliged to pay Harvard an annuity as compensation. Furthermore, the annuity payable to the college by the Charles River Bridge was extended from forty to seventy years; that is, to the year 1856.

John Hancock, now governor of Massachusetts, had a notion to veto the bill. Interested speculators, however, had outmaneuvered this champion of the people and made a veto seem unbecoming by publishing a newspaper advertisement announcing the sale of shares. It began: "As *all* citizens have an *equal* right to propose a measure that may be beneficial to the public or advantageous to themselves, and as no body of men have an *exclusive* right to take to themselves such a privilege, a number of gentlemen have proposed to open a new subscription for the purpose of a bridge from West

Boston to Cambridge, at such a place as the General Court may be pleased to direct."

Although Hancock, ever attentive to the public voice, did not withhold his approval from the bill, he had not felt helpless to protect his own investment. He used his influence to have the bridge established "near the Pest House" on the Boston side, and he arranged to have the proprietors of the new bridge pay Harvard £300—one hundred more than his own was paying! The principal proprietor of the new venture, Francis Dana, who had served during the Revolution as the first American minister to Russia, did not find the location as objectionable as his adversaries had hoped, because the Pest House was at the point nearest to Cambridge. Dana, however, protested strenuously the £100 difference between his obligation and that of the Hancock interests, and he succeeded in having the annuity payment reduced to £200.

When Dana's West Boston Bridge was opened on November 23, 1793, it was hailed for its beauty immediately. Many people thought it outclassed the Charles River Bridge by far. The *Columbian Centinel* exulted that the "elegance of workmanship" and "the magnitude of the undertaking are perhaps unequalled in the history of enterprises." The first pedestrian to traverse this wonderwork was the patriot Elbridge Gerry, a signer of the Declaration of Independence and later vice president of the United States.

The Boston community was now enjoying the convenience of two bridges, and Harvard College was enjoying annually the use of £400 in compensatory payments. As the traffic on both spans increased, the tolls poured in and the value of the stock grew apace. How fascinating it was that so much money could be made out of the transit of people and goods from one side of the Charles to the other! By 1805 the value of a share of Charles River Bridge stock had risen to $1,650. A few years later the cautious overseers of Harvard College bought two shares at $2,080 each, deeming them a prudent investment.

But shortly their judgment seemed questionable. New outlooks were forming, and a new world was in the making. By the 1820s perceptive people were being persuaded that charters which tended to be exclusive in practice, like the one granted to the Charles River Bridge proprietors, hindered rather than helped the growth of business. Emerging leaders had not yet become fully convinced that competition was the life of trade, but they were inclining toward that view. For the moment they focused their energy on arguing that the Charles River Bridge monopoly was a costly bottleneck in the circulation of people and goods in the busy city of Boston. Public support to end the old exclusivity seems to have developed parallel with the spirit of Jacksonian democracy, which ultimately destroyed the greatest monopoly of all: the Bank of the United States.[1]

A sign of the new stirring was the petition introduced in the Massachusetts legislature by a group of merchants in 1823 to build another bridge over the Charles, this one for foot passengers, to be wholly toll-free. Not least of the spurs to action was rising irritation that the tolls on the Charles River Bridge—unchanged since 1786, when the traffic was only half as great—were handsomely rewarding the proprietors while unjustly burdening the community. Comparable petitions followed at subsequent sessions of the legislature were rejected each time. The Charles River Bridge proprietors insisted that the building of a new bridge would flagrantly damage their property interests. Estimating the value of their bridge at $280,000, they declared, in answer to the charge that it had paid back its original shareholders many times over, that the majority of the equity was "holden by persons who have purchased stock within the last ten or fifteen year—by widows, by orphans, by literary and charitable institutions. The erection of another bridge from Charlestown to Boston would annihilate at once two-thirds of this property." Besides, the proprietors regarded a new span as quite unnecessary. They maintained that advocates of it were interested not in *another* bridge but in a *free* one. The proprietors declared in a pamphlet they issued that "scarcely a man . . . would be in favour of a new bridge if the charter contained a provision for taking a foot toll." The Harvard Corporation vigorously backed the proprietors' argument.

By the end of the 1820s the tone of the remonstrances for a new bridge had become more strident and, in fact, the general atmosphere of the discussion was changing. Opponents of the new bridge had lost their easy confidence that the law would unfailingly protect charters in their exclusivity. The issue was dragged into the political arena, with the Democrats arrayed on the side of permitting

[1]See Chapter III, "The Bank Cases."

the new bridge and the Whigs, strengthened and emboldened by the involvement of revered Harvard College, firmly committed to opposing it.

For the Whigs, nothing less than the good faith of government seemed to be at stake in the controversy. In 1827, vetoing a proposal for a new bridge, Governor Levi Lincoln said it this way: "To the interest and confidence of private associations we must look for investment of funds in the prosecution of valuable and useful objects, and it is only from a firm reliance on the most scrupulous regard to rights under acts of incorporation that they will be encouraged to action." Lincoln's eyes were fixed not only on the plight of his alma mater but also on the canals and new steam railroads just being developed and the possibilities they opened for revolutionizing transportation. Only the year before, the first railroad had been incorporated in Massachusetts. It was a small one, designed to carry granite from the quarries of Quincy to the Neponsit River, but the handwriting was on the wall and, to him, clear: If people were to be encouraged to invest in railroads, railroad charters must be sacrosanct. Two questions cried out for an answer: Could the state destroy the equity of a corporation it had once helped to create? And yet, could the state disregard the current requirements and interests of its citizens by holding them to be less important than contracts drawn in an earlier day when public needs were different?

These questions could not easily be settled with justice to all parties. But a solution could not be indefinitely delayed. The growing size of Boston helped to hasten the day of reckoning. The population of the city had leaped from 39,000 in 1810 to 54,000 in 1820. The census of 1830 would show it to be over 85,000. The city's economy, already expanding phenomenally, would not be restrained by the sophistries and tortuous reasoning of bridge-toll collectors. Is it any wonder that there was continual talk of a free bridge over the Charles, and that it became a perennial issue in state politics?

Under increasing pressure to yield, the Charles River Bridge proprietors proposed surrendering their property to the state for a sum to be agreed upon by impartial commissioners. Alternatively, they said they would surrender their bridge without payment of any kind after eight more years of operation. Confident of the intention of Massachusetts to defend their rights, they expressed a desire to be relieved of the need to argue their case periodically before committees of the legislature, or ultimately in the courts.

On the surface, the issue was between the old and the new. But it also partook of a tug-of-war between urban and rural Massachusetts. The rural portion was contending for the right to enter Boston free of charge; the city fathers, possibly better attuned to the virtue of observing contracts, defended the toll collectors. The legislature, showing no more determination to stand against the force of public sentiment than do most representatives of the people, on March 12, 1828, approved a charter for a new span to be known as the Warren Bridge, in honor of Joseph Warren, a martyr of Bunker Hill.

The proprietors of the Warren Bridge, under the charter's terms, would collect tolls until the cost of construction plus 5 percent had been recovered. After that time, passage across the bridge would be toll-free. In any event, the term of toll collecting was not to exceed six years. Until the bridge became free, its proprietors agreed to assume one-half of the annuity of £200 required to be paid to Harvard College by the Charles River Bridge. Despite strenuous protest by a number of the leading citizens of Massachusetts—for the most part, alumni of Harvard—Governor Lincoln, who prided himself on being part of a new generation of leadership, signed the enactment. Thereupon began officially the saga of the Warren Bridge.

Immediately, the proprietors of the Charles River Bridge sought a preliminary injunction against the building of the proposed span. Counsel for the Charles River Bridge were the incomparable Daniel Webster and Lemuel Shaw, later chief justice of the Massachusetts supreme court. Of primary concern to the proprietors was the estimate that the Warren Bridge would easily absorb two-thirds of the traffic over the river. At the Charlestown end the new bridge, when completed, would be only 260 feet away from the Charles River Bridge; at the Boston end the distance would be a mere 916 feet. The roads leading from them would come within 26 feet of each other. Clearly, the traffic—and the tolls—on the Charles River Bridge would cease altogether when the Warren Bridge reverted to the state in six years. To show the amount of their equity at stake, the proprietors offered in court the fact that from 1786 to 1827 the Charles River Bridge had collected $824,798 in tolls. Although the court did not grant the preliminary injunction, it left the door open for future litigation. The opinion was rendered by Chief Justice Isaac Parker, who until a year and a half before had held the Royall Professorship at the Harvard Law School, which he had helped to establish.

In anticipation of the opening of the Warren Bridge on Christmas Day, 1828, the stockholders of the Charles River Bridge reckoned anew the anticipated loss in tolls. Harvard College felt particularly a victim. When the new bridge became free in 1834, Harvard stood to lose an annuity of £200 that had twenty-three more years to run and the value of its Charles River Bridge stock, which would, of course, become virtually worthless.

In their next proceeding for legal relief, the Charles River Bridge proprietors asserted that the creation of the new company violated their charter and in so doing also violated the contract clause of the United States Constitution, and further that to be deprived of property without compensation was a violation of the Massachusetts Constitution.

The defendants filed their answers early in December 1828, even before they had collected their first toll, and the titanic court battle was thus joined. Their strategy was to seek delay until the successful operation of their bridge drew public sentiment to their side. Not until more than a year later, on January 12, 1830, were the opinions handed down. The court proved to be evenly divided: two of the justices declared the statute creating the new bridge unconstitutional and two upheld it. Chief Justice Parker, in attacking the law, expressed the interesting view that the high profits earned over the years by the Charles River Bridge had willy-nilly adversely affected the case for indemnifying its proprietors. He observed that if the Warren Bridge had been authorized without appropriate compensation in 1787, when the Charles River Bridge was only a year old, "the opinion of the injustice would have been universal."

On the other side was the no less stern view of Judge Marcus Morton, an appointee of Governor Lincoln. He declared that to accept the arguments of the Charles River Bridge proprietors meant that "no improved road, no new bridge, no canal, no railroad, can be constitutionally established. For I think, in the present state of our country, no such improved channel of communication can be opened without diminishing the profits of some old corporation."

The court was aware that railroad interests were watching the outcome closely. Until the extent of charter rights could be ascertained, potential investors would view askance the railroad securities now beginning to appear throughout the country.

Morton, for many years an overseer of Harvard, was also a devout Jacksonian and may be said to have been uttering the anticorporation sentiments of his political constituents. He ran for governor on the Democratic ticket in every election year from 1828 to 1843, not stepping down from the bench until be was finally elected in 1839.

Without delay, the issue was taken to the United States Supreme Court. It was set to be argued in the following year. This final drama would be inseparably interwoven, as the whole question had been from the first, with the name of Harvard College. The Supreme Court, presided over by the aging John Marshall, included Joseph Story, who in 1829 had been appointed the Dane Professor at the Harvard Law School. A brilliant letter writer, he kept his family and friends in Cambridge well informed about the arguments presented in those five crowded days in March 1831, when the case was heard. The pleadings held the charm for him not only of a competition carried to its conclusion, but also of a gladiatorial spectacle delicious for its own sake. Yet his personal sympathy for the Charles River Bridge cause was always apparent.

Chief counsel for the Charles River Bridge was Daniel Webster, without peer among the lawyer-advocates of his day. At Webster's side was Warren Dutton, another prominent attorney, who had a personal interest in the Charles River Bridge. For the Warren Bridge, chief counsel was William Wirt, who had been attorney general under James Monroe, and John Quincy Adams, and at his side was Walker Jones, a District of Columbia lawyer of repute. Wirt, who earlier had served as prosecuting attorney in Aaron Burr's trial for treason, was a master of the courtroom. Story, deeply moved by the intellectual excitement of the trial, wrote to a Harvard colleague:

We . . . have heard the opening counsel on each side in three days. Dutton for the plaintiffs made a capital argument in point of matter and manner, lawyerlike, close, searching and exact; Jones on the other side was ingenious, metaphysical, and occasionally strong and striking. Wirt goes on to-day and Webster will follow tomorrow.

But for all the brilliance of the argument, the court was not yet ready to decide. Owing to the illness, indisposition, and death of several justices, it would be another six years before the verdict came down. A decision of this importance, it seemed, ought not to be made with less than the full court in attendance. Meanwhile, the cast of characters significantly changed.

Marshall died in 1835. (We will never be certain where he stood on the issue, although it might be inferred from the Dartmouth College case that he would have defended as inviolable the rights conferred by the Charles River Bridge charter.) Two other members of the court also died. So did William Wirt, on February 14, 1834. The case, patently, would have to be reargued before a reconstituted court by a reorganized defense.

When at last President Jackson filled the vacancies on the Supreme Bench, the membership included a new chief justice, Roger B. Taney of Maryland. Taney was the product of a different political tradition than Marshall. His career measured the road over which the new country had traveled in the generation that separated him from his great predecessor. Born in Maryland, he grew up in a family of wealthy slave owners who raised tobacco. Entering politics after graduation from Dickinson College, he became a staunch Federalist. He broke with his party's leadership when it opposed the War of 1812, but not yet with the party itself. That rupture did not come until 1824, when he committed his political future to the Jacksonians. In 1831 he accepted an appointment as Jackson's attorney general. Then, as the third in the line of secretaries of the Treasury that Jackson appointed, Taney obeyed the President's order to remove the government's deposits from the Bank of the United States in the famous struggle with "the Monster."

In 1835, at the age of fifty-eight, Taney had been designated by Jackson to be an associate justice of the Supreme Court. Marshall had personally approved of the appointment, but an angry Senate, regarding Taney as a pliant tool of the President, had rejected it. The membership and the mood of the Senate changed quickly, however, and the following year, when Jackson nominated Taney to be Marshall's successor in the chief justiceship, he was quickly confirmed. A New York newspaper commented sourly: "The pure ermine of the Supreme Court is sullied by the appointment of that political hack." This was a partisan judgment, for Taney was a man of conviction with a good legal mind. The first Supreme Court chief to wear trousers rather than knee breeches, he was an obvious threat to the past. It was misleading to judge him by his gentle appearance, to which deep-set, collie-like eyes lent an almost melancholy air; his manner was leonine and his purpose firm.

Taney's fault in the view of his adversaries was that on economic matters he faced the future. Taney had formulated his position on one of the principal questions of the day, namely the role of the corporation which performs public services: what we today call the public utility. In an opinion written in 1832 as attorney general, Taney had said that corporations engaged in providing services to the community, such as the building and maintaining of roads and bridges, bore special responsibilities. The charters of such corporations, he explained, can "never be considered as having been granted for the exclusive benefit of the corporators. Certain privileges are given to them in order to obtain a public convenience; and the interest of the public must, I presume, always be regarded as the main object of every charter for a toll-bridge or a turnpike road."

Cognizant like Marshall of the formative role he could play, Taney intended to write *his* economic views into the Constitution. The Charles River Bridge case, the first case he would hear, could not help but appeal to Taney. Not only was its substance made to order for him, but the impact of the decision would be considerable. Further delay, moreover, was indefensible, not least of all because in the half-dozen years since the case was first argued, fresh complications had developed at the Charles River.

By 1837 the commuters of Boston had put the *Warren* Bridge under attack. Its very success was the cause. The bridge had paid for itself within two years of its completion, and almost immediately a general cry arose that its use be made toll-free immediately. The legislature could not permit such a public benefit, lest an unfavorable decision by the Supreme Court in the Charles River Bridge case impose heavy damages and consequent financial liabilities on the Warren Bridge proprietors.

Therefore the collection of tolls was extended annually. In 1835, however, the legislature took from the proprietors of the Warren Bridge all further interest in the tolls, and provided that subsequent collections be earmarked for use exclusively in the maintenance and repair of the bridge and for "such sums of money as may be recov-

ered by the proprietors of Charles River Bridge in any suit in law
or equity." When the Warren Bridge became free of tolls at last in
April 1836, Charlestown held a celebration. Robert Rantoul, the
reformer whose legal arguments and victory on behalf of labor in
the case of *Commonwealth* v. *Hunt* a few years hence established a
towering landmark in the history of unionization in America, was
publicly thanked for his unceasing efforts, now rewarded. Gloomily,
the proprietors of the Charles River Bridge opened their draw and
suspended operations.

The Harvard College Corporation was thoroughly discomfited.
With the Warren Bridge free, the annuity from it had ceased to be
payable. Furthermore, the Charles River Bridge stock was now practically valueless and the proprietors were unable to pay the annuity
to which they were pledged.

This was the situation when, at the end of January 1837, the case
was reargued in Washington. For the Charles River Bridge, counsel
was once again the imposing Daniel Webster, senior senator from
Massachusetts, and Warren Dutton; for the Warren Bridge proprietors, Simon Greenleaf, holder of the Royall Professorship at the
Harvard Law School, and John Davis, junior senator and former
governor of Massachusetts. It is noteworthy that twenty-six-year-old
Charles Sumner (destined also to sit in the Senate for Massachusetts) substituted for Greenleaf at the Harvard Law School in the
weeks of Greenleaf's absence in Washington. Harvard had dutifully
given Greenleaf permission to defend the Warren Bridge side of the
issue. He had formally inquired whether the Harvard Corporation
would permit him to engage in the practice of law as his predecessor
had. If the Harvard authorities were irritated that he was on the
"other side" of the issue they gave no hint, granting him leave for
two weeks "for the purpose of arguing an important cause before
the Supreme Court of the United States."

Still sitting like the spokesman for old New England, pained but
gripped in this hour when Massachusetts men were turned upon
one another with the welfare of society and Harvard at stake, was
Joseph Story of the class of 1798. He wrote his son of the proceedings:

We have been for a week engaged in hearing the Charles River Bridge
cause. It was a glorious argument on all sides, strong and powerful and apt.

Mr. Greenleaf spoke with great ability and honored Dane College—Mr. Webster pronounced one of his greatest speeches. Mr. Dutton was full of learning and acute remarks, and so was Governor Davis—"Greek met Greek."

And a few days later Story was writing to Sumner: "On the whole it was a glorious exhibition for old Massachusetts; four of her leading men brought out in the same cause, and none of them inferior to those who are accustomed to the lead here."

The decision, then, could not fail in one way or another to be an intellectual triumph. But not, as it turned out, for Harvard. In a powerful decision rendered on February 12, 1837, Taney spoke for the majority of a court split 7–2. He arrayed himself unequivocally on the side of "progress," declaring that grants by state legislatures such as the charter for the Charles River Bridge cannot be construed as exclusive unless specifically stated to be so. His language seemed crystal clear:

The whole community are interested in this inquiry and they have a right to require that the power of promoting their comfort and convenience, and of advancing the public prosperity, by providing safe, convenient, and cheap ways for the transportation of produce and the purposes of travel, shall not be construed to have been surrendered or diminished by the state unless it shall appear by plain words that it was intended to be done.

And what, he asked, would happen if the Court took an opposite position and permitted an exclusive right for the Charles River Bridge? In that event, he averred, America would "find the old turnpike corporations awakening from their sleep and calling upon this court to put down the improvements which have taken their place." The building of canals and railroads would be arrested and the country would have to wait until the old turnpike companies had been satisfied and were ready to permit Americans "to avail themselves of the lights of modern science, and to partake of the benefit of those improvements which are now adding to the wealth and prosperity, and the convenience and comfort, of every other part of the civilized world." Story in his eloquent dissent stood where he always had in decrying any "encroachment upon the rights and liberties of the citizens, secured by public grants [of charter rights]. I will not consent to shake their title deeds by any speculative niceties or novelties."

Webster testily predicted that the decision would be overturned. He proved to be wrong. As the construction of railroads went forward in the next generation, the Court's holding became the basis for limiting the rights granted by their charters. The effect on the railways themselves was not always salutary. Ruinous competition often enervated roads financially and left them with inadequate rolling stock and roadbeds.

Fears that the courts were weakening in their defense of property rights proved illusory and foolish. Not so the defense of monopoly. Charles Warren, an eminent historian of the Supreme Court, regarded the Charles River Bridge case as one of the two great antitrust cases of the country's early national history (the other being *Gibbons* v. *Ogden*),[2] creating precedents that have been followed even in the present century.

For decades the implications of Taney's decision for the Commonwealth of Massachusetts itself continued to reverberate. In 1837 the Massachusetts legislature appointed a joint committee to examine the question of compensation for the Charles River Bridge proprietors. Such indemnification seemed unlikely. But in 1841 the issue was resolved with the payment of $25,000 for the surrender to the state of all rights held by the proprietors. The Charles River Bridge was now reopened to travel, after having been closed for about five years, and a toll was once again charged. The same act of the legislature made the Warren Bridge a toll bridge again! And in 1847 the state of Massachusetts compensated Harvard College for the annuities it had lost by awarding it the sum of $3,330. Harvard's treasurer recorded: "It is agreeable to see the disposition manifested by the state, once more to do something for education at Cambridge after the lapse of so long an interval in her patronage."

Tolls on the bridges were removed at the end of 1843. Except for a short time between 1854 and 1858, the bridges remained free ever after. In 1887 the right and title to the Charles River Bridge were transferred to the city of Boston. This opened the way, when the Boston Transit Commission made ready to build a still more modern form of transportation—a subway—to demolish the old bridge and build a new one, of steel and stone, called the Charlestown

[2]See Chapter IV, "The Steamboat Case."

Bridge. Just as the nineteenth century was drawing to a close the last of the Charles River Bridge was hauled away, victim of disrespectful demolition crews and the ravages of time. Yet in its fashion it still stands, an indestructible monument to the dogged struggle between property rights and human needs that once assailed the New England conscience.

DRED AND HARRIET SCOTT.

The Dred Scott Case VI

BY DON E. FEHRENBACHER

(*Dred Scott* v. *Sandford*, 19 Howard 393)

*Constitutional questions relating to the rights of blacks began to attract the
attention of American courts in the 1780s, when a Massachusetts man, Nathaniel Jennings, was indicted for attacking one Quock Walker. Jennings's
defense was that Walker was his slave, but the Massachusetts Supreme Court
ruled (1783) that "slavery is inconsistent with our . . . [State] Constitution,"
thus effectively abolishing the institution in the Commonwealth. Other Northern Courts followed this Massachusetts precedent.*

*However, the federal Constitution recognized the "peculiar institution" as
a matter for state control and in Article IV included an authorization for a
national fugitive slave law. Congress passed such a law in 1793. In the case
of* Prigg v. *Pennsylvania (1842), the Supreme Court upheld the constitutionality of this act, and eight years later, as part of the Compromise of 1850,
Congress passed a very stringent Fugitive Slave Act which denied jury trials
to accused fugitives apprehended in free states.*

*A still more important constitutional question was that of the power of
Congress to regulate slavery in the territories. For decades this power was
assumed. The Ordinance of 1787 banned the institution from the old Northwest Territory, and the Missouri Compromise of 1820 outlawed it in the
Louisiana Territory north of 36 degrees, 30 minutes north latitude, except for
the state of Missouri. Some Southerners, however, most notably John C. Calhoun of South Carolina, argued that Congress was bound by the Constitution
to maintain slavery in the territories, since its abolition in these regions discriminated against one class of citizens, those who owned property in the form
of slaves. Of course, nearly all Northerners objected violently to this doctrine.
The Supreme Court took it upon itself to settle this argument in the case
described by Don E. Fehrenbacher, author of* The Dred Scott Case, *which
won a Pulitzer Prize.*

On March 15, 1836, the United States Senate confirmed the appointment of Roger B. Taney as chief justice of the Supreme Court. Later that same spring, an army medical officer accompanied by his black servant, Dred Scott, traveled up the Mississippi River to a new assignment in federal territory where slavery had been forbidden by the Missouri Compromise. The historical convergence of these two unrelated but nearly simultaneous events lay twenty years in the future. Yet the forces that would ultimately bring them together were already visible.

By 1836, the new wave of radical abolitionism had turned Congress into a battleground over antislavery petitions, and in that year the House of Representatives dealt with the problem by imposing its notorious "gag rule." The ensuing uproar continued for almost a decade. It was also in 1836 that the American settlers in Texas won their struggle for independence from Mexico and established an independent republic. Soon the antislavery petitioners in the United States were concentrating their efforts on a campaign against the proposed annexation of Texas. Thus the issue of the expansion of slavery, presumably settled for good in the Missouri Compromise of 1820, began once again to shake the foundations of the Union. In 1846, when the annexation of Texas led to war between the United States and Mexico, the expectation of further American expansion prompted the introduction in Congress of the Wilmot Proviso, which proposed to exclude slavery from any territory that might be acquired as a result of the conflict. Although it failed to become law, the Proviso inaugurated a new and dangerous phase of the sectional struggle over slavery. It was during that same critical year that Dred Scott took the first steps in his legal fight for freedom.

Scott, a little man scarcely five feet tall, was then about forty-five years old. A St. Louis newspaper later described him as "illiterate but not ignorant," with "strong common sense" that had been sharpened by his many travels. It is possible that he acquired his unusual name belatedly, after having been known simply as "Sam" in his younger years. According to the scanty historical record, he was probably born in Virginia and migrated to Missouri by way of Alabama with his master, Peter Blow. Shortly before or soon after Blow's death in 1832, Scott was sold to John Emerson, a St. Louis physician about to enter military service.

Dr. Emerson, despite his Pennsylvania origins, apparently felt no qualms about slave owning. During the winter of 1833–34, he took Scott with him to his first post at Rock Island in the free state of Illinois. Some two years later, as a result of army orders, master and slave moved farther north to Fort Snelling, located in federal territory near the site of modern St. Paul, Minnesota. At that frontier outpost, Scott met and was allowed to marry a slave named Harriet Robinson, the servant of the local Indian agent.

With a new wife and duties that were less than arduous, Dred Scott presumably found life relatively pleasant at Fort Snelling, but his master was dissatisfied. Emerson wrote to the surgeon general complaining about the effect of the cold weather on his health and was promptly transferred to Fort Jesup in western Louisiana. There he became acquainted with Irene Sanford, a lovely young Virginia woman visiting the fort. They were married after about two months of courtship, but Emerson hated Louisiana and his complaints won him reassignment to Fort Snelling. He could not in fact be comfortable anywhere, for he was suffering from the secondary effects of syphilis, contracted, apparently, on the eve of his entry into the army. It may have been his increasingly querulous behavior that brought about another transfer in 1840—this time to Florida, where the Seminole War was still being fought.

The Scotts were with Emerson at Fort Jesup and made the trip back to Fort Snelling with him and his bride. They did not go to Florida, however, but instead accompanied Mrs. Emerson to St. Louis, where she settled down to await her husband's return. It was probably at this point that Dred, now the father of two daughters, renewed his ties with the Blow family. Emerson, meanwhile, served in Florida until 1842 and then, after complaining once too often to the surgeon general, was awarded an honorable dismissal from the service. He died the next year. At about this time, the Scotts were apparently hired or loaned to Mrs. Emerson's brother-in-law, an army officer, and Dred as a consequence may have traveled as far away as Texas before being sent back to St. Louis in the spring of 1846.

In the litigation about to begin, Scott had some influential support, especially from the Blows. The motives on both sides were unquestionably straightforward and personal. Dred Scott wanted freedom for himself and his family; Irene Emerson wanted to retain ownership of her slaves. There is no evidence of an attempt to contrive a test case.

After certain preliminaries required by Missouri law, Scott and his wife brought separate suits against Mrs. Emerson. The facts and arguments were so similar, however, that the two cases were eventually treated by stipulation as one. The attorneys for Scott claimed that Emerson, by holding him as a slave in the free state of Illinois and in federal territory where slavery was prohibited, had thereby emancipated him. Although judicial precedent in Missouri was clearly on Scott's side, the decision of the state circuit court went against him because of a technical deficiency in the preparation of his case. The judge granted a motion for a new trial. Mrs. Emerson's counsel challenged that action in the Missouri supreme court, which ruled in Scott's favor. Other delays followed, and the second trial did not take place until 1850, that memorable year of sectional crisis and compromise. This time, Dred Scott won. The court declared him to be a free man, but Mrs. Emerson carried an appeal to the state supreme court. There, in 1852, Scott became a political pawn. The court by a 2–1 vote repudiated Missouri precedent and angrily declared that the state would no longer enforce the antislavery law of other jurisdictions against Missouri's own citizens. Dred Scott's residence elsewhere was pronounced irrelevant. In Missouri, he remained a slave.

Scott's only remaining hope, it appeared, was an appeal to the Supreme Court of the United States. However, a recent decision in another case apparently convinced Scott's attorneys that the Court would refuse to accept jurisdiction. They decided instead to file a new suit for freedom in the United States circuit court for Missouri. Such a suit in federal court was possible only between citizens of different states. Mrs. Emerson had in fact moved to Massachusetts and become a citizen of that state, but naming her as defendant again would have been more like resuming the old suit than commencing a new one. Furthermore, it would have amounted to taking an appeal from the highest court of a state to a lower federal court and might have been turned aside for that reason.

Scott's lawyers needed a new defendant and found him in the person of Mrs. Emerson's brother, John F. A. Sanford of New York, who had been acting as her agent in the Dred Scott litigation and may even have become the slave's owner. So there took shape the famous case of *Dred Scott* v. *Sandford* (with Sanford's name misspelled in the official record). It came to trial in May 1854, just as the inflammatory Kansas-Nebraska Act was being maneuvered toward final passage in Congress and inspiring a political revolution.

In Dred Scott's suit against Mrs. Emerson, the central issue had been how residence on free soil affected the legal status of a slave. This was a familiar issue that had been dealt with in a number of state court decisions. During the early decades of the Republic, a kind of sectional accommodation had developed. Southerners were generally able to take their personal servants temporarily into free states without interference. At the same time, there was general acceptance of the rule that a slave kept more or less permanently in a free state became forever free. This arrangement began to break down in the 1830s, however, largely because of antislavery pressure. A number of Northern states withdrew the sojourning privilege, and there was growing acceptance of the view that any slave other than a fugitive became free the moment he set foot on free soil. To Southerners, the change was not only inconvenient but insulting, and they looked for ways to retaliate.

Dred Scott v. *Sandford,* by its very nature, raised an additional issue of great importance. In order to maintain a suit in federal court, Scott had to claim that he was a citizen of Missouri. Sanford's counsel challenged this assertion by arguing that blacks were *not* citizens and that the court therefore lacked jurisdiction. The question of Negro citizenship had arisen previously in a number of state courts, but it remained unsettled, partly because of the marginal position of free blacks in American society, and partly because the term "citizen," though used in the United States from the time of the Revolution, was not authoritatively defined until after the Civil War. Hostility to Negro citizenship prevailed throughout most of the country and was especially intense in the South, where unrestricted control of the free black population seemed essential to the security of the slave system.

Few white Americans wanted blacks to enjoy all the privileges associated with citizenship. But at the same time, few were determined to strip them of all rights. Could it not be argued, then, that a free Negro, whatever his other disabilities, was enough of a citizen to have access to the federal courts? The Taney Court had already arrived at just such a compromise in determining the legal status of corporations, and this was the course followed by the trial judge in *Dred Scott* v. *Sandford*. He ruled that any person residing in a state and legally capable of owning property there was qualified to bring suit under the diverse-citizenship clause of the Constitution. In the trial on the merits of the case, however, the judge instructed the jury in favor of the defendant. Like the Missouri supreme court in *Scott* v. *Emerson*, he declared that Scott's status, after returning to Missouri, depended entirely upon the law of that state, without regard to his residence in free territory. The jury accordingly brought in a verdict for Sanford.

The case then proceeded on writ of error to the United States Supreme Court, a judicial body more powerful, said Alexis de Tocqueville, than any other tribunal known to history. The Court at this time consisted of five Southern Democrats, two Northern Democrats, one Northern Whig, and one Republican. Chief Justice Taney, almost eighty years old, had become a venerable public figure, seemingly far removed from his controversial days as a Jacksonian politician and cabinet officer. Fairly tall, but stooped and frail, with a withered, homely face and the stained teeth of a heavy cigar smoker, he presided over his fellow justices in a gentle manner that only partly concealed a strong-willed personality. Taney's most important judicial opinions to date, such as the one delivered in the *Charles River Bridge* case,[1] had been concerned with business enterprise and its regulation by state governments. But in the few slavery cases coming before the Court, he had revealed himself as a resolute defender of Southern interests.

Having a crowded docket, the Court did not hear arguments in *Dred Scott* v. *Sandford* until February 1856. When it did, another new issue was injected into the case—the one that gave the Dred Scott decision its prominent place in American history. Now, for the first time, Sanford's counsel argued that Scott had not become free in federal territory because the law prohibiting slavery there was unconstitutional. This was the issue, of course, that had inflamed national politics for the preceding decade and would continue to do so in the final years of sectional crisis.

Congressional regulation of slavery in the territories had begun with the Northwest Ordinance of 1787. The constitutionality of

[1]See Chapter V.

such regulation had not been seriously challenged until the Missouri controversy of 1819–20, and it did not become a major public issue until after introduction of the Wilmot Proviso in 1846. Yet a tendency to "constitutionalize" difficult political issues had been present ever since Jefferson first clashed with Hamilton about the Bank of the United States.[2] Perhaps it was inevitable in a system of government founded on a written constitution.

Constitutionalizing a political argument was a way of stamping "imperative" on one's own doctrines and "illegitimate" on those of the opposition, but in the slavery controversy it also served as a strategy of evasion. The survival of the major political parties as national organizations seemed increasingly to require that quarrels over slavery be kept out of national politics, and so, beginning in 1848, there was strong bipartisan support for turning the territorial question over to the judiciary. At about the same time, certain leaders of the Democratic party began to advocate another strategy of evasion. Congress, they said, must keep its hands off the problem entirely and let the people of each territory decide for themselves whether to establish or prohibit slavery. In the terms then used, this meant "nonintervention" by Congress and "popular sovereignty" in the territories. Let the Supreme Court decide, or let the territorial population decide—either way the disruptive issue would presumably be banished from the halls of Congress. Both solutions were incorporated in the Compromise of 1850 and in the Kansas-Nebraska Act of 1854.

By 1856, with the new and aggressive Republican coalition having replaced a disintegrating Whig organization as the major opposition party, the Democrats were relying heavily on the principle of nonintervention to maintain a semblance of unity under the stress of sectional conflict. Congress, they generally agreed, should not and indeed could not establish or prohibit slavery in the territories. But concerning the closely associated principle of popular sovereignty there was no such agreement. Senator Stephen A. Douglas and many other Northern Democrats believed that a territorial legislature could make the critical decision for or against slavery as soon as it was organized. Southerners insisted, however, that the decision could be made only at the *end* of the territorial period,

[2]See Chapter III, "The Bank Cases."

when inhabitants of the territory framed a constitution and applied for statehood.

Facing a presidential election, Democratic leaders in Congress sought to suspend and camouflage their disagreement by turning it also over to the Supreme Court. Republicans hastened to exploit the division in enemy ranks and kept demanding a clearer definition of popular sovereignty. Did a territorial legislature have the power to prohibit slavery or did it not? The same answer echoed back again and again from the Democratic side: "It is a judicial question–a judicial question—a judicial question."

So there were *two* important constitutional issues related to slavery in the territories, both of which had been laid informally before the Supreme Court by politicians who considered them too dangerous to handle. One, in essence the issue between the Republican party and the slaveholding South, was whether *Congress* had the power to forbid slavery in the territories. This was the question recently introduced into the Dred Scott case by defense counsel, but in national politics it had become largely a theoretical question since the failure of the Wilmot Proviso and passage of the Kansas-Nebraska Act. In short, there was no urgent public need for judicial resolution of this issue. The other issue, the one dividing Northern and Southern Democrats, was whether a *territorial legislature* had the power to forbid slavery. This was the question upon which congressional debate centered in 1856 and which Democrats solemnly passed on to the Supreme Court. It was a question, however, that did not arise in the Dred Scott case. Furthermore, the fragile structure of Democratic unity depended upon continuing the evasion— that is, upon leaving the question to the judiciary without ever receiving an answer. Still, the Supreme Court was the one major agency of government that had not yet tried its hand at resolving the sectional conflict, and more than a few Americans hoped that at its command, agitation of the slavery question would subside.

The spring of 1856 was a season of mounting violence in Kansas, angry debate in Congress, and ominous talk about disunion if the Republicans should succeed in electing their presidential candidate. It was plainly not an auspicious time for judicial intervention in the slavery controversy. Prudently, the Court ordered the Dred Scott case to be reargued at its next session. In December 1856, after the election of James Buchanan had quieted fears of disunion, the justices again listened to arguments of counsel, and on March 6, 1857, two days after Buchanan's inauguration, the Court finally announced its decision.

Although Taney spoke officially for the Court, every other justice had something to say, and only one of them explicitly concurred with the chief justice in every particular. One thing alone was perfectly clear: Dred Scott had lost his eleven-year battle for freedom. Seven of the nine justices agreed that at law he was still a slave. Beyond that, the results of the contest were open to dispute.

In his opinion, Taney emphatically excluded blacks from citizenship and denied Congress the power to prohibit slavery in the territories. But were these declarations authoritative? Concerning the first, there was doubt that it had the support of a majority of the justices, while the second was promptly challenged with the label *"obiter dictum."*

The insistence of certain contemporary critics and later historians that Taney, in ruling against Negro citizenship, did not speak for a majority of the Court rests upon the assumption that only those justices explicitly agreeing with him are to be counted on his side. Yet, since Taney's opinion was the authorized opinion of the Court, it seems more appropriate to regard only those justices expressly *disagreeing* with him as constituting the opposition. By this standard, the opinion never encountered dissent from more than two justices on any significant point. More conclusive, however, is the fact that five of the nine justices, in their opinions, spoke of the Negro citizenship question as having been decided by the Court.

Far better known is the complaint that Taney indulged in an *obiter dictum* when he ruled that Congress had no power to prohibit slavery in the territories. That is, after deciding that Dred Scott was not a citizen and therefore could not bring suit in a federal court, the chief justice, it was asserted, had no right to go on and review the merits of the case. Republicans were especially fond of this argument because it enabled them to defend the main plank of their party platform by treating the Court's ruling on territories as without legal effect. What the argument ignored or rejected was Taney's insistence that throughout his opinion he was dealing with the question of jurisdiction. Having concluded that Scott could not be a citizen because he was a *Negro,* the chief justice chose to reinforce the conclusion by also demonstrating that Scott could not be a citizen because he was a *slave*, which entailed examination of the facts of the case. That a judicial opinion may legitimately offer more than one reason for reaching a decision is well established. And such reinforcement was especially appropriate in the Dred Scott case because of the confusion surrounding the citizenship question. The judgment issued by Taney, it should be noted, did not reverse the decision of the circuit court on the merits of the case. Instead it ordered that court to dismiss the case for want of jurisdiction.

Thus it is by no means evident that any of Taney's major rulings were unauthoritative. The charge that one of them was extrajudicial does not stand up well under close scrutiny, and the evidence indicates that in each instance he did present the opinion of the Court. Furthermore, in all branches of government and in popular thought, the "Dred Scott decision" came to mean the opinion of the chief justice.

Taney devoted 44 percent of his opinion to the question of Negro citizenship, 38 percent to the territorial question, and just 2 percent to the original question of whether residence on free soil had the legal effect of emancipating a slave. From beginning to end, it was a proslavery document, written with sectional passion and yielding no concessions whatever to critics of the slaveholding system.

The citizenship issue obviously concerned only free Negroes, not slaves, but Taney ignored the distinction and persistently grouped them together as one degraded class of beings. They had been "subjugated by the dominant race," he declared, "and, whether emancipated or not, yet remained subject to their authority." Thus all blacks, in his view, stood on the same ground, having "no rights or privileges but such as those who held the power and the Government might choose to grant them." Manumission made no difference because the status of the free Negro was fixed forever by the fact that he or his ancestors had once been enslaved. In a later passage, Taney added the notorious statement that will always be associated with his name. At the time of the framing of the Constitution, he declared, the Negro "had no rights which the white man was bound to respect." This was not merely historical commentary, as some defenders of the chief justice have maintained. He also held that the constitutional status of blacks had not changed since 1787.

This obviously meant that in 1857 they *still* had no rights *under the federal Constitution* that whites were bound to respect. The effect of Taney's ruling was to exclude blacks not only from citizenship, but also from every protection given to *persons* by the Constitution of the United States.

As for the more critical territorial question, one might expect that the controlling clause of the Constitution would have been the one authorizing Congress "to dispose of and make all needful rules and regulations respecting the territory or other property belonging to the United States." But Taney began by dismissing that clause as irrelevant. He held that it applied only within the original boundaries of the United States, and that in any case it involved only a power to dispose of public lands, not a power to govern. Congressional authority over the Western territories, he said, came from the clause authorizing the admission of new states, and nothing in that clause or in any other part of the Constitution conferred upon Congress any power concerning slavery in the territories, except "the power coupled with the duty of guarding and protecting the owner in his rights." At one point in his argument, the chief justice seemed about to conclude that congressional prohibition of slavery in the territories was contrary to the due process clause of the Fifth Amendment, but he never actually arrived at that conclusion. Instead, he held that the antislavery provision of the Missouri Compromise was "not warranted" by the Constitution, a vague bit of phrasing that did not clarify his reasoning.

Having thus outlawed the main plank of the Republican platform, Taney went on to strike a heavy blow against the Douglas Democrats and their doctrine of popular sovereignty. If Congress could not prohibit slavery in a territory, he said, neither could it authorize a territorial legislature to do so. "It could confer no power on any local government, established by its authority, to violate the provisions of the Constitution." This statement, being on a subject that had not arisen in the case, was *dictum,* pure and simple, but it exemplified Taney's determination to provide slavery with comprehensive judicial protection.

There remained the problem of whether Dred Scott's two-year residence in the free state of Illinois had made him a free man. Here, Taney simply echoed the ruling of the lower federal court and of the Missouri supreme court in *Scott* v. *Emerson.* Scott's status after his return to Missouri, said the chief justice, depended entirely on Missouri law, and by that law he was still a slave.

The flaws in Taney's opinion were devastatingly exposed by the dissenting justices, John McLean and Benjamin R. Curtis, and by a host of antislavery critics, who promptly launched a violent attack upon the decision. Horace Greeley's New York *Tribune* set the pace with editorials almost every day denouncing this "atrocious," this "wicked," this "abominable" judgment, and scores of other Republican newspapers followed suit. Of course Southerners were delighted with the decision, and most Northern Democrats joined them in rejoicing that Republican doctrine was cast beyond the fringe of constitutionality. In Andrew Jackson's reign, Democrats had been fiercely critical of the Supreme Court, but now they spoke of it in reverent tones as the "august and incorruptible" guardian of the Constitution. At the same time, they denounced its assailants as dangerous men verging not only on sedition but on sacrilege.

Long before then, the two principals in the case had become mere pawns in the sectional struggle, and the verdict of the Court meant little to either of them. John Sanford, the winner, was languishing in an insane asylum at the time. He died two months after the reading of the decision. Dred Scott, the loser, was soon manumitted, but he lived only sixteen months as a free man before succumbing to tuberculosis.

The general legal effect of the decision was likewise relatively slight. In its ruling on the Missouri Compromise, the Court invalidated a law that was already largely repealed, and it denied a power that Congress was no longer disposed to exercise. In ruling against the citizenship of free blacks, the Court did, to be sure, further impair the status of an already scorned and deprived minority, but its influence in this respect was cut short by the Civil War and the Fourteenth Amendment. As judicial precedent, then, the substance of *Dred Scott* v. *Sandford* proved to be unimportant. Yet this was the first instance in which a major federal law was ruled unconstitutional. The decision is therefore a landmark in the development of judicial review and in the growth of judicial power.

Most important, of course, was the immediate influence of the decision on national politics and the slavery controversy. No doubt it did contribute significantly to the sectional animosity that had already reached a dangerously high level. Taney's vehemently proslavery opinion lent credence to the fear of many Northerners that an aggressive slave power was determined to extend its peculiar institution throughout all the federal territories and perhaps even into the free states. At the same time, the fierce Republican attack on the Court's action confirmed many Southerners in the fear that no amount of judicial vindication could protect their slaveholding society against increasing Northern aggression. The decision also aggravated the split in the Democratic party by eliciting Douglas's "Freeport doctrine" and inspiring Southern demands for a territorial slave code. Still, there were many other causes of the hostility between North and South. By itself, the Dred Scott decision probably did not make the difference between sectional compromise and civil war, but it was a conspicuous part of the pattern of events and conditions that caused disruption of the Union.

SALMON P. CHASE.

The Case of the Copperhead Conspirator

VII

BY ALLAN NEVINS

(*ex parte Milligan*, 4 Wallace 2)

In a sense the Civil War represented an attempt by the Southern states to erase the gloss that the Supreme Court had placed upon the Constitution during the first half of the nineteenth century. Secession could be legally justified only by restoring to the states much of the authority that John Marshall's decisions had assigned to the national government. Thus the defeat of the Confederacy permanently established the Marshall view of the Constitution, although it by no means ended the debate over the exact limits of federal and state authority.

The war also brought new constitutional issues to the fore, the most important being the power of the government to restrict civil liberties in time of crisis. Early in the conflict Lincoln authorized the suspension of the writ of habeas corpus under certain circumstances. In May 1861, a citizen of Baltimore, John Merryman, was arrested and imprisoned by the military without trial or formal charge. He petitioned Chief Justice Taney for a writ ordering his captors to bring him into federal circuit court for a hearing. Taney granted this plea, but the local commander, General George Cadwalader, refused to obey, citing Lincoln's order. Taney then filed an opinion, ex parte Merryman, denying the right of the President to suspend habeas corpus. Only Congress could do this, he argued. Lacking executive support, Taney was unable to free the prisoner, but eventually Merryman was turned over to the civilian courts and released without being brought to trial.

During the remainder of the Civil War practices such as that adopted in the Merryman affair continued to be employed by the military authorities.

*Taney died in 1864 without ever having been vindicated. But the issue
remained. It was finally settled by the case described here by Allan Nevins,
author of the multivolume study* The Ordeal of the Union.

On an August day in 1835 a group of young men in St.
Clairsville, the seat of Belmont County in eastern Ohio, passed the
rudimentary examination in law required of them and were admitted to the bar. One was destined to write his name high in the annals
of the nation: Edwin McMasters Stanton, later secretary of war
under Lincoln and Andrew Johnson. Another was to take a different
road to fame—or infamy: the road of disunion activities and subversive conspiracy that narrowly missed, if it did not reach, treason. His
name was Lambdin P. Milligan, and although he is now forgotten
by all but students of civil liberties, he was briefly a national celeb-
rity. The paths of Stanton and Milligan were later to cross in dramatic fashion.

Within a dozen years both men removed to new fields, Stanton
settling in Pittsburgh and Milligan in Huntington County in north-
eastern Indiana. Stanton was soon securely established as one of the
nation's leading attorneys. For a time Milligan also did well, although handicapped by ill health. Records speak vaguely of spinal
meningitis, and when he finally stood military trial he asked for
special consideration on the ground of bodily ailment. However, by
the time that Stanton won his famous victory in preventing the
erection of a bridge over the Ohio at Wheeling as certain to obstruct
Pennsylvania steamboats, Milligan was one of the more distinguished Indiana lawyers. He was interested in railroad promotion,
and the scrappy, uncertain accounts of his antebellum years indicate
that he was counsel for short Indiana lines later incorporated in the
Wabash and Erie systems.

In the 1850s, if not before, Milligan began to cherish political
ambitions. He was a zealous Democrat, an admirer of Thomas Jefferson and to a lesser degree Andrew Jackson, and a fervent states'
rights man. He brought to politics certain gifts. He was generously
hospitable, giving dinners to fellow attorneys, railroad men, and
politicians all the way from Fort Wayne to Indianapolis. He was an
interesting conversationalist, entertaining hearers by his wit, legal
lore, and anecdotes of party leaders. A devout Catholic, he was a
man of integrity and principle. But it is plain from the cloudy facts

preserved about him that as the Civil War approached he became grimly fanatical. Indiana had been settled largely by Southerners descending the Ohio or crossing from Kentucky, and part of it was a hotbed of Southern feeling. All Milligan's sympathies lay with the South, and with the measures of Franklin Pierce and James Buchanan friendly to slave-state interests. He did not carry his predilections as far as Jesse D. Bright, the Indiana leader who owned slaves on Kentucky soil and was expelled from the Senate in 1861 for writing Confederate president Jefferson Davis a letter recommending a friend for employment. But he carried them as far as the demagogue Daniel Vorhees, "the tall sycamore of the Wabash," who would cheerfully have made Kansas the fifteenth slave state and was willing to accept secession; in fact, a good deal further.

Nobody ever thought Milligan a great or important man. He and his friends hoped in 1864 that he might be nominated for governor, but he was not of sufficient caliber. He was merely a disturbing zealot, a rider of the wave of sectional passion. It is not the man who merits attention, but the terribly perilous situation which, in the midst of the Civil War, created the dramatic case of which he was the center.

I

The fierce conflict between North and South no sooner gained headway, straining the old-time fealties of countless men, than the government in Washington had to meet two crucial questions: How should the nation be safeguarded against traitors? And just what should be regarded as treasonable conduct? Inevitably, radical opinion on these issues differed from conservative opinion as night from day.

After four months of Lincoln's administration, declared the New York *Daily News* on July 1, 1861, civil liberties were prostrate. The sacred privilege of habeas corpus had been thrust aside; homes were illegally entered and searched; the private papers of citizens were seized without warrant; men were arrested without legal process, and held behind bars without a hearing. "Almost every right which American citizens have been taught to consider sacred and inalienable," this proslavery daily asserted, "has been trampled upon by Mr. Lincoln and his Administration." Yet at the same time some Republican editors, some members of Congress, and many military commanders believed that the government was grossly negligent in ferreting out traitors and that its mildness imperiled the life of the Republic.

Late in April 1861, Lincoln had authorized General Winfield Scott to suspend the writ of habeas corpus in the communications zone between Philadelphia and Washington, and Scott had deputed this power to his principal subordinates. Military arrests began immediately. The Constitution provided that the writ might be suspended if, in time of rebellion or invasion, the public safety demanded it. A few dim precedents existed. During the Revolution the Pennsylvania authorities had suspended the writ, and in 1815 Andrew Jackson had put New Orleans under martial law and arrested a judge who tried to intervene. Lincoln believed that he rather than Congress had the power and boldly exercised it. He had to deal promptly with men trying to stop the vital movement of troops from the North to the capital, and majority opinion in the critical weeks after Sumter upheld him.

In due course Lincoln made his theoretical approach to the field of disloyalty, martial arrests, and civil liberties perfectly clear. He felt a tremendous anxiety for the safety of the government he had sworn to protect and uphold. The preservation of the Union seemed to him far more important than the uninterrupted maintenance of privileges and immunities which could later be restored. As he put it, a limb might well be amputated to save a life, but a life ought never to be sacrificed to save a limb. "I felt that measures, otherwise unconstitutional, might become lawful by becoming indispensable to the preservation of the Constitution, through the preservation of the nation."[1] As a broad guiding rule, most people in the North apparently (we cannot be sure) regarded his statement as sound. They were willing to let the military authorities arrest suspected traitors in an endangered area, throw them into jail, and hold them behind bars until the danger was past.

Nevertheless, so deeply ingrained in Americans was their attach-

---

[1] According to one member of his Cabinet, Lincoln's difficulty was his inability to administer this policy effectively. "The President . . . wishes well to his country, but lacks the faculty of control, the *will* to punish the abuses of his power, which, rampant and unrebuked, are rapidly bringing him and this good cause to sorrow and shame." Edward Bates to James O. Broadhead, August 13, 1864.

ment to the principles of civil liberty as laid down by Magna Carta and subsequent Anglo-American declarations that the first military arrests aroused deep uneasiness. The imprisonment of heads of the Baltimore police force, secessionist members of the Maryland legislature, and others troubled thoughtful observers. For one reason, some of the officers who ordered arrests were mere whippersnappers: one a major of the New York militia, another a militia captain. For another reason, the grounds offered were often weak: General Banks, in immuring the Baltimore police commissioners, merely alleged that they entertained "some purpose not known to the government" but supposedly inimical to its safety. Senator Pearce of Maryland declared in July 1861 that citizens had been imprisoned "upon intimations conveyed by base and unprincipled men, who, to gratify private malignity and personal or political hostility, have rendered persons far more respectable than themselves, and quite as loyal too, the victims of this tyrannous oppression." At the same time, officers like Ben Butler, one of the first to lead national troops through Maryland, thought the government all too gentle.

When Congress met at Lincoln's call just before Bull Run, the debate showed how sensitive and difficult was the issue. Senator Pearce questioned not the suspension of habeas corpus but the unguarded nature of the step, and the more arbitrary of the acts committed under its shelter. He recalled how reluctant Great Britain had been to use martial law in the Jacobite revolts of 1715 and 1745 and the stormiest period of the French wars, and how carefully the British government had limited the period during which persons arrested for treason might be held without bail or mainprise. When the Senate Judiciary Committee proposed a bill to authorize, define, and regulate the use of martial law, angry comment came from two quarters, its proponents and opponents.

Everybody agreed that in suppressing rebellion the military authorities needed large powers in imperiled districts and would certainly take them; no general would let his forces be hamstrung. But to define these powers was a difficult matter. Some feared the definition would not go far enough; others that it would go too far. Senator Edgar Cowan of Pennsylvania saw "difficulty environing us everywhere." Senator Lyman Trumbull of Illinois pleaded eloquently for a cautious measure as a safeguard. "I think that the idea that the rights of the citizen are to be trampled upon, and that he is to be arrested by military authority, without any regulation by law whatever, is monstrous in a free government," he said. Conservative members pointed out that loyal and disloyal people were inextricably mingled in some communities, and that suspicion often fell upon the wrong persons. Radicals urged for severity because loyalty oaths meant nothing to scoundrels, and because in some places military tribunals would be more trustworthy than the civil courts.

In the end Congress dropped the Judiciary Committee bill. It contented itself with passing a mild Conspiracies Act, punishing any plot to overthrow the government or levy war against it by a fine not exceeding $5,000 and imprisonment for not more than six years. Trumbull, a staunch defender of civil liberties, urged its passage. Eight border senators, however, signed a protest declaring that its vagueness as to indictments and evidence offered a dangerous latitude to improper prosecutions. The sphere of military control remained vaguely defined, primarily because some congressmen wanted a broad grant of powers, while others insisted upon a very narrow delimitation. The sequel of this failure to set clear bounds around the authority of the government and army to deal with alleged disloyalists offers one of the unfortunate chapters of wartime history.

II

Arbitrary arrests became a commonplace of Northern life. Not only did no plain law exist; the administration made matters worse by failing to create a careful, well-organized, and responsible machinery for operating in the twilight zone. The government lawyers could not assume the task, partly because Attorney General Edward Bates was too old, slow, and erratic, and partly because he was outspokenly hostile to military arrests. ("I am resolved," Bates wrote in 1864, "that the records of my office shall bear testimony that at least *one* member of the Government did, sometime, resist capricious power and the arbitrary domination of armed forces.") Lincoln at first deputed the labor to William H. Seward. The secretary of state was able, prompt, and shrewd, but he had all he could really manage in conducting foreign affairs and was often distressingly casual, circuitous, and flippant in his methods. History will never forget his remark that whenever he wanted an offender seized, he tapped a little bell on his desk, and the man was soon in durance. As the complexity of the problem of disloyalty increased, and Seward found the burden insupportable, Lincoln took advantage of the appointment of Stanton to the War Department early in 1862 to hand him the responsibility. This was by executive order on February 14, 1862.

Theoretically, much could be said for giving the civilian head of the war machine responsibility for military arrests. Practically, however, this transfer of functions was open to grave objections. Of all the members of the Cabinet Stanton had the least judicial mind, and was the most prone to violent and unfair acts. His handling of the lamentable case of Brigadier General Charles P. Stone at once illustrated his worst qualities. Congressional radicals who controlled the Committee on the Conduct of the War mistakenly held Stone responsible for the Ball's Bluff disaster of October 1861, in which more than half of a seventeen-hundred-man Union force was killed or captured in a battle on the Potomac upstream from Washington. Stanton ordered Stone's arrest, kept him in Fort Lafayette for more than six months on charges never specified, gave him no real trial, and finally released him without acquittal. Stone's career was blasted, and he had later to rebuild it under the Egyptian flag. Few grosser breaches of civil liberty in our history can be found than his long and causeless confinement. Other acts by Stanton were equally arbitrary.

The total of arrests continued to grow as 1861 passed into 1862. Meanwhile, a few cases—far too few—came into court for a hearing. The situation produced so much irritation that in the session of 1861–62 Lyman Trumbull introduced a resolution calling on the executive to report the total number of alleged disloyalists held in prison, and to state under just what law they had been detained. Various colleagues expostulated with him. Henry Wilson, chairman of the Senate Committee on Military Affairs, declared that Lincoln had done quite right in making an example of leading subversionists, that "the turning of the doors of Fort Lafayette and Fort Warren on their hinges silenced innumerable traitors in the loyal States." Dixon of Connecticut asserted that if Lincoln and Seward had not seized the dangerous men undermining the federal government, *they* would have been guilty of treason—at any rate, "moral treason."

However, powerful editors ranged themselves on Trumbull's side. William Cullen Bryant of the *Evening Post* denounced methods which savored of the old *lettres de cachet.* "For months we have read of arrests without a single cause of them having been specified." Horace Greeley had a *Tribune* correspondent hand Seward a letter declaring that whenever the government arrested decent citizens without strong reason, "you tear the whole fabric of society." And the editor of the Washington *National Intelligencer* wrote (February 12, 1862): "The neglect to bring a single person to trial when so many have been arrested, does not authorize any very satisfactory inference with regard to the efficiency of the government in ferreting out real traitors, or in preserving the innocent accused from the unlawful detention."

It was to Lincoln's credit that early in 1862, when General McClellan was about to advance upon Richmond and hopes of an early victory ran high, he ordered that all political prisoners in military custody be released upon parole and granted an amnesty for past offenses. Extraordinary arrests by the military authorities would continue: all spies, secret agents, and conspirators whom the secretary of war regarded as dangerous to the public safety would be taken up and kept in custody. But the old slate was wiped clean. And it was to Stanton's credit that he adopted a sensible course for sifting the great body of prisoners held on various charges, and releasing most of them. He appointed John A. Dix and Edwards Pierrepont as commissioners to examine those held in the New York area and render a quick verdict. Visiting Fort Lafayette and other prisons, by April 1862 they had practically finished their work. The judge advocate of the army for the Washington area was empowered to dispose of prisoners arrested in the Federal District and adjacent Virginia. Governor David Tod of Ohio was authorized to use a special agent to investigate cases, with a promise that any prisoner would be released on his recommendation.

Early in 1863, however, after the bloody disaster at Fredericksburg, discontent and disloyalty rose to new heights, and nowhere more threateningly than in the Middle West. Lincoln's Emancipation Proclamation became final on New Year's Day. It not only angered friends of the South, but aroused fears that a host of liberated blacks would inundate Ohio, Indiana, and Illinois. Losses on Mississippi Valley battlefields were heavy, and Democratic families bore their full share. A great many voters who had supported the struggle while it was simply a national war for the Union took a hostile attitude when it seemed to become a Republican war to destroy slavery, establish a strong central government, and hold the South in subjection.

Nor were real economic grievances wanting. Astute farmers of the Middle West saw plainly that the new high tariffs which enriched industry were injurious to agriculture, for they limited the ability of Europe to buy farm products. Daniel Voorhees delivered resentful speeches in the House on the subject. Western agrarians perceived also that while they suffered from a glut of grain and rising freight and elevator charges, Eastern manufacturers got most of the fat war contracts, and Eastern capitalists pocketed the large profits made by banks and railroad lines.

Naturally a cry for peace went up in many quarters. Early in 1863 the Democratic central committee in Indiana published an address which urged the "great duty of pacification or honorable adjustment" and advocated "compromise." Naturally, too, volunteering sank, and as army morale declined many soldiers went absent without leave. "Desertions [are] occurring daily, and encouraged at home," wrote General Lew Wallace. Union enthusiasts demanded more arrests. When the impetuous General Burnside took command of the Department of the Ohio (which included Indiana) early in 1863, he issued a general order asserting that he would not tolerate declarations of sympathy for the enemy, or any other form of "express or implied treason." Implied treason was something new to the jurisprudence of English-speaking countries.

The stage was being set for the arrest of the Ohio copperhead Clement L. Vallandigham—and for the case *ex parte Milligan.* For Milligan was coming under suspicion for his supposed connection with what was later termed the great Northwestern Conspiracy. Beyond a doubt a conspiracy to array large groups in the old Northwest against the war did take form in 1862–63. But how formidable was it?

III

From the beginning of the war many Southerners had cherished a hope that, once Confederate victories bred a spirit of defeatism in the North, Indiana, Illinois, Missouri, and possibly Iowa would desert the struggle. Some Northern copperheads, sharing the hope, laid plans to realize it. How could this colossal defection be accomplished? By the formation of a Northwestern Confederacy.

"All people will recollect," wrote Stephen A. Douglas's old-time lieutenant, James A. Sheahan, in his Chicago *Post* of July 12, 1864, a paper for war Democrats,

[that the Northwestern Confederacy] was a common topic of conversation in the spring of 1862 among "Northern men of Southern principles," who scouted the idea that Grant would take Vicksburg as they are now pooh-poohing the idea that he will take Richmond. In all the larger cities of the Northwest, and in many of the smaller ones, these Northwestern Confederacy disunionists were bold in avowing and vociferous in advocating the traitorous scheme, whenever it could be done without personal danger. It was even supported in the columns of Mr. Vallandigham's shameless newspaper in this city [Sheahan meant Wilbur F. Storey's Chicago *Times*], and the subject was not allowed to drop until the fall of Vicksburg reopened the Mississippi, and put an end to all immediate hopes of its realization.

Later it was revived.

Milligan, as a Northerner with Southern principles, violently detested the warlike governor of Indiana, Oliver P. Morton. He opposed Morton's successful effort in 1861–62 to maintain a state arsenal for supplying Indiana regiments with ammunition. He was outraged by the movement of Grant's troops into Kentucky and the capture of Forts Henry and Donelson. When Lincoln, in the summer of 1862, after McClellan's failure, called for 300,000 more troops, and Governor Morton worked valiantly to fill Indiana's quota of 31,350 recruits, Milligan did everything in his power to discourage enlistments. The patriotic Indianapolis *Daily Journal* castigated him, along with Voorhees and Thomas A. Hendricks, in burning terms. These seditionists cheered for Jeff Davis, it declared; they gloated over Union losses; they plotted to obstruct volunteering; and while weeping for slavery, they had not a single tear for the death of brave Union boys.

By 1863 government policy was more severe. Liberalized in the first half of 1862, it became stringent during the second half. As successive Northern defeats and the rebirth of fears for the safety of Washington made disloyalty bolder, the administration felt less inclined to take risks. Moreover, the first limping draft law in the summer of 1862 resulted in an ebullition of evasion and resistance which the War Department thought it had to repress by the use of extraordinary powers. Any man who left his community to escape conscription, or encouraged or abetted such evasion, was subject to abrupt military arrest. Public sentiment generally approved the apprehension of "skeedaddlers," forty of whom were caught in a single day at Rouses Point on the Canadian boundary. Yet when a number of prominent Democratic politicians were jailed for their denunciations of the war and administration policy, angry protests arose. Horatio Seymour of New York and Vallandigham of Ohio were particularly vocal.

Lincoln made matters worse by a most unfortunate proclamation of September 24, 1862, announcing that "all Rebels and Insurgents, their aiders and abettors within the United States, and all persons discouraging volunteer enlistments, resisting militia drafts, or guilty of any disloyal practise . . . shall be subject to martial law and liable to trial and punishment by Courts Martial or Military Commission." This was going far, indeed, in overriding the civil courts. Moreover, as it came two days after the Emancipation Proclamation, it seemed to offer a threat of overcoming all opposition to that measure by harsh punitive arrests.

Meanwhile, Milligan's bitter opposition to the war in 1862–63 attracted nearly as much attention in Indiana as Vallandigham's activities in Ohio. General Burnside, determined to punish "implied treason," had failed in his effort to extend martial law over Indiana, but federal agents followed Milligan closely, noting his actions, taking down his speeches, and watching for any support he gave to plans for a Northwestern Confederacy. They found evidence, according to subsequent allegations, that on or about October 1, 1863, he conspired with William A. Bowles, Andrew Humphreys, Stephen Horsey, and other Indiana copperheads to overthrow the government, and for this purpose helped organize a secret society, the Order of American Knights, or Order of Sons of Liberty— "erected on the dissolved fragments of the Knights of the Golden Circle," which had become discredited. One conspirator identified by government agents was a Kentuckian, Joshua F. Bullitt, and another a Missourian, J. A. Barrett, suggesting that the group might be formulating a broad Northwestern plan. They met in Indianapolis in complete secrecy.

Federal agents also gathered evidence that about a month later the group distributed arms to various malcontents for resisting the draft. They further alleged that the plotters held another meeting in Indianapolis on or about May 16, 1864, for flagrantly disloyal purposes. This time Milligan, Bowles, and others crossed the line of treason, for they communicated details of their scheme for an armed uprising later in the year to the Confederates, and asked for the cooperation of Confederate forces.

With this evidence in hand, the military authorities took action. They went further than with Vallandigham, whose seizure on flimsy grounds by General Burnside in May 1863 had caused Lincoln so much embarrassment, and had ended merely in temporary deportation. On October 5, 1864, they arrested Milligan at his home, under orders of General Alvin P. Hovey, commanding in Indiana. Keeping him in close confinement, Hovey brought him on October 21 before a military commission in Indianapolis. This body found him guilty of inciting insurrection and giving aid and comfort to the enemies of the United States, and sentenced him to be hanged on May 19, 1865. Milligan, expert in law, at once petitioned the Federal Circuit Court for the District of Indiana to be discharged from what he termed his unlawful imprisonment, and in due course the case came before the Supreme Court in Washington.

The rigor shown by General Hovey, and the celerity with which the military tribunal imposed a death sentence, owed much to the fact that just before the arrest and trial the so-called Northwestern Conspiracy had come to a head. The plot, as given final form, had fantastic scope. It was nothing less than a plan to use the Sons of Liberty to seize federal and state arsenals in Ohio, Indiana, and Illinois; to release the prisoners of war held in Camp Douglas (Chicago), Camp Morton (Indianapolis), Camp Chase (Columbus, Ohio), and on Johnson's Island in Lake Erie; to arm these prisoners from the arsenals; and after creating terror by arson and pillage, to march against the Union troops in Missouri and Kentucky, where Confederate forces would be ready to lend assistance.

The boldness of the scheme was impressive, but how much support did it have in men and money? Apparently a good deal, for

Confederate leaders and Eastern copperheads were actively involved. Jacob Thompson, a Mississippian who had been secretary of the interior under Buchanan, C. C. Clay, former senator from Alabama, and Ben Wood, congressman from New York, owner of the New York *Daily News* and brother of Fernando Wood, were all participants. The summer of 1864 found this trio in Canada. They hoped that the Northwestern uprising and a New York outbreak akin to the Draft Riots might be timed to occur simultaneously. This fact is revealed in a letter, hitherto unpublished, which Clay sent to Jacob Thompson on August 3, 1864, from St. Catherine's in Canada:

I have just parted from Ben Wood, who expected to see you in Toronto. He knows nothing more of our speculations than he knew before meeting me. He had an impression of the storm impending and about to burst in the West, and expressed a willingness to see it and even to help it rage. He says there is a large body of laboring men in New York who can be commanded any day to aid in throwing off the yoke of the tyrant, if they had the arms. He thinks these can easily be obtained. If there be insurrection in the West, a riot in New York would checkmate any effort to suppress it. You will understand without fuller explanation.

Ben Wood was doubtless revolving plans for getting the needed weapons by sacking arms shops and breaking into regimental armories. Thompson was perfecting a pleasant scheme, later put into effect, for setting fires in New York hotels. Money was not a problem, for Clay went on to explain to Thompson that he had plenty from rebel sources. According to federal agents, the Confederacy had supplied half a million dollars.

"Holcombe arranges with me," Clay continued (Judge J. P. Holcombe of Virginia being a Confederate commissioner in Canada),

that we can invest twenty thousand dollars in New York with profit especially to assist the other operation in the West. The former will secure the fruits of the latter. I sent ten thousand dollars to X according to his and Holcombe's understanding with you. I have advanced to Captain C. [John B. Castleman of Kentucky] $250 for the purpose on which you sent him to the Falls . . . If you see Ben Wood you can confide more than I have done to him, I think, for he is among the staunchest and boldest of our friends.

A full history of this sinister but utterly impracticable Northwestern Conspiracy, of the work of the officers detailed from the Southern army to assist it—Colonel St. Leger Grenfell and Captain T. H. Hines being the chief—of the attempts to capture the U.S.S. *Michigan,* a little vessel of eighteen guns stationed on Lake Erie, and of the gathering of desperate men in Chicago, would require more space than it is worth, for it all came to naught. General Basil W. Duke declared later that "visionary and desperate" as the scheme appeared, "it was in reality very nearly the last hope the South had of prolonging the war." Grant's hammer blows in Virginia were plainly bringing the conflict close to its end. The conspirators' plan was to time the outbreak for the Democratic National Convention meeting in Chicago the last week in August 1864.

"August 28th," writes the author of a sensational account of the conspiracy, "dawned upon at least a hundred thousand strangers in Chicago, both gentlemen of the Convention and the ruffians of the Sons of Liberty." Their numbers had been swollen by fugitives from the draft. Some were well armed, a few even possessing muskets. Weapons for at least ten thousand men, according to another sensational record, had been smuggled into the city. But Colonel B. J. Sweet, commandant at Camp Douglas, had obtained ample warning of the plot and was watching suspicious characters like a sharp-taloned hawk. Guards at the camp and garrisons elsewhere in the Northwest had been reinforced. As the Sons waited for orders, word reached their leaders that a government agent, Felix G. Stidger, had wormed his way into the central recesses of the Sons of Liberty, obtained full particulars of their designs, and carried them to Union headquarters. They saw at once that the game was up. While the Democratic Convention still continued, they told their followers that the precaution of the military authorities made any attack impossible.

The frustrated Sons hastily left Chicago, some for home, some for Canada, and some for the border states, but all uttering threats of vengeance. Colonel Grenfell and a few others remained in the city, totally impotent. The Northwestern Conspiracy, in which Milligan was undoubtedly implicated—though nobody knows how far— had proved an utter fiasco. But as the press learned a good deal about it, while army officers knew more, it had an influence on the stern action of the military commission which condemned Milligan and two others to death. Fortunately for Milligan, the war ended before the date of his execution. After Lincoln's assassination, President Andrew Johnson first respited him, and then commuted his sentence to life imprisonment.

IV

The issue which came before the Supreme Court in April 1866 in *ex parte Milligan* was simple. It was the question of whether the government had the power, in an area free from invasion or rebellion, and not a theater of military operations—an area where the civil courts were in full discharge of their duties—to suspend the constitutional immunities of a citizen and consign him to a military commission for arrest, trial, and sentence. The guilt or innocence of Milligan was not in question. What was challenged was the right of a military commission, deriving its powers entirely from martial law, to try and punish him. Lincoln had declared in his proclamation of September 24, 1862, that all insurgents, with their aiders and abettors, should be subject to martial law. Was this declaration valid in places where ordinary grand jury presentments and jury trials were still available, or was it valid only where this system of justice was paralyzed?

Four distinguished men, James A. Garfield, Jeremiah S. Black, Joseph Ewing McDonald, and David Dudley Field, appeared for Milligan. The logical force and eloquence of their pleas, the interest of the precedents they cited, and the far-reaching import of the Court's decision combined to make the case one of the most memorable in our history. Milligan's personal record, however heinous, could be set aside. The all-important question was the nature of the line to be drawn around the powers of government in internal war, and the limits of the line protecting civil liberties. In the published proceedings, the opening plea of the government attorneys, James Speed, Henry Stanbery, and Benjamin F. Butler, occupies less than eight pages. The plea of Garfield, however, fills twenty-seven pages, that of Black twenty-six, and that of Field sixty pages. Ben Butler then made a reply of fourteen pages.

The weight as well as the volume of the arguments was heavily against the government. Field showed that when the military trial began, no known enemy in arms could be found in the state of Indiana; none within hundreds of miles. He showed that on the day set for Milligan's execution as an act of military necessity, Confederate resistance had ceased, and all was submission from the Rio Grande to Katahdin. Black recalled that when Washington called out troops to quell the Whiskey Rebellion, he never thought of suspending constitutional guarantees in Pennsylvania. The court was reminded that liberal members of the House of Representatives, late in the war, had attached to an appropriation bill an amendment declaring that, except for military personnel or alleged spies, "no person shall be tried by court-martial or military commission in any State or Territory where the courts of the United States are open," and when congressmen objected, these liberals defeated the appropriation rather than recede.

Particularly telling were the precedents from Anglo-American history which Garfield cited. He showed that in 1745 a Lieutenant Frye serving on the British warship *Oxford* in the West Indies was ordered by his superior to arrest another officer, but doubting the legality of the action, he demanded a written directive. For this he was himself arrested and tried by a naval court, which sentenced him to fifteen years' imprisonment and debarred him forever from the royal service. He at once brought an action in a civil court in England against the president of the naval tribunal. This court awarded him one thousand pounds for illegal detention and sentence, and informed him that he might arrest and sue *any* member of the naval tribunal. The incensed Frye promptly had two more members arrested.

After this, fifteen naval officers headed by a rear admiral met and formally declared it a gross insult to the British navy that any civil officer, however highly placed, should cause the arrest of a naval officer for any of his official acts. Thereupon Lord Chief Justice Willes had all fifteen men arrested and brought before him. Despite their efforts to enlist the king, this courageous judge persevered so energetically in his determination to maintain the supremacy of the civil authority that after two months' examination the fifteen signed a humble letter of apology. This letter the Lord Chief Justice placed in the Remembrance Office "as a memorial to the present and future ages, that whoever set themselves up in opposition to the laws, or think themselves above the law, will in the end find themselves mistaken."

Still more impressive, as cited by Garfield, was the case of Governor Joseph Wall of the African colony of Goree. In 1782 the brutal

Wall, suspecting that the garrison was about to mutiny, assembled five hundred British soldiers on parade, held a hasty consultation with some officers, and ordered Private Benjamin Armstrong, a supposed ringleader, seized, stripped, tied to an artillery wheel, and given eight hundred lashes with a one-inch rope. Armstrong died. Some years later Governor Wall was brought before the most august civil tribunal in England to answer for the murder of the poor private. Three eminent jurists listened to the pleas. Wall's counsel argued that as governor and military commander at Goree he held the power of life and death in time of mutiny, and was the sole judge of the necessities of the case. After a patient hearing, the jurists decisively vindicated the supremacy of the civil system of justice. They found Wall guilty of murder, sentenced him to death, and saw that he was executed.

The decision of the majority of the Supreme Court in *ex parte Milligan*, as read by Chief Justice Chase on April 3, 1866, was decisive. It declared that since the civil courts had been open in Indiana, and the state far removed from the battlefront, the military commission had possessed no legal jurisdiction for trying and sentencing Lambdin P. Milligan. Of course, no judicious person had any sympathy with the zealot who had apparently wished to see the Confederacy triumph, the Union riven asunder, and the institution of slavery preserved. He (like many others) had been severely penalized, by his long illegal imprisonment while the Supreme Court was waiting to rule on the constitutionality of military arrests and trials, but in view of the impediments he had offered the prosecution of the war, he got off rather lightly. He had a certain compensation, too, in the immortality he received in the lawbooks and constitutional histories; in the fact that, as Chief Justice Warren declared in 1962, his case was a landmark which firmly established the principle that "when civil courts are open and operating, resort to military tribunals for the prosecution of civilians is impermissible."

Many observers then and later believed with John W. Burgess of Columbia University that the decision drew too rigid a line around the powers of the government in dealing with disloyalty in time of war or civil commotion. Radical leaders in Reconstruction days hotly denounced it. "That decision," said Thaddeus Stevens on January 3, 1867, "although in terms not as infamous as the Dred Scott decision, is yet far more dangerous in its operation upon the lives and liberties of the loyal men of this country." His view was that only military tribunals could protect carpetbaggers and blacks against seditious enemies of the national government in some parts of the South. In the First Reconstruction Act of 1867, Congress provided for military jurisdiction and for trial by military commissions of the precise kind that the Milligan decision had stigmatized as illegal. Although such trials were clearly unconstitutional, efforts to prevent the enforcement of the military provisions by injunction suits broke down when the Supreme Court, intimidated by Congress, dismissed the suits as outside its competence.

But the Milligan decision nevertheless represented a great triumph for the civil liberties of Americans in time of war or internal dissension. The cautious Supreme Court might temporarily sidestep its implications, but it stood. No less respected a historian than William A. Dunning declared that Lincoln's proclamation of September 12, 1862, upon martial law and military arrests had offered "a perfect platform for a military despotism." So it had, and although Lincoln was the last man in the world to make himself such a despot, he might conceivably have a successor some day who, unless a clear line were drawn, would permit the erection of a martial autocracy. The line was now emphatically delineated. The Supreme Court established the rule that, no matter how grave the emergency, and no matter how high the public excitement, the civil authority is supreme over military authority; that wherever such civil authority is established and its ordinary judicial procedures are operating, its protections of the citizen shall remain absolute and unquestionable. The heart of this decision is the heart of the difference between the United States of America and Nazi Germany or the Soviet Union.

The Case of the Unscrupulous Warehouseman

VIII

BY C. PETER MAGRATH

(*Munn* v. *Illinois*, 94 U.S. 113)

American businessmen have never opposed government activity in the economic area per se. Indeed, ever since Hamilton's day "propertied" interests have looked to the government for aid, advocating protective tariffs, land grants for railroads, and other forms of assistance. However, as the economy grew more complex, the need for government regulation of some aspects of the economy became manifest, and this businessmen have been far less eager to accept. Inevitably, their resistance to regulation brought constitutional questions to the fore. What were the limits of the government's power to control economic development? C. Peter Magrath, President of the University of Missouri, discusses the controversy which more than any other provided an answer to this question. Magrath is the author of a biography of Chief Justice Morrison R. Waite, whose Court decided this case.

One fine November day in 1848 a railroad locomotive christened the "Pioneer" chugged westward out of Chicago a distance of eight miles. It pulled only a single coach, a baggage car temporarily outfitted to carry a handful of prominent Chicagoans being treated to one of the first runs of the Galena & Chicago Union Railroad. Spotting a farmer driving an oxen wagon filled with wheat and hides toward Chicago, two of the passengers purchased the goods and transferred them to the baggage car. The train then returned to its home city. This simple event foreshadowed the future course of Chicago's development: within twenty years the modest railroad comprising ten miles of track became the giant Chicago & North Western, one of the roads that made Illinois the nation's leader in railroad mileage. The city, which numbered 30,000 in 1848, grew tenfold. The inflow which had begun when that one-car

Ira Y. Munn.

train hauled a few bushels of wheat amounted by 1868 to tens of millions of bushels annually.

"Let the golden grain come, we can take care of it all," cried a Chicago newspaper of the 1850s. And come it did. Illinois was a major grain producer and Chicago—"the New York of the West"— enjoyed a strategic location that made it the key transfer point for transcontinental trade. Systems like the Chicago & North Western and the Illinois Central funneled in wheat, corn, and barley from the immense cereal carpet that lay to the city's west and northwest. During the 1860s it became one of the world's primary grain markets; through the wonder of the telegraph, fluctuations in the Chicago market were communicated to the rest of the world, affecting prices in New York and faraway Liverpool. At the center of these transactions stood the Chicago Board of Trade, the focal point for the buying and selling of grains, flour, and other foodstuffs. A contemporary called the Board "the Altar of Ceres," and the label was apt. Grain, or rather the money it might bring, was indeed a goddess to be worshiped by the restless merchants of the Board of Trade.

To accommodate the quantities of grain which flowed in and out of Chicago a most lucrative business developed, that of storing the grain in warehouses until it was sold and shipped East. These warehouses or grain elevators were huge skyscrapers capable of holding 500,000 to 1,000,000 bushels in elongated perpendicular bins which were mechanically loaded by dump buckets fastened to conveyor belts. Warehousemen facilitated sales to merchants and speculators by issuing them receipts to represent the grain in storage. These receipts were regarded as stable tokens of value comparable to bank bills, and presumably a warehouseman, like a banker, held a position of public trust demanding a high level of integrity. The presumption, however, often proved to be quite unjustified.

The history of the great Chicago grain elevators is reflected in the rise and fall of Munn & Scott, a firm founded in Spring Bay, Illinois, in 1844. The two partners, Ira Y. Munn and George L. Scott, ran a small (about 8,000 bushels capacity) warehouse, located on the Illinois River, which served the north-central part of the state. Munn, who was the firm's driving spirit, soon expanded his operations. Taking advantage of the opportunities presented by the growing commercial ascendancy of Chicago, he established a 200,000-

bushel grain elevator there in 1856 under the name of Munn, Gill & Company. Two years later it became Munn & Scott, one of thirteen firms in Chicago with a combined storage capacity of over four million bushels.

The next decade was enormously prosperous for Munn & Scott. They expanded to four elevators with a total capacity of 2,700,000 bushels; their warehouses could daily receive as much as 300,000 bushels and ship out twice that amount. With success came power and prestige. Ira Munn emerged as a leading Chicago businessman; he was prominent in the affairs of the Board of Trade, serving as its president in 1860 and as president of the city's chamber of commerce in 1868. During the Civil War he participated conspicuously in activities supporting the Union cause. At the same time, good capitalist that he was, Munn diversified his enterprises by engaging in wholesale grain speculation and by investing in newspapers and banks.

On the surface all seemed well for Munn & Scott, but prosperity brought its problems. These, in large measure, were of the company's own making; the age of enterprise was also an age of corruption, and the Chicago warehousemen were not at war with the spirit of their age. By 1868 Munn & Scott and four other firms dominated the field. They were interlocked in a pool, each owning a part interest in the others' businesses. In consequence they could administer prices and force farmers, who had to store their grain prior to sale, to pay high storage fees. There were also cruder forms of chicanery. The warehousemen commonly made deals with the railroads whereby they were assured of receiving all the grain carried by a particular line, regardless of the shipper's consignment. Munn & Scott, for instance, received most of their grain from the Chicago & North Western. Another practice was to misrepresent the quality of grain by mixing inferior grains with superior ones. The warehouses also systematically issued bogus receipts not backed by actual grain. Yet another favorite trick, performed in league with allied speculators, was to spread false rumors that the grain was spoiling; unsuspecting merchants would hasten to unload their grain receipts at depressed prices, thus setting up a juicy profit for the warehousemen.

While this sophisticated graft pleased the profiteers, it aroused its victims. As early as 1857 Chicago's grain merchants, acting through the Board of Trade, sought to impose a system of self-regulation upon the grain elevator owners. Their aim was to get impartial inspectors into the warehouses whose presence would prevent improper mixing of grades and who could report on the condition and the quantity of the grain in storage. A related objective was to make the Board a central registration agency which would record the receipt of grain and validate its sale so as to eliminate the practice of issuing bogus receipts. The warehousemen naturally resisted, claiming that as private owners they had an inherent right to exclude outside parties from their property. Since the elevator proprietors also had representation on the Board of Trade, they were usually able to turn the regulatory proposals into meaningless compromises. The upshot was the semblance but not the substance of regulation: grain weighers who were in the employ of the warehousemen; inspectors whose admission into the elevators depended upon the owner's goodwill and who were vulnerable to bribes; and unverifiable reports filed by the warehousemen, which were as worthless as many of their grain receipts.

The Munn & Scott firm was both notoriously unscrupulous in its business practices and a leader in the fight against effective control by the Board. In 1861, after warehouse "wheat doctors" had camouflaged a huge quantity of spoiled grain by mixing it with good grades, open charges of fraud were voiced. The Board appointed an investigating committee, but by tacit agreement its report was suppressed. When Joseph Medill's crusading Chicago *Tribune* suggested that the report was shelved because it incriminated many elevator men, Munn & Scott succeeded in getting *Tribune* reporters expelled from Board meetings. Similar newspaper charges hinting at Munn & Scott frauds appeared in 1865; another public furor followed, but the lax inspection procedures remained unchanged.

Four years later almost all of Chicago's receivers, shippers, and dealers of grain united in demanding a system of real inspection. The immediate cause of these renewed demands was a rise in storage rates and the imposition of an extra charge for grain that spoiled while in storage. New Board regulations designed to eliminate fraudulent issues of grain receipts were adopted early in 1870; once again the warehousemen, including Munn & Scott, asserted their right to control matters within their own elevators. The fight intensified. Elections for Board of Trade officers in the spring of 1870 split the membership into two factions—one supported the warehousemen; the other, which won most of the offices, insisted that their power be broken.

Businessmen are not customarily champions of governmental regulation, but the warehouse situation had become intolerable. The conduct of complex business relationships, after all, depends in a significant part on mutual trust. Unable to control the warehousemen, the Board of Trade turned to the state, asking that Illinois subject them to public regulation. It was necessary, declared the Board president in 1870, to destroy "a monopoly highly detrimental to every interest in the city." Joseph Medill, whose newspaper made warehouse regulation its cause, put it more colorfully when he described the warehousemen as "rapacious, blood sucking insects." These demands went before the state's constitutional convention of 1869–70, then in session. The result was one of those strange yet almost typical alliances of American politics: a temporary pact between two normally opposed interests, the grain merchants and the grain producers. Together they induced the convention to adopt constitutional articles which the state's voters overwhelmingly ratified; these authorized public regulation of warehouses and railroads.

The farmer-merchant alliance was an unusual one for 1870 because that year found the Midwestern farmer in bitter revolt against the forces of capitalism. The reasons were rooted in the economic depression which gripped agricultural America. Beyond a doubt, the economic balance of the post–Civil War period was heavily weighted against the American farmer. Between 1861 and 1865 he had rapidly expanded production to meet burgeoning needs, but the postwar market could absorb only part of his increased output of wheat, corn, and other grains. The farmer, moreover, sold in an unprotected world market at a time of falling prices: wheat, which sold at $1.45 a bushel in 1866, fell to seventy-six cents a mere three years later. As prices dropped, the value of money appreciated and the farmers, who had borrowed in the wartime flush of inflationary optimism, had to meet debts with a scarce and hard-earned currency. Manufacturers, by contrast, were protected by a high tariff, which pushed up the cost of the farmers' tools and domestic necessities.

The farmers of the West and Midwest had yet another grievance, which became the focus of all their discontents—the great railroad systems whose shiny rails crisscrossed the farm country. No one had welcomed the coming of the railroad more than Western farmers since it opened up new markets for their products and made farming feasible in otherwise remote areas. Many had mortgaged their property to buy railroad securities; others had cheerfully accepted high local taxes to finance the bonds that lured the iron horse into their territory. Unfortunately, the harvest was a bitter one. Once established, the railroads treated their clientele with disdain. Company officials were overbearing; freight rates were high and discriminated in favor of large shippers, who received special discounts. Precisely because the railroads were so essential, they could act arrogantly; in any one area a single line usually enjoyed a monopoly and thus had the power to raise rates as high as, or even higher than, the traffic would bear. The railroads of course defended their charges as moderate, sufficient only to compensate for the immense speculative risks that they had taken.

The farmers were unimpressed. To them the dominant fact was that freight costs ate up a frightful percentage of their income, so that they were often reduced to burning their corn as fuel rather than shipping it to market. Almost inevitably their profound discontent found an organized outlet. Oddly, what became the major vehicle for agrarian protests had its start as a fraternal order intended to provide isolated farmers with social and educational opportunities. In 1867 an idealistic government clerk in Washington, Oliver Hudson Kelley, founded the National Grange of the Patrons of Husbandry. At first his organization existed more on paper than in reality, but Kelly was an indefatigable worker—and also a shrewd observer. He broadened the Grange's appeal by making its primary objective cooperative purchasing and control of monopolies. These tactics paid off, and the Grange spread like prairie wildfire. It soon blanketed the nation, reaching its peak in 1874 when representatives of 800,000 farmers convened in St. Louis to proclaim "the art of agriculture" as "the parent and precursor of all arts, and its products the foundation of all wealth."

Although the term "Granger" became a synonym for all the agrarian movements of the 1870s, there were other highly vocal farmer associations which intervened in their states' politics throughout the Midwest. Many antedated the Patrons of Husbandry, but all shared the same goals: elimination of the middle-man's profits, lowered interest charges, and, most insistently, rail-road rate regulation. "We were all grangers," a farmer later re-called. "I never belonged to the order but I was a granger just the same." What he and his fellow farmers wanted had been well sum-marized by a Granger publicist who wrote simply and directly: "We want cheap coal, cheap bread, cheap transportation, cheap cloth-ing."

In Illinois the farmers scored one of their first victories when they joined with Chicago's merchants in getting the state's constitutional convention to authorize railroad and warehouse regulation. Like the Board of Trade, Illinois farmers had just cause for wanting to see the elevators controlled. Typically, a farmer might ship a thou-sand bushels of wheat to Chicago, receiving a warehouse receipt for 950. After paying costly storage charges he might be told that his grain was "heating" and that, to avoid a complete disaster, he should sell his receipt back to the warehouseman at a loss of ten cents per bushel. Later, the hapless farmer would learn that his grain, perfectly sound, had been sold at a nice profit. But beyond their joint desires to clean up a dirty business, the farmers were interested in comprehensive regulation. The Board of Trade merely wanted to make normal business relationships based on supply and demand possible; the farmers wanted a stringent limitation on the rates charged by railroads and warehouses.

Acting in response to these pressures, the 1871 legislature for-bade railroad discriminations and prescribed maximum freight and passenger rates. The warehousemen's fraudulent practices were outlawed, storage rates were limited, and a Railroad and Warehouse Commission was created to enforce the regulations. Enforcement, however, was not easy; the warehousemen claimed that the law was unconstitutional and ignored its requirements. Munn & Scott refused to take out the license required by the law and denied the state-appointed registrar of grain access to their elevators. The state then sued the firm, but the trial proceedings were delayed because of the mass destruction of records by Chicago's Great Fire of 1871. In July 1872, the state won a judgment of $100; Munn & Scott promptly appealed to the Illinois Supreme Court.

Meanwhile, a series of related events brought the downfall of Munn & Scott. Despite the state regulation (which at first had no practical impact), the Board of Trade continued to seek inspection of the warehouses during 1871 and 1872. Some elevators cooperated with Board inspectors in measuring their grain, but Munn & Scott remained defiant. Finally, in 1872, the firm consented to admit inspectors. It requested, however, that its elevators be inspected last in order to give it time to consolidate its grains and to avoid any implication that Munn & Scott were particularly distrusted. The Board agreed. The firm used this reprieve to floor over the tops of several bins in its northwestern elevator, covering the false bottoms with grain so as to give the illusion of full bins. The inspectors were fooled until an employee divulged the secret; then it came out that Munn & Scott grain receipts totaled 300,000 bushels more than the actual grain in their elevators.

Deplorable as the corruption was, its revelation merely confirmed what had long been suspected. More immediately damaging were Munn & Scott's financial misadventures in the summer of 1872. Along with three other speculators the firm attempted to corner all the wheat pouring into Chicago, hoping to dictate its ultimate price in world markets. For a while the corner worked; the price of wheat rose to $1.40 a bushel. Then, as it rose still further, farmers marketed all their reserves. This was the crucial point and it destroyed the corner. Unable to raise a million-dollar loan from Chicago's banks, the speculators had to stop buying. Their scheme collapsed, and wheat prices plummeted forty-seven cents in a twenty-four-hour period. Munn & Scott were ruined, their grain receipts thoroughly discredited. To avoid a complete panic, the powerful George Armour & Company bought up the Munn interests and quietly set about purchasing grain to make its receipts good. Munn and Scott themselves went into bankruptcy; the ensuing court proceedings, as summarized in newspaper headlines, told the story of the Chicago elevator business:

Ira Y. Munn on Stand Lays Bare Elevator Combination—Profits Divided—Agreement in 1866—Included Northwestern Elevators, West Side Elevators, Galena and Wheeler & Munger—A General Pool—History of Contracts with Northwestern Railway Beginning in 1862 and Renewed in 1866.

On December 3, 1872, Munn & Scott were expelled from the Board of Trade.

Although Ira Munn and George Scott thus passed into oblivion, the regulatory impulse that they and their fellow warehousemen had helped trigger continued unabated. The year 1873 was one of economic panic; grain prices dropped further and a severe shortage of credit forced numerous mortgage foreclosures. The Granger movement reached flood tide, and its political power was felt in all the Midwestern states. Granger votes elected legislators, governors, and judges pledged to lowering railroad rates; as the governor of Minnesota inelegantly phrased it, "It is time to take robber corporations by the scruff of the neck and shake them over hell!"

The period was indeed a hellish one for the railroads. Illinois strengthened its regulatory laws, creating the nation's first "strong" railroad commission. Unlike "weak" commissions with purely advisory powers such as existed in Rhode Island and Massachusetts, the Illinois Commission could set maximum rates, eliminate discriminations, and initiate court actions. Iowa and Minnesota adopted legislation akin to that of Illinois, and Wisconsin enacted unusually harsh legislation, the Potter Law, which lowered freight rates radically (25 percent, the railroads exaggeratedly claimed).

The Granger laws, cursed as communistic in Eastern business and financial circles, were a tribute to the political power of organized farmers. But the objects of their wrath—they might be described as the patrons of capital—soon showed why they were renowned for skill and resourcefulness. Having failed to prevent this legislation, they retaliated with a variety of weapons. Railroad agents fought to appeal or weaken the laws and to convince the public of their undesirability. They insisted that regulation was against the farmers' best interests and threatened that it would discourage further construction—an effective point, for even the bitterest foes of "the octopus" wanted increased railroad service at a fair price.

Resistance took other forms as well. In some cases the railroads aimed to make the laws unpopular; because of technical loopholes they were able to equalize their rates (thus formally ending discriminations) by raising them as much as 50 percent in areas where they had been low. In other cases they reduced service and forecast its complete abandonment. Wisconsin customers, for example, were treated to dilapidated cars and erratic service—"Potter cars, Potter rails, and Potter time"—that the railroads suavely blamed on the new law. Alternatively, the railroads pretended the laws were nonexistent. The president of the Chicago, Burlington & Quincy ordered his subordinates to ignore Iowa's "mousing RR commrs." "We have and shall pay no attention to the Iowa law," he told them. "We shall increase our rates on certain kinds of freight so as to make any reductions we are compelled to make good, and probably something more."

Mostly, however, the corporations put their faith in the judiciary, not the elective state courts where decisions were likely to mirror popular desires, but the United States Supreme Court. For the railroads were confident that rate regulation, no matter how moderate, violated the Constitution in at least three ways. First of all, the laws contravened the federal contract clause by impairing their right to set rates, a right which they declared had been granted by the states' charters of incorporation. Here the railroads cited the Dartmouth College doctrine of 1819. (They conveniently overlooked the Supreme Court's later ruling in the *Charles River Bridge* case. Furthermore, the railroads' charters had been issued under state constitutions granting the legislatures the authority to amend such franchises.) Second, the corporations claimed that the laws tampered with interstate transportation, thereby impinging on Congress's plenary power over interstate commerce. And lastly, they argued that public rate setting was a radical innovation unknown to the American experience. It was, they contended, an illegal confiscation of private property which violated the Fourteenth Amendment's prohibition against depriving persons of property without due process of law.

This resistance quickly led to specific cases in the state and federal courts. Wisconsin produced four, *Stone* v. *Wisconsin; Chicago, Milwaukee, & St. Paul* v. *Ackley; Lawrence* v. *Chicago & North Western;* and *Piek* v. *Chicago & North Western.* The Piek and Lawrence cases, which had been arranged at a New York meeting of the Chicago & North Western's directors, were carefully planned bondholders' and shareholders' suits against the Potter Law. From Iowa came the case of *Chicago, Burlington & Quincy* v. *Iowa,* which involved another powerful line. At a conference in Boston the Burlington's principal attorney, the capable Orville Hickman Browning, who had served in President Andrew Johnson's Cabinet, persuaded its directors that their proper course was to deny absolutely any state power to set rates, no matter how reasonable the rates might be. The Supreme

Court, argued Browning, "must decide in our favor." His confidence was echoed by James M. Walker, the Burlington's president, who was "certain" that the Iowa and Illinois laws would fall because according to their original charters "the railroad Companies have the exclusive right to fix rates of transportation." Minnesota gave rise to *Winona & St. Peter* v. *Blake* and *Southern Minnesota Railroad* v. *Coleman.*

The Illinois Railroad Act became bogged down in jurisdictional squabbles. However, *Munn* v. *Illinois* was litigated. The Chicago warehousemen who had succeeded to the Munn & Scott properties had continued to defy the Warehouse Act, unsuccessfully carrying their case to the state supreme court. The state, declared the Illinois judges, might regulate all subjects "connected with the public welfare" in order "to promote the greatest good of the greatest number."

Despite this and other reverses in the lower courts, the business interests were confident of ultimate victory. The assurances of their high-priced lawyers were soothing. An advisory opinion prepared for the Chicago & North Western by three distinguished attorneys, including former Supreme Court justice Benjamin R. Curtis, pronounced Wisconsin's Potter Law unconstitutional. The prestigious *American Law Review* featured numerous articles during 1874 and 1875, all of them agreeing that the "assault upon private property" embodied in the Granger laws would be turned back. Well might the chairman of the Burlington line, John N. Denison, conclude that "we shall be annoyed very much," but "happily we have the law on our side." Thus convinced, the corporations appealed their cases; in 1873 and 1874 *Munn* v. *Illinois* and seven railroad cases, which became known as the Granger Railroad Cases, all made their way to the United States Supreme Court.

The confidence of the railroad leaders, however, was grossly misplaced; the Court of the 1870s did not regard itself as the judicial handmaiden to entrepreneurial capitalism. Its chief justice, Morrison Remick Waite, was a moderate whose deep faith in representative democracy made him tolerant of legislative experimentation. His predisposition to trust the people had been shaped in frontier Ohio, where he had settled in 1838. As a lawyer who practiced in Toledo, Waite was active in local and state affairs. His politics were solidly Republican, but his experiences in a close-knit community where personal honesty and character mattered as much as business acumen made Waite a typical member of the antebellum class of professional and mercantile men to whom wealth was not an end in itself.

Ironically, this honest man owed his appointment as chief justice to the tawdry maneuverings of the Grant era. President Grant's blundering efforts to please his malodorous entourage after a vacancy had occurred in the chief justiceship in 1873 created a nine-month national scandal that saw three dubious candidates considered for the post. The muddled President finally selected Waite, whose respectability assured his confirmation. An unassuming, middle-aged man of medium height, his face clothed in one of those ample beards that were then the style, Waite proved an excellent chief justice. While his intelligence was keen, Waite's most valuable assets were an amiable personality and a knack for leading men. "Policy" and "diplomacy" were his self-proclaimed guidelines. In seeking to influence men, he once wrote, it was better to move slowly rather "than jumping at once to the lead without having built behind."

These qualities served him well because Waite's associates on the Court were men of uncommon ability; their vanities and ambitions could easily have mired the Court in a morass of personal conflicts. Unquestionably the best mind and the most learned jurist on the Waite Court was Joseph P. Bradley. A self-made man, Bradley enjoyed a successful career representing some of New Jersey's leading railroads until put on the Court in 1870 by President Grant. Once on the bench, he showed marked independence of the corporate interests he had formerly defended, frequently upholding economic regulation. Another Court giant was Samuel Freeman Miller. Beginning as a poor Kentucky farm boy, Miller had two careers, one as a country doctor and, after studying law on his own, another as a rural attorney. Moving to Iowa in 1850, he fast became a leader of the Western bar and was active in Republican politics. Appointed by Lincoln in 1862, Miller stressed in his judicial philosophy the importance of personal liberties and reflected a hostility to corporate and financial wealth. Blunt, self-confident, somewhat vain, he was a dominant figure on the postwar Court.

Ward Hunt, Noah H. Swayne, Nathan Clifford, and David Davis, four of the tribunal's lesser lights, generally followed Waite's lead in economic regulation cases. Like Waite, all of them had grown to maturity in Jacksonian America, and they retained a democratic faith which made them favorably disposed to laws passed by the people's representatives. Most of them had been attorneys for corporations, yet had not tied themselves to any single interest. Their image of what America should be remained essentially Jacksonian; Waite and the majority valued property rights, but had no real commitment to the immense concentrations of financial and corporate property which emerged in the post–Civil War years. To this general characterization there were two exceptions: William Strong, a conservative judge sympathetic to corporate claims, and Stephen J. Field. A transplanted New Englander who prided himself on being a rugged Californian, Field was tactless, querulous, and given to fits of self-righteous moralizing. Yet, for all his faults, this "War Democrat" whom Lincoln had placed on the Court in 1862 was a remarkable judge. Through a service of nearly thirty-five years Field outspokenly defended the claims of American business—a bench of nine Stephen Fields would have handsomely rewarded the railroads' initiative in bringing their grievances before the Supreme Court.

Judicial processes are rarely speedy, and the Court of the 1870s moved with majestic deliberation. Overburdened with a lengthy docket, it usually required about three years to reach decisions. The first Granger case to be considered, a challenge to Minnesota's rate law, arrived in October 1873, and the Illinois, Iowa, and Wisconsin cases were docketed the next year. Oral arguments occupied two sessions during the 1875 term; the *Granger Railroad Cases* were heard in October 1875, and *Munn* v. *Illinois,* the elevator case, was argued early in 1876. For the oral arguments the business interests marshaled the elite of the nation's bar. William M. Evarts, Orville H. Browning, David Dudley Field (Justice Field's brother), and Frederick M. Frelinghuysen were among the assembled legal talent. They contended that the laws unconstitutionally confiscated property, impaired the obligation of contracts, and interfered with interstate commerce. To these constitutional arguments they added the charge that, except for certain minor categories, rate regulation was unheard of in America. Almost hysterically, they described the Granger laws as forerunners to the total confiscation of private property, "the beginning of the operations of the [Paris] commune in the legislation of this country." In reply, the state attorneys defended the laws as reasonable measures to protect the general welfare against the exactions of uncurbed monopolies whose businesses had in effect become public.

Despite the brilliance of the railroad attorneys and the eloquence of their arguments, seven of the justices cast their votes for the Granger laws. Only Field and Strong dissented when, on November 18, 1876, all eight cases were decided together. Chief Justice Waite assigned himself the opinions, well aware of their importance: this was the Supreme Court's first major statement on the constitutionality of regulating the new industrial capitalism. He chose the elevator case, *Munn* v. *Illinois,* for his main opinion. Unlike the companies involved in the Granger Railroad Cases, Munn & Scott were unincorporated partners and their business was not interstate transportation. Their case therefore presented the crucial issue of rate regulation in pure form, uncomplicated by the contract and commerce questions raised in the other disputes.

The chief justice devoted the winter to preparing the opinions, later remarking that "they kept my mind and hands at work all the time." He wrote at home, sitting at a long and cluttered library table in his private study, where he worked in the morning's early hours and often into the night. Admittedly "old-fashioned," Waite spurned secretaries and the newfangled typewriters, writing his drafts in longhand. A glimpse of his labors on the *Munn* opinion is preserved on a lined sheet of paper on which he jotted down earlier illustrations of American business regulation:

MILLS
1. Ohio regulated tolls from 1799 until present time—No distinction between water & steam mills—
   Ferries—same—any stream
   Auctions

TAVERNS—
   In New Jersey—County Court was authorised to fix rates of charge Revision of 1821 P. 281.

LICENSES BY CITIES IN OHIO
   Ferries
   Shows

(continued)

LICENSES BY CITIES IN OHIO *(continued)*
        Hawkers & Peddlers
        Venders of Gunpowder
        Taverns
        Hucksters
        Vehicles
        Undertakers
        Pawn Brokers
TAVERNS.
        County Courts fix rates in Mississippi—
        Dig Stat Miss. 7 397—Pub. in 186

These references to historical practice, some of which appeared in the final opinion, were pertinent. Those challenging the Granger laws had strongly contended that regulation was alien to America; to demolish their claim Waite naturally referred to the state he knew best, citing numerous precedents drawn from Ohio history.

As Waite prepared the *Munn* opinion, he turned for assistance to Justice Bradley, his closest collaborator on the Court. Bradley, in fact, deserves recognition as coauthor, for he prepared a lengthy "Outline of my views on the subject of the Granger Cases" from which the chief justice freely borrowed. In refuting the business arguments, Bradley, a confirmed legal antiquarian, dug up an obscure seventeenth-century English legal treatise, *De Portibus Maris*. Written by Lord Chief Justice Hale, it justified regulation of the fees charged by enterprises in public ports with the following language: "For now the wharf and crane and other conveniences are affected with a publick interest, and they cease to be *juris privati* only." Waite quoted the statement and so introduced the public-interest doctrine into American constitutional law. Late in February he circulated the draft opinions among the brethren for final approval. Bradley, the former railroad attorney, responded enthusiastically: "terse, correct, & safe." Miller found the opinions "equal to the occasion which is a very great one."

With these endorsements, the Court released its opinions on March 1, 1877, ruling that the Constitution sanctioned economic regulation in the public interest. Waite's opinion in *Munn* v. *Illinois* began by stressing the power of the Chicago grain elevators, which, standing at the gateway of commerce to the East, "take toll from all who pass." Their business, he argued, citing Lord Hale, "tends to a common charge, and is become a thing of public interest and use" subject to state control. Noting earlier instances of American price regulation, Waite summarily dismissed the contention that such laws unconstitutionally destroyed private property. Underlying these conclusions was the root assumption of *Munn* v. *Illinois*—that popularly accountable legislatures should be the judges of the wisdom of regulatory laws. "For protection against abuses by legislatures the people must resort to the polls, not to the courts," Waite wrote, thus enunciating one of the Supreme Court's major declarations in favor of judicial self-restraint in economic regulation cases.

With the Warehouse Act sustained, the Granger Railroad Cases fell easily into place. In brief opinions Waite disposed of them by relying on the *Munn* public interest doctrine. He rejected the commerce clause argument, finding that none of the regulations extended to commerce beyond state lines. Waite found the claim that the rate laws impaired contract rights to be equally without merit; the states' constitutions had reserved the power to amend charters. Justice Field wrote a fiery dissent labeling the *Munn* decision "subversive of the rights of private property," and he predicted that its reasoning implied an almost unlimited scope for the regulatory power: "If the power can be exercised as to one article, it may as to all articles, and the prices of everything, from a calico gown to a city mansion, may be the subject of legislative direction."

Although Field's gloomy prediction that property rights would be destroyed proved false, he was essentially correct in calling attention to the broad implications of the *Munn* decision. In modern-day America the scope of governmental regulation is immense; no one doubts that "the prices of everything"—even calico gowns and city mansions—may be regulated. And this intervention by government in economic affairs finds much of its constitutional sanction in *Munn* v. *Illinois* and the line of cases which are its progeny. During the 1870s and 1880s, the years when Waite and his majority sat on the Court, the public interest doctrine and the underlying assumption that legislative acts are valid unless completely arbitrary led to further expansions of regulatory power. State railroad regulations were repeatedly upheld, as were laws setting the rates charged by water companies, outlawing businesses that engaged in the liquor trade or operated lotteries, and scaling down the interest and principal owed to the holders of state bonds. Congress's power to regulate federally chartered corporations was similarly upheld in the Sinking Fund Cases of 1879, a decision which infuriated corporation and financial leaders.

Later, roughly between 1895 and 1937, judges far more committed to industrial capitalism than Waite, Bradley, and Miller often found in the general prohibitions of the due process clauses of the Fifth and Fourteenth Amendments reasons for invalidating economic regulations. *Munn* v. *Illinois* was never overruled, but its public interest doctrine was radically reinterpreted. In the 1920s the Taft Court decided that only a narrow category of businesses—enterprises traditionally regulated and large monopolies—were affected with a public interest, and it struck down a number of state regulatory laws as unconstitutional.

All this came to an end in the next decade. In the 1934 case of *Nebbia* v. *New York,* sustaining a comprehensive scheme of state milk price regulation the Supreme Court returned to a sweeping view of the public interest doctrine. "A state," Justice Roberts announced in words that Waite would have approved, "is free to adopt whatever economic policy may reasonably be deemed to promote the public welfare, and to enforce that policy by legislation adapted to its purpose." Three years later in the case of *NLRB* v. *Jones & Laughlin Steel Corporation,* when the justices began the process of upholding the economic regulation of the New Deal, the permissive spirit of Waite's *Munn* opinion again triumphed. For now his insistence on judicial toleration of legislation regulating economic relationships was the supreme law of the land.

This, then, is the ultimate meaning of *Munn* v. *Illinois*—one of the landmark pronouncements of American constitutional law on the subject of economic regulation. But the case also had a more contemporary impact. The proprietors of the city's grain elevators, the Chicago *Tribune* reported a few days after the Supreme Court's decision, "are thoroughly reconstructed. They bow to the inevitable." They lowered their rates and began cooperating fully with the state's Railroad and Warehouse Commission. Two decades of arrogance by the warehousemen had come to an end: not only were their opponents politically dominant, but the elevator business itself was in a period of relative decline. Competing grain centers at Milwaukee and Minneapolis, and especially the growing practice of shipping grain directly through Chicago, weakened the warehouse-men's power. In 1876 13 percent of the grain arriving in Chicago was not stored; by 1885 the figure had jumped to 57 percent, though the volume of grain handled by the elevators was still impressive.

The state's railroads also complied with the *Munn* decision. Many of the Midwestern states, responding to powerful railroad lobbies, repealed or drastically loosened their regulatory laws. Illinois, however, remained a leader in strong railroad regulation: the farmers' influence prevented the repeal of the laws, which were sustained by the state's highest court in 1880 and by the Supreme Court in 1883.

A few final words on the parties whose behavior and maneuvering contributed to *Munn* v. *Illinois* are appropriate, for the case well illustrates the many ironies of constitutional litigation in America. By 1877 the Patrons of Husbandry, which had provided much of the political pressure behind the regulatory laws, was but a shadow of its onetime strength. Organizational dissensions and the collapse of its cooperative enterprises sharply reduced membership and destroyed its political influence. In fact, the Grange gradually reverted to its original social purposes and is today a thriving fraternal order.

The unsavory firm of Munn & Scott was also no longer a factor in 1877. It had long since passed out of existence, bankruptcy forcing the dispersal of its properties. Eventually three of its four elevators came under the control of Munger, Wheeler & Company, a firm which enjoyed a near monopoly of the Chicago grain storage business.

Chicago's Board of Trade, having finally curbed the warehouse-men, had second thoughts about the wisdom of public control. Through the 1870s and 1880s its leaders vigorously, though unsuccessfully, sought to return the power of regulating the warehouses to their hands. Other businessmen, too, had cause for regret. As the decisions of 1877 showed, the warehousemen who succeeded to Munn & Scott, and particularly the railroad leaders who deliberately forced the Granger Railroad Cases to a final decision, had disastrously miscalculated the Court's judicial position.

But ultimately more significant than the immediate results and the conflicting motives of the many participants was the constitutional residue left by the struggles of the 1870s: the clear announcement that legislatures might regulate business on behalf of the public interest, a principle that received additional vitality from Chief Justice Waite's assertion that the Court should be reluctant to upset regulatory laws passed by the people's representatives. This was the meaning of *Munn* v. *Illinois,* and it provided a leading precedent for the day when the Patrons of Capital would find themselves under effective and continuing governmental regulation.

The Case of the Prejudiced Doorkeeper

IX

BY ALAN F. WESTIN

(*U.S.* v. *Singleton,* etc. [The Civil Rights Cases], 109 U.S. 3)

The Civil War, caused in part by Chief Justice Taney's dictum in the Dred Scott case that Congress could not bar slavery from the territories, resulted, of course, in the destruction of slavery. The Thirteenth Amendment formally abolished the institution. The Fourteenth and Fifteenth Amendments, which the defeated Southern states were forced to ratify in order to get back into the Union, made blacks citizens, prohibited the states from depriving "all persons" of life, liberty, or property without due process of law, and made it illegal to deny anyone the right to vote "on account of race, color, or previous condition of servitude."

For a time, backed by federal bayonets, former slaves in the South were able to exercise their civil rights fairly effectively. But the dominant white element in the former Confederacy resisted every effort to grant them real freedom and equality, and with the passage of time the determination of Northerners to force Southern whites to do so began to flag. Gradually the blacks were forced back into a state of second-class citizenship.

Naturally they resisted this trend, calling upon the courts to protect them against discrimination. How the Supreme Court reacted in this situation is described below. Alan F. Westin, professor of public law and government at Columbia University, is editor of Freedom Now! The Civil Rights Struggle in America.

On November 22, 1879, Messrs. Poole and Donnelly, managers of the Grand Opera House in New York City, were looking forward to a well-attended Saturday matinee. The Thanksgiving season was on, and Edwin Booth, the famous tragedian and brother of the late John Wilkes Booth, was in the middle of a record-breaking, four-week engagement. His *Hamlet, Othello,* and *Richelieu* had been lauded by the critics, and the attempt of a mad-

JOHN MARSHALL HARLAN.

man to shoot him during a performance of *Richard II* a few months earlier had made the actor a center of attention. "I am jamming the Grand Opera House," he wrote happily to a friend on November 16, and turned to putting the final touches on his scheduled Saturday appearance in Victor Hugo's *Ruy Blas.*

One person who had decided to see Booth that Saturday was William R. Davis, Jr., a tall, handsome and well-spoken man of twenty-six. He was the business agent of the *Progressive-American,* a weekly newspaper in New York City. This happened to be a black newspaper, and Davis happened to be black, born a slave in South Carolina in 1853. At ten o'clock Saturday morning, Davis's girlfriend, described by the press as "a bright octoroon, almost white," purchased two reserved seats at the box office of the Opera House. At 1:30 P.M., Davis and his lady presented themselves at the theater, only to be told by the doorkeeper, Samuel Singleton, that "these tickets are no good." If he would step out to the box office, Singleton said, Davis could have his money refunded.

That Davis was either surprised or dismayed by Singleton's action is unlikely. In 1875, shortly after passage of the federal Civil Rights Act forbidding racial discrimination in places of public accommodation, William R. Davis, Jr., had been refused a ticket to the dress circle of Booth's Theater in New York. He had sworn out a warrant against the ticket seller but a federal grand jury had refused to return an indictment, apparently because Davis's witnesses failed to show up at the hearing. In light of this earlier episode, Davis's appearance at the Grand Opera House this Saturday in 1879 could well have been a deliberate test of Messrs. Poole's and Donnelly's admission policies. There is more than a slight possibility that this was so, for the 1870s were unique years of testing for race relations in America.

During the 1870s, no state in the Union, whatever its relation to the Mason-Dixon line, had laws requiring separation of whites and blacks in places of public accommodation. Admission and arrangement policies were generally a matter of choice for individual owners. In the North and West, many theaters, hotels, restaurants, and public carriers served black patrons without hesitation or discrimination. Others accepted them for second-class accommodations, such as smoking cars on railroads or balconies in theaters; here, blacks sat beside white customers who could not afford first-class tickets. Some Northern and Western establishments refused black patronage entirely.

The situation was much the same in the larger cities of the border states and in the Deep South. Most establishments admitted blacks to second-class facilities. Some gave first-class service to blacks with high social status, such as federal and state public officials, army officers, newspapermen, and traveling clergymen. On the other hand, many places, particularly in rural areas, were closed to them whatever their wealth or status.

From 1865 through the 1870s, the general trend in the nation was toward wider acceptance of black patronage. The federal Civil Rights Act of 1866, which guaranteed them the "equal benefit of the laws," had set off a flurry of test suits—for denying sleeper accommodations to blacks on a Washington–New York train; for refusing to sell theater tickets to them in Boston; for restricting them to the front platforms of Baltimore streetcars; and for barring black women from the waiting rooms and parlor cars of railroads in Virginia, Illinois, and California. Ratification of the Fourteenth Amendment in 1868 had spurred on the challenges, and three Northern states had passed laws making it a crime for owners of public accommodation businesses to discriminate. Similar laws were enacted during the Reconstruction period in several Southern states. Most state and federal court rulings on these statutes between 1865 and 1880 held in favor of black rights, and the rulings served as a steady pressure on owners to relax racial bars.

Laws were not the only pressure. In many communities, blacks won recognition of their legal rights through direct action. A typical campaign took place in Louisville, Kentucky, during the spring of 1871. Although blacks paid the same five-cent fare as white passengers on the horse-drawn streetcars of Louisville, the companies did not permit them to sit inside; they had to stand on the open platforms at the front of the cars. Company officials were encouraged to maintain this policy by antiblack Democratic administrations in the city of Louisville and the state of Kentucky.

In April of 1871, a black named Robert Fox entered the Walnut Street car, deposited his nickel in the fare box, and attempted to take a seat. He was put off forcibly by the driver. Fox sued the company in federal district court for assault and battery, and the presiding judge instructed the jury that under federal law the company was obligated as a public carrier to serve passengers without regard to color. The jury awarded Fox $15, plus $72.80 in legal costs.

Armed with this legal precedent, and encouraged by the local white Republican leadership, Louisville blacks began what today would probably be termed a "ride-in." At 7:00 P.M. on May 12, 1871, near the Willard Hotel, a black youth paid his fare and took a seat. Following company policy adopted after the Fox decision, the driver did not try to eject him but simply stopped the car, refusing to drive on until he got out. A large crowd gathered swiftly, including the governor, the city chief of police, and other prominent citizens, as well as many white teenagers. The police were under orders not to intervene.

As the crowd grew, cries of "Put him out," "Hit him," "Kick him," and "Hang him" were heard. White teenagers climbed into the car and shouted in the face of the boy, who sat quietly in his seat. Then they dragged him out by force. He was pushed away from the car and beaten until he finally turned and began to fight back. At this point, two policemen seized him and took him to jail.

The "ride-in" demonstrators were prosecuted immediately in Louisville city court for disorderly conduct. The judge ruled that there was no common-law duty commanding streetcar companies to carry blacks inside the cars and that all federal legislation passed since 1865 to guarantee their rights was "clearly unconstitutional," whatever other federal and state judges might have said to the contrary. The defendants were fined and warned that further attempts would result in jail sentences.

By now, the nation was watching, and Northern newspapers carried full accounts of the final round of the Louisville contest. Blacks returned to the "ride-ins." For several days, violence erupted sporadically. Some were forced from the cars by groups of white newsboys. One was thrown out of a car window. On several occasions, in various parts of the city, blacks stayed on the cars, the drivers got off, and the black passengers drove to their destination, accompanied by cheers from black spectators. As the situation approached riot proportions, Kentucky newspapers warned of another "Bloody Monday" such as Louisville had experienced in the 1850s between Know-Nothing and Catholic groups.

The blacks' determination and the support they received from federal officials proved decisive. The streetcar company managers met and agreed that "it was useless to try to resist or evade the enforcement by the United States authorities of the claim of the Negroes to ride in the cars." To "avoid serious collisions," the company would allow all who paid their nickels to take seats. The Louisville press during the 1870s records no history of violence following this integration. In fact, the peaceful way in which the two races occupied the streetcars was cited by many observers as proof that, once facilities were opened, "Southern mores" could accommodate successfully. Never again would Louisville streetcars be segregated.

Despite civil rights laws and test cases, stories of exclusion or separation were a steady diet in the press during the early 1870s. The rulings of a substantial minority of state and federal courts that there was no duty to serve blacks created a cloudy legal atmosphere, and the United States Supreme Court did not pass on this issue during the decade. To settle the question "once and for all" and to harvest the political benefits of this "final protection" for the new freedmen, congressional Republicans led by Senator Charles Sumner pressed for a new statute. Democrats and conservative Republicans warned in the debates that such a law would violate states' rights and would never be upheld by the Supreme Court, a view which was echoed by influential journals such as the *New York Times* and the *Nation.* Sumner had the votes, however. On March 1, 1875, "An Act to Protect all Citizens in their Civil and Legal Rights" went into force. Its preamble declared that "the appropriate object of legislation [was] to enact great fundamental principles into law," and such principles were involved here:

> [I]t is essential to just government [that] we recognize the equality of all men before the law, and . . . it is the duty of government in its dealings with the people to mete out equal and exact justice to all, of whatever nativity, race, color, or persuasion, religious or political.

Section 1 declared that "all persons within the jurisdiction of the United States shall be entitled to the full and equal enjoyment of the accommodations . . . of inns, public conveyances on land or water, theaters and other places of public amusement; subject only to the conditions and limitations established by law, and applicable alike to citizens of every race or color." Section 2 provided that any person violating the Act could be sued in federal court for a penalty of $500, could be fined $500 to $1,000, or could be imprisoned from thirty days to one year. Other provisions provided for jurisdiction by the lower federal courts and review by the Supreme Court regardless of the amount in controversy. An additional section forbade racial discrimination in the selection of juries.

Reaction to the law was swift—and varied. Several hotels in Baltimore and Alexandria closed temporarily. In Chattanooga, some hotels turned in their licenses and filed to become private boardinghouses. A group of blacks was refused admission to the orchestra of the Public Library Hall in Louisville. (They were offered balcony seats and all but one accepted these. The lone holdout walked over to Macauley's Theater, where he and a friend were sold tickets to the dress circle and sat through the play among the white patrons without incident.) But in Washington, D.C., two blacks were served at the bar of the Willard Hotel, and in Chicago a black man was admitted for the first time to McVicker's Theater.

In other episodes, blacks were not successful. Several visited restaurants and barbershops in Richmond, Virginia, two days after the Act became law, but were refused service at each establishment. In Montgomery, Alabama, a party was refused admission to the dress circle to see Cal Wagner's Minstrels. In New Orleans, a man and his wife were refused accommodations on the steamboat *Seminole.* Suits were filed in many cities. A few of the resulting court cases were dismissed, with comments by federal commissioners or district judges that the Civil Rights Act was unconstitutional. Other cases resulted in verdicts against the owners, as in Galveston, Texas, where the manager of the Tremont Opera House was fined $500 for refusing to admit a black. In both types of situation, appeals began their slow march upward through the federal courts.

This was the situation in 1879, when William R. Davis, Jr., was turned away from the Grand Opera House. Convinced that the operators of the theater were acting out of "prejudice against his race," he had no intention of pocketing a refund and walking away. Seeing a small white boy standing on the sidewalk near the theater, Davis gave him a dollar, plus ten cents for his trouble, and had him purchase two more tickets to the matinee. When Davis presented himself, his lady, and these tickets to Samuel Singleton, the lady was admitted, "perhaps because her complexion deceived the doorkeeper," as the press speculated. But Davis was again told that his ticket "was no good." Singleton ordered him to move out of the entrance, and when Davis argued with him, a policeman was called. The officer told Davis that Messrs. Poole and Donnelly did not admit colored persons to the Opera House. "Perhaps the managers do not," Davis retorted, "but the laws of the country [do]." He announced that he would see to their enforcement at once.

On Monday, November 24, Davis filed a criminal complaint and on December 9, Singleton was indicted. The press described this as the first criminal proceeding under the Act to go to trial in New York. When the case was heard, on January 14, 1880, counsel for Singleton, Louis Post, adopted the position that the Act of 1875 was invalid. "It interferes with the right of the State of New York to provide the means under which citizens of the State have the power to control and protect their rights in respect to their private property." Assistant United States Attorney Fiero replied that such a conception of states' rights had been "exploded and superseded long ago." It was unthinkable, he argued, that "the United States could not extend to one citizen of New York a right which the State itself gave to other of its citizens—the right of admission to places of public amusement." The presiding judge referred the constitutional question to the circuit court at its February term. Justice Samuel Blatchford of the Supreme Court, assigned to the Southern District of New York, and District Judge William Choate reached opposite conclusions on the issue and certified it to the United States Supreme Court "on division of opinion between the judges."

Perhaps a hundred such cases were tried and appealed during the late 1870s and early 1880s. Federal judges in Pennsylvania, Texas, Maryland, and Kentucky, for example, ruled the Act constitutional; in North Carolina, New Jersey, and California, the Act was held invalid. In New York, Tennessee, Missouri, Kansas, and other states, divided federal circuit courts certified the issue to the Supreme Court for decision.

The Supreme Court was in no hurry to settle the issue, however. Two cases reached the Supreme Court in 1876 and a third in 1877. The attorney general of the United States, Charles Devens, filed a brief in 1879 defending the constitutionality of the Act. Yet the Court simply continued the cases on its docket. In 1880, three additional cases were filed and the solicitor general of the United

States filed a new brief in 1882. The Court's ruling did not come down until late in 1883. Even though they were badly delayed on their docket in the 1880s, it is difficult to resist the conclusion that the justices preferred to accumulate the civil rights act cases and let them "ripen" a while before decision.

William R. Davis, Jr.'s, case reached the Supreme Court in 1880, under the title of *U.S.* v. *Singleton.* Four similar cases accompanied it. *U.S.* v. *Stanley* involved the refusal of Murray Stanley in 1875 to serve a meal at his hotel in Topeka, Kansas, to Bird Gee. *U.S.* v. *Nichols* presented the refusal in 1876 of Samuel Nichols, owner of the Nichols House in Jefferson City, Missouri, to accept W. H. R. Agee as a guest. *U.S.* v. *Ryan* involved the conduct of Michael Ryan on January 4, 1876, as doorkeeper of Maguire's Theater in San Francisco, in denying George M. Tyler entry to the dress circle. In *U.S.* v. *Hamilton,* James Hamilton, a conductor on the Nashville, Chattanooga & St. Louis Railroad, on April 21, 1879, had denied a black woman with a first-class ticket access to the ladies' car and had restricted her to "a dirty disagreeable coach known as the smoking car." These five cases all were criminal prosecutions and presented as their issues the constitutionality of the Act of 1875.

The sixth case had a different setting. On the evening of May 22, 1879, Mrs. Sallie J. Robinson purchased two first-class tickets at Grand Junction, Tennessee, for a trip to Lynchburg, Virginia, on the Memphis & Charleston Railroad. Shortly after midnight, she and her nephew, Joseph C. Robinson, described as "of light complexion, light hair, and light blue eyes," boarded the train and started into the parlor car. The conductor, C. W. Reagin, held Mrs. Robinson back ("bruising her arm and jerking her roughly around," she alleged) and pushed her into the smoking car. He called her "girl" and when asked why he refused them entry, replied brusquely, "Why do you people try to force yourselves in that car?" A few minutes later, when Joseph informed the conductor that he was Mrs. Robinson's nephew, the conductor looked surprised. He said that in that case they could go into the parlor car at the next stop. The Robinsons finished the ride in the parlor car, but they filed complaints with the railroad about their treatment and then sued for $500 under the Act of 1875. At the trial, Reagin testified that he had thought Joseph to be a white man with a black woman, and his experience was that such combinations were "for illicit purposes." Couples of this sort usually "laughed, drank, smoked and acted disorderly, and were objectionable to other passengers" in the parlor car.

Counsel for the Robinsons objected to Reagin's testimony, on the ground that his actions were based on race and constituted no defense. The railroad admitted the constitutionality of the Act for purposes of the trial, but contended that the action of its conductor did not fall within the statute. The district judge ruled that the motive for excluding persons was the decisive issue under the Act; if the jury believed that the conductor had acted because he thought Mrs. Robinson "a prostitute travelling with her paramour," whether "well or ill-founded" in that assumption, the exclusion was not because of race and the railroad was not liable. The jury found for the railroad, and the Robinsons appealed.

The brief that Solicitor General Samuel F. Phillips submitted for the United States in 1882 was a strong presentation. It reviewed the cases involved, described the history of the war amendments and civil rights laws, and stressed the importance of equal access to public accommodation facilities. Four times since 1866, Phillips noted, a Congress led by men who had fought in the Civil War and had framed the war amendments had enacted civil rights legislation. These men knew that "[e]very rootlet of slavery has an individual vitality, and, to its minutest hair, should be anxiously followed and plucked up."

They knew also that if blacks were denied accommodations "by persons who notably are sensitive registers of local public opinion," and if the federal government allowed this to continue, the warning of Junius would be applicable, that "What upon yesterday was only 'fact' will become 'doctrine' tomorrow."

On the afternoon of October 15, 1883, Justice Joseph Bradley disposed of five of the six cases with an opinion holding the Act of 1875 to be unconstitutional. (*U.S.* v. *Hamilton* was denied review on a procedural point.) Bradley, who was the spokesman for eight members of the Court, was probably the most powerful intellect among the justices, a disciplined craftsman in his opinions, a tough-minded constitutional logician, and, despite his background as a leading lawyer for New Jersey railroads and insurance companies, a justice who supported liberal values. He had originally been a Whig in New Jersey politics of the 1850s, had struggled for a North-

South compromise in the darkening months of 1860–61, and had swung to a strong Unionist position with the firing on Fort Sumter. He ran for Congress on the Lincoln ticket in 1862, and in 1868 he headed the New Jersey electors for Grant. He had given firm support to the Thirteenth and Fourteenth Amendments when they were adopted, and his appointment to the Supreme Court by Grant in 1870 drew no criticism from friends of blacks.

Those who joined Bradley in the majority position were an uncommonly talented group of justices. Chief Justice Morrison Waite, underrated today, was a good judge and a courageous spokesman for Jacksonian values in the Gilded Age. Samuel Miller was a sophisticated constitutional lawyer who left issues glowing clearly after he had written on them. Stephen J. Field had the power and arrogance of an Old Testament prophet, and his pounding opinions forged American constitutional law in a laissez-faire pattern in these decades. Horace Gray was a tower of erudition and master of legal procedure. William Woods, Stanley Matthews, and Samuel Blatchford, while lesser men, were still better-than-average justices. All except Field were Republicans, and even he had been appointed by Lincoln. All had made their careers in Northern, Midwestern, or Western states.

Bradley's opinion had a tightly reasoned simplicity. The Thirteenth Amendment forbade slavery and involuntary servitude, Bradley noted, but its protection against reinstituting the incidents of slavery could not fairly be stretched to cover "social" discriminations such as those involved here. As for the Fourteenth Amendment, it was addressed specifically to *state* deprivations of liberty or equal protection and did not encompass private acts of discrimination. Thus there was no source of constitutional power in the war amendments to uphold Congress's attempt to control private actions in the Act of 1875. Even as a matter of policy, Bradley argued, the obvious intention of the war amendments to aid newly freed blacks had to have some limits. There must be a point at which the black ceased to be "the special favorite of the laws" and took on "the rank of mere citizen."

When Bradley finished reading his opinion, Justice John Marshall Harlan of Kentucky—the Court's only Southerner, a former slaveholder, and a bitter critic of the war amendments in the 1860s— announced that he did not agree with his colleagues. Without summarizing his reasons for the onlookers, he stated he would file a dissent later.

At the Atlanta Opera House that evening, the end man of Haverly's Minstrels interrupted the performance to announce the decision. The entire orchestra and dress circle audience rose and gave three cheers. Blacks sitting in the balcony kept their seats, "stunned" according to one newspaper account. A short time earlier, a black had been denied entrance to the dress circle at the Opera House and had filed criminal charges against the management under the Act of 1875. Now, his case—their case—was dead.

In Washington, D.C., Frederick Douglass, the noted black publicist, lashed out at the decision. Southerners are gloating, he said, that they have now got the black "just where they want him."

They can put him in a smoking car or baggage car . . . take him or leave him at a railroad station, exclude him from inns, drive him from all places of amusement or instruction, without the least fear that the National Government will interfere for the protection of his liberty.

Most of the nation's press supported the Court. Newspapers like the *New York Times,* Chicago *Tribune,* Washington *Post,* and Louisville *Courier-Journal* found the opinion well reasoned and wise, a salutary restoration of "constitutional government" after years of "Congressional excess." Those newspapers that disagreed with the majority ruling, such as the New York *World* and the Chicago *Interocean,* commented that the nation was awaiting Justice Harlan's dissent with intense interest.

Harlan's odyssey from slave supporter to civil rights champion makes a fascinating chronicle. Like Bradley, he had entered politics as a Whig and had tried to find a middle road between secessionist Democrats and antislavery Republicans. Like Bradley, he sought compromise between North and South in the months of indecision after Lincoln's election. Like Bradley, the firing on Fort Sumter sent him without hesitation into the Union camp. Here the parallels end. Although Harlan entered the Union army, he was totally opposed to freeing the slaves, and his distaste for Lincoln and the "Radicals" was complete. Between 1863 and 1868, he led the Conservative party in Kentucky, a third-party movement which supported the war but opposed pro-black and civil rights measures as "flagrant invasions of property rights and local government."

By 1868, however, Harlan had become a Republican. The re-sounding defeat of the Conservatives in the 1867 state elections convinced him that two-party politics were finally emerging in Kentucky. Harlan had moved from the Democratic, antiblack city of Frankfort to the more cosmopolitan atmosphere of Louisville, center of such urbane and talented Republicans as Benjamin Bristow, with whom Harlan entered into a law partnership. Harlan's antimonopoly views and his general ideas about economic progress conflicted directly with state Democratic policies. Thus, when the Republicans nominated his field commander, Ulysses S. Grant, in 1868, Harlan was one of the substantial number of conservatives who joined the GOP.

He changed his views on black rights also. The wave of "vigilantism" against white Republicans and blacks which swept Kentucky in 1868–70 convinced Harlan that federal guarantees were essential. He watched blacks in Kentucky move with dignity and skill to become useful citizens, and his devout Presbyterianism led him to adopt a "brotherhood-of-man" outlook in keeping with the position of his church. That sixty thousand Kentucky blacks would become voters in 1870 was not lost on Harlan as a realistic political leader of the Republicans.

Thus a "new" Harlan took the stump in 1871 as Republican gubernatorial candidate. He opened his rallies by confessing that he had formerly been antiblack. But "I have lived long enough," he said, "to feel that the most perfect despotism that ever existed on this earth was the institution of African slavery." The war amendments were necessary "to place it beyond the power of any State to interfere with . . . the results of the war." The South should stop agitating the race issue, and should turn to the rebuilding of the region on progressive lines. When the Democrats laughed at "Harlan the Chameleon" and read quotations from his earlier speeches, Harlan replied: "Let it be said that I am right rather than consistent."

Harlan became an influential figure in the Southern Republican wing, and when President Hayes decided to appoint a prominent Southern Republican to the Supreme Court in 1877, Harlan was a logical choice. Even then, the race issue rose to shake Harlan's life again. His confirmation was held up because of doubts by some senators as to his "real" civil rights views. Only after Harlan produced his speeches between 1871 and 1877 and party leaders supported his firmness on this question was he approved.

Once on the Supreme Court, Harlan could have swung back to a conservative position on civil rights. Instead, he became one of the most intense and uncompromising defenders of black rights of his generation. Perhaps his was the psychology of the convert who defends his new faith more passionately, even more combatively, than the born believer. Harlan liked to think he had changed because he knew the South, and realized that any relaxation of federal protection of the rights of blacks would encourage the "white irreconciliables" to acts of discrimination and then of violence, destroying all hope of racial accommodation.

This was Harlan's odyssey on civil rights. When he sat down in October of 1883 to write his dissent in the Civil Rights Cases, he hoped to set off a cannon of protest. But he simply could not get his thoughts on paper. He worked late into the night, and even rose from half-sleep to write down ideas that he was afraid would elude him in the morning. "It was a trying time for him," his wife observed. "In point of years, he was much the youngest man on the Bench; and standing alone, as he did in regard to a decision which the whole nation was anxiously awaiting, he felt that . . . he must speak not only forcibly but wisely."

After weeks of drafting and discarding, Harlan seemed to reach a dead end. The dissent would not "write." It was at this point that Malvina Harlan, bred in an abolitionist New England household, contributed a dramatic touch to the history of the Civil Rights Cases.

When the Harlans had moved to Washington in 1877, the justice had acquired from a collector the inkstand which Chief Justice Roger Taney had used in writing all his opinions. Harlan was fond of showing this to guests and remarking that "it was the very inkstand from which the infamous *Dred Scott* opinion was written." Early in the 1880s, however, a niece of Taney, who was engaged in a collection of her uncle's effects, visited the Harlans. When she saw the inkstand she asked Harlan to contribute it to this reconstruction, and the justice agreed. The next morning, Mrs. Harlan noted her husband's reluctance to part with his most prized possession, so without telling him, she arranged to have the inkstand "lost." She hid it away and the justice was forced to make an embarrassed excuse to Taney's niece.

Now, on a Sunday morning, probably early in November of 1883, after Harlan had spent a sleepless night working on his dissent, Mallie Harlan remembered the inkstand. While the justice was at church, she retrieved it from its hiding place, filled it with a fresh supply of ink and pen points, and placed it on the blotter of his upstairs desk. When the justice returned from church, she told him, with an air of mystery, that he would find something special in his study. Harlan was overjoyed to recover his symbolic antique. It broke his writer's block at once. As Mrs. Harlan explains:

> The memory of the historic part that Taney's inkstand had played in the Dred Scott decision, in temporarily tightening the shackles of slavery upon the negro race in those ante-bellum days, seemed, that morning, to act like magic in clarifying my husband's thoughts in regard to the law . . . intended by Summer to protect the recently emancipated slaves in the enjoyment of equal "civil rights." His pen fairly flew on that day and, with the running start he then got, he soon finished his dissent.

How directly the recollection of Dred Scott pervaded Harlan's dissent is apparent to anyone who reads the opinion. Harlan noted that the pre–Civil War Supreme Court had upheld, by *implication* from the Constitution, congressional laws forbidding individuals to interfere with recovery of fugitive slaves. To strike down the Act of 1875 meant that "the rights of freedom and American citizenship cannot receive from the Nation that efficient protection which heretofore was unhesitatingly accorded to slavery and the rights of masters."

Harlan argued that the Act of 1875 was constitutional on any of several grounds. The Thirteenth Amendment had already been held to guarantee "universal civil freedom"; Harlan stated that barring blacks from facilities licensed by the state and under legal obligation to serve white persons without discrimination restored a major disability of slavery days and violated that civil freedom. As for the Fourteenth Amendment, its central purpose had been to extend national citizenship to blacks, reversing the rule of *Dred Scott;* the final section of the Fourteenth Amendment gave Congress power to pass appropriate legislation to enforce that affirmative grant as well as the section barring state action which denied liberty or equality. Now the Supreme Court was deciding what legislation was appropriate and necessary for those purposes, although that role belonged to Congress, not the federal judiciary.

Even under the "state action" clause of the Fourteenth Amendment, he continued, the Act was constitutional; it was well settled that "railroad corporations, keepers of inns and managers of places of public accommodation are agents or instrumentalities of the State." Finally, Harlan attacked the majority's unwillingness to uphold the public carrier section of the Act under Congress's power to regulate interstate trips. That was exactly what was involved in Mrs. Robinson's case, he reminded his colleagues, and it had never been true before that Congress had to recite the section of the Constitution on which it relied.

In a closing peroration, Harlan replied to Bradley's comment that blacks had been made "a special favorite of the laws." The war amendments had been passed not to "favor" them but to include black men and women as "part of the people for whose welfare and happiness government is ordained."

Today, it is the colored race which is denied, by corporations and individuals wielding public authority, rights fundamental in their freedom and citizenship. At some future time, it may be that some other race will fall under the ban of race discrimination. If the constitutional amendments be enforced, according to the intent with which, as I conceive, they were adopted, there cannot be in this republic any class of human beings in practical subjection to another class.

One of the major results of the Civil Rights Cases was predicted by one of Harlan's friends from Kentucky shortly after the decision. "I greatly fear the Court's action will invite assaults upon the colored people from the worst class of whites in the country," John Finnell speculated. The Southern states would give blacks no legal protection against discrimination. "As long as it was understood that the Federal Government felt bound to protect the Negro, there was a healthy fear of the Federal Government by these poor whites. The Negro, except in certain localities in the far South, was getting along passably well." Now, the "patriotic vagabonds of the South" will move against the blacks.

Actually, the Civil Rights Cases ruling did two things. First, it destroyed the delicate balance of federal guarantee, black protest, and private enlightenment which was producing a steadily widening area of peacefully integrated public facilities in the North and South during the 1870s and early 1880s. Second, it had an immediate and profound effect on national and state politics as they related to blacks. By denying Congress power to protect their rights to equal treatment, the Supreme Court wiped the issue of civil rights from the Republican party's agenda of national responsibility. At the same time, those Southern political leaders who saw antiblack politics as the most promising avenue to power could now rally the "poor whites" to the banner of segregation.

If the Supreme Court had stopped with the Civil Rights Cases of 1883, the situation of blacks would have been bad but not impossible. Even in the South, there was no immediate imposition of segregation in public facilities. During the late 1880s, they could be found sharing places with whites in many Southern restaurants, streetcars, and theaters. But increasingly, Democratic and Populist politicians found blacks an irresistible target. As Solicitor General Phillips had warned the Supreme Court, what had been tolerated as the "fact" of discrimination was now being translated into "doctrine": between 1887 and 1891, eight Southern states passed laws requiring railroads to separate all white and black passengers. The Supreme Court upheld these laws in the 1896 case of *Plessy* v. *Ferguson*. [1] Then in the Berea College case of 1906, it upheld laws forbidding private schools to educate black and white children together. Both decisions aroused Harlan's bitter dissent. In the next fifteen or twenty years, the chalk line of Jim Crow was drawn across virtually every area of public contact in the South.

Today we may reflect on what might have been in the South if the Act of 1875 had been upheld, in whole or in part. Perhaps everything would have been the same. Perhaps forces were at work between 1883 and 1940 too powerful for a Supreme Court to hold in check. Perhaps Sumner's law was greatly premature. Yet the notion that total, state-required segregation was inevitable in the South after the 1880s is hard to credit. If the Supreme Court had taken the same laissez-faire attitude toward race relations that it took in economic affairs in these decades, voluntary integration

[1]See Chapter X, *The Case of the Louisiana Traveler.*

would have survived as a counter tradition to Jim Crow and might have made the transition of the 1950s less painful than it was. At the very least, one cannot help thinking that Harlan was a better sociologist than his colleagues, a better Southerner than the "irreconciliables." American constitutional history has a richer ring to it because of the protest that John Marshall Harlan finally put down on paper from Roger Taney's inkwell in 1883.

The Case of the
Louisiana Traveler

X

BY C. VANN WOODWARD

(*Plessy* v. *Ferguson*, 163 U.S. 537)

Despite the discouraging decision in the Civil Rights Cases, not all American blacks stood idly by while the country undid the progress that had been made during the Civil War and Reconstruction. C. Vann Woodward, professor emeritus of history at Yale University and author of many important books, including The Strange Career of Jim Crow, *describes some of these efforts, culminating in one of the most decisive cases in the history of the Supreme Court. Professor Woodward revised this essay when he published it in* American Counterpoint (1971), *a collection of his articles on slavery and racism. With the exception of the first two pages, that version, minus the annotation, is here reprinted.*

In the spring of 1885, Charles Dudley Warner, Mark Twain's friend, neighbor, and onetime collaborator from Hartford, Connecticut, visited the International Exposition at New Orleans. He was astonished to find that "white and colored people mingled freely, talking and looking at what was of common interest," that blacks "took their full share of the parade and the honors," and that the two races associated "in unconscious equality of privileges." During his visit he saw "a colored clergyman in his surplice seated in the chancel of the most important white Episcopal church in New Orleans, assisting the service."

It was a common occurrence in the 1880s for foreign travelers and Northern visitors to comment, sometimes with distaste and always with surprise, on the freedom of association between white and black people in the South. Yankees in particular were unprepared for what they found and sometimes estimated that conditions below the Potomac were better than those above. Segregation was,

ALBION W. TOURGÉE.

HENRY B. BROWN.

after all, a Yankee invention. It had been the rule in the North before the Civil War and integration the exception. In the South slavery and, afterward, its heritage of caste had so far served to define blacks' "place" in the eyes of the dominant whites. There was discrimination, to be sure, but that was done on the responsibility of private owners or managers and not by requirement of law. As Alan Westin points out in the previous chapter, after the Supreme Court's decision in the Civil Rights Cases federal law gave no protection from such private acts.

Where discrimination existed it was often erratic and inconsistent. On trains the usual practice was to exclude blacks from first-class or "ladies" cars but to mix them with whites in second-class or "smoking" cars. In the old seaboard states of the South, however, blacks were as free to ride first class as whites. In no state was segregation on trains complete, and in none was it enforced by law. The age of Jim Crow was still to come.

The first genuine Jim Crow law requiring railroads to carry blacks in separate cars or behind partitions was adopted by Florida in 1887. Mississippi followed this example in 1888, Texas in 1889, Louisiana in 1890, Alabama, Arkansas, Georgia, and Tennessee in 1891, and Kentucky in 1892. The Carolinas and Virginia did not fall into line until the last three years of the century.

Blacks watched with despair while the foundations for the Jim Crow system were laid and the walls of segregation mounted around them. Their disenchantment with the hopes based on the Civil War amendments and the Reconstruction laws was nearly complete by 1890. The American commitment to equality, solemnly attested by three amendments to the Constitution and elaborate civil rights acts, was virtually repudiated. What had started as a retreat in 1877, when the last Federal troops were pulled out of the South, had turned into a rout. Northern radicals and liberals had abandoned the cause; the courts had rendered the Constitution helpless; the Republican party had forsaken the cause it had sponsored. A tide of racism was mounting in the country unopposed. Blacks held no less than five national conventions in 1890 to consider their plight, but all they could do was to pass resolutions of protest and confess their helplessness.

The black community of New Orleans, with its strong infusion of French and other nationalities, was in a strategic position to furnish leadership for the resistance against segregation. Within these groups were people of culture, education, and some wealth, as well as a heritage of several generations of freedom. Unlike the great majority of blacks, they were city people with an established professional class and a high degree of literacy. By ancestry as well as by residence they were associated with Latin cultures at variance with Anglo-American ideas of race relations. Their forebears had lived under the Code Noir decreed for Louisiana by Louis XIV, and their city faced out upon Latin America. When the Jim Crow car bill was introduced in the Louisiana legislature, New Orleans blacks organized to fight it.

On May 24, 1890, a few days after the railroad segregation bill was reported in the legislature, that body received a memorial entitled "Protest of the American Citizens' Equal Rights Association of Louisiana Against Class Legislation." Signed by a committee of seventeen members of the Association, all apparently black, the memorial denounced the proposed separate-car law as "unconstitutional, un-American, unjust, dangerous and against sound public policy." Such a law, the protest continued, would be "a free license to the evilly disposed that they might with impunity insult, humiliate and otherwise maltreat inoffensive persons, and especially women and children who should happen to have a dark skin."

Two of the signers of the memorial, Louis A. Martinet and Rudolphe L. Desdunes, black members of the French-speaking community of New Orleans, were to figure prominently in carrying the fight against the law to the United States Supreme Court. The son of a Creole father and a slave mother, Martinet was a young attorney and physician of the city who had been a Democrat but had recently gone over to the Republicans. In 1889 he founded the *New Orleans Crusader,* a militant weekly paper devoted to the cause of black rights. Desdunes, descendant of free blacks of New Orleans, was a friend of Martinet, a contributor to the *Crusader,* a poet, and later the author of a history of his people, *Nos Hommes et Notre Histoire,* published in 1911.

Under the prodding of the *Crusader,* the eighteen black members of the legislature, with the aid of railroad interests who opposed the bill, succeeded in stalling the progress of the separate-car legislation for a while. But on July 10, 1890, the assembly passed the bill, the governor signed it, and it became law. Rightly or wrongly,

Martinet and Desdunes in separate articles published in the *Crusader* placed a heavy share of the blame for passage of the bill on the black Republican members of the legislature. According to Desdunes, they had been promised votes against the Jim Crow bill in exchange for votes to overturn the governor's veto of the unpopular Louisiana Lottery bill and these promises were then broken. "The Lottery bill could not have passed without their votes," wrote Martinet; "they were completely the masters of the situation" had they only withheld their support. "But in an evil moment our Representatives turned their ears to listen to the golden siren," and "in emulation of their white colleagues, they did so for a 'consideration.' "

Putting aside recrimination, Martinet declared: "The Bill is now a law. The next thing is what we are going to do." He thought there was merit in Desdunes's idea of boycotting the railroads, but he was more interested in fighting the case in the courts. "The next thing is . . . to begin to gather funds to test the constitutionality of this law. We'll make a case," wrote the young lawyer, "a test case, and bring it before the Federal Courts on the ground of the invasion of the right of a person to travel through the States unmolested." Nothing came of the proposal for more than a year. Then, on September 1, 1891, a group of eighteen "men of color," all but three of them with French names, such as Esteves, Christophe, Bonseigneur, and Labat, including Desdunes and Martinet, formed a Citizens' Committee to Test the Constitutionality of the Separate Car Law. Money came in slowly at first, but by October 11, Martinet could write that the committee had already collected $1,500 and that more could be expected "after we have the case well started." Even before the money was collected, Martinet had opened a correspondence about the case with Albion Winegar Tourgée, of Mayville, New York, and on October 10 the Citizens' Committee formally elected Tourgée "leading counsel in the case, from beginning to end, with power to choose associates."

This action called back into the stream of history a name prominent in the annals of Reconstruction. Albion W. Tourgée was in 1890 probably the most famous surviving carpetbagger. His fame was due not so much to his achievements as a carpetbagger in North Carolina, significant though they were, as to the six novels about his Reconstruction experience that he had published since 1879. Born in Ohio, of French Huguenot descent, he had served as an officer

in the Union army and in 1865 moved to Greensboro, North Carolina, to practice law. He soon became a leader of the Republican
party, took a prominent part in writing the radical constitution of
North Carolina, and served as a judge of the superior court for six
years with considerable distinction. On the side he helped prepare
a codification of the state law and a digest of cases.

Tourgée's Southern enemies questioned his public morals and
his political judgment, but not his intelligence and certainly not his
courage. They knew him too well. "Tourgée was a special case," as
Edmund Wilson shrewdly remarked. "He was a Northerner who
resembled Southerners: in his insolence, his independence, his
readiness to accept a challenge, his recklessness and ineptitude in
practical matters, his romantic and chivalrous view of the world in
which he was living. . . . And he evidently elicited *their* admiration
or he could never have survived as so provocative an antagonist
fourteen years, as he did, in their midst." Although he entitled his
most successful novel on Reconstruction *A Fool's Errand,* he had by
no means lost the convictions that inspired his crusade for the
freedmen of North Carolina, and he brought to the fight against
segregation in Louisiana a combination of zeal and ability that the
Citizens' Committee of New Orleans would have found impossible
at that time to equal.

In a period of mounting racism, when former friends of the
blacks had died off, grown silent, or changed their views, Tourgée
stood out, as his biographer says, as "the most vocal, militant,
persistent, and widely heard advocate of racial equality in the
United States, black or white. He was the Garrison of a new struggle," all the more conspicuous because "the times were wrong." In
speeches, articles, books, and after 1888 in his weekly column in the
Chicago *Interocean,* he kept up a passionate, polemical, and unre-
lenting attack on the enemies and wrongs of blacks. In October
1891, when the New Orleans committee opened correspondence
with him, Tourgée was just beginning a drive to organize a biracial
National Citizens Rights Association (NCRA), with himself as provi-
sional president, for the defense of black rights. Two or three hundred letters a day were arriving from recruits, many of them in the
South, and within six months he claimed over one hundred thousand members. George W. Cable of Louisiana, with whom Martinet
and his friends were in touch, served on the executive board of

Tourgée's association, and a local branch of the NCRA was soon established in New Orleans. Martinet, speaking for the Citizens' Committee on the Jim Crow law, had ample reason to write Tourgée, "We know we have a friend in you." He informed his friend that the committee's decision electing him their counsel was made "spontaneously, warmly, and gratefully."

To assist Tourgée with local procedure, the committee employed a white Republican lawyer, James C. Walker. Tourgée served throughout without fee. In keeping with a strategy he had in mind, his first suggestion was that the person chosen as defendant in the test case be "nearly white," but that proposal raised some doubts. "It would be quite difficult," explained Martinet, "to have a lady *too* nearly white refused admission to a 'white' car." He pointed out that "people of tolerably fair complexion, even if unmistakably colored, enjoy here a large degree of immunity from that accursed prejudice. . . . To make this case would require some tact." He would volunteer himself, "but I am one of those whom a fair complexion favors. I go everywhere, in all public places, though well-known all over the city, & never is anything said to me. On the cars it would be the same thing. In fact, color prejudice, in this respect, does not affect me. But, as I have said, we can try it, with another." An additional point of delicacy was a jealousy among the darker members of the black community, who "charged that the people who support our movement were nearly white, or wanted to pass for white." Martinet discounted the importance of this feeling, but evidently took it into account. The critics, he said, had contributed little to the movement.

Railroad officials proved surprisingly cooperative. The first one approached, however, confessed that his road "did not enforce the law." It provided the Jim Crow car and posted the sign required by law, but told its conductors to molest no one who ignored instructions. Officers of two other railroads "said the law was a bad and mean one; they would like to get rid of it," and asked for time to consult counsel. "They want to help us," said Martinet, "but dread public opinion." The extra expense of separate cars was one reason for railroad opposition to the Jim Crow law. It was finally agreed that a white passenger should object to the presence of a black in a "white" coach, that the conductor should direct the passenger to go to the Jim Crow car, and that he should refuse to go. "The conductor will be instructed not to use force or molest," reported Martinet, "& *our* white passenger will swear out the affidavit. This will give us our *habeas corpus* case, I hope."

On the appointed day, February 24, 1892, Daniel F. Desdunes, son of Louis Desdunes, bought a ticket for Mobile, boarded the Louisville & Nashville Railroad, and took a seat in the white coach. All went according to plan. Desdunes was committed for trial to the criminal district court in New Orleans and released on bail. On March 21, Walker, the local attorney associated with Tourgée in the case, filed a plea protesting that his client was not guilty and attacking the constitutionality of the Jim Crow law. He wrote Tourgée that he intended to go to trial as early as he could.

Between the lawyers there was not entire agreement on procedure. Walker favored the plea that the law was void because it attempted to regulate interstate commerce, over which the Supreme Court held that Congress had exclusive jurisdiction. Tourgée was doubtful. "What we want," he wrote Walker, "is not a verdict of not guilty, nor a defect in this law but a decision whether such a law can be legally enacted and enforced in any state and we should get everything off the track and out of the way for such a decision." Walker confessed that "It's hard for me to give up my pet hobby that the law is void as a regulation of interstate commerce," and Tourgée admitted that he "may have spoken too lightly of the interstate commerce matter."

However, the discussion was ended abruptly and the whole approach altered before Desdunes's case came to trial by a decision of the state supreme court handed down on May 25. In this case, which was of entirely independent origin, the court reversed the ruling of a lower court and upheld the Pullman Company's plea that the Jim Crow law was unconstitutional insofar as it applied to interstate passengers.

Desdunes was an interstate passenger holding a ticket to Alabama, but the decision was a rather empty victory. The law still applied to intrastate passengers, and since all states adjacent to Louisiana had by this time adopted similar or identical Jim Crow laws, the exemption of interstate passengers was of no great importance to the blacks of Louisiana and it left the principle against which they contended unchallenged. On June 1, Martinet wired Tourgée on behalf of the committee saying, "Walker wants new case wholly within state limits," and asked his opinion. Tourgée wired his agreement.

One week later, on June 7, Homer Adolph Plessy bought a ticket in New Orleans, boarded the East Louisiana Railroad bound for Covington, Louisiana, and took a seat in the white coach. Since Plessy later described himself as "seven-eighths Caucasian and one-eighth African blood," and swore that "the admixture of colored blood is not discernible," it may be assumed that the railroad had been informed of the plan and agreed to cooperate. When Plessy refused to comply with the conductor's request that he move to the Jim Crow car, he was arrested by Detective Christopher C. Cain and charged with violating the Jim Crow car law. Tourgée and Walker then entered a plea before Judge John H. Ferguson of the Criminal District Court for the Parish of New Orleans, arguing that the law Plessy was charged with violating was null and void because it was in conflict with the Constitution of the United States. Ferguson ruled against them. Plessy then applied to the state supreme court for a writ of prohibition and certiorari and was given a hearing in November 1892. Thus was born the case of *Plessy* v. *Ferguson.*

The court recognized that neither the interstate commerce clause nor the question of equality of accommodations was involved and held that the sole question was whether a law requiring "separate but equal accommodations" violated the Fourteenth Amendment. Citing numerous decisions of lower federal courts to the effect that accommodations did not have to be identical to be equal, the court, as expected, upheld the law. "We have been at pains to expound this statute," added the court, "because the dissatisfaction felt with it by a portion of the people seems to us so unreasonable that we can account for it only on the ground of some misconception."

Chief Justice Francis Tillou Nicholls, who presided over the court that handed down this decision in 1892, had signed the Jim Crow act as governor when it was passed in 1890. Previously he had served as the "Redeemer" governor who took over Louisiana from the carpetbaggers in 1877 and inaugurated a brief regime of conservative paternalism. In those days, Nicholls had denounced race bigotry, appointed blacks to office, and attracted many of them to his party, Martinet among them. Martinet wrote Tourgée that Nicholls in those years had been "fair & just to colored men" and had, in fact, "secured a degree of protection to the colored people not enjoyed before under Republican Governors." But in November 1892, the wave of Populist radicalism was reaching its crest in the South. Not only were black and white farmers aroused, but New Orleans workers of both races had just shaken the city by a militant general strike. Forty-two union locals with over 20,000 members, who with their families made up nearly half the population of the city, struck for a ten-hour day, overtime pay, union recognition, and a closed shop. Business came to a halt and bank clearings were cut in half. It has been described by one historian as "the first general strike in American history to enlist both skilled and unskilled labor, black and white, and to paralyze the life of a great city." The governor of the state proclaimed martial law, and under threat of force the strikers agreed to a weak compromise. This was the immediate background of the court's decision, though it would probably have gone the same way anyhow. But the course of Judge Nicholls since 1877 typified the concessions to racism that conservatives of his class were making—and had been making—to divert white farmers and workers from their course of rebellion.

Tourgée and Walker were denied a rehearing but obtained a writ of error, which was accepted by the United States Supreme Court. There ensued a delay of three years before the Supreme Court got around to hearing the case argued. The delay, oddly enough, pleased Tourgée. What he most feared was an unfavorable (and irreversible) decision. He was convinced that time worked in his favor and that with more years of agitation and crusade by the new National Citizens Rights Association, the tide of public opinion could be turned. The tide, of course, continued to mount against his cause. The brief that Albion Tourgée filed with the Supreme Court in behalf of Plessy in October 1895 breathed a spirit of equalitarianism that was more in tune with his carpetbagger days than with the prevailing spirit of the mid-1890s. And it was no more in accord with the dominant mood of the Court than was the lone dissenting opinion later filed by Justice John Marshall Harlan, which echoed many of Tourgée's ringing phrases.

At the very outset, however, Tourgée advanced an argument in behalf of his client that unconsciously illustrated the paradox that had from the start haunted the American attempt to reconcile strong color prejudice with equalitarian commitments. Plessy, he contended, had been deprived of property without due process of law. The "property" in question was the "reputation of being white." It was "the most valuable sort of property, being the master-key that unlocks the golden door of opportunity." Intense race prejudice excluded any man suspected of having Negro blood "from the friendship and companionship of the white man," and therefore from the avenues to wealth, prestige, and opportunity. "Probably most white persons if given the choice," he held, "would prefer death to life in the United States as colored persons."

Since Tourgée had proposed that a person who was "nearly white" be selected for the test case, it may be presumed that he did so with this argument in mind. He doubtless hoped thereby to appeal to the preferential treatment the Supreme Court notoriously gave to property rights. Of course, this was not a defense of the blacks against discrimination by whites, but a defense of those "nearly" white against the penalties of color. From such penalties blacks admittedly had no defenses. The argument, whatever its merits, apparently did not impress the Court.

Tourgée went on to develop more relevant points. He empha-sized especially the incompatibility of the segregation law with the spirit and intent of the Thirteenth and Fourteenth Amendments, particularly the latter. Segregation perpetuated distinctions "of a servile character, coincident with the institution of slavery." He held that "slavery was a caste, a legal condition of subjection to the dominant class, a bondage quite separable from the incident of ownership." He scorned the pretense of impartiality and equal pro-tection advanced in defense of the "separate but equal" doctrine. "The object of such a law," he declared, "is simply to debase and distinguish against the inferior race. Its purpose has been properly interpreted by the general designation of 'Jim Crow Car' law. Its object is to separate the Negroes from the whites in public convey-ances for the gratification and recognition of the sentiment of white superiority and white supremacy of right and power." He asked the members of the Court to imagine the tables turned and themselves ordered into a Jim Crow car. "What humiliation, what rage would then fill the judicial mind!" he exclaimed.

The clue to the true intent of the Louisiana statute was that it did not apply "to nurses attending the children of the other race." On this clause he observed:

The exemption of nurses shows that the real evil lies not in the color of the skin but in the relation the colored person sustains to the white. If he is a dependent, it may be endured: if he is not, his presence is insufferable. Instead of being intended to promote the *general* comfort and moral well-being, this act is plainly and evidently intended to promote the happiness of one class by asserting its supremacy and the inferiority of another class. Justice is pictured blind and her daughter, the Law, ought at least to be color-blind.

Looking to the future, Tourgée asked, "What is to prevent the application of the same principle to other relations" should the separate-car law be upheld? Was there any limit to such laws?

Why not require all colored people to walk on one side of the street and the whites on the other? Why not require every white man's house to be painted white and every colored man's black? Why may it not require every white man's vehicle to be of one color and compel the colored citizen to use one of different color on the highway? Why not require every white business man to use a white sign and every colored man who solicits customers a black one? One side of the street may be just as good as the other and the dark horses, coaches, clothes and signs may be as good or better than the white ones. The question is not as to the *equality* of the privileges enjoyed, but the *right of the State to label one citizen as white and another as colored* in the common enjoyment of a public highway as this court has often decided a railway to be.

Two other briefs in support of Plessy's case, both by Southern whites out of the Radical Reconstruction past, were laid before the court. One was by James C. Walker of Louisiana, Tourgée's associate in the case. The other was by Samuel F. Phillips of North Carolina, an old friend and onetime Scallawag colleague of onetime carpetbagger Tourgée. Thirteen years before the *Plessy* decision Phillips, then United States solicitor general, had suffered defeat before the same court in the Civil Rights Cases of 1883.

The Supreme Court did not hand down a decision on *Plessy* v. *Ferguson* until 1896. In the four years that had intervened since Homer Plessy was arrested in New Orleans, the South had quickened the pace of retreat from its always reluctant commitment to equality and the Fourteenth Amendment, and it had met with additional acquiescence, encouragements, and approval in the North. New segregation laws had been adopted. Lynching had reached new peaks. Frightened by Populist gains in 1892 and 1894, Southern conservatives raised the cry of black domination and called for white solidarity. Two states had already disfranchised blacks, and several others, including Louisiana, were planning to take the same course. In New Orleans, Louis Martinet's valiant *Crusader* had folded and his forces were in disarray. In 1892, Congress defeated the Lodge Bill to extend federal protection to elections, and in 1894, it wiped from the federal statutes a mass of Reconstruction laws for the protection of equal rights. And then, on September 18, 1895, Booker T. Washington delivered a famous speech embodying the so-called Atlanta Compromise which was widely interpreted as an acceptance of subordinate status for blacks by the foremost leader of the race.

Given the strong tide of reaction in public opinion on race relations, the weakness of white friends of blacks, and the seeming acquiescence of blacks themselves, it may well have appeared to the court that it was not within the capabilities of the judicial process to stem the tide—even if the court had been so disposed. If in this case, however, the court acted out of fear of public opinion or deference to majority will, it had certainly shown no such timidity in defying public opinion the previous year, 1895, when it handed down a succession of extremely unpopular opinions in defense of property rights. By 1896 the court may not have been able to stem the tide of segregation, as it might have earlier. On the other hand, it was under no obligation or necessity to give impetus to reaction by the rhetoric in which it couched its opinion.

On May 18, 1896, Justice Henry Billings Brown, of Michigan residence and Massachusetts birth, delivered the opinion of the court on the case of *Plessy* v. *Ferguson*. His views upholding the separate-but-equal doctrine were in accord with those of all his brothers, with the possible exception of Justice Brewer, who did not participate, and the certain exception of Justice Harlan, who vigorously dissented. In approving the principle of segregation, Justice Brown was also in accord with the prevailing climate of opinion and the trend of the times. More important for purposes of the decision, his views were in accord with a host of state judicial precedents, which he cited at length, as well as with unchallenged practice in many parts of the country, North and South. Furthermore, there were no federal judicial precedents to the contrary.

Whether Brown was well advised in citing as his principal authority the case of *Roberts* v. *City of Boston* is another matter. The fame of Chief Justice Lemuel Shaw of the Massachusetts Supreme Court was undoubtedly great, and in this case he unquestionably sustained the power of Boston to maintain separate schools for blacks and rejected Charles Sumner's plea for equality before the law. But that was in 1849, twenty years before the Fourteenth Amendment, which, as Tourgée pointed out, should have made a difference. More telling was Brown's mention of the action of Congress in establishing segregated schools for the District of Columbia, an action endorsed by Radical Republicans who had supported the Fourteenth Amendment and sustained by regular congressional appropriations ever since. Similar laws, wrote Brown, had been adopted by "the legislatures of many states, and have been generally, if not uniformly, sustained by the courts."

The validity of such segregation laws, the justice maintained, depended on their "reasonableness." And in determining reasonableness, the legislature "is at liberty to act with reference to the established usages, customs, and traditions of the people, and with a view to the promotion of their comfort, and the preservation of the public peace and good order."

In addition to judicial precedent and accepted practice, Justice Brown ventured into the more uncertain fields of history, sociology, and psychology for support of his opinion. The framers of the Fourteenth Amendment, he maintained, "could not have intended to abolish distinctions based upon color, or to enforce social, as distinguished from political, equality." The issue of "social equality" was hardly in question here, but there were certainly grounds for maintaining that the framers of the amendment were under the impression that they intended to abolish all legal distinctions based on color.

The sociological assumptions governing Justice Brown's opinion were those made currently fashionable by Herbert Spencer and William Graham Sumner, but the dictum of Chief Justice Shaw in 1849 that prejudice "is not created by law, and probably cannot be changed by law," can hardly be attributed to the influence of either of those theorists. "We consider the underlying fallacy of the plaintiff's argument," said Brown,

to consist in the assumption that the enforced separation of the two races stamps the colored race with the badge of inferiority. If this is so, it is not by reason of anything found in the act, but solely because the colored race chooses to put that construction upon it. . . . The argument also assumes that social prejudices may be overcome by legislation, and that equal rights cannot be secured by the negro except by an enforced commingling of the two races. We cannot accept this proposition. . . . Legislation is powerless to eradicate racial instincts, or to abolish distinctions based upon physical differences, and the attempt to do so can only result in accentuating the difficulties of the present situation. If the civil and political rights of both races be equal, one cannot be inferior to the other civilly or politically. If one race be inferior to the other socially, the constitution of the United States cannot put them upon the same plane.

The most fascinating paradox in American jurisprudence is that the opinions of two sons of Massachusetts, Shaw and Brown, should have bridged the gap between the radical equalitarian commitment of 1868 and the reactionary repudiation of that commitment in 1896, and that a Southerner should have bridged the greater gap between the repudiation of 1896 and the radical rededication of the equalitarian idealism of Reconstruction days in 1954. For the dissenting opinion of Justice Harlan, embodying many of the arguments of Plessy's ex-carpetbagger counsel, foreshadowed the court's eventual repudiation of the *Plessy* v. *Ferguson* decision and the doctrine of "separate but equal" more than half a century later.

John Marshall Harlan is correctly described by Robert Cushman as "a Southern gentleman and a slaveholder, and at heart a conservative." His famous dissent in the Civil Rights Cases of 1883 had denounced the "subtle and ingenious verbal criticism" by which "the substance and spirit of the recent amendments of the Constitution have been sacrificed." In 1896, the "Great Dissenter" was ready to strike another blow for his adopted cause.

Harlan held the Louisiana segregation law in clear conflict with both the Thirteenth and Fourteenth Amendments. The former "not only struck down the institution of slavery," but also "any burdens or disabilities that constitute badges of slavery or servitude." Segregation was just such a burden or badge. Moreover, the Fourteenth Amendment "added greatly to the dignity and glory of American citizenship, and to the security of personal liberty," and segregation denied blacks the equal protection of both dignity and liberty. "The arbitrary separation of citizens, on the basis of race, while they are on a public highway," he said, "is a badge of servitude wholly inconsistent with the civil freedom and the equality before the law established by the constitution. It cannot be justified upon any legal grounds."

Harlan was as scornful as Tourgée had been of the claim that the separate-car law did not discriminate against blacks. "Every one knows," he declared, that its purpose was "to exclude colored people from coaches occupied by or assigned to white persons." This was simply a poorly disguised means of asserting the supremacy of one class of citizens over another. The justice continued:

But in view of the constitution, in the eye of the law, there is in this country no superior, dominant, ruling class of citizens. There is no caste here. *Our constitution is color-blind,* and neither knows nor tolerates classes among citizens. In respect of civil rights, all citizens are equal before the law. The humblest is the peer of the most powerful. The law regards man as man, and takes no account of his surroundings, or of his color when his civil rights as guaranteed by the supreme law of the land are involved. . . . We boast of the freedom enjoyed by our people above all other peoples. But it is difficult to reconcile that boast with a state of law which, practically, puts the brand of servitude and degradation upon a large class of our fellow citizens—our equals before the law. The thin disguise of "equal" accommodations for passengers in railroad coaches will not mislead any one, nor atone for the wrong this day done.

The present decision, it may well be apprehended, will not only stimulate aggressions, more or less brutal and irritating, upon the admitted rights of colored citizens, but will encourage the belief that it is possible, by means of state enactments, to defeat the beneficent purposes which the people of the United States had in view when they adopted the recent amendments of the constitution.

If the state may so regulate the railroads, "why may it not so regulate the use of the streets of its cities and towns as to compel white citizens to keep on one side of a street, and black citizens to keep on the other," or, for that matter, apply the same regulations to streetcars and other vehicles, or to the courtroom, the jury box, the legislative hall, or any other place of public assembly? "In my opinion," concluded the Kentuckian, "the judgment this day rendered will, in time, prove to be quite as pernicious as the decision made by this tribunal in the Dred Scott Case."

The country received the news of the *Plessy* v. *Ferguson* decision with a response that differed from the way it had reacted to the decision in the Civil Rights Cases thirteen years earlier. In 1883, the news of the court's action had precipitated hundreds of editorials, some indignant rallies, congressional bills, a Senate report, and much general debate. Otto H. Olsen has made a systematic survey of the national reaction to the *Plessy* decision which indicates that the news was not received without dissent, that hostility was not confined to the black press, and that the presumption of consensus about segregation in 1896 is an exaggeration. Nevertheless, it is clear that a great change had taken place since 1883 and that the court gave voice to the dominant mood of the country. Justice Harlan spoke for the convictions of a bygone era.

The racial aggressions that the justice foresaw came in a flood after the decision of 1896. Even Harlan indicated by his opinion of 1899 in *Cummings* v. *Board of Education* that he saw nothing unconstitutional in segregated public schools. Virginia was the last state in the South to adopt the separate-car law, resisting it until 1900. Up to that year, this was the only law of the type adopted by a majority of the Southern states. But on January 12, 1900, the editor of the Richmond *Times* was in full accord with the new spirit when he asserted: "It is necessary that this principle be applied in every relation of Southern life. God Almighty drew the color line and it cannot be obliterated. The negro must stay on his side of the line and the white man must stay on his side, and the sooner both races recognize this fact and accept it, the better it will be for both."

With incredible thoroughness the color line *was* drawn and the Jim Crow principle applied—even to areas that Tourgée and Harlan had suggested a few years before as absurd extremes. In sustaining the constitutionality of the new Jim Crow laws, courts universally and confidently cited *Plessy* v. *Ferguson* as the leading authority. They continued to do so for more than half a century.

On April 4, 1950, Justice Robert H. Jackson wrote old friends in Jamestown, New York, of his surprise in running across the name of Albion W. Tourgée, once a resident of the nearby village of Mayville, in connection with segregation decisions then pending before the Supreme Court. "The Plessy case arose in Louisiana," he wrote,

and how Tourgée got into it I have not learned. In any event, I have gone to his old brief, filed here, and there is no argument made today that he would not make to the Court. He says, "Justice is pictured blind and her daughter, The Law, ought at least to be color-blind." Whether this was original with him, it has been gotten off a number of times since as original wit. Tourgée's brief was filed April 6, 1896, and now, just fifty-four years after, the question is again being argued whether his position will be adopted and what was a defeat for him in '96 be a post-mortem victory.

Plessy v. *Ferguson* remained the law of the land for exactly fifty-eight years, from May 18, 1896, to May 17, 1954. Then, at long last, came a vindication, "a post-mortem victory"—not only for the ex-carpetbagger Tourgée, but for the ex-slaveholder Harlan as well.

The Case of the Monopolistic Railroadmen

XI

BY R. W. APPLE, JR.

(*Northern Securities Co. et al.* v. *U.S.*, 193 U.S. 197)

The growth of large corporations after the Civil War led Congress to pass the Sherman Anti-Trust Act of 1890, which declared illegal combinations "in restraint of trade or commerce among the several States, or with foreign nations." The constitutionality of the Sherman Act was never questioned; it clearly fell within the power of Congress under the "commerce clause," which John Marshall had defined so broadly in the Steamboat *case. But the law was vague. What constituted "restraint" of trade and commerce?*

During the 1890s, the Supreme Court limited the scope of the Sherman Act, especially in the E. C. Knight case (1895), in which it held that the control over the manufacture of more than 90 percent of the sugar refined in the United States was not ipso facto a violation of the law. Congress had not attempted "to deal with monopoly directly," Chief Justice Melville Fuller declared in the Knight decision, and the government had offered no proof that the sugar refiners had intended to restrain trade. As a result of this and other court tests, by 1900 the Sherman Act had become practically a dead letter.

This was the situation when the events leading up to the case described by New York Times *correspondent R. W. Apple, Jr., took place.*

On January 7, 1901, for the first time in history, two million shares changed hands on the New York Stock Exchange, and brokers were pushed to the edge of exhaustion by the pace of trading. Less than two months later came the formation of the billion-dollar United States Steel Corporation, the climax of ten years of breathtaking industrial consolidation. President William McKinley had just been assured of another four years, the specter of Bryanism was banished, and the road to prosperity looked as smooth and as clear as the New York Central's best straightaway.

EDWARD H. HARRIMAN.

JAMES J. HILL.

More than any other, the man who epitomized the era was the awesome figure in the glass-paneled office at 23 Wall Street. At sixty-three, J. Pierpont Morgan was a brusque and lordly man, with steel-gray hair, a big, straggling mustache, a bulbous red nose, and hazel eyes of an almost hypnotic intensity. Looking into his eyes, said the photographer Edward Steichen, was like staring at the headlight of an onrushing express train at night. During the preceding decade, he had reorganized four great railroads—the Southern, the Erie, the Reading, and the Norfolk and Western. The power of the House of Morgan grew with each reorganization, because Morgan saw to it that directors loyal to him were installed on the boards of each line.

Only one railroad man had both the bravado and the means to challenge the House of Morgan. His name was Edward H. Harriman, and he commanded, in addition to the considerable assets of the Union Pacific and the Southern Pacific, the support of William Rockefeller and Henry H. Rogers—the "Standard Oil boys." Small, frail, myopic, unkempt, he made a striking contrast to Morgan the Magnificent. When he assumed the leading role in the affairs of the Union Pacific in 1897, it had liabilities of $81 million, antiquated rolling stock, a poorly ballasted roadbed, and little traffic. It was scarcely more than a ribbon of rust. Three years later, the Union Pacific was free of debt, paying dividends regularly, and earning $20 million a year. "Bet-You-a-Million" Gates called it "the most magnificent railroad property in the world."

J. J. Hill's Great Northern and Morgan's Northern Pacific ran almost parallel from Minnesota to the coast; Ned Harriman's Union Pacific stretched across the plains from Omaha to Ogden, Utah. East of them lay the Chicago, Burlington & Quincy, reaching from the great marketplace on Lake Michigan northwest toward St. Paul and southwest across Iowa and Nebraska. The Burlington had a strategic position, and the man who controlled it would have a tremendous competitive advantage.

Harriman tried first. Early in 1900, he instructed Jacob Schiff of the investment banking house of Kuhn, Loeb & Company to acquire 200,000 shares of Burlington in the open market. Schiff's operatives went to work in May, but on July 25 Harriman gave up, having been able to buy only 80,300 shares.

The next year, it was Morgan's turn. He told his ally Hill, "Go ahead and see what you can do with the Burlington." A grim, craggy old man, Hill was the personification of the frontier myth. Perhaps his dress was a bit more elegant than it had been when he arrived in the raw village of Pig's Eye, Minnesota, as a young man. But then Pig's Eye was more elegant, too—it was now called St. Paul—and even fastidious clothes couldn't hide Hill's long, shaggy beard or his volcanic temper. Hill had no intention of trying to buy control of the Burlington on the Exchange. Instead, he went straight to the road's directors and offered them $200 a share, although the stock's market price was only $180. In March 1901 the Burlington accepted, agreeing to sell one-half to the Great Northern, one-half to the Northern Pacific.

Harriman, frozen out, was furious. At a meeting with Hill in the home of New York financier George F. Baker a few weeks later, he demanded a one-third interest in the Burlington. Only in this way, he insisted, could peace be maintained in the country west of the Missouri. Hill refused. "Very well," said Harriman, "it is a hostile act and you will have to take the consequences." But Hill remained unconcerned. He had the Burlington, hadn't he? How could Harriman hurt him? Hill left for Seattle to look after the affairs of the Great Northern, and Morgan sailed for France to enjoy the sun at Aix-les-Bains.

The plan now concocted by Harriman was so audacious that even Morgan would never have believed it, had it not become a crushing reality. He would steal the Northern Pacific itself while Hill and Morgan congratulated themselves on their coup. It would be a gargantuan project—the Northern Pacific's stock was worth $155 million, so it would take $78 million to buy control—but that appealed to the little man's sense of grandeur.

Quietly, carefully, he put Schiff to work early in April. By April 15, the banker had 150,000 of the 800,000 shares of common and 100,000 of the 750,000 shares of preferred. The Hill-Morgan forces slumbered on. One of Hill's closest friends sold Kuhn, Loeb 35,000 shares, and a subsidiary of the Northern Pacific sold 13,000 shares from its treasury. On May 2, irony of ironies, the House of Morgan itself disposed of 10,000 shares.

Out in Seattle, Jim Hill finally became alarmed. He hurried to New York, stormed into the office of Jacob Schiff, and demanded an explanation. Schiff, for once, was not evasive; he told his agitated visitor he was buying for Harriman's account. "But you can't get control," Hill said. "The Great Northern, Morgan and my friends were recently holding thirty or forty million of Northern Pacific stock, and so far as I know, none of it has been sold." Answered Schiff, "That may be, but we've got a lot of it."

Schiff's confidence was well founded. By May 3, a Friday, the Union Pacific held 370,000 shares of common—a shade less than half—and 420,000 shares of preferred—more than half. Taking the two classes together (and both had voting rights), it held 790,000 of 1,550,000 shares—a clear majority and hence enough for control. But to Harriman, alert though too sick with excitement to leave his bed, it was not enough. He knew the preferred could be retired at the beginning of the next year by vote of the board of directors, and he was sure Morgan would try to do so. So he called Kuhn, Loeb on the morning of the fourth and placed an order for 40,000 more shares of common. Unfortunately for Harriman, the devout Schiff was at the synagogue. When the order was finally relayed to him, he ordered it held up, convinced that Harriman was wasting his money.

By Monday it was too late. Hill and Robert Bacon, partner-in-charge at 23 Wall Street while Morgan was in Europe, had at last decided that they were in danger. Led by James R. Keene, the most proficient market manipulator of his day, the Morgan forces were everywhere, snapping up N.P. for whatever price was asked. By Tuesday night, they had 410,000 shares of common, a clear majority.

And then the brokers began counting. If Harriman had 370,000 shares, and he did, and Morgan had 410,000, and *he* did, that left only 20,000 in other hands. Many more than that must be in strong-boxes and mattresses on both sides of the Atlantic. The answer lay with the "shorts"—that is, speculators who had sold N.P. shares they did not own, certain they could buy them back later, before they had to make delivery, at a lower price. If, for some reason, the price stayed up for several days, they could borrow shares from brokers for a nominal fee. All of this was—and is—a normal part of the Wall Street routine. But these were not normal times, as the first clicks of the ticker on Wednesday morning made painfully evident.

It was a brutal day. Brokers fought, elbows flailing, to get at their posts. Prices melted away as the shorts unloaded their other holdings to get enough money to buy Northern Pacific. First Burlington, then Erie, then the whole list broke. Only Northern Pacific rose— to 160, to 170, finally to 180. After the din subsided, one desperate man paid $25,000 for the use of 500 shares overnight.

Old Jim Hill was still playing possum. "I have not bought a share of Northern Pacific in six months," he told a reporter. But the hundreds of men who filled the Waldorf-Astoria that night, milling from the café through the billiard room into the bar and back again, were not so sure. "It looks," said one of them, "as if the little boys have commenced something while the big boy was away."

Thursday, May 9, brought gray skies to New York and a slow, depressing drizzle. Huge crowds gathered in the financial district long before the opening. The suspense did not last long. Liquidation began with the opening bell, and soon the whole market was swept away—hundreds of millions of dollars in values were destroyed—as the hysterical shorts jettisoned every share they had. "In the [first] hour, the nearest to hell I ever saw in Wall Street," said one broker many years later, "the bottom seemed to drop out of everything." At first the declines were a point or so, then five, then ten, then twenty. The panic was on. Atchison, which had been at 90 the week before, touched 43; U.S. Steel fell from 54 to 24, Amalgamated Copper from 125 to 90. An elderly woman, arriving at the Exchange about eleven-thirty, asked a bystander where Steel preferred was selling. "Eighty-three," he said. "God help me," she gasped. "I'm ruined."

Above the whole list, like some loathesome star, hung the one stock that had caused it all, the one stock that was all but impossible to buy—Northern Pacific. The frenzied shorts bid it up to 300, to 650, to 800, and finally, just before noon, to $1,000. A man from Schenectady sold his 100 shares at a profit of $55,000; a man from Connecticut sold his 100 at a profit of $60,000. Shortly after noon, the madness ebbed. The bankers made available several millions in short-term credit, and Bacon and Schiff, after unforgivable vacillation, announced that the shorts would be allowed to settle for $150 a share.

The contest for control of the Northern Pacific remained substantially unchanged, with each side convinced it had effective control. Morgan and Hill thought they could delay the stockholders' meeting long enough to retire the preferred stock, and Harriman had the word of five corporation lawyers that this was illegal. Finally, Harriman decided, either on his own or at the suggestion of his Standard Oil friends, to accept a compromise. He agreed to a peace treaty, signed May 31 at the Metropolitan Club. On July 17, Morgan —as provided in the agreement—named five new Northern Pacific directors, including Harriman himself and two others considered his allies.

But to Morgan and Hill, it was an uneasy truce. Each feared that another raid might be launched from another direction. Hill, moreover, had long cherished the idea of putting the Great Northern stock that he and his friends owned into a holding company so it would not be dispersed after his death. It was decided to create a gigantic company to hold the stocks of the Great Northern, the Northern Pacific, and the Burlington. Accordingly, on November 12, under the particularly accommodating laws of New Jersey, the Northern Securities Company was incorporated. Its capital was a whopping $400 million—"large enough," said Morgan, "so that nobody could ever buy it."

Just a few moments after the close of the stock market on September 14, a pack of excited newspapermen had burst into the sanctum at 23 Wall Street. Almost at the front door they came upon the redoubtable Morgan, on his way to an East River pier to board his yacht. "Mr. Morgan," the first one shouted, "President McKinley is dead." For a moment there was silence; then one of the bolder reporters asked the great man for a comment. "It is the saddest news I ever heard," came the reply. "I can't talk about it."

For once, the reaction of Morgan was no different from that of the average American. Men in all stations of life were shocked and saddened by the terrible news from Buffalo. But if the death of William McKinley affected the Indiana farmer and the Boston shopkeeper like the death of a beloved uncle, it must have seemed to J. P. Morgan like the loss of a general in the midst of battle. Business had contributed more than $4 million to McKinley's campaign, and business leaders thought they had bought four years' worth of insurance against government "meddling." With his good friend Mark Hanna sitting at the President's elbow, Morgan had concluded, the government was as sound as any government made up of politicians could be.

Theodore Roosevelt, heir to the McKinley administration, had been assistant secretary of the navy, governor of New York, and, of course, vice president. He had formulated nothing approaching an organic economic philosophy, but there were enough scattered indications of heterodoxy to give the business classes pause. Roosevelt had early conceived a dislike for mere wealth—especially wealth gained in speculation, an activity which offended his almost puritanical sense of morality. "The commercial classes," he had written at the age of twenty-eight, "are only too likely to regard everything from the standpoint of 'Does it pay?' " In 1894, he told Brander Matthews: "I know the banker, merchant, and railroad king well . . . and *they* also need education and sound chastisement." Such sentiments, a mild potion indeed compared to the heady brew of Bryanism, were nevertheless a distinct departure from those of McKinley.

Yet in 1884 Roosevelt had opposed so primitive a measure of government control as a bill to limit the workday of streetcar conductors to twelve hours. And the bloody Pullman strike, which had moved Hanna to shout, "Any man who won't meet his men halfway is a God-damn fool," had elicited from Roosevelt a very different comment: "I like to see a mob handled by the regulars, or by good state guards, not overscrupulous about bloodshed."

Nowhere was the ambivalence of Roosevelt's attitudes more evident than on the question which meant most to Morgan—corporation control. "The quack who announces he has a cure-all," Roosevelt insisted, "is a dangerous person." Still, with his suspicion of great wealth, Roosevelt was unwilling to let corporations run roughshod over all other elements in society. "There *are* real abuses," he conceded. He announced his determination to "see that the rich man is held to the same accountability as the poor man."

Sometime early in 1902, probably in January, Roosevelt asked his attorney general, Philander Chase Knox, for an opinion on the legality of the Northern Securities Company. An old-line Republican from Pittsburgh who had once been Andrew Carnegie's lawyer, Knox had never shown the slightest inclination to interfere with business. But poring over the incorporation papers of the Securities Company, he came to the conclusion that it had the power to restrain trade in the Northwest, and that its capitalization would force it to exercise its power. More than 30 percent of its $400 million of stock, Knox decided, was pure water, and only by gouging customers could it hope to earn a reasonable return on such a top-heavy capital structure. On February 19, after the close of the stock market, he issued a terse memorandum to the newspapers. "Some time ago," it said, "the President requested an opinion as to the legality of this merger, and I have recently given him one to the effect that in my judgment it violates the Sherman Act of 1890." On March 10, a suit was filed in the federal court in St. Paul, just a few blocks from Jim Hill's office.

The attack on the Northern Securities Company was a symbolic act, not a grudge fight. "The men creating [the Securities Company] had done so in open and above-board fashion," Roosevelt wrote years later, "acting under what they, and most of the members of the bar, thought to be the law." As his later career made clear, Roosevelt considered regulation, not prosecution, the ultimate answer to the problems created by the New Industrialism. First, however, it was necessary to make sure that the forces of the left did not take matters into their own hands, that Debs and Bryan did not, like Marat and Robespierre, bring down the whole social structure. And it was necessary to make sure that Morgan and his friends did not, like Louis XIV and his courtiers, make revolution inevitable by their blindness. "When I became President," Roosevelt wrote later, "the question as to the *method* by which the United States Government was to control the corporations was not yet important. The absolutely vital question was whether the Government had the power to control them at all." The Northern Securities case was the test in which he sought to establish that power.

Governmental secrets were, as a rule, no better kept in the first decade of the twentieth century than they are in the ninth, but the Northern Securities suit was an exception. Even Secretary of War Elihu Root, usually Roosevelt's closest Cabinet confidant, was taken aback by Knox's announcement.

The surprise of Root was nothing, however, compared with the utter astonishment of Morgan. The financier was at home having dinner when he got the word. His face reflecting a kind of appalled dismay rather than the seething anger of which he was capable, Morgan spoke over and over of the unfairness of the President's action. The President, Morgan felt, had violated the rules of gentlemanly behavior. If a gentleman thought a friend was doing something out of bounds, he mentioned it to him discreetly. If the Securities Company had to be dissolved, Morgan told his friends, Roosevelt should have asked *him* to do it.

Morgan arrived in Wall Street an hour earlier than usual the next morning and spent the day in conference with Charles Steele and George W. Perkins, two of the firm's partners. Across the street, there was pandemonium. In the first twenty minutes of trading on the outdoor Curb Exchange—the ancestor of the American Stock Exchange—Northern Securities stock lost almost ten points before Morgan allies could shore it up. Speculators, of course, were furious at the President, because they were the ones who stood to lose the most in a short, violent swing of the market. The investors and underwriters, more concerned with the long term, were considerably less angry. "It is a good thing," said a prominent banker. "A decision by the highest authority is needed to let people know where they stand." Thomas Woodlock's editorial in the *Wall Street Journal* the next morning put the matter a little less delicately. "If securities combinations are legal," he wrote, "[the financiers] wish to be able to take full advantage of the fact. If they are not legal, the quicker the fact is established, the quicker some other method of accomplishing desired results can be sought."

On the twenty-second, Morgan, Hanna, William Rockefeller, and several other businessmen went to the White House to get the President's views firsthand. Apparently the meeting was not a success, for Morgan met privately later that afternoon with Roosevelt and Knox. Why, Morgan wanted to know, had he not been consulted in advance? "That," said the President, "is just what we did not want to do." Morgan was not easily put off. "If we have done anything wrong," he persisted, "send your man to my man and they can fix it up." "That can't be done," said Roosevelt, and Knox snapped, "We don't want to fix it up. We want to stop it."

This last must have impressed Morgan, because his next question was defensive. "Are you going to attack my other interests, the Steel Trust and the others?" "Certainly not," the President replied, "unless we find out that in any case they have done something that we regard as wrong." After Morgan had departed, obviously enraged, Roosevelt added a postscript. "That is a most illuminating illustration of the Wall Street point of view," he said to Knox. "Mr. Morgan could not help regarding me as a big rival operator who either intended to ruin all his interests or else could be induced to come to an agreement to ruin none."

Hill, who was in St. Paul, was too busy to go to Washington, but his irritation was evident. "If [this is] a grandstand play, of course, we shall hear little more about it," he said. "But if they do fight they will have their hands full, and they will wish they had never been born before they get through." In mid-March, a group of his friends paid a call on Senator Hanna at the Arlington Hotel in Washington. They asked Hanna to intercede with the President, but the senator would have none of it. "I warned Hill that McKinley might have to act against his damn company last year," he grunted. "I'm sorry for Hill, but just what do you gentlemen think I can do?" When they pressed him further, Hanna put them off with another question: "The Senate passed the Sherman Anti-Trust Law; how can I take it off the books?"

All through the summer and fall of 1902, a special examiner heard testimony from Morgan, Hill, Harriman, Perkins, Schiff, and scores of lesser figures. There was a good deal of pulling and hauling as the government sought to establish its case and the high-priced battery of defense attorneys, headed by the suave Francis Lynde Stetson, Morgan's top lawyer, sought to keep it from doing so. The responses of the great capitalists were marked by an ingenuousness that is as unconvincing today as it was to the trial court. Schiff, for example, maintained that his firm had bought Northern Pacific for its own account, not for that of Harriman. And Morgan, he of the prodigious mathematical mind, found himself unable to recall any significant portion of the details of the transactions he had handled.

As to the pivotal questions involved, there was general disagreement. The government contended that the Great Northern and the Northern Pacific had been "engaged in active competition with one another"; the defense insisted that less than 2 percent of the total interstate business in the Northwest had been competitive. The government charged that the Burlington purchase had been part of a general scheme to put the Great Northern and Northern Pacific under common control; the defense ridiculed the allegation. The government argued that the Securities Company had been organized specifically to "restrain and prevent" railroad competition in the Northwest; the defense asserted that the company was designed solely to protect the Great Northern and the Northern Pacific from further raids like Harriman's. Finally, each side made a climactic extralegal appeal. If the Securities Company was not dissolved, the government brief contended, every railroad in the country could be "absorbed, merged and consolidated, thus placing the public at the absolute mercy of the holding corporation." The government was invoking that great rhetorical abstraction, The People, but Stetson had the perfect answer: he wrapped his clients in the Constitution. To dissolve the Securities Company, he said, echoing the phraseology of the Fourteenth Amendment, would be to deprive citizens of their property without due process of law "by taking away from them their right to sell it as their interest may suggest."

The circuit court decision was announced at St. Louis on April 9, 1903, by Judge Amos Thayer, speaking for a unanimous four-man court. It must have been clear to the defendants almost as soon as Judge Thayer began reading that their cause was lost, for the sixth sentence of his opinion began: "These railroads *are,* and in public estimation have ever been regarded, as parallel and competing lines." This was a key point. If the situation were otherwise, how could the court hold that trade was being restrained? Not much later, Thayer applied the *coup de grâce.* "The [Northern Securities] scheme," he said, "destroyed every motive for competition" between the two roads. "We must conclude that those who conceived and executed the plan" intended to do so. It did not matter whether competition had, in fact, been lessened; it was enough that there was a likelihood that it would be.

Eleven days later, the defendants filed notice of their intention to appeal the decree, and on May 11, 1903, the seventeen hundred closely printed pages comprising the record in the case now styled *Northern Securities Company et al.* v. *The United States* reached the Supreme Court.

Since 1895, the Supreme Court had been engaged in doing all it could to protect the rights of property. Few were the occasions when the court had seemed willing to admit that war and the industrial explosion which followed had wrought the slightest change in American life. As a result, the Sherman Act had remained, for nearly fifteen years after its enactment, an almost toothless tiger in a jungle of carnivores. Although robust enough to deal with price fixing by railroads or an occasional restraint of trade case, against the awesome industrial trusts—the targets of its authors—it was impotent.

Perhaps the Northern Securities case would change all this. Not since the Dred Scott decision in 1857 had the country been so fascinated by a lawsuit. Every captain of industry in the country, the *New York Times* said, awaited the court's decision "with the deepest anxiety." The *Times* forgot to mention it, but there were millions of other people anxious to know the outcome, too. Would the court decide for Hill and Morgan and Harriman? Or would it go along with Teddy Roosevelt?

On December 14, at the table reserved for the press, James Creelman, a reporter from the New York *World,* watched the justices file in. First came little Chief Justice Melville W. Fuller, looking like a dilettante poet; then John Marshall Harlan, with his shining bald head; Rufus W. Peckham, tall, silver-haired, and pallid; Oliver Wendell Holmes, towering over the rest, ramrod straight; David J. Brewer, who reminded Creelman of a medieval archbishop, except that he wore no beard; Edward D. White, square of jaw and resolute; Joseph McKenna, wearing glasses and a pointed little gray beard; William R. Day, small and emaciated. Only Henry B. Brown, ill with an eye infection, was missing.

Then John G. Johnson of Philadelphia was on his feet, addressing the Court in his almost conversational tone of voice. Nine years before, he had defended the Sugar Trust; now, massive and gray, he was speaking as the chief defense counsel of the Northern Securities Company. This Court, he began, had always held that it was the use of power, not the mere possession of it, that constituted the offense. But the circuit court had decided that the Securities Company was guilty because it had *the power to restrain trade.* Was that not in conflict with settled law? "Few of us have a desire to commit murder," he told the Court, "but many of us use a razor, which gives us the power to murder." Pacing about the courtroom, swinging his glasses on the end of their string, occasionally raising his hands above his head to drive home a point, Johnson asked the Court to put itself in the position of Hill and Morgan after the Harriman raid. "What was to be done?" he asked them. "Remain quiet and allow these people, who were waiting like the fox under the tree for something to drop, and let them have the prize, or protect the alliance?" The second course was the only sensible one, he submitted, and the method chosen was entirely legal.

When C. W. Bunn of the Northern Pacific had finished his brief supplementary argument, Attorney General Knox, handsome and immaculate, rose from the chair where he had been sitting watchfully all afternoon. Slowly and calmly at first, then with rising passion, he laid out the government's case. Just before the adjournment, he went to the heart of the matter—the spot Justice Holmes liked to call the jugular. "The Securities Company," he said, "is guilty of the mischief the law is designed to prevent—namely, it brings transportation trade through a vast section of country under the controlling interest of a single body."

The next morning, Knox had but one point to make. "To deny that this is a combination challenges common intelligence," he said. "To deny that it is in restraint of trade challenges the authority of this court." He finished in only ninety minutes, less than half the time allotted to him. In rebuttal George B. Young of the Great Northern insisted that the holder of railroad stock was no more engaged in interstate commerce than the holder of stock in a baseball team was engaged in playing baseball, and asked that the lower court ruling be reversed. Then the lawyers gathered up their papers and departed, and the Court passed to a consideration of less dramatic matters. In New York, Jim Hill told a reporter: "I am just as sure that the Northern Securities Company is lawful as I ever was."

Three months later the drama was reenacted. Again the courtroom was packed with visitors, although the Court had tried to keep the decision date secret. The speculation was that the government would win, but no one could be sure, despite the rumor that Justice White had prepared a dissent weeks ago. When Justice Holmes opened the proceedings by reading the decision in an obscure probate case, the air of expectancy subsided. But then the chief justice nodded almost imperceptibly to Harlan, who began shuffling a great stack of papers in front of him. When he said "Case Number 277," a murmur went through the courtroom. As Harlan read on, a chain of messengers began feeding reports to newspapermen outside—noncommittal at first, because Harlan in his unhurried way was beginning with a recital of the whole Sherman Act and a long description of the facts of the case. Finally he came to the phrase "no scheme or device could more certainly come within the words of the act." The Associated Press sent out a bulletin: "NORTHERN SECURI-TIES DECISION AFFIRMED."

The opinion was vintage Harlan. It was blunt, interminably long, full of rhetorical questions. Most important, it bore on almost every page the marks of Harlan's impatience with legal formalism and his determination to look beyond the form of a transaction to its essence. "No scheme or device," the most telling passage began,

could more certainly come within the words of the [Sherman] act . . . or could more effectively and certainly suppress free competition between the constituent companies. This combination is, within the meaning of the act, a "trust"; but if it is not it is a *combination in restraint of interstate and international commerce;* and that is enough to bring it under the condemnation of the act. The mere existence of such a combination . . . constitute[s] a menace to, and a restraint upon, that freedom of commerce which Congress intended to recognize and protect. . . . If such a combination be not destroyed . . . the entire commerce of the immense part of the United States between the Great Lakes and the Pacific at Puget Sound will be at the mercy of a single holding corporation.

The decision simply pulverized the defendants' carefully wrought arguments. The suggestion that the federal government could not interfere with the Securities Company because it was acting pursuant to a state charter, Harlan wrote, "does not at all impress us." The contention that the Court was sanctioning the regulation of stock ownership rather than the regulation of commerce, he added, "is the setting up of mere men of straw to be easily stricken down." Justice Brown, Justice McKenna, and Justice Day voted with Harlan, and Justice Brewer agreed with their conclusion, although he arrived at it by slightly different reasoning. The other four members of the Court dissented.

Both Holmes and White wrote opinions taking Harlan to task. White's essay was one long wail of anguish over what he regarded as the nonlogic of the majority's stand. At least a half-dozen times he used the words "I fail to perceive . . ." and it was evident that the whole pattern of Harlan's thought had escaped him. In White's view, all the unknowns could be factored out of the case save one —whether "the ownership of stock in railroad corporations" was interstate commerce. Convinced that the answer was no, he argued that this meant Congress could not, under the Constitution, regulate such ownership.

If the central thesis of White's dissent was that Congress *could not* regulate the ownership of stock, the whole thrust of Holmes's was that it *had not*. He was happy, he said, that only four members of the Court had adopted the most extreme view—a view which, in his opinion, would

disintegrate society so far as it could into individual atoms. If that were its intent I should regard calling such a law a regulation of commerce as a mere pretense. It would be an attempt to reconstruct society. I am not concerned with the wisdom of such an attempt but I believe that Congress was not entrusted with the power to make it and I am deeply persuaded that it has not tried.

It was necessary, Holmes said, to consider dispassionately what the Sherman Act meant, to "read the words before us as if the question were whether two small exporting grocers shall go to jail."

The two key phrases in the statute are "contract in restraint of trade" and "combination in restraint of trade," Holmes wrote, and each has a settled meaning at English common law. In a *contract* in restraint of trade, A enters into an agreement with B under which the activities of A are restricted. Clearly this did not apply to the Securities Company. In a *combination* in restraint of trade, on the other hand, A and B join to exclude C from some field of endeavor. But, Holmes continued, the restraint does not begin until something is done to prevent the third party from competing with the combination. To be guilty of violating the Act's prohibition of combinations in restraint of trade, the Securities Company would have had to prevent another railroad from competing with the three it owned. Had this happened? Since the Sherman Act specifically had put corporations and individuals on equal footing, the best test was to inquire whether an individual who had done what the Securities Company had done would be guilty. "I do not expect to hear it maintained," he said, "that Mr. Morgan could be sent to prison for buying as many shares as he liked of the Great Northern and the Northern Pacific, even if he bought them both at the same time and got more than half of the stock of each road."

According to Holmes, the difficulty with the court's decision was that it had confounded the two terms. "If I am [wrong]," he concluded, "then a partnership between the two stage drivers who had been competitors in driving across a state line . . . is a crime. For . . . if the restraint on the freedom of the members of a combination" —rather than on outsiders—"caused by their entering into partnership is a restraint of trade, every such combination, as well the small as the great, is within the act."

"Great cases," said Justice Holmes in his dissent, "make bad law." There is no question that Harlan's opinion was marred by its refusal to consider the theses set forth so doggedly by White and so eloquently by Holmes. Nor did the decision succeed in fostering increased competition, either between the Great Northern and the Northern Pacific or among other corporations. Morgan and Hill continued to run the railroads in tandem, much as they had in 1900, and the merger trend continued. ("You cannot make men fight who have evolved the good sense to work together," said one journal.) There were, as Alexander Dana Noyes pointed out, some beneficial side effects—the minority holdings in the two roads were again in public hands, and the possibility that there would be other securities companies, each with dangerously watered stock, was averted. But these were, after all, relatively minor points.

Only a few people, apparently, understood at the time what gave the decision its real importance and dulled the edge of all the criticism. It had nothing at all to do, in the deepest sense, with farmers in Minnesota, or even with railroads. It had to do with power; specifically, with the power of the government vis-à-vis business. Power is part substance and part symbol, and the Northern Securities decision was to become a symbol of the government's right to control the activities of business. It helped to give Roosevelt the leverage he needed to exercise stricter supervision and control over the corporations. And it is at least part of the reason we remember Roosevelt—and not Taft, who brought far more suits under the Sherman Act—as the "trust-buster." An anonymous writer for *The Outlook* saw this, as did few of his contemporaries, only two weeks after the decision. The important thing about the decision, he said,

is not that it prevents the consolidation of two competing railways, but that it paves the way to Governmental regulation of those railways after they shall have been consolidated; not that it cures a particular abuse of corporation powers, but that it establishes more firmly than ever the sound political and industrial doctrine that corporations deriving their existence from the hands of the people must submit to regulation by the people.

The significance of the legal issues in the Northern Securities case has been eroded by eight decades of Supreme Court opinions in the antitrust field, especially the opinion of Justice Holmes in the Swift case and that of Justice White in the Standard Oil case. The economic philosophy of which it was an expression has been made obsolete by the realization, first during World War I and later during the railroad financial crisis of the 1950s, that unlimited railway competition creates more problems than it solves. But by creating at a crucial moment in history a moral climate in which government could effectively control the power of business, the decision helped to work a permanent change in American life.

The Case of the Overworked Laundress

XII

BY ALPHEUS THOMAS MASON

(*Muller* v. *Oregon*, 208 U.S. 412)

By the beginning of the twentieth century laws regulating the conditions and hours of labor were being passed by state legislatures all over the country. These acts were a "response to industrialism," attempts to adjust to new conditions resulting from the growth of giant corporations, the increased mechanization of industry, and other factors. Inevitably, the Supreme Court was asked to answer the question of how these laws squared with the Constitution of the United States, drafted in a preindustrial age. As Professor Alpheus T. Mason of Princeton University's department of politics explains, this was a difficult problem and it took the Court many decades to find a satisfactory solution. No one contributed more to the search than Louis D. Brandeis, first as a lawyer and then as a member of the Court. The story of his work and influence begins with the case described here. Professor Mason is the author, among other books, of Brandeis: A Free Man's Life.

Nearly half a century separates *Muller* v. *Oregon* (1908), a judicial landmark unscarred by criticism, from the Supreme Court's unanimous decision of May 17, 1954, outlawing racial segregation in the public schools. The latter ruling, the most controversial judicial pronouncement since *Dred Scott,* stirred mixed reactions. Certain Southern lawyers and lawmakers denounced the decision as based "solely on psychological and sociological conclusions," instead of on law and "factual truths." A few social scientists, noting Chief Justice Warren's sympathetic reference to the findings of modern sociological and psychological authorities, were ecstatic. The Warren Court had provided "the greatest opportunity ever accorded sociologists to influence high level decisions." Louis D. Brandeis's novel brief-making technique, introduced in the

Louis D. Brandeis.

Muller case, had at long last, it was thought, paid off.

Ex facto jus oritur—out of facts springs the law—must prevail, Brandeis pleaded, if we are to have a living law. Justice David J. Brewer, speaking for a full bench in the Muller case, had apparently nodded his approval. The Warren Court, in language strikingly similar to Brewer's, had also yielded, it seemed, to the imperatives of authentic empirical data. Chief Justice Warren, like Justice Brewer, had responded favorably to Brandeis's blunt caveat: "A lawyer who has not studied economics and sociology is very apt to become a public enemy."

These assumptions, pleasant or shocking depending on one's point of view, may be illuminated by exploring the peculiar circumstances leading to Brandeis's participation in the Muller litigation. Prior to 1908 the constitutionality of statutes restricting working hours had been argued almost entirely on their legal merits. Briefs of counsel had been confined chiefly to the states' authority, under the police power, to enact such measures. Even on this narrow basis and despite interference with "freedom of contract" guaranteed by the Fourteenth Amendment, public health and welfare legislation was sometimes sustained. Increasingly, however, the justices looked askance at government encroachment on the right to purchase or sell labor, recognized as part of the "liberty" protected by the Constitution. No state, the Fourteenth Amendment enjoined, shall deprive "any person of life, liberty, or property without due process of law." With no precise criteria of contested legislation, no measure of validity save that most elastic yardstick "due process," the Court became final arbiter of economic and social policy. If predilection was not to have free rein, the justices would have to go beyond the customary bounds of constitutional exegesis. But the legal profession had developed no technique whereby the Court could be furnished with relevant social data and statistics. Briefs of counsel as well as judicial opinions were steeped in the convention that law, despite the tangles of sociology and economics, was to be mastered only by a series of syllogisms, informed (or misinformed) by "general knowledge" or "common understanding."

Forward-looking enactments did not suffer so long as the justices followed the self-imposed rule—to presume in favor of constitutionality until violation is proved beyond all reasonable doubt. But once the Court took the position that the states must show special

justification for legislation restricting "liberty of contract," the need
for a new method of brief-making became imperative.

The desperate urgency of a more realistic approach was highlighted in *Lochner* v. *New York* of 1905, known as the Bakeshop Case,
a decision so far reaching in its power-crippling implications as to
evoke Justice Holmes's classic indictment—the Constitution "does
not enact Mr. Herbert Spencer's Social Statics." In the Lochner case
the Court was confronted with a New York statute limiting the
working hours of bakers to ten a day or to a sixty-hour week. "Is this
law," Justice Rufus W. Peckham asked, "a fair, reasonable, and
appropriate exercise of the police power of the state . . . ?" Five
justices answered "No." "There is," they said, "no reasonable
ground for interfering with the liberty of persons or the right of free
contract, by determining the hours of labor in the occupation of a
baker." "This is not a question," Peckham added somewhat defen-
sively, "of substituting the judgment of the Court for that of the
legislature." To reconcile what seems to be an obvious contradic-
tion, one must understand the justice's theory of the judicial process. His ruling against the New York law was not reached as an
evaluative judgment, nor was it based on any factual investigation.
The decision rested on "common knowledge" that "the trade of a
baker, in and of itself, is not an unhealthy one to that degree which
would authorize the legislature to interfere with the right to labor."

By 1907 events had taken place which were destined to undermine Justice Peckham's assumptions. In that year Curt Muller, an
obscure laundryman of Portland, Oregon, was arrested for violating
the state's ten-hour law for women. Muller tried unsuccessfully to
build a defense on Justice Peckham's predilections in the Bakeshop
Case. "Statutes of the nature of that under review," Peckham had
observed, "are mere meddlesome interferences with the rights of
the individual. . . . This interference seems to be on the increase.
. . . We do not believe in the soundness of the views which uphold
this law." Muller naturally appealed his conviction to the United
States Supreme Court, where Brandeis, as counsel in defense of the
Oregon statute, had a chance to demonstrate by recourse to facts
that the Oregon legislators could reasonably have believed their
ten-hour law to be an appropriate remedy for a probable evil. The
dragon to be slain was judicial preference, the rugged dogma of
laissez-faire.

As was his invariable practice, Brandeis did not volunteer his services. Through the good offices of the National Consumers' League, John Manning, the district attorney in charge of the case in Oregon, invited the Boston lawyer to cooperate. Organized in 1899, the League had as its first general secretary Florence Kelley, a member of Hull House and a distinguished social worker. Among its first activities was the Consumers' League label, precursor of the now familiar union label. As preliminary to according its stamp of approval, reports were requested from local Boards of Health and state factory inspectors. The label stitched on a manufacturer's product meant that "the state factory law is obeyed; all the goods are made on the premises; overtime is not worked; children under sixteen years of age are not employed." The League also drafted legislation regulating hours, wages, and working conditions and propagandized in support of its enactment. Not content merely to get laws on the statute books, it waged legal battles in the courts. *Muller* v. *Oregon* was the first effort of this type to gain national prominence.

On being alerted by the Oregon State Consumers' League that the Muller case was on its way to the U.S. Supreme Court, the national organization began to give serious consideration to the ammunition needed to meet the attack. More than the Oregon statute was at stake, for similar legislation had been passed in nineteen other jurisdictions. Massachusetts had earlier sustained an hours-of-work law for women, but the courts of Illinois had found its own legislation in conflict with both the state constitution and the Fourteenth Amendment. The record in the United States Supreme Court was not wholly encouraging. In 1896 Utah's eight-hour limit on hazardous employment in mines had been upheld, but within a decade a 5–4 decision set aside, as we have seen, the New York Bakeshop law. Even as the League received word of the Oregon case it was swallowing still another bitter pill in New York State. The attorney general had just decided to delay defense of a state labor law until after the November election.

At this critical juncture, the League decided to tap the best legal talent in the country. In Mrs. Kelley's absence, the male members of the League's Policy Committee secured for her an appointment with Mr. Joseph H. Choate, then leader of the New York bar. Superficially, a retainer from a lawyer of Choate's standing seemed a grand stroke. The New Yorker, however, was not interested. Choate could not see, as he said, why "a big husky Irishwoman should not work more than ten hours if she so desired." The next day Kelley was in Boston talking to the eminent corporation lawyer Louis D. Brandeis.

Turning to Brandeis was not accidental. Louis's parents, Adolph and Frederika Dembitz Brandeis, had come to America, along with other "forty-eighters," in search of the freedom Europe denied them. Trained as a lawyer, he emerged at the turn of the century as an uncommonly gifted reformer. The trait that distinguished him from the entire miscellany of liberals was his inductive, factual approach to evil conditions and immoral practices. "Seek for betterment," he advised, "within the broad lines of existing institutions. Do so by attacking evils *in situ;* and proceed from the individual to the general." The unsurpassed grasp thus gained of social and economic complexities developed in him a profound sense of urgency, an uncanny premonition that one generation's failure to resolve its own problems complicates tomorrow's issues.

The national spotlight first fell on Brandeis in 1897 when he spoke up for consumers before a congressional committee amid the jeers of tariff-supporting legislators. He came into the public eye again five years later when Clarence Darrow consulted him while preparing the mineworkers' case for the Anthracite Coal Strike Commission created by President Theodore Roosevelt. Serving as counsel, without pay, in various public welfare contests in the Bay State had won for him the title "People's Attorney." The National Consumers' League sought his services, however, not as reformer but as lawyer. There was little or no expectation that he would resort to novelty. Direction of the League's court cases was in the hands of Josephine Goldmark, Brandeis's sister-in-law. As chairman of the Committee on Legislation, Miss Goldmark had to keep the Executive Committee informed about all legislation concerning the objects in which the organization was interested. Recalling Brandeis's participation in the Muller Case, she observed:

What he would say, we had no idea. After all, he had had no hand in shaping the legal record nor in presenting the defense in the state courts. The verdict of the highest courts in Oregon was in our favor; but in the U.S. Supreme Court the adverse *Lochner* decision invalidating an hour law stood

menacingly in our path. The time to prepare a brief was very short, probably not more than a month.

Brandeis went to work quickly. Realizing that the crux of the
matter lay in human facts, in diverse medical and sociological data,
he enlisted the services of nonlawyers, amassing the authoritative
statements and testimony of medical and lay experts. He would
need, Brandeis told Goldmark, *"facts,* published by anyone with
expert knowledge of industry in its relation to women's hours of
labor, such as factory inspectors, physicians, trade unions, economists, social workers." Aided by ten readers, Miss Goldmark delved
into the libraries of Columbia University, the Astor Library, and the
Library of Congress. A young medical student devoted himself
solely to research on the hygiene of occupations. Meanwhile, Brandeis constructed the legal argument.

The finished brief contained only two scant pages of "law" and
over a hundred of extralegal sources. Besides the testimony of
scholars and special observers, here and abroad, the brief included
extracts from over ninety reports of committees, bureaus of statistics, commissioners of hygiene, and factory inspectors. A generation
of experience in Europe and America had not only demonstrated
the widespread evil of long working hours but also the physical,
moral, and economic benefits of shorter hours. "Production not
only increased but improved in quality. . . . Regulation of the working day acted as a stimulus to improvement in processes of manufacture. . . . Factory inspectors, physicians and working women were
unanimous in advocating the ten-hour day. . . ." Some experts
considered ten hours too long. "Long hours of labor are dangerous
for women primarily because of their physical organization."

No one knew whether the Court would notice a brief so unconventional. In all previous cases in which social legislation had been
invalidated, the judges, by recourse to abstract logic, had confidently denied any "reasonable" relation between the legislation and
its stated objective of improved public health. In 1905, Justice Peckham had asserted categorically that "it is not possible, in fact, to
discover the connection between the number of hours a baker may
work in a bakery and the healthy quality of the bread made by the
workman." One could not be sure that the Court would recognize
the factual relation even if it were shown.

No lawyer, except Brandeis, had this faith either in the justices or in himself. Shrewdly playing down the revolutionary aspect of his brief, he tried to show that the Court had practically asked for a convincing demonstration of public health needs, not merely a logical array of precedents. The legal portion of his argument listed five rules established in the Bakeshop Case. He accepted them all, including Peckham's insistence that "No law limiting the liberty of contract ought to go beyond necessity." Brandeis diverged from Justice Peckham only in contending that in the determination of necessity, logic is not enough. "There is no logic that is properly applicable to these laws except the logic of facts," he said.

Brandeis appeared in oral argument January 15, 1908, before a Court dominated by superannuated legalists, including Chief Justice Melville W. Fuller and Justices Peckham, Brewer, and William R. Day. Rattling the dry bones of legalism, William D. Fenton, counsel for Muller, argued that "women, equally with men, are endowed with the fundamental and inalienable rights of liberty and property, and these rights cannot be impaired or destroyed by legislative action under the pretense of exercising the police power of the state. Difference in sex alone does not justify the destruction or impairment of these rights."

But this time the Court could not be screened from knowledge of the living world. "Common knowledge" was reinforced by the testimony of experts. "The disinguishing mark of Mr. Brandeis's argument," Miss Goldmark recalled,

was his complete mastery of the details of his subject and the marshaling of evidence. Slowly, deliberately, without seeming to refer to a note, he built up his case from the particular to the general, describing conditions authoritatively reported, turning the pages of history, country by country, state by state, weaving with artistic skill the human facts—all to prove the evil of long hours and the benefit that accrued when these were abolished by law.

"We submit," Brandeis told the justices, "that in view of the facts of common knowledge of which the Court may take judicial notice and of legislative action extending over a period of more than sixty years in the leading countries of Europe, and in twenty of our states, it cannot be said that the Legislature of Oregon had no reasonable ground for believing that the public health, safety, or welfare did not require a legal limitation of women's work in manufacturing and mechanical establishments and laundries to ten hours in one day."

The justices listened with interest and admiration. In what Brandeis said they could discern no wholesale erosion of established principles, no "creeping socialism." Taking the Brandeis brief in stride, the Court's spokesman, Justice Brewer, mentioned the Boston lawyer by name and commented on his very "copious collection of material from other than legal sources." Continuing, the justice struck a cautious note, observing that "Constitutional questions are not settled by even a consensus of present public opinion." Yet, he added, "when a question of fact is debated and debatable, and the extent to which a special constitutional limitation goes is affected by the truth in respect to that fact, a widespread and long-continued belief concerning it is worthy of consideration."

The Court's mention of Brandeis by name was unusual; the lawyer's factual approach was novel. As to the judgment reached, however, Brandeis's facts were corroborative, not decisive. What everybody knows, judges are presumed to know. It is general knowledge that women are mothers of the race. "Woman's physical structure," Justice Brewer declared, "and the performance of maternal functions place her at a disadvantage in the struggle for existence. . . . We take judicial cognizance of matters of general knowledge."

Thus the Court upheld the Oregon law, though without overruling the bakeshop decision. The mighty laissez-faire barrier had been penetrated. Requests for the Brandeis brief poured in from lawyers, economists, college professors, and publicists. The Russell Sage Foundation reprinted it in quantity, and the National Consumers' League aided in its distribution. Brandeis, the National Consumers' League, and the American people had taken an important step toward a living law. *The Outlook* of March 7, 1908, called the Muller decision "a victory for posterity," "unquestionably one of the momentous decisions of the Supreme Court," "immeasurable in its consequences, laden with vast potential benefit to the entire country for generations to come." More prophetic, however, was the magazine's observation, a month earlier, that the Supreme Court had not "always been strictly uniform" in passing on the constitutionality of social legislation.

The National Consumers' League, encouraged by this signal victory, pressed on, voting to set up a permanent committee in defense of labor laws. Brandeis appeared for oral argument in other states and sent briefs to fourteen different courts. Expanding its legislative campaign in Oregon, the League won in 1913 establishment of the Industrial Welfare Commission to regulate wages and hours and prescribe safety, health, and welfare measures for industrial employees. The Commission immediately promulgated minimum wages for women in factories and stores. When the validity of this order was contested on December 17, 1914, before the United States Supreme Court, Brandeis was on hand for oral argument. With "facts," he fused compelling moral and humane considerations.

"Why should the proposition be doubted," he asked, "that wages insufficient to sustain the workers properly are uneconomical? Does anybody doubt that the only way you can get work out of a horse is to feed the horse properly? . . . Regarding cows we know now that even proper feeding is not enough; or proper material living conditions. . . . Experience has taught us that harsh language addressed to a cow impairs her usefulness. Are women less sensitive than beasts in these respects?" Brandeis's earthy and elemental argument was overpowering. An eyewitness, Judge William Hitz of the District of Columbia supreme court, reported:

I have just heard Mr. Brandeis make one of the greatest arguments I have ever listened to. . . . He spoke of the minimum wage cases in the Supreme Court, and the reception he wrested from that citadel of the past was very moving and impressive to one who knows the Court. . . . When Brandeis began to speak, the Court showed all the inertia and elemental hostility which courts cherish for a new thought, or a new right, or even a new remedy for an old wrong, but he visibly lifted all this burden, and without orationizing or chewing the rag he reached them all. . . . He not only *reached* the Court but *dwarfed* the Court because it was clear that here stood a man who knew infinitely more, and who cared infinitely more, for the vital daily rights of the people than the men who sat there sworn to protect them.

Before the Court could reach a decision, Brandeis was immortalized in a way that transcended his famous factual briefs. It was January 28, 1916. The nation's capital was relatively serene. Suddenly Washington and the rest of the country were stunned as if struck by a salvo from an unseen zeppelin. That day President

Wilson nominated Louis D. Brandeis associate justice of the United States Supreme Court.

Within a year after taking his seat on the bench the greatest gain derived from his brief-making technique was recognized and enforced. Having rejected—thanks in part to Brandeis's innovations—the freedom-of-contract fiction as to working women, the Court recognized an implied obligation to insist—certainly before setting legislation aside—upon a factual showing of the sort Brandeis introduced in 1908. The case was *Bunting* v. *Oregon,* involving an Oregon ten-hour factory law. Three additional hours might be worked at a time-and-one-half pay rate. Bunting employed a laborer for thirteen hours without complying with the overtime requirement. Indicted and found guilty, he appealed to the United States Supreme Court. A bulky sociological brief in behalf of the Oregon law was presented by Professor Felix Frankfurter. Later on, an edition of four thousand copies was printed in book form and sent to 462 law schools, colleges, and libraries in forty-five states. In this particular case the effort seemed quite unnecessary. Presuming constitutionality, the Court, voting 5–3 (Brandeis not participating), cast the burden of proving the act's alleged invalidity on Bunting. "There is a contention made," the Court observed, "that the law, even regarded as regulating hours of service, is not either necessary or useful 'for the preservation of the health of employees in mills, factories or manufacturing establishments.' The record contains no facts to support the contention, and against it is the judgment of the legislature and the [State] Supreme Court." The record being barren of any factual demonstration tending to show unreasonableness, the act was sustained. This by-product of the Brandeis brief has been of incalculable importance. It set the pattern Brandeis himself followed as a Supreme Court justice.

Though the Court in the Muller case may not have been decisively influenced by Brandeis's facts, the justices, nevertheless, approved his method. Even that was challenged in 1923, when the Supreme Court set aside a District of Columbia minimum wage law for women. Justice Sutherland, speaking for a majority of six and reversing the stand taken in the Bunting case of 1914, presumed unconstitutionality. "Freedom of contract is the general rule and restraint the exception," he said. The justice thereby called upon those who favored the restraint to justify the exception. Professor

Frankfurter, again following Brandeis's example of 1908, had sub-mitted a brief heavily freighted with facts. But Justice Sutherland considered these wholly irrelevant.

> We have . . . been furnished with a large number of printed opinions [by special observers, students of the subjects, etc.] approving the policy of the minimum wage, and our own reading has disclosed a large number to the contrary. These are all proper enough for the consideration of lawmaking bodies, since their purpose is to establish the desirability or undesirability of the legislation; but they reflect no legitimate light upon the question of its validity, and that is what we are called upon to decide.

Nevertheless, the Brandeis way caught on. In recent years his type of brief has become the lawyer's stock in trade, particularly in cases involving racial discrimination. As part of the effort to induce the courts to create a new legal rule in the enforcement of restrictive covenants based on race, sociologists were called in as expert wit-nesses and queried about population patterns, availability and con-dition of housing, and the effect of racial ghettos on health, crime, and juvenile delinquency. The special sociological memorandum introduced in these cases was the precursor of the Social Science Statement appended to appellant's brief in the School Segregation Cases, in which more than a score of psychologists and sociologists appeared as expert witnesses. In opposition Virginia called two psychologists and a psychiatrist. Prior to this dramatic develop-ment, government lawyers, using statistical and related data, were markedly successful in lawsuits against private corporations. Op-posing lawyers soon began to file briefs of the same kind. The results, however, were not altogether satisfying for those promoting the factual brief as the champion of social advance. "There are ways of rigging your statistics," Charles Edward Sigety, teacher of statisti-cal method, observed, "so that almost any conclusion can be reached from the same basic information."

The point was illustrated in the Supreme Court case of *Jay Burns Baking Co.* v. *Bryan* (1927). In 1926 the Nebraska legislature, in an effort to prevent fraud, prescribed the maximum and minimum limits for the weight of bread. When this act came before the High Court, counsel on both sides, employing the Brandeis method, flooded the justices with special reports of chemists and others dealing with the technical phases of bread making. Faced with conflicting expert testimony, the Court collected "facts" of its own. Seven justices, after exhaustive research, sustained the contentions of the plaintiff; two, presumably as well versed in the science of baking, were convinced that the state had proved its case. Justice Brandeis, dissenting, then set in clearer focus the role of social and economic statistics in the judicial process:

Put at its highest, our function is to determine, in the light of all facts which may enrich our knowledge and enlarge our understanding, whether the measure, enacted in the exercise of the police power and of a character inherently unobjectionable, transcends the bounds of reason. That is, whether the provision as applied is so clearly arbitrary or capricious that legislators acting reasonably could not have believed it to be necessary or appropriate for the public welfare.

To decide, as a fact, that the prohibition of excess weights "is not necessary for the protection of the purchasers against imposition and fraud by short weights"; that it "is not calculated to effectuate that purpose"; and that it "subjects bakery and sellers of bread" to heavy burdens, is, in my opinion, an exercise of the power of a super-legislature—not the performance of the constitutional function of judicial review.

For Brandeis the Court's function was equally circumscribed when confronted with a legislative policy he approved. In 1925 the Oklahoma legislature provided that no one could engage in the manufacture of ice for sale without obtaining a license. If on investigation the state commission found that the community was adequately served, it might turn down the bid of a would-be competitor, and in this way, perhaps, advance monopoly. On its face, this legislation encouraged precisely the trend Brandeis had tried to prevent. "The control here asserted," the Court ruled in a 6–2 opinion setting aside the act, "does not protect against monopoly, but tends to foster it." Yet Brandeis, in dissent, voted to uphold the regulation. "Our function," he wrote, "is only to determine the reasonableness of the legislature's belief in the existence of evils and in the effectiveness of the remedy provided."

The case was decided in 1932, the low point of economic depression. In an emergency "more serious than war," Brandeis observed,

There must be power in the States and the Nation to remold, through experimentation, our economic practices and institutions to meet changing social and economic needs. . . . This Court has the power to prevent an experiment. We may strike down the statute which embodies it on the ground that, in our opinion, the measure is arbitrary, capricious, or unreasonable. . . . But in the exercise of this high power, we must be ever on guard, lest we erect our prejudices into legal principles.

Brandeis's factual brief had been invented in response to a particular need. At the turn of the century, the evils of long hours, low wages, and improper working conditions were well known. Legislative attempts to provide correctives had been impressive. Required was a new weapon to neutralize the paralyzing effects of the laissez-faire dogma in judicial decisions. Among lawyers and judges particularly, effective support for an alternative gospel was crucial—laissez-faire for legislative reform. Brandeis's facts were prompted by Justice Peckham's disregard of the presumptive principle. For effective remedial action, facts had to be marshaled on a specific front and given moral voltage.

Failure to grasp Brandeis's purpose has led to the notion that he laid the groundwork for the Warren Court's alleged reliance on extralegal data in the desegregation decision of 1954. Those thus inclined to invoke Brandeis's authority make a twofold error. First, they exaggerate the effect of the Brandeis technique both in the Muller case and in the school decision. Second, they reverse the intent or aim of his method. As a lawyer and as a dissenting judge he amassed social facts to buttress the presumption of legislative reasonableness; when writing for the Court, he relied solely on the presumption rule. In neither situation did he utilize facts in an attempt to prove that legislators had been unreasonable—indeed, in the *Jay Burns* case he protested against this practice.

Justice Brewer in 1908, like Chief Justice Warren in 1954, referred sympathetically to extralegal findings. In a footnote Brewer cited sources drawn from Brandeis's brief. Similarly, Chief Justice Warren, referring to the supporting data found in "modern authority," listed six sociological and psychological studies in the now famous footnote eleven. Like Brandeis's "authorities," these were merely indicative of "widespread belief" as to the psychological effects that had now become common knowledge. There was the further consideration, noted by Justice Frank Murphy in another context, that "racial discrimination is unattractive in any setting" and "utterly revolting among a free people who have embraced the principles set forth in the Constitution of the United States." The irony is that Chief Justice Warren's corroborative footnote eleven, tending to show the *unconstitutionality* of state action, ignited hot fires of protest, whereas Justice Brewer's footnote endorsement of Brandeis's findings, tending to support the *constitutionality* of state action, stirred not a ripple of discontent from any quarter. Tactically, footnote eleven has hurt more than it has helped.

Brandeis would have applauded the use of the so-called task force as prerequisite to informed action in any area of the governing process—including constitutional interpretation. He would have concurred in Justice Harlan F. Stone's judgment of 1936 as to the need for "an economic service—a small group of men, trained as economists and statisticians, and thus qualified to assemble material for use of the Court." "Knowledge," Brandeis said, "is essential to understanding; and understanding should precede judging." In the role of dissenter, as in that of counsel, he would open the "priestly ears" to the call of extralegal voices. In the decision-making process, however, social science data are only one among the factors requiring consideration.

Without exception the opinions Justice Brandeis embellished with social facts and statistics are in dissent. His factual dissenting opinion, like the factual brief, was an imposing apparatus to support his conviction that "the most important thing the justices do is not doing." In man's eternal pursuit of the more exact, Brandeis recognized that there are facts and facts. Facts have to be interpreted. For him "economic and social sciences are largely uncharted seas." Social science experiments rarely exhibit convincing proof comparable to that achieved in a laboratory of physics or chemistry. One can never be sure all the facts are assembled, and even if this were possible, exploration and study of them would rarely point to only one conclusion. Policy decisions are too complex to be left to statisticians. Their findings need to be informed by opinions based on less specialized knowledge. As to whether the shoe pinches and where, we want the verdict of the wearer, not that of the skilled craftsman who made it.

"Government," Brandeis said, "is not an exact science." When the validity of its use as an instrument of social improvement is at issue, public opinion concerning the evils and the remedy "is among the important factors deserving consideration." He therefore attached great weight, as we have seen, to presumption of constitutionality, and objected vigorously when the Court in defiance of this principle, and on the basis of its own "facts," used its awesome power to strike down a novel and perhaps socially useful experiment. More than once, when his colleagues interposed the judicial veto because the measure seemed to them unwise or foolish, he admonished: "To stay experimentation in things social and economic is a grave responsibility. . . . If we would guide by the light of reason, we must let our minds be bold." Only in reviewing statutes affecting First Amendment freedoms and legislation directed against religious, national, or racial minorities need the Court subject legislation to "more exacting judicial scrutiny." Brandeis suggested that such encroachments run counter to "a fundamental principle of American government."

The primacy of facts, of informed action, is the hallmark of Brandeis's life and work. His brief in the Muller case is symbolic of his inflexible conviction that for wise action there must be "much and constant enquiry into facts." He relied on experts, utilizing their findings, not their commands. Knowledge, along with promptings of the heart, alerted him to the perils of inaction in the face of evils no one could deny. The solution of society's problems could not wait until every aspect was explored, every relevant fact presumably known. Overwhelming factual demonstrations alone do not account for the intensity of Brandeis's moral indignation and reformist zeal. "Mr. Brandeis," a friend once asked, "how can you be so sure of your course of action?" "When you are 51 percent sure," the justice replied, "then go ahead."

The Case of the Miscreant Purveyor of Scandal

BY PAUL L. MURPHY

(*Near* v. *Minnesota*, 283 U.S. 697)

Throughout its history, the Supreme Court has had frequently to deal with controversies involving civil liberties, and not merely with those of blacks. Generally speaking, the Court has stood firmly for freedom of speech, religion, and the press and for guaranteeing that procedural rights such as trial by jury are properly protected. There are, however, necessary limits to individual freedoms when they conflict with the interests of society. The right of free speech, as Justice Oliver Wendell Holmes pointed out in an important 1919 decision, "would not protect a man in falsely shouting fire in a theater and causing a panic."

But could a person say or publish something that libeled an individual or that was grossly offensive to a large segment of society? Clearly, anyone making libelous statements could be called to account. But could the libeler be prevented from publishing false or maliciously motivated statements? The right of what is known as "prior restraint" was the issue in the case discussed here by Paul L. Murphy of the University of Minnesota. Professor Murphy is the author of The Constitution in Crisis Times: 1918–1969, *a volume in Harper & Row's New American Nation series.*

        Chiseled in marble on the facade of the *Chicago Tribune* building is a statement by Chief Justice Charles Evans Hughes. Taken from the 1931 Supreme Court case *Near* v. *Minnesota*, it reads:

The administration of government has become more complex, the opportunities for malfeasance and corruption have multiplied, crime has grown to most serious proportions, and the danger of its protection by unfaithful officials and of the impairment of the fundamental security of life and

JAY M. NEAR.
FROM *The Minneapolis Tribune*,
APRIL 19, 1936.

The Saturday Press

Vol. 1, No. 4　　　Minneapolis, Minn., Oct. 13, 1927　　　Price 5 Cents

A Direct Challenge to Police Chief Brunskill

The Chief, in Banning This Paper from News Stands, Definitely Aligns Himself With Gangland, Violates the Law He Is Sworn to Uphold, When He Tries to Suppress This Publication, The Only Paper in the City That Dares Expose the Gang's Deadly Grip on Minneapolis. A Plain Statement of Facts and a Warning of Legal Action.

Respectfully Submitted

FRONT PAGE OF
The Saturday Press,
OCTOBER 13, 1927.

property by criminal alliances and official neglect, emphasize the need of a vigilant and courageous press, especially in great cities. The fact that liberty of the press may be abused by miscreant purveyors of scandal does not make any less necessary the immunity of the press from prior restraint in dealing with official misconduct.

The case that produced this landmark ruling also generated a massive body of argumentation on both sides as to the true meaning of freedom of the press, its history as a concept and instrument, and its role in relation to the Constitution and constitutional government. The ruling has become vital in the censorship area, as its frequent use as a precedent attests.

The ruling involved a small newspaper, widely recognized as a scandal sheet; a future mayor of Minneapolis; a future governor of Minnesota; two publishers, one a millionaire and the other a pauper; a national civil liberties organization; and the First Amendment to the Constitution. The time was the famous Jazz Age—the socially irrepressible but politically conservative Twenties. The fact that the case drew extended national attention was a measure of the sensitive, vital, and often contradictory national feelings it tapped.

Along with flappers, bathtub gin, speakeasies, and hoods, the 1920s had seen developments in communications that had a multitude of serious and troubling overtones. "The business of America is business," President Calvin Coolidge told the Society of American Newspaper Editors in 1925, and this spirit infused almost every aspect of American life. Combined with this new spirit was business consolidation and growth, the rapid development of huge metropolitan centers, and a massive movement of people from the country to the city, all of which produced an increasingly depersonalized urban culture characterized by the automobile, the radio, and the motion picture. These homogenizing tendencies broke down the uniqueness of small-town culture and created a greater national synthesis. Anomie increased among many urban dwellers, and the comfort, convenience, and gossip of the small town were no longer accessible. Urban newspaper owners quickly saw a potential market for a type of journalism that would reach this audience. Other businesses viewed the newspaper as a means to induce customers to buy their products. Thus during the decade the press shifted its emphasis to meet the needs of a new mass market; as a result, the content and orientation of newspapers tended to change in several ways. As big business operations, newspapers became increasingly dependent upon advertising for support and, consequently, upon burgeoning circulation figures. The attempt to appeal to a popular audience required the increased subordination of serious news and thoughtful editorial content to what the critic Silas Bent, in a devastating exposé of the industry in the 1920s, called "the art of Ballyhoo." This yellowing journalism frequently tended to be irresponsible and based upon half-truths. It often employed the exposé as a surefire method of selling newspapers. Pages were filled with details of crime, sex and sexual perversion, not-too-subtle attacks on minority religious and racial groups, grossly exaggerated accounts of the questionable morality of public officials, and scandals surrounding the private lives of prominent citizens.

One casualty of this development was the decline of older style, editorially oriented, political journalism tailored to inform people accurately about public issues. That journalism also considered the complex administration of government and the need to bring certain kinds of pressure to force it to deal with corrupt politicians, malfeasance in office, and suspected liaisons between organized crime and politicians. Hence, particularly with the rise of the tabloid, 1920s journalism offended many older, more serious Americans, who were still guided by a vigorous Victorian-Progressive morality and decorum. They objected to everything about the tabloid: its fraudulent and harmful advertising, its gross misrepresentation of facts, its deliberate invention of tales calculated to excite the public, and its wanton recklessness in the use of headlines. Also offensive to many was the graphic detail of the tabloid's portrayals of scandals and divorce of rich or prominent people; its pictures of vicious criminals, prizefighters, and bathing beauties; its "sob stuff"; and its xenophobic jingoing and ill will toward other nations. As Felix Frankfurter wrote at the time: "A low tone, emotionalism, off-emphasis, irrelevance, and neglect are . . . the outstanding sources of newspaper shortcomings. These qualities of news matter fashion the mind of the public. The public, in its turn, is stimulated to want this kind of news."

There was, however, a further dimension to these developments. The 1920s also saw the emergence of a number of cheap, ephemeral scandal sheets, which were used for extortion, blackmailing petty crooks, or pressuring concessions from venal public officials. Many, however, while their tone was deplorable, actually filled an information gap. In a number of cities, the politicians *were* in collusion with the business world, which was closely tied to big newspapers and more interested in circulation based upon scandal and gossip than in performing honest public information functions. As with the newspapers, the response of a fair segment of the "respectable" public to the scandal sheets was hostile. In the public mind the two rather disparate forms of journalistic endeavor tended to blur together and become synonymous. Moreover, the respectable public felt victimized and powerless to retaliate against them all, particularly when suggestions of regulation or curtailment inevitably met the argument that the First Amendment protected these journalistic activities.

The Minnesota situation was not atypical. Because of Prohibition, the state had become a crossroads in the illegal Canadian liquor trade, and with such law defiance had come vice and crime, both in Duluth and in Minneapolis and St. Paul. Ordinary law-abiding citizens looked the other way, concerning themselves with their private affairs, leaving law enforcement and civic administration to corrupt politicians and gangsters. Numerous gang killings accompanied gambling and trade in illegal booze. Respectable newspapers refused to investigate the association between the law breakers and law enforcement officials, and scandal sheets moved in to fill the void. In Duluth, John Morrison's *Duluth Rip-Saw* trumpeted sin, vice, and corruption so raucously and attacked vulnerable politicans so aggressively that the Minnesota legislature, responding to public demands for censorship, enacted a statute in 1925 to protect the community against the evils of these forms of business. The law was pushed by State Senator Mike Boylan and State Representative George Lommen, both of whom had been targets of the *Rip-Saw.* Subsequently dubbed the Minnesota Gag Law, it permitted a judge, acting without a jury, to stop the publication of a newspaper if the judge found it "obscene, lewd, and lascivious" or "malicious, scandalous, and defamatory." More specifically, it provided that the county attorney or, in his absence, the attorney general or any citizen acting in behalf of the county attorney, might petition the district court for a temporary restraining order against any periodical that allegedly had violated the provisions of the act.

After a trial on the merits of the case, the district court judge could grant a permanent injunction, by which, in the language of the law, "such a nuisance may be wholly abated." Thus, the law allowed the enjoining of any publication which, in the opinion of a single judge, was contrary to public morals. It was, as a popular commentator wrote later, "a shining example . . . of that kind of police power which makes for governmental tyranny." If the law was effective, political corruption and business fraud could flourish without fear of exposure. Failure to comply with the order of the court would be contempt, punishable by a fine of a thousand dollars or a year in the county jail.

Minnesota's experiment quickly drew warm national approval as a "wise and desirable remedy" for these evils. In fact, the law was seen as a model; the national student debate topic for 1930 was "Resolved: That the Minnesota Nuisance Law Should Be Adopted by Every State in the Union."

The arguments for supporting the law ran as follows. The complications of ordinary censorship, or prior restraint, make such censorship impractical: it would be impossible to have government censors read every magazine and delete every falsehood, exaggeration, indecency, or obscenity. Censorship would require an enormous, highly trained staff and would, therefore, be expensive and unworkable. Legal actions against undesirable publications also fail completely. Prosecutions under the criminal libel statutes do not result in effective repression or suppression of such literature. Further, civil actions for damages cannot prevent the harm done or even a repetition of the offense. The publicity given to trials sometimes does more harm than good. In addition, the expense of trials and appeals puts this remedy out of the reach of all except the wealthy. Supporters argued that the Minnesota law could be applied promptly and could stop obscenity, indecency, falsehood, and defamation, as well as end the publication of scandal sheets completely. It could, in other words, make the journalistic profession responsible again, intimidate the criminal element among writers and publishers, and encourage reputable newspapers and magazines. Freedom of the press would not be impaired—it never meant a license to publish scandalous, malicious, obscene, or indecent matters. Finally, Gag Law advocates contended that the First Amendment did not limit the power of the state governments; it merely limited

Congress. Each state could properly regulate its own newspapers, magazines, and news agencies under its police power.

Clearly the law created positive regulatory overtones. It sought to protect the property rights of certain individuals against black-mailers and scandalmongers who might damage their reputation and standing in the community, injuring them financially. The purpose of the law placed the public welfare above any First Amendment rights that people might claim. To the extent that it protected "liberty," the law saw liberty as the citizen's freedom from the evil impacts of this new journalistic development; certainly it was not liberty of members of the "fourth estate" to publish freely what they wanted.

Jay M. Near and Howard Guilford had established the *Saturday Press* in 1927. Both had come to the Twin Cities a decade or so earlier, Near from Fort Atkinson, Iowa, and Guilford from Northampton, Massachusetts. They had previously practiced a brand of journalism that teetered on the edge of legality, and frequently toppled over. Guilford had had a particularly checkered career. Though never convicted of any crime, he had been indicted nineteen times. Rumor had it that he was a skillful con man who was not above blackmail and extortion. He had founded a weekly paper, *The Reporter,* in St. Paul in 1913. It was a sensationalist sheet that exposed gambling, prostitution, and the sexual adventures of the Twin Cities elite. In 1916, Guilford hired Near as a reporter. Near, who was something of a dandy, had a different flair. He was anti-Catholic, anti-Semitic, antiblack, and antilabor, frequently blasting the "Communist unions." These values crept into even his exposé stories about the Twin Cities establishment. Political corruption, and the truce between bootleggers, gamblers, and prostitution merchants and the police and city fathers, provided endless material for the two. But although their articles were sensational and often over-stated, much that they published was true, or at least more true than false.

The *Saturday Press,* the object of the *Near* case, was to be a paper primarily to reveal corruption, including corrupt ties between the police and the Twin Cities underworld. Minneapolis Chief of Police Frank Brunskill learned of its purpose, as did figures with whom he was working. He sought to ban it before a single issue was published, threatening to send out his men to get it off the newsstands. He failed, but shortly after the first issue did hit the streets, a touring car overtook Howard Guilford on his way home, and before he could pull his own gun, two assailants pumped four bullets into his car. The last struck him in the abdomen as the car careened to a stop. Guilford was rushed to the hospital in critical condition. "I headed into the city on September 26, ran across three Jews in a Chevrolet, stopped a lot of lead and won a bed for myself in St. Barnabas Hospital for six weeks," he later reported. "Wherefore, I have withdrawn all allegiance to anything with a hook nose that eats herring." The respectable Minneapolis *Morning Tribune,* in reporting the episode, included an editorial indicating that "gangland [which clearly included people like Guilford] cannot settle its differences with impunity in our streets."

But in the next issue of the *Saturday Press,* Near made clear that there were links between gambling syndicates and the police. He warned the mob and the police that: "If the ochre-hearted rodents who fired those shots into the defenseless body of my buddy thought for a moment that they were ending the fight against gang rule in this city, they were mistaken." The paper went on from there to get particularly tough with city and county government officials, attacking among others the county prosecutor, Floyd B. Olson, who later became a three-term Minnesota governor. It called him a "Jew Lover" and accused him of dragging his feet in the investigation of gangland pursuits.

Olson was enraged. Politically ambitious and savvy about whom to play ball with, Olson had occasionally blinked at some of the minor infractions of small-time gamblers. Having certain Robin Hood proclivities, he hoped to build a base from which to move into state politics, and he certainly wanted no insinuations as to his motives. He promised to "put out of business forever the *Saturday Press* and other sensational weeklies."

On November 21, 1927, Olson filed a complaint with Hennepin County District Judge Mathias Baldwin, alleging that the *Saturday Press* had defamed Mayor George Leach, Police Chief Brunskill, and Charles G. Davis, head of the Law Enforcement League, as well as the Minneapolis *Tribune,* the Minneapolis *Journal,* the Hennepin County Grand Jury, Olson himself, and the entire Jewish community. He described the paper as a "malicious, scandalous, and defamatory publication" and asked that "said nuisance be abated." He wanted the court to issue a temporary restraining order barring Near and Guilford or anyone else from "conducting or maintaining said nuisance under the name of the *Saturday Press,* or any other name." Judge Baldwin complied, and went on to forbid Near and Guilford "to produce, edit, publish, circulate, have in their possession, sell, or give away any publication known by any other name whatsoever containing matter of the kind alleged in the plaintiff's complaint."

Near and Guilford promptly demurred, arguing that the statute was unconstitutional. Thomas Latimer, a prominent Minneapolis attorney, agreed to defend the almost destitute defendants, although he deplored the *Saturday Press.* At the hearing on December 1, he argued that the law was a "subterfuge to get away from the state's constitution and libel laws" and contended that only Italy and Russia had such statutes. Judge Baldwin sided with Olson, however, and rejected the demurrer. The paper was harmful to the community at large, he said, and the public should be protected against it.

However, the Minnesota constitution contained a clear statement that "the liberty of the press shall forever remain inviolate, and all persons may freely speak, write, and publish their sentiments on all subjects." Baldwin, conscious of this guarantee, certified an appeal of the case to the Minnesota supreme court, leaving to it the question of the law's constitutionality.

The removal of the *Saturday Press* from the streets was popular in the Twin Cities. Few people understood the technical difference between a temporary restraining order and a permanent injunction, and many praised Floyd B. Olson's actions and Judge Baldwin for backing them up. But its removal did little to hinder criminal action. In fact, shortly after the ban, a county grand jury began probing various charges of misconduct against Chief Brunskill, a number of which had first been lodged against him in the *Saturday Press.* County prosecutor Olson called seventeen witnesses (including Guilford!) and the grand jury listened to testimony ranging from charges of political impropriety to allegations of covering up criminal behavior.

Three months after the request for an expedited hearing, the Minnesota supreme court convened to hear oral arguments on the constitutionality of the 1925 Public Nuisance Bill. If the court sustained it, the case would then be sent back to Baldwin's court to decide whether the *Saturday Press* had violated the law and whether the temporary restraining order should be made permanent. By this time Guilford's interest was waning. Nursing his gunshot wound, he left it to Near to fight the law and keep the case in the courts. However, Thomas Latimer (who in 1935 became mayor of Minneapolis) made an eloquent argument that the law was indeed a violation of the state constitution and was "null, void and invalid, being in contravention of the Fourteenth Amendment to the Constitution of the United States." Latimer also stressed the denial of a jury trial, guaranteed by the Sixth Amendment, and contended that the entire concept of freedom of the press guaranteed by the First Amendment had been breached. He further argued that the due process clause of the Fifth Amendment, which had been made applicable to the states with the passage of the Fourteenth Amendment, had been violated.

The court was unimpressed. It ruled unanimously to uphold the state law. Comparing the *Saturday Press* to houses of prostitution and noxious weeds, Chief Justice Samuel B. Wilson asserted that the legislature had the power to do away with such nuisances. In Minnesota, Wilson argued, no one could stifle the truthful voice of the press, but the Constitution's drafters never intended it to protect malice, scandal, and defamation.

Before the issue returned to Judge Baldwin's courtroom, national actions began. In both New York and Chicago the "Minnesota Gag Order" was viewed with alarm. Near had contacted the New York–based American Civil Liberties Union and its founder, Roger Baldwin, responded by sending money for Near's legal defense. The step was typical of the ACLU: Near, the right-wing bigot, was being defended by an organization committed to tolerance. Baldwin had spent a year in a federal prison during World War I for refusing military service. The ACLU board also included such prominent liberals as Clarence Darrow, Felix Frankfurter, and Norman Thomas, all of whom were seen by conservatives, including the powerful *Chicago Tribune*, as practically Bolshevik in their orientation.

The ACLU lawyers focused on the doctrine of "prior restraint." Heretofore, the only control of the press had been through prosecution for criminal or libelous matter after the material had been printed. "We see in this new device for previous restraint of publication a menace to the whole principle of the freedom of the press," the ACLU stated. It also saw the Public Nuisance Law as a dangerous model. "If the Minnesota law is constitutional, then the Fourteenth Amendment and inferentially the First Amendment no longer protect the press against prior restraint."

Minneapolis newspapers refused to see the broader implications which sustaining the Gag Law carried. To them, the issue was the damage blackmailers and scandalmongers would do the community. They scoffed at the fears of the ACLU.

But the editor of the Chicago *Tribune* was not nearly so myopic. Colonel Robert Rutherford ("Bertie") McCormick admired Near for many of the same reasons that the ACLU was apprehensive about him. Rich and powerful, isolationist in his politics, and constantly at battle with Chicago officials over crime and corruption in that city, McCormick disliked blacks, Jews, and other minorities, to say nothing of labor unions. He had fought many legal battles over exposé-type articles published in his newspapers. He certainly did not want the Illinois legislature to copy the Minnesota Gag Law. The interests of the rich publisher in Chicago and those of the poor scandalmonger in Minnesota coincided. McCormick therefore committed the *Tribune*'s resources to the case, indicating that he would strongly consider providing representation for Near in future legal proceedings.

Weymouth Kirkland had been a former law partner of the Colonel and was one of his few lifelong friends. When apprised of the Near situation he was outraged that a judge, without a jury, had suppressed a newspaper by a writ of injunction. He was quick to appreciate that if the Gag Law was upheld, this method of curbing the press would become a model. He rapidly became the chief strategist in the fight for the First Amendment. McCormick was pleased, but increasingly irate. As he wrote later, "Whenever the corruption and the effrontery of the politicians in power reaches a sufficient debasement, action must be taken." Kirkland was skeptical of the ACLU, however. He nudged that body out of the case.

When Judge Baldwin called his court to order in Minneapolis in October 1928, sitting beside Thomas Latimer at Near's table were two *Tribune* lawyers, William H. Symes and Charles Rathbun. When

Floyd B. Olson rose to ask that the temporary restraining order be made permanent, he realized, from these new faces, that the proceedings would be just another detour on the way to the United States Supreme Court. His and Latimer's arguments were almost perfunctory. Baldwin then declared the Public Nuisance Law constitutional and made the temporary order against the *Saturday Press* permanent. "Let said nuisance be abated," he ordered.

Near and his attorneys had little doubt that the Minnesota supreme court would uphold the injunction, since it had already upheld the Gag Law. Nevertheless, they appealed. The step was essential to ensure a final appeal to the U.S. Supreme Court. As expected, the Minnesota supreme court agreed that the *Saturday Press* was a public nuisance. The judges did say that the defendants could publish a newspaper "in harmony with the public welfare." Yet such a paper would hardly be the *Saturday Press*.

Before going to the Supreme Court, McCormick sought to muster further clout. Enter here the American Newspaper Publishers' Association. The ANPA had been founded in 1887 as a daily-newspaper trade association. In the 1920s it represented the great majority of American newspapers, serving principally as an instrument for treating conflicts with advertisers, labor, competitors in other media, newsprint makers, and the government. It opposed government interference with the press and in 1923 had set up a committee to "exercise its utmost effort to maintain freedom of the press whenever and wherever it may be threatened." It also was afraid that the public would regard the press solely as a business enterprise and not as a vital information source protected by the First Amendment. Sensitive to the growing criticism as to the press's sins of both commission and omission, particularly in its highly partisan treatment of many political issues, it found itself increasingly on the defensive.

McCormick's connection with the ANPA had been lengthy. In 1928, partly in response to the first prosecution under the Minnesota Gag Law, he had accepted the chairmanship of the new ANPA Committee on Freedom of the Press. The committee promptly adopted a resolution condemning the law as "one of the gravest assaults upon the liberties of the people . . . since the adoption of the Constitution. The action of the Minnesota legislature and courts," the committee contended, "will render all guarantees of free speech valueless in Minnesota, and such choking of thought and expression can be extended further if not checked."

The action the ANPA should take was less clear. Many members were concerned about the high cost of litigation, but McCormick was more interested in the sanction than the money. He thus maneuvered an ANPA referendum on the issue itself, and gained 254 of 259 members' votes to support the appeal to the Supreme Court, the understanding being that the *Chicago Tribune* would assume most of the financial responsibility. The next day the *New York Times* published an editorial calling the Minnesota statute "a vicious law." Other newspapers followed suit.

McCormick was determined to use the Committee to further educate the public. At the 1929 ANPA general meeting, he submitted a Committee report decrying the statute as "tyrannical, despotic, un-American and oppressive," as resuscitating "obsolete libels on the government," and as "permitting suppression of publications exposing corruption in government." The report asserted that courts of equity should not be permitted to censor the press and suppress writing in advance of publication, and that "this statute was the first attempt of a legislature since the foundation of the Union to gag the press in so drastic a manner." At its 1930 meeting the entire APNA adopted a further resolution condemning the Minnesota act as "a violation of the First and Fourteenth Amendments to the Constitution of the United States, a peril to the right of property and a menace to republican institutions . . . and as a dangerous and vicious invasion of personal liberties."

So the stage was finally set for Near, with McCormick's help, to bring his case to the United States Supreme Court, and on April 26, 1930, the clerk of the Court notified the Minnesota supreme court that *Near* v. *Minnesota* had been docketed. Thus the highest court in the land for the first time took a freedom-of-the-press case involving the vital and ancient principle of prior restraint.

The Supreme Court that was to hear the *Near* case had undergone important shifts in personnel shortly before the case was argued. Chief Justice William Howard Taft, a conservative, property-conscious jurist, had been replaced by the more liberal and rights-oriented Charles Evans Hughes. In addition, the death of Justice Edward T. Sanford of Tennessee had produced an unusual situation. President Hoover's first nominee was Federal District

Court Judge John J. Parker of North Carolina, but Parker's antilabor and antiblack record created a furor. The Senate rejected the nomination. Hoover then turned to the more liberal Owen J. Roberts of Pennsylvania, who had been a determined prosecutor of the Teapot Dome oil scandals, which had sent several members of the Harding administration to prison. A wealthy Philadelphia lawyer, Roberts was seen as a moderate, even though his attitudes toward public regulation of business were hostile and critical. His views on the First Amendment were generally not known, but supporters of the *Near* position hoped he could be reached more easily on a "liberty" question than either Sanford or Parker, given his oft-expressed belief in what he called "good old-fashioned Anglo-Saxon individualism."

In some respects, however, the most important justice on this issue was Louis D. Brandeis. Brandeis had been steering the Court for a decade toward protecting freedom of speech and the press against state legislation by stressing the term "liberty" in the due process clause of the Fourteenth Amendment. Further, he had prepared himself assiduously for the *Near* case, even probing into the ousting of Police Chief Brunskill, an action that was not unrelated to the attacks upon that official by the *Saturday Press* itself.

At 12 noon on Friday, January 30, 1931, the Supreme Court justices entered, for one of the last times, their courtroom in the old Senate chamber of the Capitol. Neither Near nor McCormick was present, but their attorneys were. Weymouth Kirkland was the first to address the Court. He summarized the arguments presented in the sixty-seven-page formal brief, arguments similar to those presented to the Minnesota supreme court. The injunction was a prior restraint; it violated the First and Fourteenth Amendments. The Constitution guaranteed freedom of the press as a fundamental right. No state could take that right away through the prior restraint process.

Moving to more practical considerations, Kirkland argued that state punishment of utterances not as criminal libels of individuals but as general injuries to the public welfare abridged freedom of the press unless the statements advocated the violent overthrow of the government or a breach of the law. Freedom of the press, he contended, was protected by the Fourteenth Amendment, and the Gag Law deprived his client of the liberty that amendment guaranteed.

The *Saturday Press* articles were "defamatory," he admitted, but "so long as men do evil, so long will newspapers publish defamation. Every person does have a constitutional right to publish malicious, scandalous, and defamatory materials, though untrue and with bad motives, and for unjustifiable ends." Such a person could be punished afterward, but the remedy was not prior censorship of the offending newspaper. Rather, the states should bring specific criminal charges against such a newspaper after it published the material.

The counsel for Minnesota was Deputy State Attorney General James F. Markham, along with William C. Larson, and Arthur I. Markve, representing the Hennepin County prosecutor's office, which had brought the original injunction. Markham argued that the law was constitutional and that the injunction was not a prior restraint. He defended the Public Nuisance Law as being well within the police powers of the state. He hinted strongly that it was the responsibility of the state to interpret the provisions of the state constitution, the implication being that the federal constitution had not been violated. Chief Justice Hughes interrupted Markham: "You need not argue further whether or not freedom of the press was a privilege or immunity under the Fourteenth Amendment." Hughes made clear that in his mind "prior decisions of the Court had established that point clearly." He then asked Markham to address the basic question of prior restraint, and whether in this case Near had been deprived of his liberty without due process. Markham denied the action. He indicated that no injunction had been issued until the *Saturday Press* had defamed public officials and become a nuisance, contending that the punishment then was intended to deal with earlier wrongs. He further contended that the law was beneficial to newspapers because it had the effect of "purifying the press."

Brandeis then quietly but firmly entered the fray. Having read the articles in the *Saturday Press,* he pointed out that Near and Guilford had sought to expose combinations between criminals and public officials in conducting and profiting from gambling halls. He conceded that such allegations were hard to prove, but pointed out that such criminal combinations did exist in many communities and that these men had taken on the responsibility of trying to expose them. Turning to Markham, he asked: "How else can a community secure protection from that sort of thing if people are not allowed to engage in free discussion of such matters?" Not waiting for an answer, he further conceded that there was defamation. "You cannot disclose evil without naming the doers of evil. It is difficult to see how one can have a free press and the protection that it affords in the democratic community without the privilege this act seems to limit." This question, he stated, is of prime interest to every American citizen and should be privileged communication. "Assuming it to be true," Markham countered. "No," Brandeis snapped. "Even if it was not true, a malicious and scandalous statement could not be restrained before publication. A newspaper cannot always wait until it gets the judgment of a court." Near and Guilford, he argued, went forward with a definite program and acted with great courage. They invited suit for criminal libel if what they said was not true. Now if that campaign was not privileged, if that was not one of the things for which the press chiefly existed, then for what did it exist?

Markham had no answer, so he turned to Oliver Wendell Holmes for support. But Holmes made clear that although in a 1907 case (*Patterson* v. *Colorado*) he had permitted a Colorado judgment wherein a newspaper publisher was penalized for criticizing judges, he now, he said quietly, "had a different view," and he did not see his earlier ruling as a precedent for permitting the Minnesota statute to stand. For those anxiously sizing up the justices, Holmes was now seen as clearly with Brandeis. On the other hand, Pierce Butler, the one Minnesotan on the bench, had made clear in his questioning that he was very much on the other side, and McReynolds, Van Devanter, and Sutherland were obviously with him. Thus whether or not the Minnesota law would stand depended on where Stone and Roberts came down.

In the meantime, back in Minnesota, a significant development had taken place. Sensing the growing unpopularity of his behavior and of the attempt to gag the press, Floyd B. Olson, now governor of the state, suddenly urged the legislature to repeal the Gag Law. Interestingly, George Lommen, the architect of the measure, agreed to lead the repeal forces. Colonel McCormick, in Chicago, promptly became apprehensive. He did not want a moot case, and he very much demanded that the law be left on the books so that it could be tested by the U.S. Supreme Court. Minnesota lawmakers were not as conciliatory as their governor. Although the Minnesota House of Representatives did vote to repeal the Public Nuisance

Law, five days after the oral arguments in Washington, the state Senate would not go along and the test case became the crux of whether the measure was valid.

In the secret conference among the justices which followed the oral arguments, Chief Justice Hughes, from the scraps of information that are extant, demonstrated a particular interest in the *Near* decision. He was aware that many state legislatures would be watching the Court's action to determine whether or not to copy the Minnesota statute. The chief justice opened the discussion on *Near,* emphasizing that the decision about the liberty of the press was applicable to the states. Brandeis and Holmes agreed, and argued that the Nuisance Law was a suppression not just of defamatory material but of any future publication, and a clear violation of the guarantee of no prior restraint. All three were willing to concede that there were times, for example when a nation was at war, when a paper might be enjoined. But those examples, they contended, were exceptions, and in the absence of such circumstances, no prior restraint could possibly be justified. Pierce Butler disagreed vigorously. He could not understand how Hughes, Holmes, and Brandeis could give First Amendment protection to scoundrels such as Near and Guilford. With the support of the other conservative members, he defended the Public Nuisance Law, arguing it was not suppression but punishment for an injustice already committed. Finally, after further often acrimonious discussion, the chief justice called for a vote on the constitutionality of the Minnesota statute. Five members, Stone and Roberts joining the liberals, voted no. Four voted yes.

Appreciative of the importance of the case and the narrowness of the vote, Hughes assigned himself the task of writing the majority opinion, and by May of 1931 both it and the minority view were circulated among the justices. In his opinion, Hughes made clear early on that "in the present case, we have no occasion to inquire as to the permissible scope of subsequent punishment." The subject was the "no prior restraint" doctrine and its protection of the publication of material that could well be the subject of subsequent punishment under criminal libel or other laws. His argument was far more historical than analytical. As First Amendment expert Thomas Emerson has pointed out, "the Court never undertook to explain the functional basis of the prior restraint doctrine." It preferred to find in the "general conception" of liberty of the press, as adopted by the federal Constitution, the essential attribute of freedom from prior restraint, which the majority was convinced the statute violated. On the other hand, possibly reflecting the emerging legal realism movement of the day, Hughes did not care to be drawn into the abstract question of whether the Minnesota law authorized prior restraint. Rather, he believed the test was whether in operation the law worked that way—whether in its administration and techniques of enforcement, it served to preclude in advance the dispersal of certain ideas and information. Proceeding from these assumptions, Hughes ruled that the Minnesota law was an unconstitutional infringement of the freedom of the press safeguarded by the due process clause of the Fourteenth Amendment. He asserted finally, 150 years after the writing of the Constitution, the principle that restraint before publication was unconstitutional.

In reducing the broad prohibition against prior restraint to a working principle of constitutional law, Hughes recognized that minor exceptions existed. The four suggested exceptions were publication of critical war information, obscenity, publication inciting acts of violence against the community or violent overthrow of the government, and publications invading private rights. Contemporary commentators, however, viewed the exceptions as insignificant and hypothetical. The broader implications of the majority opinion gave the decision its historical significance as a turning point in American law and public policy.

Months passed with no word from Washington as to when the decision would be announced to the public. Near and Colonel McCormick grew increasingly impatient. Finally, on the last day of the term, rumor had it that the decision would be announced. That day, June 1, 1931, had been set aside for a memorial service to Chief Justice Taft and Justice Sanford. Hughes's comments during the service were straws in the wind. He paid particular homage to Sanford's majority opinion in the 1925 *Gitlow* case, which had upheld the principle of applying First Amendment freedoms to the states through the term "liberty" in the due process clause of the Fourteenth Amendment. And Hughes made clear in his remarks that Sanford's wisdom was to be followed in the future. There came next the announcement of a string of technical decisions, read by Justice Brandeis and then by Justice Van Devanter. And finally, the chief justice, making clear its importance, began to read the *Near* opinion from beginning to end. Warming to the task, Hughes stated, "It is no longer open to doubt that the liberty of the press and of speech is within the liberty safeguarded by the due process clause of the Fourteenth Amendment from invasion by state action." He then went on "throwing all his ardor into his delivery," as Chicago *Tribune* correspondent Arthur Sears Henning wrote, borrowing from Blackstone, adamantly insisting that libel laws, not suppression, were the proper solutions to false accusations and defamation, quoting James Madison on the First Amendment, and generally defending a free press as an essential ingredient of good government.

Hughes then turned to Pierce Butler, three chairs to his left, and signaled with a nod that it was now the four dissenters' turn to be heard. Butler was intense, angry, and emotional. Although he was speaking for a lost cause, he was determined to speak with fervor. The decision of the Court in this case, he contended, "declares Minnesota and every other state powerless to restrain by injunction the business of publishing and circulating among the people malicious, scandalous and defamatory periodicals that in due course of judicial procedure have been adjudged to be a public nuisance." The ruling, Butler charged, "gives to freedom of the press a meaning and scope not heretofore recognized and construes 'liberty' in the due process clause of the Fourteenth Amendment to put upon the states a federal restriction that is without precedent." He based most of his dissent upon the facts of the particular case, pointing out that Near did precisely what the law was intended to prevent and that Near was, by his own admission, tainted with blackmail. He also quoted at length from the alleged malicious articles appearing in the *Saturday Press*.

A considerable portion of his analysis questioned whether the Minnesota law actually constituted prior restraint in the historical sense of that term. Butler denied sharply that it did, quoting the petitioner: "Every person had a constitutional right to publish malicious, scandalous and defamatory material though untrue and with bad motives and for unjustifiable ends in the first instance, though he is subject to responsibility therefore afterwards." The malice, once it was established by reading the published writing, was perfectly susceptible to control through the exertion of the state's police power, a power which the justice viewed as being broad authority to prohibit a full range of questionable activities. The use of this type of police power was essential for practical reasons. Subsequent punishment, he argued, was inadequate to protect against the sort of evil confronted here, since legislative libel laws were "inadequate effectively to suppress evils resulting from the kind of business and publications that are shown in this case." Thus Butler, whose previous position had generally been that "a state may not, under the guise of protecting the public, arbitrarily interfere with private business, or prohibit lawful occupations or impose unreasonable and unnecessary restrictions upon them," now took the position that protection of legitimate businesses from this kind of illegitimate behavior justified new levels of control. Although Near's business had not been regulated, but closed down totally, Butler did not see this as any threat to property rights, despite the argument of Near's attorneys to the contrary. Since he was threatening the morals, peace, and good order of the state, Near's behavior was a nuisance. Any way that such a nuisance could be legally suppressed appeared to be condonable in the justice's eyes.

The immediate reaction to the decision was overwhelmingly positive. The nation's press, needless to say, was generally gratified and relieved. Many newspapers quoted Colonel McCormick's statement that "the decision of Chief Justice Hughes will go down in history as one of the greatest triumphs for free thought." (The irrepressible Colonel even wrote a letter to the chief justice stating: "I think your decision in the Gag Law case will forever remain one of the buttresses of free government.") McCormick's competitor, the Chicago *Times,* graciously praised the *Tribune* for performing "a public service of high order when it carried the Minnesota case to the Supreme Court." The *New York Times* called the decision "weighty and conclusive," although it added a note of caution: "Freedom of the press, now again happily vindicated and affirmed, is not freedom to be a 'chartered libertine.' " The *New York Herald-Tribune* observed that "the very fact the exercise of liberty of the press in this momentous case came before the Supreme Court in the least favorable light adds a buttress of steel to the constitutional guarantee."

Retrospectively, the implications of the decision were many. It brought to a significant new stage Brandeis's long crusade for redefining the term "liberty" in human-rights rather than in property-rights terms. By actually using that concept to strike down a state law, the decision also logically extended the incorporation theory as it related to freedom of the press. It also shifted the presumptions regarding the constitutionality of state laws. Laws restricting personal liberties now demanded new and vigorous justification, while laws restricting property rights were to be given the judicial benefit of the doubt. Thus, the ruling culminated more than sixty years of struggle over the proper relationship among the federal government, the states, and the citizen regarding First Amendment issues. The press now joined speech in being protected not only from formal federal government restraint but from state restraint and more subtle forms of local restraint such as those authorized by the Minnesota law.

In the First Amendment area, the ruling was clearly a reflection of "marketplace" theory. It strongly stressed the importance in a democratic society of the press being free to carry out its proper function of informing the electorate, particularly about the behavior of the people's public officials. The behavior of the editors of the *Saturday Press* obviously troubled the chief justice—the form of exposé writing they engaged in clearly was styled to arouse passion rather than to dispense information. The opinion, however, in some ways blurred this distinction, stressing instead the importance of editors being able to criticize public officials and downplaying any illicit motives they might have. Hughes focused upon what was defensible about Near's operation, rather than what was indefensible. In this regard, the opinion came directly to terms with the changing and modernizing conditions that produced much of the new journalism. Arguing, with good historical justification, that journalistic abuse of American institutions and the people who ran them characterized the early period in which our institutions took shape, Hughes pointed out, in the statement later chiseled on the *Chicago Tribune* tower, that the need to expose modern corruption was equally great and equally justified.

The subsequent history of the *Near* case is impressive. The list of cases in which it has been cited takes up two full pages of *Shepard's U.S. Citations* and includes Supreme Court cases, lower federal court cases, and cases in the supreme courts of many states. Its standard held for forty years, without successful challenge, and as late as May 17, 1971, Chief Justice Warren E. Burger reaffirmed it in a decision upholding the right of an interracial group in Chicago to distribute leaflets charging a real estate broker with "blockbusting" sales tactics. Burger reiterated the "heavy presumption" against "the constitutional validity" of any prior restraint of expression.

Its most well-known use as a precedent, however, came a month later when the Washington *Post* and the *New York Times* began publishing the *Pentagon Papers,* based upon a forty-seven-volume secret history of the Vietnam War and detailing aspects of the reasons behind American involvement. The papers were promptly met with a federal injunction against continuation of that series of articles, filed by the Nixon administration. In the fireworks that followed, *Near* v. *Minnesota* was cited frequently by both sides. In the resulting lower federal court adjudication involving the *Post,* Judge Gerhard A. Gesell wrote a 600-word opinion that relied heavily upon Hughes's opinion in the *Near* case. He stressed the historical reasons supporting the total freedom of the press. He contended that the government was misusing the Espionage Act, under which the injunction had been sought, since that law was never intended to provide for "any preexisting restraint or censorship of the press."

In the *New York Times* case, U.S. Attorney Whitney North Seymour focused on the *Near* exception. He argued that Chief Justice Hughes's "troop ship" doctrine in *Near,* setting out the potential areas where prior restraints were justified, was merely a symbolic one, intended to cover a broad range of national defense activities. The top-secret classification of the *Papers,* in and of itself, should be accorded "great deference" by the courts, he argued, but if that were not enough, the witnesses which the government had produced had made, he contended, a compelling case that "disclosure of the material in the *Times*'s possession would gravely endanger the security of the United States." Federal Judge Murray I. Gerfein, however, was not persuaded, and ruled against the government.

Eleven days later the United States Supreme Court agreed to try to untangle the various lower court opinions. It noted, however, that all the arguments in all the briefs and opinions were dominated by the theory of no prior restraint. Not insignificant, however, was the citing by the supporters of the newspapers of Chief Justice Warren Burger's opinion in the Chicago leafletting case and his acceptance of the no-prior-restraint principles.

The Supreme Court met hastily on Saturday, June 25, and five days later announced its 6–3 decision. Relying heavily on *Near,* the majority held that the heavy burden of justifying the imposition of prior restraint had not been met by the government. It required nine opinions for the Supreme Court to explain its votes. *Near* was cited ten times. Justice William O. Douglas, in an opinion joined by Justice Hugo Black, quoted long passages from the Hughes majority opinion. Black himself argued that both the history and the language of the First Amendment supported the view that the press must be left free to publish news, whatever the source, without censorship, injunctions, or prior restraints. "Only a free and unrestrained press," he argued, "can effectively expose deception in government." He went on to say that in revealing to the public workings of the government that led to the Vietnam War, the newspapers did precisely what the founders had hoped and trusted they would do.

In the dissents of Burger, Harlan, and Blackmun, Hughes's exceptions to the prohibitions against prior restraint were cited. But the concept itself was not challenged. The outcome was that the Court lifted the government's prior restraint on the *New York Times,* the Washington *Post,* and twenty other newspapers that were prepared to publish sections of the *Pentagon Papers,* secure in their confidence that "there is no greater safety valve for discontent and cynicism about the affairs of government than freedom of expression in any form." That statement had come from Federal Judge Murray I. Gerfein in his earlier ruling, a ruling that he later revealed he had written "in the light of *Near,* with Hughes' opinion in front of me."

Near would have been pleased. However, he was long dead. After his vindication in 1931, he had again started up the *Saturday Press,* with a new banner bearing the caption: "The Paper That Refused to Stay Gagged." Another slogan of the paper was the slightly exaggerated statement, "The only paper in the United States with the Supreme Court record of being right; the only paper that dared fight for freedom of the press—fought and won." But the *Saturday Press* went back to it usual hyperbole and defamation and muckraking, taking on the Minneapolis police and again making allegations of linkage with the underworld. Near quickly got in financial trouble and turned to his old partner Howard Guilford for support. But Guilford wanted to push the paper heavily toward sex scandals, and

Near therefore quit. He came back to publish it, however, a year later when Guilford announced he would run for mayor of Minneapolis on a clean-up-the-city and expose-the-mob ticket. But on September 6, 1934, while driving home from work, Guilford was crowded to the curb by a black sedan and a shotgun blast at close range practically blew his head off.

Near charged that Guilford's assassins had been hired by communists. But the appeal of such exposé journalism was dwindling, and when Near died in April 1936, he was virtually penniless and almost completely forgotten. His longest obituary was published, not surprisingly, in the Chicago *Tribune*. There four paragraphs were devoted to *Near* v. *Minnesota* and the *Tribune*'s role in bringing it to the Supreme Court.

As Fred Friendly has written, "No other nation on earth has a constitutional tradition against prior restraints comparable to those which sprang from Hughes' sweeping opinion." But there remains one vital question which the *Near* decision did not answer: Hughes's frequently overlooked statement that the First Amendment was not absolute still troubles. What, if any, information should be exempted from the First Amendment's protection, particularly under claims of national security, a term that can be abused by government? This is a concern when the definition of national security is in the hands of officials who might seek to use their powers in dubious ways by blacking out public information and crippling the censorial role which the American people have come to feel is their birthright.

The Sick Chicken Case

BY FRANK FREIDEL

(*Schechter* v. *U.S.*, 295 U.S. 495)

*The Great Depression of the 1930s, which everyone recognized as a major
national crisis, led President Franklin D. Roosevelt and the New Deal Congress to experiment with a variety of new laws in an effort to restore good times.
These laws obviously carried federal power to the outer limits of constitutionality. But did they go beyond these bounds? Many individuals and corporations,
injured or restricted in some way by their operations, thought that they did, and
went to court to prove the point.*

*Among hundreds of controversies, many came eventually to the Supreme
Court. The Court was in a difficult position, for while the times called for
experimentation and broad government power, much of the new legislation was
hastily conceived and also path-breaking. Much hung on how the Court acted.
None of the cases considered at this time was more significant than the one that
Frank Freidel, professor of history at the University of Washington, describes.
Professor Freidel is the author of a major biography of Roosevelt, four volumes
of which have so far appeared.*

It was no easy matter to earn one's living in the depres-
sion-haunted, racket-ridden wholesale poultry trade of the New
York area in the 1930s. Joseph, Alex, Martin, and Aaron Schechter
could view with pride their achievement in building, despite these
hazards, the largest such business in the Brooklyn area. The brothers owned two firms, the A. L. A. Schechter Company and the
Schechter Live Poultry Market, Inc. In a trade so plagued by gangsters that within it had originated the term "racket," the Schechters
managed to succeed. Once, at the beginning of the 1930s, the
stocky, shrewd boss of the business, Joe Schechter, tried to evade
the outrageous rental that gangsters were charging for coops and

The NRA Eagle.

for his pains had two cups of emery powder poured into the crank-case of his truck. The government, trying to eradicate racketeering, forced Schechter to testify as one of its witnesses before a grand jury, and ultimately in 1934 won its case against the racketeers before the United States Supreme Court.

Meanwhile, in 1933 the Schechters themselves became subject to extensive federal regulation when they, together with fellow poultry dealers, joined the National Recovery Administration, displayed its emblem, the Blue Eagle, and promised to adhere to the numerous provisions of the Code of Fair Competition for the Live Poultry Industry of the New York Metropolitan Area. Like most business-men, large and small, the Schechters hoped that the NRA would provide the magic formula for restoring prosperity through govern-ment intervention.

The optimism of the summer of 1933, when the NRA was an-nounced, soon evaporated, and before long critics began to chal-lenge the constitutionality of the program. The transcendent ques-tion was: "Under the Constitution can the government regulate business in an effort to restore prosperity?" The critics' answer was an emphatic "No," but there were various legal precedents which would indicate that the NRA might well be operating within the bounds of the Constitution.

Litigation over the NRA marked a significant phase in the strug-gle to shift interpretation of the Constitution from a late-nineteenth-century to a twentieth-century view. From the Federalist period through Reconstruction the Supreme Court had placed few impediments in the way of state or federal regulation of the econ-omy. Then in the 1880s and 1890s the laissez-faire and social-Darwinist ideology so fashionable at the time became the doctrine of the Court. In a series of decisions it narrowly interpreted the power over the economy vested in either state governments or the national government. In later years, decisions in such controversies as the *Northern Securities* case and in *Muller v. Oregon* had indicated the Court's willingness to allow a wider degree of government con-trol, but in the 1920s it had again veered toward a narrower inter-pretation.

However, at the time the New Deal legislation was drafted most observers thought the Court would again take a broad view of the question. Times had changed and with the times, presumably, the way in which the Supreme Court would view the Constitution. True enough, during the terrible depressions of the nineteenth century the federal government had done little to restore prosperity beyond bolstering public confidence through its efforts to maintain government solvency. But when the nation plummeted into the severe depression of the 1930s, few people expected the government to remain inactive.

The aged secretary of the treasury, Andrew Mellon, recalling the depression of the 1870s, recommended to President Hoover that the government keep hands off, since he earnestly believed that the liquidation of a large part of the economy would be beneficial. Although himself a "rugged individualist," Hoover disagreed:

I, of course, reminded the Secretary that back in the seventies an untold amount of suffering did take place which might have been prevented; that our economy had been far simpler sixty years ago, when we were 75 per cent an agricultural people contrasted with 30 per cent now; that unemployment during the earlier crisis had been mitigated by the return of large numbers of the unemployed to relatives on the farms; and that farm economy itself had been largely self-contained.

Mellon tried to answer by suggesting that however the economy had been altered, human nature never changed. This was true enough, but human expectations of the federal government had, in fact, changed a great deal, especially as a result of the experience of World War I, when the government had established an array of agencies regimenting the economy. Through the War Industries Board it had regulated industry, through the Food Administration it had stimulated farm production, and through the War Finance Corporation it had made loans. No fear of unconstitutionality had inhibited Congress in establishing these regulatory bodies; the war emergency seemed to override whatever narrow interpretation the courts might in peacetime place on the Constitution. This assumption, however, had not been tested because at the end of the war the new government agencies were quickly liquidated, and no test cases concerning them came before the Supreme Court. In any case, numerous people argued, could not the federal government reconstitute similar emergency agencies in time of depression in order to make war on the depression?

President Hoover, who had achieved a towering world reputation through his supervision of the relief of Europe's hungry millions during and after the war, had himself been head of the Food Administration. During the 1920s he had added to his fame by promoting voluntary cooperation between business and government. Now, as the depression blackened, he enlisted the federal government in the struggle for recovery. He enormously increased public works spending and persuaded Congress to establish the Reconstruction Finance Corporation, a loan agency somewhat analogous to the War Finance Corporation. Some businessmen, remembering the War Industries Board, urged him to create a similar government agency, which would put the force of federal law behind business efforts to stop price-cutting and overproduction. Hoover rejected these proposals indignantly. Earlier as secretary of commerce he had helped to promote voluntary trade associations, but had opposed giving them power to stabilize prices and control distribution. This power, he believed, would lead to the decay of American industry, the creation of monopolies, the destruction of human liberty, and, ultimately, the imposition of fascism or socialism.

After Franklin D. Roosevelt became president in the spring of 1933, he expressed no such qualms. Like President Hoover, he was ready to enlist the full powers of the federal government to bring about recovery. Like Hoover, he was ready to call for voluntary cooperation on the part of business and agriculture. Unlike Hoover, he felt that these so-called voluntary recovery programs, if they were to be effective, must have behind them the force of federal law. His own personal experience led toward this conclusion, since in the 1920s he had been head of a voluntary trade association, the American Construction Council, which had proved powerless to bring order into the chaotic building industry.

Trade association agreements had been weak even in prosperous years; during the depression they were practically impotent. Many retailers in order to obtain business were shaving profit margins and advertising "loss leaders." They could remain solvent only if they forced their employees to work mercilessly long hours for pathetically low wages. Many wholesalers and small manufacturers were caught in the same relentless bind. In some industries, like bituminous coal and petroleum, overproduction was glutting the market and wasting national resources. In the spring of 1933 a barrel of petroleum in some Texas fields sold for less than a bottle of the newly legal 3.2 percent beer.

The National Industrial Recovery Act of June 1933 proposed the road to recovery that businessmen themselves had been advocating. Business obtained the right to draw up its own regulations in the form of codes of fair practices, which had behind them the force of federal law. In return, workers were granted certain objectives they had long been seeking: minimum wages, maximum working hours, and the right of collective bargaining. The law also protected consumer interests. By granting concessions to businessmen, employees, and consumers alike, the New Dealers hoped to aid business in breaking the disastrously deflationary spiral and in pushing prices up to a prosperity level. To raise buying power, employees should receive more money for working fewer hours. To further "prime the pump" of the economy, the Roosevelt administration was authorized to spend $3.3 billion on public works.

The National Recovery Administration began operations amid widespread fanfare and optimism. President Roosevelt described the enabling act as "the most important and far-reaching legislation ever enacted by the American Congress." He appointed as administrator one of the liveliest figures on the American scene, General Hugh S. Johnson, who had served with Bernard Baruch on the War Industries Board during World War I. During the war, he had advanced from lieutenant to brigadier general in two years; afterward he had become vice president of the Moline Plow Company, which failed in the agricultural depression of the 1920s.

Johnson had a flair for words. Early in his career he wrote two boys' books, both very popular, which combined the worst qualities of Rudyard Kipling and Horatio Alger. As head of the NRA, Johnson whipped up excitement for the recovery program, delighting the public with his vigorous, colorful language. Unfortunately, he brought little except words to the task at hand. He had hoped to preside over both recovery functions—simultaneously to draw up codes of fair practice for industries and to pour public works money into especially depressed spots in the economy. But Roosevelt allowed him to preside only over the code making, entrusting the spending power to the cautious, slow-moving secretary of the interior, "Honest Harold" Ickes.

General Johnson, despite his enormous public acclaim, had little real authority. There was nothing to back up his energetic denunciation of "chiselers" impeding the recovery effort. From the outset, Johnson was aware of the difficulties he faced. "It will be red fire at first and dead cats afterwards," he remarked when he became administrator. "This is just like mounting the guillotine on the infinitesimal gamble that the ax won't work."

For a few weeks there was red fire aplenty as an inspired nation heeded Roosevelt's request to accept an interim blanket code, the President's Re-employment Agreement, abolishing child labor and establishing maximum hours of thirty-five or forty per week and minimum wages of thirty to forty cents per hour. In this one sweeping agreement the NRA achieved what reformers had sought since the dawn of the Progressive era. Parades and rallies helped persuade employers to sign the NRA agreement and display the Blue Eagle emblem and its slogan, "We Do Our Part." Consumers pledged themselves to buy only where they saw the Blue Eagle insignia.

Then began the drawn-out process of negotiating specific codes to cover each major industry. Manufacturers rushed to turn out goods before costs of material and labor went up under the codes, hiring quantities of workers for the few weeks they operated their plants at capacity. Wholesalers likewise bought in increased volume in anticipation of higher prices. The index of production (calculated at 100 for the boom year 1929) skyrocketed from 56 in March 1933 to 101 in July. Payrolls also went up, but only from an index figure of 37.1 to 50.8. With prices rising more quickly than buying power, Secretary Ickes nevertheless followed President Roosevelt's wishes and only very slowly authorized public works expenditures. Before the end of the summer the NRA boomlet collapsed.

Meanwhile, as the negotiation of codes for the major industries went on, minor industries also clamored for individual codes. The result by February 1934 was, accordingly, not a handful of codes as had originally been planned, but 557 basic codes and 208 supplementary codes. Each of these had been negotiated by the representatives of a particular industry in association with representatives of labor and consumers. The representatives of the industries so thoroughly dominated these negotiations that in effect the business leaders were allowed to draft their own codes of fair practices—in some instances copying them word for word from earlier trade association agreements. There were codes not only for the steel, automobile, textile, and bituminous coal industries but also for the mop-stick, corn-cob pipe, and powder puff industries; for burlesque theaters, investment banking houses, and pecan shellers. The retail trade code covered nearly three and a half million employees, the animal soft-hair industry a mere forty-five. Some sixty-two codes covered fewer than five hundred employees each, yet almost all of them contained intricate regulations.

In return for the government's prohibition of unfair practices, each industry had to guarantee its employees fair wages and hours and the right to bargain collectively. There were long enumerations of unfair practices: four fifths of the codes tended to bolster minimum prices, three fourths prohibited rebates, and a few major codes even set production quotas. It was of vital significance that the first code, regulating the textile industry with its 400,000 employees, set the minimum wage for forty hours of work at twelve dollars in the South and thirteen in the North. It also provided that no minor under sixteen could be employed, and that production machinery could not be operated for more than two shifts of forty hours each. But many codes contained numerous petty regulations. The macaroni code stipulated that noodles must contain not less than 5.5 percent of egg or egg yolk solids and must not be artificially colored or packaged in yellow wrappers that would deceive the purchaser.

Altogether the businessmen's committees included within the different codes more than a thousand provisions regulating 130 different trade practices. Their aim was not so much the protection of the consumer as the elimination of unfair competition. Laudable though such regulations might be, they created an administrative problem for the NRA. Each code, when signed by President Roosevelt, had behind it the force of the National Industrial Recovery Act, and any violation of a code was a violation of the law.

When public enthusiasm over the Blue Eagle was running high, relatively mild threats were sufficient to bring successful enforcement. If a retailer did not comply with the President's Re-employment Agreement after receiving a warning, he received a telegram that sternly ordered him to return his Blue Eagle poster and other NRA paraphernalia to the nearest post office. Presumably, consumers would then boycott the offender's establishment. When public enthusiasm waned, removal of the insignia no longer sufficed. The NRA increasingly had to resort to litigation, but of 155,102 cases docketed by the NRA state offices, only 564 reached the courts.

Ironically, it was the regulation of trade practices so eagerly sought by businessmen rather than the enforcement of wages-and-hours and collective bargaining agreements that caused the most trouble. The public was sympathetic toward exploited employees, but had no enthusiasm for rules that might keep purchasers from obtaining "bargains." Consumer interest might coincide with that of the mayonnaise manufacturers in upholding the regulation that mayonnaise substitutes labeled "salad dressing" must meet minimum standards, but consumers could only feel that they were being deprived of bargains by regulations that forbade the sale of second-quality plumbing fixtures or the manufacture of bedding from secondhand materials. The drafters of the codes had argued that the sale of substandard merchandise depressed the prices of standard products, and they wished zealously to enforce these and similar trade provisions. It was difficult, they realized, to obtain evidence of evasion that would be acceptable in a court, yet if the evaders went unpunished, general compliance was likely to break down. Highly competitive businesses were especially faced with compliance problems; many a small businessman argued that evasion was the only alternative to bankruptcy.

For most Americans the NRA honeymoon was soon over. After the upturn in the summer of 1933, prices steadied and General Johnson emphasized that they must not go up further until buying power had risen. Yet Clarence Darrow, the iconoclastic lawyer who headed the National Recovery Review Board, was widely supported when he charged in the spring of 1934 that the NRA was under the domination of big business, and that big business was forcing living costs upward. There were other complaints. Those who feared union labor were alarmed over the great organizing drives launched by John L. Lewis and others and were outraged by the numerous strikes that accompanied the new militancy on the part of the unions. Workingmen, on the other hand, feeling that they had gained but little from the NRA codes or the collective bargaining guarantees, wisecracked that the initials NRA stood for "National Run Around."

Even as General Johnson had predicted, in the fall of 1934 he became the victim of the guillotine. President Roosevelt replaced him with a five-man board, which tried to make the NRA more acceptable by remodeling and simplifying its activities along more enforceable lines. But it was by no means certain that Congress would renew the Act as its date of termination approached in the spring of 1935. Also, by that time, the issue of constitutionality was becoming increasingly troublesome.

In the exciting spring of 1933 the question of constitutionality had not seemed very important. Public opinion was overwhelmingly behind President Roosevelt's call for drastic powers with which to combat the depression, and there was considerable feeling that the crisis made it possible to act in ways that in ordinary times might not be legal. Whether emergency New Deal legislation would be sanctioned by the Supreme Court remained to be seen. In any event, the drafters of the National Industrial Recovery Act argued that it was within the power of Congress to regulate commerce among the states. Since the 1895 sugar decision (the *Knight* case), the Supreme Court had broadened its interpretation of the commerce clause, so there seemed to be adequate precedent. However, the New Dealers could not be entirely sure. While handing down strong decisions in protection of civil liberties, the Court was split into two wings on questions that involved government regulation of the economy.

Because of the unpredictability of the Supreme Court, the Roosevelt administration was not dismayed that a test of the NRA was delayed into 1935. In addition to the certain opposition of the conservative wing of the Court, there was the possibility that the NRA might run afoul of moderate Chief Justice Charles Evans Hughes's dislike for the practice of delegating broad regulatory powers to administrative agencies. In 1931, addressing the American Bar Association, Hughes had warned that this tendency threatened to overwhelm American institutions. Moreover, there was the possibility that Justice Brandeis, long a foe of industrial giantism, might object to the way the NRA had in effect suspended the antitrust laws.

Nevertheless, by the spring of 1935, with criticism of the NRA mounting and defiance of the codes spreading, a Supreme Court decision had become essential. While there was a danger that the Court might act unfavorably, in two cases which it had decided early in 1934 it had seemed to regard the depression emergency as justifying drastic economic regulation by the states. These were a Minnesota case involving a mortgage moratorium and a New York case fixing the price of milk. In the mortgage decision Chief Justice Hughes pointed out that "While emergency does not create power, emergency may furnish the occasion for the exercise of power."

But these two cases involved state, not federal, legislation. Early in 1935, when cases involving the federal prohibition against making payment on contracts in gold (the gold clause cases) were decided, the government won by an uncomfortably close 5–4 margin, made more unpleasant because the majority through Chief Justice Hughes castigated the administration for its immorality. It was on this occasion that Justice James C. McReynolds in dissenting added extemporaneously, "As for the Constitution, it does not seem too much to say that it is gone."

The "hot-oil" decision, involving a provision of the National Industrial Recovery Act that authorized the President to prohibit or not, as he saw fit, the transportation in interstate and foreign commerce of petroleum produced in excess of legal quotas, was still more ominous. With only Justice Benjamin N. Cardozo dissenting, the Court held that Congress had unconstitutionally delegated too much discretionary power to the President. This setback to the New Deal led the solicitor general on April 1, 1935, to drop a Southern lumber case (*United States* v. *Belcher*) which it had been generally assumed would serve as the test of the NRA. The lumber case was too close to the "hot-oil" cases for the government attorneys to feel comfortable.

Since opposition newspapers were thundering editorially that the New Dealers were welching, it was necessary to find another test case in a hurry. At this point the government won in the circuit court of appeals a case that involved the New York live poultry code. The defeated defendants petitioned for a Supreme Court review, and there was not much the Department of Justice could do except to use this not entirely satisfactory case for its test of the NRA. Thus the fate of the NRA, and to a considerable degree the power of the government to aid business in fighting the depression, came to depend upon how the Supreme Court would look upon the right of the federal government to punish Brooklyn poultry dealers who, among their other offenses, had sold a sick chicken. The dealers were the Schechter brothers.

The Code of Fair Competition for the Live Poultry Industry of the Metropolitan Area in and about the city of New York was one of the multitude of lesser codes that contained lists of especially applicable unfair practices, the enforcement of which had made the course of the NRA so difficult. It was not one of the dozen or more major industries indisputably lying athwart interstate commerce, the sort that the framers of the NRA had contemplated regulating. On the other hand, most counts in the case had been decided unanimously in favor of the government by the three distinguished justices of the circuit court of appeals, of whom one was Learned Hand. Further, the Supreme Court justices themselves had given some indication that they regarded the racket-ridden New York live poultry industry as falling within the scope of interstate commerce. Only a year before, when the racketeers had appealed against a federal injunction on the grounds that their acts did not interfere with interstate commerce, the Court had sustained the injunction.

Racketeering and cutthroat competition had lead the operators of kosher wholesale poultry slaughterhouses in the New York area to seek the protection of a code. The code established a minimum wage of fifty cents an hour and a maximum work week of forty-eight hours and prohibited the sale of poultry that was either uninspected or unfit for human consumption. It also required "straight killing" (customers purchasing less than a full coop must take "run of the coop" rather than pick out the best birds).

The four Schechter brothers, earlier in federal court as witnesses for the government against racketeers, now found themselves back in court as defendants. They were charged with having violated the wages-and-hours and several of the trade-practice provisions of the code in order to beat their prices below those of their rivals. For example, they had allowed customers to select the best chickens out of a coop. But above all, witnesses testified at a jury trial before Judge Marcus B. Campbell of the United States district court in Brooklyn, they had sold thousands of pounds of diseased chicken at four to eight cents per pound below the market price.

This would seem of little consequence if, as one NRA inspector reported, they had merely sold chickens that were "egg-bound"— that is, unable to lay eggs. What made their offense a menace was that many of the chickens suffered from tuberculosis, which was communicable to human beings. One witness testified to thirty-seven instances in which persons had contracted tuberculosis from sick chickens. Before passage of the NRA code, New York had served as a national dumping ground for diseased poultry. Rejects from Western packing stations—"anything with a head on it," said one witness—had been shipped east. Others estimated that although only 2 percent of the poultry sold in New York prior to the code was unfit for human consumption, these birds had so disgusted unwary purchasers that thereafter many refused to eat any chicken. As a result, poultry consumption fell about 20 percent. The bargain prices also depressed the market price for good poultry. After a three-week trial the Schechters had been found guilty on seventeen counts, given brief jail sentences, and fined $7,425. The circuit court had reversed the conviction on the wages-and-hours counts, but upheld the conviction on the unfair-trade-practices counts.

In preparing their brief for the Supreme Court the government attorneys made the most possible use of the fact that the Court had earlier considered the New York poultry business as affecting interstate commerce. But in the criminal conviction of the Schechter brothers the government attorneys had a liability, since the Supreme Court might well balk at sending anyone to jail because of a code violation.

The government's brief pointed out that over 96 percent of the live poultry marketed in the New York area came from other states; that some thirty-five states, chiefly in the Midwest and the South, shipped to New York; and that 175 to 200 freight carloads a week arrived at the New York markets, more than the combined shipments made to all other large cities. Detailed evidence was presented to prove that the market price of live poultry in New York set the price of poultry throughout the United States. It was argued that unfair trade and labor practices in the live poultry business in New York City tended to lower poultry prices throughout the country, and that these practices therefore contributed to the obstruction of interstate commerce. The brief also cited numerous earlier Supreme Court decisions as precedents: "Under the decisions of this Court, the Code provisions which the petitioners violated are within the commerce power of the Congress," the government lawyers asserted.

The Schechter case was argued before the Supreme Court on May 2 and 3, 1935, in the small, red-plush courtroom in the Capitol which had once been the Senate chamber. Solicitor General Stanley Reed (who was himself later to sit on the Court) used one of the government's allotted two hours to expound the constitutional arguments. A distinguished New York lawyer, Frederick H. Wood, who had become associated with the defense, countered learnedly that when the chickens were delivered to the commission merchants in New York they "came to rest," and were no longer involved in interstate traffic.

At the close of the first session, Justice McReynolds ominously quizzed Solicitor General Reed on two points:

McReynolds: "Were these defendants among those who agreed to the live poultry code?"

Reed: "They were not, but I may add that they were present at all the conferences which preceded the adoption of the code."

McReynolds: "What does unfair competition mean? Is it anything industry says is unfair?"

Reed: "The only standard is what industry considers unfair, plus the judgment of the President as to whether they are fair trade provisions."

The second session, the next day, was more lively. The Schechters' original lawyer, Joseph Heller, stole the limelight from his constitutionalist associate Wood as in uninhibited and colloquial language he strove to convince the Court of the local nature of the Schechter poultry business. Heller described the problems of the Schechters in doing business under the code in a fashion that convulsed the justices with laughter and did serious damage to the government's case. He parried the charge that the Schechters had been selling diseased poultry, pointing out that the one sick chicken purchased by the NRA agent had only been "egg-bound" and earlier had been passed by a government inspector.

When he was asked what straight killing meant, he explained, "Straight killing means you have got to put your hand in the coop and take out whichever chicken comes to you. You hand the chicken over to the rabbi, who slaughters it."

"And it was for that your client was convicted?" Justice McReynolds inquired.

"Yes, and fined $5,000 and given three months in jail."

In summation for the government, Chairman Donald Richberg of the National Industrial Recovery Board was less entertaining but more eloquent. He emphasized that the NRA was a vital response to the effects of the depression upon interstate commerce. "The NRA law was enacted for the purpose of checking the progressive destruction of industry, to make possible an orderly advance by industry rather than a disorderly retreat," he asserted. "Congress alone could deal effectively with the causes contributing to this breakdown of interstate commerce." If Congress could not stop the "vicious cycle of wage-cutting, then it is impotent indeed," he declared. Trying to lift the case above the "run-of-the coop" and "egg-bound" level, Richberg declared: "For the court to pass on this case only as if it fitted into the Schechter poultry case would be like trying to diagnose a case of scarlet fever by examining one small spot on the skin."

Decision day came on Monday, May 27. Solicitor General Reed and Chairman Richberg, both in fine spirits, took their places at the counsel table. "I feel," smiled Richberg, "as though I were waiting for a jury to come in—guilty or not guilty." When the nine justices filed in, they also seemed cheerful, but almost immediately events took an ominous turn. Justices George Sutherland and Louis D. Brandeis each read a lesser decision; both were unanimous and unfavorable to the New Deal. Then Chief Justice Hughes announced that he would read the Schechter decision. Richberg stiffened and paled as Hughes launched into a detailed discourse on the background of the case. The crowd of congressmen and lawyers who filled the small chamber fidgeted expectantly. The chief justice went on and on. Finally, looking Olympian as he stroked his white beard, he read the crucial sections, slowly and vehemently. They were devastating.

"Extraordinary conditions do not create or enlarge constitutional power," Hughes declared. "Congress cannot delegate legislative power to the President to exercise an unfettered discretion to make whatever laws he thinks may be needed or advisable for the rehabilitation and expansion of trade or industry." Against the government's assertion that the Schechters' transactions were in interstate commerce, he stated, "So far as the poultry here in question is concerned, the flow in interstate commerce had ceased. The poultry had come to a permanent rest within the State."

The chief justice provided precedents for all these points from earlier Supreme Court decisions (even as the government lawyers had backed their pleas with a different set of precedents). What of the decision only a year earlier, restraining New York poultry racketeers from interfering with the flow of poultry in interstate commerce? This earlier case *(Local 167* v. *United States)* was different, Hughes said.

The proved interference by the conspirators "with the unloading, the transportation, the sales by marketmen to retailers, the prices charged and the amount of profits exacted" operated "substantially and directly to restrain and burden the untrammeled shipment and movement of the poultry" while unquestionably it was in interstate commerce. The intrastate acts of the conspirators were included in the injunction because that was found to be necessary for the protection of interstate commerce against the attempted and illegal restraint.

As Hughes read off the crucial sentences Richberg slumped in his chair and cupped his chin in his hands. A newspaperman scribbled a note and passed it to him: "Can there be a new Recovery law?" Richberg inscribed a large question mark. Reed and Richberg left the courtroom unable to conceal their gloom.

In the Department of Justice office, Attorney General Homer S. Cummings put down a ham sandwich he had been munching and entered into a hurried conference with them. Late in the afternoon the three men went to the White House, there to spend two hours studying the Court's decision with President Roosevelt. When Richberg came out of the President's office he announced: "This decision of the Supreme Court makes all codes of fair competition unenforceable as a matter of law." From his headquarters Chairman Richberg wired orders to suspend immediately all enforcement of NRA codes. Businessmen were now liberated from the machinery they had themselves created. They could again engage in whatever trade practices they pleased and treat their employees as they saw fit. They were freed from government interference. But they were also left without protection against unscrupulous competitors.

Throughout the nation there was an excited, though mixed, reaction. The National Association of Manufacturers was jubilant. "As a result of the court's notable decision the opportunity is again afforded to industry to go forward on a basis of voluntary self-government," its spokesman proclaimed. Anti-New-Deal senators exulted. "The Constitution is re-established," William E. Borah announced. Carter Glass, who as early as August of 1933 had dubbed the Blue Eagle a "black buzzard," commented: "I have always been opposed to any such exercise of tyranny." The stock market shot upward, then swiftly dropped, as investors on second thought demonstrated their fear of deflation. The commodity market was shaken. Retail stores quickly revived trade wars that the NRA had held in abeyance. Gimbel's cut the price of Modern Library books from fifty-six cents to twenty-nine cents. Some stores reduced the price of a carton of cigarettes to little more than the tax on them.

Many retailers found it necessary to recoup such price cuts by lengthening the working hours of their employees. Only days later the head of the Food and Grocery Distributors' Code Authority declared that already 90 percent of all grocery employees were being obliged to work sixty-five to seventy-two hours per week rather than the forty-eight-hour NRA week. Of some seven hundred telegrams that arrived at the White House the day after the Court's decision, eight out of nine urged some sort of new NRA. The Washington *News* editorialized that critics of the NRA had "prayed for rain and got a cloudburst."

At his first press conference after the decision, on May 29, President Roosevelt had relatively little to say. Was the President going to accept the decision calmly? During the next two days excitement increased, and letters and telegrams continued to arrive at the White House.

Roosevelt did intend to reply to the Supreme Court, but in his own time and fashion. The time was eleven o'clock on the morning of Friday, May 31, and the form was not a message to Congress or a radio "fireside chat" to the American public. It was an unbroken discourse of an hour and twenty-five minutes before two hundred assembled reporters at his press conference. The newsmen were allowed to take notes, but could report the President only in indirect discourse. Through them Roosevelt would put his case to the American people.

When the reporters jammed into the President's office, he had the stage set for them. Leaning back in his swivel chair as they crowded forward, he regarded them with a laconic smile. Behind him sat Mrs. Roosevelt, knitting a blue sock. Another chair was being held for Senate Majority Leader Joseph Robinson, who arrived ten minutes late. On one side of Roosevelt's desk lay a pile of telegrams; on the other, an open copy of the Supreme Court decision.

Lighting a cigarette, he opened the conference by inquiring facetiously of the reporters: "What is the news?" Then, when the inevitable question came concerning the NRA, he launched into his disquisition. Taking the sheaf of telegrams from his desk, he remarked, "I have been a good deal impressed by . . . the rather pathetic appeals that I have had from all around the country to do something. They are very sincere as showing faith in government . . . so sincere that you feel the country is beginning to realize that something in the long run has to be done." And he read a number of excerpts from the telegrams, all of them from businessmen, most of whom complained that their businesses were already suffering from the decision. Several urged that something be done about the Supreme Court.

"The implications of this decision," Roosevelt told the reporters, "are much more important than any decision probably since the Dred Scott case." What Roosevelt felt made it significant was not the stricture against undue congressional delegation of power. That could easily be remedied through more specific instructions. Rather it was the way in which the Supreme Court had reverted to the earlier view of the power of Congress to regulate commerce, limiting it apparently to what was actually in interstate transit. "The big issue is this," Roosevelt emphasized: "Does this decision mean that the United States Government has no control over any national economic problem?" Did it mean that the government had no right to try to better national social conditions?

Roosevelt pointed out in detail the difficulties of trying to solve economic problems through forty-eight sets of state regulations. The Supreme Court decision implied that the federal government could neither legislate concerning fair trade practices and wage-and-hours regulation nor control agricultural production, stock market activities, and other areas, he said. As for self-regulation, he remarked sarcastically: "Can we go ahead as a nation with the beautiful theory, let us say, of the Hearst press, 'At last the rule of Christ is restored. Business can do anything it wants and business is going to live up to the golden rule so marvelously that all of our troubles are ended'? . . . It is a school of thought that is so delightful in its naïveté."

In sum, Roosevelt declared, these implications made the decision one of the most important ever rendered, since it raised the question as to how the nation was to proceed in the area of economic regulation. "We are the only nation in the world that has not solved that problem," he concluded. "We thought we were solving it, and now it has been thrown right straight in our faces and we have been relegated to the horse-and-buggy definition of interstate commerce."

"Horse-and-Buggy" echoed in headlines all over America, and the lines were drawn for the bitter struggle between the New Dealers and the Supreme Court. The New Dealers found it easy enough to replace the useful parts of the NRA through various separate laws: the Wagner Act (National Labor Relations Act) to protect labor in its collective bargaining; the Guffey Act, in effect reenacting the bituminous coal industry code; other legislation to protect retailers from some of the unfair trade practices. The difficulty was that these measures in turn were likely to be invalidated by the Supreme Court—and so indeed the Guffey Act soon was. Several other New Deal measures, most notably the processing tax program established by the Agricultural Adjustment Act, fell afoul of the Supreme Court. At about the same time the Court in another decision denied to states the power to regulate the economy. Such was the background of President Roosevelt's ill-fated attempt in the spring of 1937 to "pack" the Supreme Court.

Then, remarkably, in the midst of the great national furor, the Supreme Court began to take a different view of both state and federal control over the economy. Chief Justice Hughes and Justice Owen J. Roberts abandoned the conservative wing of the Court to join the liberal trio, Stone, Brandeis, and Cardozo, who by this time were ready to take an even more liberal view of federal authority. In a test case involving the Wagner Act, the Court's 5–4 decision held that labor relations in the steel industry did come within Congress's power to regulate commerce among the states. A host of similar decisions followed. A "sick chicken" might have downed the Blue Eagle of the NRA, but only two years later the Supreme Court was demonstrating that it was taking a modern rather than a "horse-and-buggy" view of the power of Congress to regulate the economy.

As for the Schechters, at first they had enjoyed emerging from the obscurity of their Brooklyn business into the national limelight. When Joe Schechter was stopped by a guard as he entered the Supreme Court chamber, he asked, "Me? You don't know who I am?" If he and his brothers thought it strange that one of the most distinguished New York law firms, Cravath, de Gersdorff, Swaine and Wood, had entered the case, associating themselves with the Schechter lawyer, Joseph Heller, they kept their opinions to themselves. Nor did they reveal who paid this high-priced firm its fee. When the favorable decision came, they and Heller celebrated with champagne. But a year later the correspondent Drew Pearson found them in distress. They had lost their business and were being forced to sell their home. "The Liberty Leaguers sent us a lot of swell letters saying they appreciated what we had done," Aaron Schechter lamented, "but they didn't put any money in the letters." And Joe Schechter added: "I honestly think the NRA could have been a good thing if there had been safeguards against racketeering. That was what wrecked us."

The Case of the Smuggled Bombers

BY ROBERT A. DIVINE

(*U.S.* v. *Curtiss-Wright Export Corp.* et al., 299 U.S. 304)

Few of the great constitutional decisions of the Supreme Court have risen out of more sordid circumstances than the one described here by historian Robert A. Divine of the University of Texas. Yet none has been wiser and not many have had such widespread and beneficial results. Professor Divine, a specialist in diplomatic history, is the author of The Illusion of Neutrality, Eisenhower and the Cold War, *and many other books.*

One June morning in 1932, a detachment of three hundred Bolivian troops stormed and overwhelmed the garrison of a Paraguayan fort in the Gran Chaco. A wild, primitive wasteland, stretching from northern Argentina to eastern Bolivia and populated by savage Guarani Indians, carnivorous piranha fish, and fierce ihenni flies, the Chaco had been in dispute between Bolivia and Paraguay since 1879. The jungle swamps and lagoons of the south and the desert plains of the north, where water holes were often fifty miles apart, offered little attraction for economic development, but land-locked Bolivia was determined to seize control of the northern Chaco to gain access to the Atlantic via the navigable Paraguay River. With a heavier population and great wealth from the world's largest tin mines, Bolivia looked forward to an easy conquest.

But Paraguay, with only 800,000 people and few natural resources, resisted fiercely. In the steamy Chaco jungles, Paraguayan bush fighters, armed only with machetes and antiquated rifles, quickly proved themselves capable of waging full-scale war. For three years the two countries fought for control of this desolate frontier in one of the least-known and most senseless wars of the twentieth century. The Chaco War wasted over 100,000 lives and

"THE NINE OLD MEN."

endangered the peace of all Latin America. It also created a vital constitutional issue affecting the foreign policy of the United States.

Bolivia won the first few skirmishes, but by the fall of 1932 Paraguay had gained the initiative. The brilliant French-trained Paraguayan general, José Estigarribia, outflanked the Bolivian forces and regained control of the central Chaco. Bolivian hopes revived in December, when General Hans Kundt, a German officer who had trained the Bolivian army, arrived to take command of the troops. Using flame throwers and tanks purchased in Europe, Kundt pushed the Paraguayans steadily southward. But then Estigarribia, bolstered by modern arms bought from Germany, England, and Italy, counterattacked. By early 1933 his troops were driving across the Chaco toward the Bolivian frontier. In desperation, the Bolivian government turned to American aircraft manufacturers for help.

These overtures came at a crucial time for the American aviation industry. After Lindbergh's transatlantic flight in 1927 convinced many people that flying was ready to leave the barnstorming stage and take its place as the new mode of transportation, the aircraft industry had boomed. Wall Street bankers took a sudden interest in aviation; in early 1929 the United Aircraft and Transport Company purchased the Pratt and Whitney Company, makers of the Wasp engines, to complete the United Aircraft combine, which also included Boeing Airplane and Chance Vought. Later in the year, to compete with this corporation, Richard Hoyt, a Harvard graduate who had married into a powerful New York investment house and gained control of the Wright Aeronautical Corporation, merged his interests with Clement M. Keys, Greek scholar, hockey player, and former Wall Street reporter, who ran the Curtiss Aeroplane and Motor Company. The new firm, christened the Curtiss-Wright Corporation, was composed of twelve operating companies with holdings in aircraft factories, engine plants, airfields, flying schools, and passenger lines. Three months after the corporation's formation, however, the stock market crashed. Soon the depression was threatening to wipe out this ambitious enterprise. In 1930 Curtiss-Wright lost $9 million; the next year, after Hoyt and Keys liquidated their more flamboyant investments, it still dropped $4 million. The bulk of the firm's business was with the United States government, but the big profits necessary to prevent bankruptcy could only come from export sales. In selling planes to the armed forces, the company set prices high enough to pay off the enormous research and development costs required for new models; then they modified the designs and sold the planes to foreign governments at the same prices. Since the engineering costs had been covered by sales to the U.S. army and navy, they doubled and sometimes even tripled their profit margins on these foreign transactions.

This lucrative trade was controlled by the Curtiss-Wright Export Corporation. Clarence K. Webster, known as "Web" to his associates, was its president. When the Chaco War broke out, Webster entered into negotiations with the Bolivian authorities, and in early 1933 he sold them two Curtis-Wright Hawks. These were single-engine pursuit planes which carried two machine guns and a bomb rack on each wing and had a top speed of 205 miles per hour. They sold for $26,000 apiece. The Bolivian pilots were delighted with the Hawks, which became the nucleus of their air force. To instruct them in the use of the planes, Webster sent Captain Clifton Travis, a retired Army pilot, to La Paz. Travis quickly won the confidence of the Bolivians, and negotiated orders for more Hawks. When Webster suggested that Travis move on from Bolivia to find other customers for Curtiss-Wright products in Latin America, the veteran pilot replied: "We cannot neglect Bolivia; they are our best customers at the present time. A small country, but they have come across with nearly half a million dollars in the past year and are good for quite a bit more if the war lasts."

Webster had no intention of neglecting Bolivia, but he also wanted to explore the possibility of selling planes to Paraguay! In February 1933 he wrote Lawrence Leon, the Curtiss-Wright agent in Buenos Aires, suggesting that he take the "rotten trip" up to Asunción to sound out the Paraguayan authorities. "If we are able to sell them anything," Webster cautioned Leon, "we will have to work very carefully and quietly, and possibly through you, as an individual, as the Bolivian Government would naturally raise 'merry hell' if they believed that we were dealing with their enemies." Though Leon was unable to sell any planes to Paraguay, Webster remained bullish about the Chaco War. "National pride and stubbornness will not permit these countries to quit until they blow up through absolute bankruptcy," he wrote to Captain Travis, "and while the show is going on, it is our job as distributors of munitions to get our share. If we don't, someone else will."

In the spring of 1933, Webster took another step toward ensuring a full share of the Bolivian business. On the advice of Travis, he made the La Paz firm of Webster and Ashton his agents in Bolivia. The Bolivian comptroller general, Castro Lopez, who passed on all contracts signed by the government, was a silent partner in Webster and Ashton, which received a 5 percent commission on all Curtiss-Wright sales to Bolivia. With Lopez's help, Webster was able to maintain an absolute monopoly over the export of military aircraft to Bolivia. In May, the Bolivian government ordered nine more planes, and Webster sent Harry Berger, a mechanic, to La Paz to aid Travis in servicing aircraft. On at least one occasion, Berger traveled down to the front lines in the Chaco to repair Bolivian planes.

Though Webster continually worried about rumors of peace in the Chaco, the war continued, with Paraguay maintaining its offensive. The Bolivians were pleased with the performance of the Curtiss Hawks, but the pilots were disappointed because they only carried 460 pounds of bombs in their wing racks. In May, Travis reported that the Bolivians had gone "bomb-minded" and were interested in purchasing several large bombers. The possible profits of such a deal were so large that Webster resigned as president of the Curtiss-Wright Export Corporation in June and formed his own export firm, which became the sole South American distributor for Curtiss-Wright. In October, he joined Travis in La Paz to negotiate a deal with Bolivian authorities for the sale of some Condor bombers, two-engine planes capable of carrying two thousand pounds of bombs in wing and fuselage racks, and selling for $70,000 apiece. Comptroller General Lopez arranged for Webster to meet with the ministers of war and finance, while Travis flew down to the Chaco with the chief of staff for a conference with General Kundt and aviation officials at the front. After prolonged negotiations, Webster signed the final contract at La Paz in February 1934. Bolivia agreed to buy nine airplanes—five fighters and four Condors—together with a large quantity of spare parts, for $629,000.

Webster was jubilant. He had now sold the Bolivians a total of thirty-four airplanes (their entire air force) and had closed a deal which represented nearly two thirds of the total exports of the Curtiss-Wright company for the previous year. The Chaco War might yet enable the company to weather the depression.

Webster's jubilation proved to be short-lived. In the first few months of 1934, a series of books and magazine articles appeared attacking the munitions makers as "merchants of death" and accusing them of fomenting and prolonging wars in the conduct of their business. In *Iron, Blood and Profits,* George Seldes described the arms makers as "organized into the greatest and most profitable secret international of our time—the international of bloodshed and profits." Leaders of the peace movement, who had been unsuccessfully advocating a curb on the munitions trade for many years, seized on the public outcry against the arms manufacturers to demand a congressional investigation of the industry. In April, Senator Gerald Nye of North Dakota, a former newspaper editor with a sharp eye for popular causes, succeeded in gaining Senate approval for an intensive inquiry into the arms trade.

Meanwhile, the League of Nations, concerned over the war between Bolivia and Paraguay, had sent an investigating committee to the Chaco. This committee recommended an arms embargo on the belligerents. But several leading members of the League doubted that such a move would be successful without the cooperation of the United States. In early May 1934, British officials sounded out the State Department on the possibility of separate but parallel action. President Franklin D. Roosevelt and his secretary of state, Cordell Hull, quickly agreed to seek congressional authorization for an embargo. Legislation was introduced in Congress on May 18. The public outcry against munitions makers forestalled opposition from developing, and on May 24 both houses passed a joint resolution empowering the President to forbid the sale of arms to the Chaco belligerents if, in his opinion, such an embargo would contribute to the reestablishment of peace. On May 28, 1934, the President issued a proclamation banning the sale of arms to Bolivia and Paraguay.

The Chaco embargo ended the possibility of future profits for Curtiss-Wright and other American companies selling weapons to Bolivia and Paraguay. However, the fate of materials contracted for and manufactured before May 28 remained in doubt. On June 14, the Justice Department seized $600,000 worth of arms and weapons at a pier in New York Harbor which were destined for Bolivia. Included were the five Curtiss-Wright fighters Bolivia had ordered in February. After vigorous protests by the Bolivian minister, the State Department announced that weapons completed before May

28 could be exported, but that any products finished after that date could not be shipped. As a result, Curtiss-Wright was able to export the five fighter planes, but the four Condor bombers, valued at $290,000, and the spare parts came under the embargo. Thus Clarence Webster lost half of his last contract with Bolivia.

Richard Hoyt, now serving as chairman of the board of Curtiss-Wright, refused to acknowledge defeat. Calling in Webster and John Allard, the new president of the Curtiss-Wright Export Corporation, Hoyt worked out a plan to get around the Chaco embargo. In the fall of 1934, at the Curtiss-Wright factory in St. Louis, workmen removed the bomb racks and the gun turrets from the four Condors and installed eighteen seats in each fuselage. Miraculously, the Condors were converted from deadly bombers into innocent passenger planes. Curtiss-Wright sold these planes to the Tampa, New Orleans, and Tampico Airlines Company, a New York corporation formed to develop air service between New York and Buenos Aires. The new company was a one-man operation headed by Hugh Wells, a World War I flier who had piloted the first airmail flight from Key West to Havana. On March 15, 1935, Wells applied to the Department of Commerce for permission to fly the four Condors to Arica, Chile, to survey the possibilities for establishing air service to Latin America. The request was sent to the State Department. The department, perhaps alerted by newspaper reports from Argentina, feared that the planes, which could easily be refitted as bombers, were destined for Bolivia. But when Wells promised not to violate the embargo, he received clearance for the flight.

On the morning of March 28, Wells, three other American pilots, and a complement of copilots and mechanics took off from a small airfield in Patterson, Louisiana, in the four Condors. Flying only by day and spending the nights at Pan American Airways facilities, the planes moved leisurely to Brownsville, Texas, south across Mexico and Central America, with a stop in Panama, and arrived in Lima, Peru, on April 2. They were preparing to leave the next day when a Department of Commerce official arrived from Washington with orders to stop the flight. Charging that Wells had deviated from his flight plan by stopping in Peru, the Commerce Department canceled the authorization for the flight, suspended the pilots' licenses, and asked the Peruvian government to ground the planes indefinitely. The local authorities complied with this request, and the four

Condors were placed under military guard at Las Palmas airport outside Lima.

Wells immediately protested and threatened to sue the United States government for damages. He told reporters that he had stopped in Lima to make arrangements for establishing air service from there to Buenos Aires. It was rumored, however, that he had planned to meet a Bolivian agent in Lima to receive the final payment for the Condors. The State Department then disclosed that it had been responsible for the seizure of the planes and announced that the Justice Department had been requested to conduct an investigation to determine if the planes were destined for Bolivia in violation of the Chaco embargo. On May 15, Martin Conboy, the United States attorney for the Southern District of New York, resigned that post to accept an appointment as special assistant to the attorney general and announced that he would go to Lima to carry out the investigation. When Conboy sailed from New York on May 18, he was accompanied by Ira A. Schiller, a lawyer hired by Wells to defend his interests.

By the time Conboy and Schiller arrived in Peru on June 1, Wells and his party had been stranded in Lima for nearly two months. They waited idly in hotel rooms for official permission to leave Peru; their only excitement came when one pilot was rushed to a hospital for an emergency appendectomy. The planes remained under close guard at Las Palmas airport. Peruvian officials even refused to allow them to be serviced, though they did permit Wells to equip them with eight extra gas tanks. The planes flew only once, when Wells and the Peruvians allowed a Cal Tech scientist working on a study of cosmic rays in the Andes to use them to gather data for his experiments at high altitudes.

The waiting ended on June 2, when Conboy began questioning the pilots and mechanics at the American embassy. On the advice of Schiller, Wells instructed his men to answer questions freely. Ten days later, Conboy completed his interrogations and left for the United States without giving any indication that he had secured incriminating information about the flight. Nevertheless, he continued his examination of the affairs of Curtiss-Wright and Wells's airline through the summer and fall of 1935. Finally, he found the evidence that he needed. When Curtiss-Wright had been building the four Condors for the Bolivian government, it had ordered twenty machine guns from the Colt firearms company, five for each bomber. Five of the machine guns had been shipped to Bolivia before the embargo went into effect, but fifteen were still in the United States on May 28, and since they were designed as part of the equipment for the Condors, the government refused to allow their export. During the summer of 1934, Webster, Allard, and a clerk for the Curtiss-Wright Corporation had placed the fifteen machine guns in the crates containing the five fighter planes which the government had permitted to be exported. The clerk had then filed an export declaration in which he failed to include the guns in the manifesto describing the contents of the crates. The guns thus left New York on September 28, 1934, and arrived in Bolivia in violation of the Chaco arms embargo.

Conboy was now ready to go to court. The machine-gun evidence confirmed his suspicions about the Condors. He still could not prove that the Curtiss-Wright officials had entered a conspiracy to deliver the planes to Bolivia, but the illegal shipment of the machine guns gave him a clear-cut case to prosecute. In October a federal grand jury began hearing the evidence and on January 27, 1936, it indicted the Curtiss-Wright Export Corporation, Clarence Webster, and John Allard on charges of conspiring to violate the Chaco arms embargo.

When the case came before Judge Mortimer J. Byers in the federal district court in New York City, lawyers for the defendants, without referring to the details of the case, asked that the charges be dismissed. They contended that the Chaco arms embargo resolution was unconstitutional because Congress had unlawfully delegated legislative power to the President. Citing the recent Supreme Court decision in the Schechter case, which had invalidated the NRA on similar grounds, Judge Byers found for the defense and dismissed the charges. The joint congressional resolution had authorized the President to decide whether an embargo would serve to reestablish peace in the Chaco before putting the ban into effect. Byers ruled that such a grant of discretionary power constituted "an attempted abdication of legislative responsibility." Congress alone could decide whether a given law would work, he concluded.

This decision had a profound impact on the Roosevelt administration. The fate of the Curtiss-Wright executives was of minor importance—the fighting had stopped in the Chaco in 1935 and the

President had revoked the arms embargo. However, in that same year, the exposures of the Nye Committee, revealing the heavy American munitions trade with the Allies from 1914 to 1917, had led Congress to pass a temporary neutrality law built around an arms embargo against all belligerents in future wars. Though the State Department had advocated a discretionary embargo which could be applied exclusively against an aggressor nation, President Roosevelt accepted the congressional view and invoked an arms embargo when Italy invaded Ethiopia in September, 1935. In the spring of 1936, this legislation was extended for another year, and Congress made it clear that it considered an impartial arms embargo essential to prevent American involvement in another world war. Government spokesmen pointed out that if Judge Byers's decision were allowed to stand, the foundation of the nation's new neutrality legislation would be undermined.

With the major tenet of American foreign policy under constitutional challenge, the Roosevelt administration appealed to the Supreme Court to reverse Judge Byers's ruling in the Curtiss-Wright case. There was little reason for optimism. In a steady series of decisions on New Deal legislation, the Court had consistently denied excessive power to the executive. In addition to its decree in the Schechter case,[1] in early 1936 the Court had invalidated the Agricultural Adjustment Act on the ground that Congress had exceeded the limits of its powers in authorizing benefit payments to farmers to induce them to restrict their acreage. Refusing to heed the argument that the emergency conditions of the depression demanded more flexible legislation, the Court seemed determined to restrict both President and Congress to traditional channels. The Curtiss-Wright case would reveal whether or not the justices would use the same standard in regard to foreign policy.

For two days in mid-November 1936, the Court heard the arguments presented by Martin Conboy, pleading the government's case, and George Z. Medalie, attorney for the Curtiss-Wright company. Both men had once served as United States attorney for the Southern District of New York, and both kept close to the constitutional issue: Did Congress have the right to delegate broad discretionary power to the President in foreign affairs? Three justices,

[1]See Chapter XIV, "The Sick Chicken Case."

George Sutherland, James C. McReynolds, and Charles Evans Hughes, gave the case unusual attention. All three had a special interest in foreign policy: McReynolds had served as attorney general under Woodrow Wilson, Sutherland was a former member of the Senate Foreign Relations Committee, and Chief Justice Hughes had served as secretary of state in the early 1920s. When Medalie echoed Judge Byers's opinion by asserting that the Chaco embargo resolution amounted to "almost an abdication of the essential functions of Congress," Hughes questioned him at length about arms embargoes enacted by Congress in 1912 and again in 1922.

Since Congress was preparing to enact permanent neutrality legislation at its next session, the Court acted swiftly. On December 18, 1936, it handed down its decision. Justice Sutherland, a staunch conservative who believed in restricting to the absolute minimum the federal government's role in domestic affairs, delivered the majority decision. Only six months before, Sutherland had voided the Guffey Coal Act, designed to bring order to a chaotic industry, by denying that the Constitution gave Congress the power to legislate for the general welfare. But now he revealed a radically different view in the field of foreign affairs. Reversing the judgment of the lower court, Sutherland stated that since the United States had existed as a sovereign nation before the adoption of the Constitution, its power in the international sphere was without constitutional limit. Then he went on to assert the supremacy of the President in conducting relations with other nations. "In this vast external realm," Sutherland maintained, "with its important, complicated, delicate and manifold problems, the President alone has the power to speak or listen as a representative of the nation." Moreover, Sutherland argued that Congress was acting within its constitutional authority in granting the President broad discretionary powers in the Chaco arms embargo. "Congressional legislation which is to be made effective through negotiation and inquiry within the international field," he concluded, "must often accord to the President a degree of discretion and freedom from statutory restriction which would not be admissible were domestic affairs alone involved." Six justices agreed with Sutherland, and only one, Justice McReynolds, dissented, though he did not file a separate opinion.

The Chaco arms embargo had been upheld, and the neutrality legislation was secure. However, for Clarence Webster, John Allard, and the Curtiss-Wright Export Corporation, the ordeal was not yet over. The Supreme Court directed that the case be continued in district court. In late 1937, another federal grand jury indicted the defendants again, and once more Martin Conboy sought a conviction. The trial proved to be a long and frustrating experience for the prosecuting attorney. After two weeks of proceedings, a member of the jury conversed with one of the defendants on the street outside the courthouse, and the judge declared a mistrial. A second jury heard the case anew and after three days of deliberation reached an ambiguous verdict—it acquitted the defendants on one count and failed to reach a decision on three others, despite a blistering lecture from the bench.

By this time, Curtiss-Wright had been caught up in the great aircraft boom brought about by the approach of World War II. In 1938 the company sold over $150 million worth of aircraft and engines to the armed forces and foreign governments, and its executives wished to avoid the adverse publicity of a third trial. Consequently, in February 1940, Webster, Allard, and the Curtiss-Wright Export Corporation pleaded guilty. The Court fined the company $260,000 and the two executives $11,000 apiece. Martin Conboy did not request prison sentences for Webster and Allard, explaining to the court that they had been acting under orders from Richard Hoyt, who had since died. Thus the search for profits in the lean years of the depression had cost Webster, Allard, and the Curtiss-Wright company years of litigation, large legal fees, and, ultimately, a fine nearly equal to the value of the planes they had tried to smuggle out of the country.

Yet by the time the case was finally settled in 1940, its importance was clear. The arms embargo section of the neutrality act had been repealed two months after the outbreak of World War II in 1939, and the illusion that the nation could ride out the European war had been shattered. But as Roosevelt transformed himself from Dr. New Deal to Dr. Win-the-War, he did not have to face another battle with the Supreme Court. Justice Sutherland's historic decision had given the chief executive wide latitude in the conduct of diplomacy at a time of great national peril. When Congress passed the Lend-Lease Act in 1941, it granted the President enormous discretion in disbursing vast sums of money to nations fighting against the Axis powers. After the German invasion of the Soviet Union, Roosevelt was able to include it among the recipients of Lend-Lease aid without consulting Congress, and thus he was able to send vital war material to the Russian front without delay at a time when Hitler's forces were threatening to destroy Soviet resistance. This significant policy, as well as the destroyers-for-bases deal, the Declaration of the United Nations, and the multitude of executive agreements which characterized American diplomacy during and since World War II, rests securely on the far-reaching opinion of the Court that the President is the sole agent of the nation in the conduct of foreign affairs.

The Case of the Wenatchee Chambermaid

XVI

by William E. Leuchtenburg

(*West Coast Hotel Co.* v. *Parrish*, 300 U.S. 379)

The controversy described in this chapter by William E. Leuchtenburg of the University of North Carolina did more than merely change the Constitution. As Leuchtenburg says, it triggered a constitutional revolution. It created a topsy-turvy situation involving radical feminists in league with mossback conservatives and the Supreme Court overruling not an errant lower tribunal, but itself. It was a landmark victory for the philosophy of the New Deal, one that ended a string of anti-New-Deal Supreme Court decisions begun when the National Industrial Recovery Act was overturned in the sick chicken case, Schechter v. U.S. *Yet it also resulted in one of the few overwhelming legislative defeats suffered by President Roosevelt, a defeat administered to him primarily by the members of his own party.*

    Professor Leuchtenburg is the author of Franklin D. Roosevelt and the New Deal *and many other books.*

       When on a spring day in 1935 Elsie Parrish walked into the office of an obscure lawyer in Wenatchee, Washington, to ask him to sue the town's leading hotel for back pay, she little realized that she was linking her fate to that of exploited women in a Brooklyn laundry a whole continent away. Still less did she think that she was setting off a series of events that would help undo President Franklin D. Roosevelt's plans for his second term. Least of all did she perceive that she was triggering a constitutional revolution that, even today, remains the most significant chapter in the two centuries of existence of the United States Supreme Court. All Elsie knew was that she had been bilked.

    Late in the summer of 1933 Elsie Lee, a woman of about forty who would soon be Elsie Parrish, had taken a job as a chambermaid at the Cascadian Hotel in Wenatchee, entrepôt for a beautiful recreation area reaching from the Columbia valley in Oregon to the Cascades and the country's foremost apple market. "Apples made Wenatchee and apples maintain it," noted the WPA guide to Washington. "It is surrounded by a sea of orchards, covered in spring with a pink foam of blossoms, mile upon mile, filling the valleys and covering the slopes; the air of the town is sweet with the fragrance." Here, in the land of Winesaps and Jonathans, where "in summer and fall the spicy odor of apples is everywhere," Parrish worked irregularly over the next year and a half, cleaning toilets and sweeping rugs for an hourly wage of twenty-two cents, later raised to a quarter. When she was discharged in May 1935, she asked for back pay of $216.19, the difference between what she had received and what she would have gotten if she had been paid each week the $14.30 minimum wage required for her occupation under state law. The Cascadian, which was owned by the West Coast Hotel Company, offered to settle for $17, but she would not hear of it. Instead, she and her husband, Ernest, brought suit for what she insisted was due her.

The Parrishes rested their case on the provisions of a statute that had been enacted by the state of Washington a quarter of a century before when, catching the contagion of reform from neighboring Oregon, it had taken steps to wipe out sweatshops. The 1913 act declared it "unlawful to employ women or minors . . . under conditions of labor detrimental to their health or morals; and . . . to employ women workers in any industry . . . at wages which are not adequate for their maintenance." To safeguard the welfare of female employees, the law established a commission that was authorized, after investigation, to call together employers, employees, and representatives of the public to recommend a wage standard "not detrimental to health and morals, and which shall be sufficient for the decent maintenance of women." On receiving that recommendation, the commission was to issue an order stipulating the minimum wage that must be paid. Under provisions of the law, a commission had set a $14.30 weekly minimum for chambermaids. Twice the statute had been challenged in the courts, and on both occasions the Washington supreme court had validated the act. Elsie Parrish appeared to have an airtight case.

Alas, any law student in the land could have told her that her case was hopeless, for twelve years before, the United States Supreme Court had ruled, in a widely reported decision in the case of *Adkins* v. *Children's Hospital,* that a minimum wage act for women was unconstitutional because it violated the liberty of contract that the Court claimed was guaranteed by the Constitution. Though the opinion by Justice Sutherland commanded only five votes and elicited vigorous dissents, it reconfirmed a notion incorporated in constitutional doctrine only a generation before: that a great corporation and its employee—even someone as powerless as a chambermaid—each had an equivalent right to bargain about wages, a fantasy that Justice Holmes dismissed as "dogma" and the renowned commentator Thomas Reed Powell of Harvard Law School called "indefensible." *Adkins,* said one commentator, "makes forever impossible all other legislation along similar lines involving the regulation of wages." The case involved an act of Congress rather than a state statute, but there was no difference in principle. Any law that transgressed the due process clause of the Fifth Amendment would, if enacted by a state, be held to transgress the due process clause of the Fourteenth Amendment. Though the Washington law remained on the statute books, it was presumed to be null and void. Hence, it startled no one when in November 1935, after hearing Elsie Parrish's case, the presiding judge of the superior court of Chelan County ruled against her, explaining that *Adkins* bound every court in the nation.

Surprisingly, the supreme court of the state of Washington took a different view. On April 2, 1936, it overturned the lower court's decision. To get around the huge obstacle of *Adkins,* the court pointed out that the U.S. Supreme Court had never struck down a *state* minimum wage law, which was true but irrelevant. The decision gave the Parrishes a moment of euphoria, but it hardly seemed likely that this opinion would survive a test in the Supreme Court, in the light of the *Adkins* ruling and given the manifest hostility of justices such as Sutherland to legislation of this nature.

Only eight weeks later, the Court settled any doubt on the matter by a decision on a case that, three thousand miles from Wenatchee, had begun to wend its way through the judicial system while Elsie Parrish was still making beds in the Cascadian Hotel. It arose out of the hope of social reformers in New York, especially women active in the Consumers' League, that the Court, despite *Adkins,*

the Court declared that there was no meaningful difference between the New York statute and the District of Columbia act that had been invalidated in *Adkins:* both violated the liberty of contract that safeguarded equally the rights of employer and employee to bargain about wages. After quoting from *Adkins* with obvious approval, the Court declared, in language that shocked champions of social legislation, "The decision and the reasoning upon which it rests clearly show that the State is without power by any form of legislation to prohibit, change or nullify contracts between employers and adult women workers as to the amount of wages to be paid." Those words all but doomed Elsie Parrish's cause, and gave cocky Joe Tipaldo the victory of a lifetime.

That victory, however, turned out to carry a very high price. "After the court decision, business looked good for a while," Joe told a reporter three months later. "I was able to undercharge my competitors a little on what I saved in labor costs." But then business started to fall off, then fell some more. "I think this fight was the cause of my trouble," he said. "My customers wouldn't give my drivers their wash." Before the summer was over the Bright Light Laundry had folded, and Joe Tipaldo was one of the army of unemployed. "I'm broke now," he confessed. "I couldn't stand the gaff."

Elsie Parrish was made of sterner stuff. She was determined to carry on her struggle, though her prospects seemed bleak indeed. Given the precedent of *Adkins,* her case had never been promising. When the attorney for the West Coast Hotel Company asked the judge who had written the opinion of the supreme court of the state of Washington sustaining that state's minimum wage law in *Parrish* how he could possibly have done so in view of what the U.S. Supreme Court had said in *Adkins,* he replied, "Well, let's let the Supreme Court say it one more time." Now, in *Tipaldo,* the Court had "one more time" stated unequivocally that minimum wage laws for women were invalid. So gloomy was the outlook that, on the advice of Ben Cohen and Felix Frankfurter, the Consumers' League did not even file a brief in *Parrish.* "We are both rather pessimistic regarding its outcome," Cohen confided. Elsie Parrish had every reason to expect the worst.

The *Tipaldo* decision, though, engendered a powerful backlash, not least from some of the members of the Supreme Court. In a strongly worded dissent, Chief Justice Charles Evans Hughes up-

might look favorably on a minimum wage law for women and minors if it was drafted to relate wage setting not just to the needs of women but to the value of the services they rendered. To that end, Felix Frankfurter of Harvard Law School and Benjamin Cohen, a former Brandeis law clerk who was to be a prominent New Dealer, crafted a model law that New York State adopted in 1933, the fourth year of the Great Depression, which had reduced some young women, living on starvation wages, to sleeping on subways. Frankfurter warned that it was "foolish beyond words" to expect the Court to reverse itself, but he hoped that the justices might be willing to distinguish this statute, with its added feature of "value of services," from the one struck down in *Adkins.* "Every word" of the New York law, explained a prominent woman reformer, was "written with the Supreme Court of the United States in mind."

In accordance with the provisions of the model legislation, New York State obtained an indictment against Joseph Tipaldo, manager of the Spotlight Laundry in Brooklyn, who had been brutally exploiting his nine female employees, first by paying them far below the minimum wage and then by pretending to pay the minimum but forcing the sweatshop laundresses to kick back the difference between what he gave them and what the state required. When Joe Tipaldo went to jail to stand trial on charges of disobeying the mandatory wage order and of forgery, the hotel industry (the same business that would be involved in the *Parrish* case) rushed to his side with an offer to bankroll a test of the constitutionality of the New York law. Since hotels were working their employees twelve hours a day, seven days a week, they had a high stake in the case. In fact, the state had already begun minimum wage proceedings against them. Consequently, each hotel put money in a kitty to finance Tipaldo's petition for a writ of habeas corpus to compel Frederick L. Morehead, warden of Brooklyn's city prison, to release him from custody. While his case was being prepared, Tipaldo, utterly shameless, renamed his firm the Bright Light Laundry and made a big investment in expanding his business. He explained, "I expect to get it back eventually on what I save in wages."

On June 1, 1936, the United States Supreme Court appeared to justify his optimism when, in a 5–4 decision in *Morehead* v. *New York ex rel. Tipaldo,* it struck down New York's minimum wage law. In a sweeping opinion written by one of the most conservative justices,

braided the majority for failing to acknowledge either that the New York law could be distinguished from the act of Congress struck down in *Adkins* or that the state has "the power to protect women from being exploited by overreaching employers." Far more biting was the separate dissent filed by Justice Harlan Fiske Stone on behalf of himself and Justices Louis Brandeis and Benjamin Cardozo. In one of the most scathing criticisms ever uttered from the bench, Stone accused the majority of indulging its "own economic predilections." He found "grim irony in speaking of the freedom of contract of those who, because of their economic necessities, give their service for less than is needful to keep body and soul together." In an impassioned warning to his brethren to exercise more self-restraint, Stone wrote: "The Fourteenth Amendment has no more embedded in the Constitution our preference for some particular set of economic beliefs than it has adopted, in the name of liberty, the system of theology which we may happen to approve."

Much of the nation shared Stone's sense of indignation about *Tipaldo.* Secretary of the Interior Harold Ickes noted angrily in his diary: "The sacred right of liberty of contract again—the right of an immature child or a helpless woman to drive a bargain with a great corporation. If this decision does not outrage the moral sense of the country, then nothing will." People of the most diverse political views were appalled by the Court's ruling, for it seemed to deny government, state or federal, any kind of authority over working conditions. New Dealers were irate, and a Republican newspaper in upstate New York declared, "The law that would jail any laundryman for having an underfed horse should jail him for having an underfed girl employee." Even Herbert Hoover asked for a constitutional amendment to give back to the states "the power they thought they already had."

Only two groups applauded the decision. One was the press in a scattering of cheap-labor towns undismayed by the fact that, following the ruling, the wages of laundresses—mostly impoverished blacks and Puerto Rican and Italian immigrants—were slashed in half. The other was a small faction of advanced feminists centered in Alice Paul's National Woman's Party. "It is hair-raising to consider how very close women in America came to being ruled inferior citizens," one of them wrote Justice Sutherland. Most women activists, though, were horrified by that view, which they believed reflected the dogmatism of upper-class ladies who had no familiarity with the suffering of workers. They were as devoted as Alice Paul to equal rights, and they must have shuddered at the paternalism implicit in earlier opinions sustaining separate treatment for women on the grounds that they were wards of the state. But they were sure that female employees required protection, and they knew that insistence on the principle of equal rights meant no minimum wage law whatsoever, since the Court, as constituted during FDR's first term, would never sanction social legislation for men. "Thus," the historian Mary Beard wrote Justice Stone, Alice Paul "plays into the hands of the rawest capitalists."

Stone himself had no doubt of the implications of *Tipaldo*. "We finished the term of Court yesterday," he wrote his sister, "I think in many ways one of the most disastrous in its history. . . . Our latest exploit was a holding by a divided vote that there was no power in a state to regulate minimum wages for women. Since the Court last week said that this could not be done by the national government, as the matter was local, and now it is said that it cannot be done by local governments even though it is local, we seem to have tied Uncle Sam up in a hard knot."

Tipaldo, handed down on the final day of the term, climaxed an extraordinary thirteen months in which the Court struck down more important socioeconomic legislation than at any time in history, before or since. During that brief period, it destroyed the two foundation stones of Roosevelt's recovery program, the National Industrial Recovery Act[1] and the Agricultural Adjustment Act; turned thumbs down on a number of other New Deal laws and state reforms; and cavalierly rebuked the President and his appointees. The NIRA ruling had been unanimous, but almost all of the others had come in split decisions, most often with the "Four Horsemen," Pierce Butler, James McReynolds, George Sutherland, and Willis Van Devanter, a quartet of adamantly conservative judges whose ideas had been molded in the heyday of laissez-faire in the late nineteenth century, voting in the negative. They were often joined by the youngest member of the bench, Owen Roberts. At the end of the term, a nationally syndicated columnist wrote, "After slaughtering practically every New Deal measure that has been dragged

[1]See Chapter XIV, "The Sick Chicken Case."

before it, the Supreme Court now begins its summer breathing spell, ending a winter's performance which leaves the stage, as in the last act of a Shakespearean tragedy, strewn with the gory dead."

Despite the enormous setbacks the New Deal had sustained, Roosevelt gave every indication that he was accepting his losses virtually without complaint. After being drubbed in the press for stating after the NIRA was struck down that the Court was returning the nation to a "horse-and-buggy" conception of interstate commerce, he had said nothing about the issue for the next year. *Tipaldo* moved him to break his silence to observe that the Court had created a "no-man's-land" where no government could function. But that was all he would say. While Elsie Parrish's feeble case was advancing toward its final reckoning in the United States Supreme Court, the President gave not the slightest indication that he had any plans whatsoever to make the justices any less refractory, for it seemed to him altogether inadvisable in the 1936 Presidential campaign to hand his opponents, who were hard put to find an issue, an opportunity to stand by the Constitution. As late as the end of January 1937, after Roosevelt had already delivered his State of the Union message and his inaugural address, the editor of *United States Law Week* wrote that "last week it was made plain that he does not at the present time have in mind any legislation directed at the Court."

But less than two weeks later, on February 5, 1937, the President stunned the country by sending a special message to Congress that constituted the boldest attempt a chief executive has ever initiated to remold the judiciary. He recommended that when a federal judge who had served at least ten years waited more than six months after his seventieth birthday to resign or retire, the President could add a new judge to the bench. Since this court was the most aged in history—its members were referred to as "the nine old men"—Roosevelt would be able to add as many as six new Supreme Court justices. He claimed he was presenting this proposal as a way of expediting litigation, but it was widely understood that what he really wanted was a more amenable tribunal. From the very first day, his program was saddled with a designation it could never shake off: "the Court-packing plan."

Though FDR's scheme provoked fierce protests, political analysts anticipated that it would be adopted. By winning in a landslide in 1936, Roosevelt had carried so many members of his party into Congress that the Republicans were left with only sixteen of the ninety-six seats in the Senate and fewer than one hundred of the more than four hundred seats in the House. So long as the Court continued to strike down New Deal reforms—and such vital legislation as the Social Security Act was still to be decided on—it was highly unlikely that enough Democrats would desert their immensely popular President to defeat the measure. The very first evidence of the attitude of the Court would come with its decision on Elsie Parrish's case, and there was every expectation that, acting not many months after *Tipaldo,* the Court would render an adverse ruling that would improve Roosevelt's already excellent chances of restructuring the Court. On the very day the *Parrish* decision was handed down, March 29, 1937, the president of the National Women's Republican Club declared, "I don't see how the President's bill can fail to get a majority."

March 29 came during the Easter holidays, always a gala season in Washington, D.C. On that bright Monday morning, a host of camera-toting tourists and children carrying Easter bunny baskets crowded the steps of the recently opened Supreme Court building and queued up in record numbers to enter the marble palace. The unusually protracted time of 103 days had elapsed since Elsie Parrish's case had been argued before the Court, and some twelve thousand visitors flocked to the building in the belief that this would be journey's end for the suit that had begun nearly two years earlier. An hour before the session was scheduled to start at noon, four thousand visitors had already been admitted to the building, where many lined up two abreast from the courtroom doorway almost to the suite of Justice Stone in the idle hope of getting a peek at the proceedings.

For some minutes it appeared that the spectators who had been fortunate enough to get into the courtroom were also to be frustrated, for the proceedings began with a recital of an opinion on another case by one of the Four Horsemen that left the audience nearly numb with boredom. But no sooner had he finished than the chief justice leaned forward in his chair, picked up some sheets of paper, and announced, "This case presents the question of the constitutional validity of the minimum wage law of the State of Washington." This was to be Elsie Parrish's day after all, and the spectators stirred in anticipation. Hughes, fully aware of the effect he was having and surely conscious of his magnificent appearance (with his patrician manner, sparkling eyes, and well-groomed beard, he was often likened to Jove), raised his voice to overcome the bustle, then paused and peered out over the crowded chamber for a moment before returning to his written opinion.

Anxious minutes passed as he labored through a reprise of the facts in the case. When he finally took up one of the arguments of Elsie Parrish's attorneys, he did so only to reject it disdainfully. It was "obviously futile," he said, for counsel to claim that the present case could be distinguished from *Adkins* on the ground that Mrs. Parrish had worked for a hotel and that the business of an innkeeper was affected with a public interest. As it happened, he noted, one of the cases *Adkins* had disposed of had dealt with a hotel employee. If the state of Washington law was to survive the day, it would need a better justification than this rickety effort. The Court was going to have to meet *Adkins* head on.

It took only a moment more for Hughes to reveal that the Court was prepared to do just that. In *Tipaldo,* the U.S. Supreme Court had felt bound by the ruling of the court of appeals of New York that the New York minimum wage act could not be distinguished from the statute in *Adkins* and hence was invalid; *Parrish,* the chief justice declared, presented a quite different situation. Here the highest tribunal of the state of Washington had refused to be guided by *Adkins* and had sanctioned the law in dispute. "We are of the opinion that this ruling of the state court demands on our part a re-examination of the Adkins Case," he continued. "The importance of the question, in which many States having similar laws are concerned, the close division by which the decision in the Adkins Case was reached, and the economic conditions which have supervened, and in the light of which the reasonableness of the exercise of the protective power of the State must be considered, make it not only appropriate, but we think imperative, that in deciding the present case the subject should receive fresh consideration." To do so properly, he observed, required careful examination of the doctrine of freedom of contract that had bulked so large in *Adkins.*

"What is this freedom?" Hughes inquired, his voice rising. "The Constitution does not speak of freedom of contract." Instead, the Constitution spoke of liberty and forbade denial of liberty without due process of law. The Constitution did not recognize absolute liberty, however. "The liberty safeguarded is liberty in a social organization," he declared. "Liberty under the Constitution is thus necessarily subject to the restraints of due process, and regulation which is reasonable in relation to its subject and is adopted in the interests of the community is due process." Hughes's delivery of the opinion in "a clear, resonant voice," noted one correspondent, "electrified and held spellbound the spectators who crowded every corner of the majestic Supreme Court chamber." As the chief justice spoke, members of the bar in the choice seats near the bench followed his every word as though transfixed.

The Court had long since established that the state had especial authority to circumscribe the freedom of contract of women, the chief justice continued. In *Muller* v. *Oregon* (1908),[2] he pointed out, the Court had fully elaborated the reasons for accepting a special sphere of state regulation of female labor. In that landmark case, the Court had emphasized, in the words of Justice Brewer, that because a woman performs "maternal functions" her health "becomes an object of public interest and care in order to preserve the strength and vigor of the race." Hence, Brewer had gone on, a woman was "properly placed in a class by herself, and legislation designed for her protection may be sustained even when like legislation is not necessary for men and could not be sustained." The state could restrict her freedom of contract, the Court had determined in *Muller,* not merely "for her benefit, but also largely for the benefit of all."

The precedents established by *Muller* and several later rulings had led the dissenters in *Adkins* to believe that the District of Columbia minimum wage law should have been sustained, and with good reason, Hughes asserted. The dissenting justices, he noted, had challenged the distinction the majority in *Adkins* had drawn between maximum hours legislation (valid) and minimum wage statutes (invalid), and that challenge remained "without any satisfactory answer." The state of Washington law was essentially the same as the Washington, D.C., act that had been struck down in *Adkins,* he acknowledged, "but we are unable to conclude that in its minimum wage requirement the State has passed beyond the

[2]See Chapter XII, "The Case of the Overworked Laundress."

boundary of its broad protective power." In that sentence, however, convoluted, Hughes had in effect said what for some minutes it had been clear he was going to say: the Supreme Court was sustaining Washington's minimum wage law. Against all odds, Elsie Parrish had won.

Lest anyone miss the implication of the Court's reasoning, the chief justice spelled it out: "The *Adkins* case was a departure from the true application of the principles governing the regulation by the State of the employer and employed." In short, *Adkins,* written by Sutherland and carrying the votes of four of Hughes's other brethren, was being put to death in its fifteenth year. In truth, Hughes maintained, one could not possibly reconcile *Adkins* with "well-considered" rulings such as *Muller.* "What can be closer to the public interest than the health of women and their protection from unscrupulous and overreaching employers?" he asked. "And if the protection of women is a legitimate end of the exercise of state power, how can it be said that the requirement of the payment of a minimum wage fairly fixed in order to meet the very necessities of existence is not an admissible means to that end?"

With an eloquence, even passion, few thought him capable of, the chief justice added:

The legislature of the State was clearly entitled to consider the situation of women in employment, the fact that they are in the class receiving the least pay, that their bargaining power is relatively weak, and that they are the ready victims of those who would take advantage of their necessitous circumstances. The legislature was entitled to adopt measures to reduce the evils of the "sweating system," the exploiting of workers at wages so low as to be insufficient to meet the bare cost of living, thus making their very helplessness the occasion of a most injurious competition.

Since many states had adopted laws of this nature to remedy the evil of sweatshop competition, the enactment of such legislation by the state of Washington could not be viewed as arbitrary or capricious, "and that is all we have to decide," Hughes said. "Even if the wisdom of the policy be regarded as debatable and its effects uncertain, still the legislature is entitled to its judgment." Delighted at what they were hearing, the New Deal lawyers in the chamber smiled broadly and nudged one another.

In his closing remarks, the chief justice advanced "an additional and compelling" reason for sustaining the statute. The exploitation of "relatively defenceless" employees not only injured those women, he asserted, but directly burdened the community, because "what these workers lose in wages, the taxpayers are called upon to pay." With respect to that reality, he said, the Court took judicial notice of the "unparalleled demands" the Great Depression had made upon localities. (That comment revealed how far he was reaching out, for the state of Washington had submitted no factual brief about any added responsibilities, and the statute in question had been enacted long before the Wall Street crash.) Hughes did not doubt that the state of Washington had undergone these tribulations, even if it had not troubled to say so. That deduction led him to state, again with unexpected acerbity: "The community is not bound to provide what is in effect a subsidy for unconscionable employers. The community may direct its law-making power to correct the abuse which springs from their selfish disregard of the public interest." Consequently, the chief justice concluded, "The case of *Adkins* v. *Children's Hospital* . . . should be, and it is, overruled," and the judgment of the Supreme Court of the state of Washington on behalf of Elsie Parrish "is affirmed." Some two years after she had changed sheets in the Cascadian Hotel for the last time, the Wenatchee chambermaid was to receive her $216.19 in back pay.

It would require some time for Court watchers to grasp the full implications of Hughes's opinion in *Parrish*—to write of "the Constitutional Revolution of 1937"—but George Sutherland's dissent revealed that the Four Horsemen understood at that very moment that their long reign, going all the way back to *Adkins* and even before, with only slight interruption, had abruptly ended. When he had spoken the final words, the chief justice nodded to Justice Sutherland seated to his left. Sutherland surveyed the chamber silently, almost diffidently, then picked up the sheaf of papers in front of him and began to read. Sensing his day had passed, Sutherland appeared barely able to bring himself to carry out his futile assignment. He started off speaking in a curiously toneless murmur, and even those near the dais had trouble at first catching his words. In the rear of the room, all was lost.

As a consequence, not a few missed altogether Sutherland's first sentence, and even those who did hear it needed a moment to take in its full import. "Mr. Justice Van Devanter, Mr. Justice McReynolds, Mr. Justice Butler and I think the judgment of the court below should be reversed," Sutherland began. A commonplace utterance. Yet that sentence signaled a historic shift in the disposition of the Supreme Court. Once again, the justices had divided 5–4, but this time, Owen Roberts had abandoned the Conservative Four to compose a new majority which on this day, and in the days and months and years to come, would legitimate the kind of social legislation that in FDR's first term had been declared beyond the bounds of governmental authority. The loss of Roberts did not go down easily. In the course of the afternoon, noted one captious commentary, "the Four Horsemen of Reaction whom he had deserted looked glum and sour."

After no more than a cursory paragraph saying that all the contentions that had just been advanced in *Parrish* had been adequately disposed of in *Adkins* and *Tipaldo,* Sutherland delivered a dissent that for quite some time constituted less a reply to Hughes and the majority in *Parrish* than to Justice Stone's 1936 calls for judicial restraint in cases such as *Tipaldo.* Undeniably, a justice was obliged to consider the contrary views of his associates, Sutherland acknowledged, "but in the end, the question which he must answer is not whether such views seem sound to those who entertain them, but whether they convince him that the statute is constitutional or engender in his mind a rational doubt upon that issue." He added:

The oath which he takes as a judge is not a composite oath, but an individual one. And in passing upon the validity of a statute, he discharges a duty imposed upon *him,* which cannot be consummated justly by an automatic acceptance of the views of others which have neither convinced, nor created a reasonable doubt in, his mind. If upon a question so important he thus surrender his deliberate judgment, he stands forsworn. He cannot subordinate his convictions to that extent and keep faith with his oath or retain his judicial and moral independence.

Though Sutherland had been directing most of his barbs at Stone (Hughes's opinion had been all but forgotten), these last words may well have had a different target. His remarks, one writer conjectured, must have been intended as a rebuke to Roberts. Perhaps so, for the minority opinion did appear to be irritating Roberts, who, after looking toward Sutherland several times, raised a handkerchief to his mouth.

Sutherland, for his part, had hit full stride. After sipping some water he seemed to gain strength, and his voice resounded throughout the chamber. Indeed, the Washington *Post* characterized the reading by "the usually mild-mannered Sutherland" as nothing less than "impassioned." The elderly judge, described in another account as "pale, grim-lipped," even went so far as to rap his knuckles on the dais as he took issue with the President, though never by name; with Justice Roberts, no longer his ally; and even more vigorously, again without mentioning him directly, with Justice Stone. In rebuttal to the chief justice's assertion that the case before the Court required a fresh examination, in part because of "the economic conditions which have supervened," Sutherland stated bluntly, "The meaning of the Constitution does not change with the ebb and flow of economic events."

When, having read nearly five pages of his opinion, Sutherland finally turned to the case before the Court, he said little more than that *West Coast Hotel* replicated the situation in *Adkins.* In every important regard, the two statutes involved had identical "vices," Sutherland maintained, "and if the *Adkins* case was properly decided, as we who join in this opinion think it was, it necessarily follows that the Washington statute is invalid." It was beyond dispute, he asserted, that the due process clause embraced freedom of contract, and Sutherland remained convinced, too, that women stood on an equal plane with men and that legislation denying them the right to contract for low-paying jobs was discriminatory. "Certainly a suggestion that the bargaining ability of the average woman is not equal to that of the average man would lack substance," he declared. "The ability to make a fair bargain, as everyone knows, does not depend upon sex."

If anyone thought that those last sentences had a hint of jocularity, they quite misperceived Sutherland's mood. The *Parrish* decision blew taps for the nineteenth-century world, and Sutherland, born in England in 1862 and reared on the Utah frontier, knew it. Having had his say, he understood that there was no point in going on any longer. Wearily, he concluded, "A more complete discussion may be found in the *Adkins* and *Tipaldo* cases cited *supra.*"

Then he carefully laid his opinion on the dais and, stern-visaged, settled back in his chair.

When news of the momentous decision, relayed swiftly to every part of the nation over press association wires, reached Sutherland's supporters, they shared his sense of dismay. Conservatives were outraged. If FDR wanted a political court, said a disgruntled senator, he had one now, for the decision was blatantly political, a transparent effort to kill the Court-packing bill by demonstrating that the judges would no longer misbehave. Ardent feminists were no less incensed. One of them wrote Sutherland: "May I say that the minority opinion handed down in the Washington minimum wage case is, to me, what the rainbow was to Mr. Wordsworth? . . . You did my sex the honor of regarding women as persons and citizens."

Most reformers, though, women as well as men, hailed the *Parrish* ruling as a triumph for social justice and a vindication for FDR, who had been accorded an altogether unexpected victory in the most improbable quarter. One outspoken Progressive, the columnist Heywood Broun, commented: "Mr. Roosevelt has been effective not only in forcing a major switch in judicial policy, but he has even imposed something of his style upon the majority voice of the court. There are whole sections in the document written and read by Chief Justice Hughes which sound as if they might have been snatched bodily from a fireside chat."

Partisans of the President jeered at the Court for its abrupt reversal of views on the validity of minimum wage legislation. Because of "the change of a judicial mind," observed Attorney General Homer Cummings sardonically, "the Constitution on Monday, March 29, 1937, does not mean the same thing that it meant on Monday, June 1, 1936." The head of one of the railway brotherhoods carried that thought a step further in noting, "On Easter Sunday, state minimum wage laws were unconstitutional, but about noon on Easter Monday, these laws were constitutional." That development perturbed some longtime critics of the Court—"What kind of respect do you think one can instill in law students for the process of the Court when things like this can happen?" Felix Frankfurter asked—but gave others no little satisfaction. A former United States senator from West Virginia wrote:

Suppose you have noticed that the untouchables, the infallible, sacrosanct Supreme Court judges have been forced to put upon the record that they are just a bundle of flesh and blood, and must walk upon the ground like the rest of human beings. I got quite a "kick" out of reading that the Supreme Court said, right out loud in meeting, that it had been wrong. Like most of the wrongs done in life, there is no compensation for the great wrongs which that old court has been doing the country; but like all democrats, I am forgiving.

The performance of the Court proved especially embarrassing for the chief justice. Commentators, observing that Hughes had once said of a nineteenth-century decision that "the over-ruling in such a short time by one vote, of the previous decision, shook popular respect for the Court," pointed out that "Now, within a period of only ten months, the Supreme Court has reversed itself on minimum wages, again by one vote." To be sure, Hughes did not admit that the Court had shifted, and years later Roberts claimed that he had voted with the Four Horsemen in *Tipaldo* only because New York had not presented the issue in the right manner. Furthermore, we now know that in *Parrish* Roberts was not responding to the Court-packing threat since he cast his vote before the plan was announced. Nonetheless, scholars, who have the advantage of information not generally known in 1937, find Roberts's contention that he did not switch unpersuasive, and at the time, no one doubted that the Court, and more particularly Mr. Justice Roberts, had crossed over. "Isn't everything today exciting?" wrote one of the women who led the National Consumers' League. "Just to think that silly Roberts should have the power to play politics and decide the fate of Minimum Wage legislation. But, thank God he thought it was politically expedient to be with us." In a more whimsical vein, *The New Yorker* remarked: "We are told that the Supreme Court's about-face was not due to outside clamor. It seems that the new building has a soundproof room, to which justices may retire to change their minds."

Yet despite all the ridicule directed at the Court, Hughes read the opinion in Elsie Parrish's case with an unmistakable note of exultation in his voice. For by being able to show that he had won Roberts to his side in *Parrish,* he had gone a long way toward defeating the Court-packing scheme. Once Roosevelt had a 5–4 majority for social legislation, there no longer appeared to be an urgent need for a drastic remedy. "Why," it was asked, "shoot the bridegroom after a shotgun wedding?" Not for nearly four months would FDR's proposal be finally rejected, and it would retain substantial backing almost to the very end, but never was it as formidable a proposition as it had been on the eve of Elsie Parrish's case. Within days after the decision was handed down, Washington insiders were regaling one another with a saucy sentence that encapsulated the new legislative situation: "A switch in time saved nine."

The Court's shift in *Parrish* proved to be the first of many. On the very day that *Parrish* was decided, "White Monday," the Court also upheld a revised farm mortgage law (the original one had been struck down on "Black Monday" in 1935) as well as other reform statutes. Two weeks later, once more by 5–4 with Roberts in the majority, it validated the Wagner Act (the National Labor Relations Act) and in the following month it turned aside challenges to the Social Security Act. Indeed, never again did the Supreme Court strike down a New Deal law, and from 1937 to the present, it has not overturned a single piece of national or state socioeconomic legislation. Many commentators even believe that the Court has forever abandoned its power of judicial review in this field. Little wonder then that analysts speak of "the Constitutional Revolution of 1937."

Battle-scarred veterans of the minimum wage movement found themselves in a universe remade. The seventeen states with minimum wage statutes on their books now took steps to enforce them, and New York made plans to enact new legislation to replace the law struck down in *Tipaldo.* Even more consequential were the implications of *Parrish* for the national government. Late in 1936, President Roosevelt had told newspapermen of an experience on the streets of New Bedford when his campaign car was mobbed by enthusiastic well-wishers, twenty thousand of them crowded into a space intended to hold a thousand:

There was a girl six or seven feet away who was trying to pass an envelope to me and she was just too far away to reach. One of the policemen threw her back into the crowd and I said to my driver, "Get the note from that girl." He got it and handed it to me and the note said this: "Dear Mr. President: I wish you could do something to help us girls. You are the only recourse we have got left. We have been working in a sewing factory . . . and up to a few months ago we were getting our minimum pay of $11 a week. . . . Today the 200 of us girls have been cut down to $4 and $5 and $6 a week. You are the only man that can do anything about it. Please send somebody from Washington up here to restore our minimum wages because we cannot live on $4 or $5 or $6 a week."

That is something that so many of us found in the Campaign, that these people think that I have the power to restore things like minimum wages and maximum hours and the elimination of child labor. . . . And, of course, I haven't any power to do it.

Now, thanks to the constitutional revolution that the Wenatchee chambermaid had detonated, Congress was able to give Roosevelt that power, and when the Fair Labor Standards Act of 1938, which set minimum wages and maximum hours for both men and women, was challenged in the courts, a reconstituted Supreme Court found no difficulty in validating it.

Long before then, Elsie Parrish had faded into the anonymity from which she had risen. When more than thirty-five years later Adela Rogers St. Johns, a reporter who had won renown as the "sob sister" of the Hearst press, tracked her down in Anaheim, California, Mrs. Parrish expressed surprise that anyone would pay attention to her. Surrounded by grandchildren, looking much younger than her years, "dressed in something pink and fresh-washed and ironed," she said that she had gotten little notice at the time "and none of the women running around yelling about Lib and such have paid any since." But she was quietly confident, she indicated to the author of *Some Are Born Great,* that she had accomplished something of historic significance—less for herself than for the thousands of women scrubbing floors in hotels, toiling at laundry vats, and tending machines in factories, who needed to know that, however belatedly, they could summon the law to their side.

The Flag-Salute Cases

BY IRVING DILLIARD

(*Minersville School District* v. *Gobitis*, 310 U.S. 586; *West Virginia State Board of Education* v. *Barnette*, 319 U.S. 624)

In 1931 the Supreme Court had determined in the case of the "miscreant purveyor of scandal" that Jay M. Near had the right under the First Amendment to defame blacks, call a decent public official a "Jew lover," and describe Minneapolis policemen as assassins and "ochre-hearted rodents." This was a relatively broad interpretation of individual rights. The decision did not, however, put an end to the controversy over the power of government to limit personal expression when the public interest was involved. The boundaries between the rights of individuals and those of society are often difficult to define. It is one thing to prevent a person from doing or saying something (as was the issue in Near v. Minnesota), *but quite another to compel a person to do something required of all individuals by law. In the following chapter Irving Dilliard, author of* One Man's Stand for Freedom: Mr. Justice Black and the Bill of Rights, *describes how the justices struggled with this question in a series of cases involving freedom of religion.*

Look closely at a map of Pennsylvania for Minersville and you will find it in semifine print in Schuylkill County, near Pottsville, about four fifths of the way from the Ohio boundary across the Keystone toward New Jersey, on an east-west line running just a little below the middle.

Geographically, Minersville is a kind of hub for central-eastern Pennsylvania, although not even the businessmen on Minersville's main street probably have ever thought of it that way. Wilkes-Barre and Scranton are north-by-northeast. Allentown and Bethlehem lie east. Philadelphia, with its museums, historic shrines and Main Line, are to the southeast. Lancaster and the steady Amish folk are due south, and Harrisburg and the state capitol with its shining dome

285

ABE FORTAS.

southwesterly. The crow that flies straight west from Minersville soon passes over the Susquehanna River.

As towns shaped up in the mid-1930s, Minersville was pretty much an average American community. It was older than many and not so old as others. Its first settlers built their cabins and began wresting a livelihood out of the forests in about 1793. Their sons drew up a plat in 1830, the year that Chicago was laid out. But the founding fathers of Minersville moved faster than their counterparts in the village on Lake Michigan. Minersville was incorporated in 1831, Chicago not until 1833.

A hundred years later the census takers of 1930 counted 9,392 souls in Minersville. This population was enough to move Minersville up the municipal scale a bit, but not enough to make it very large. It relied perhaps too much on the anthracite coal industry, though it also went in for producing clothes.

Minersville had the run of community organizations, institutions, and activities for a place its size. It had men and women and children of a variety of interests and tastes and affiliations and beliefs. Among its God-fearing citizens was the family of Walter Gobitis, pronounced "Go-bite-us."

One afternoon in 1936 Lillian Gobitis, age twelve, and her brother William, age ten, came home from public school with news that distressed their parents. The principal had told Lillian and William that they could not attend school anymore unless they would agree to salute the national flag as their classmates did at the opening patriotic exercises each morning.

Other children, along with their teachers, repeated the oath of allegiance every day. Other children saluted the flag without objection. The Gobitis children must do likewise or stop coming to public school in Minersville.

The reason Lillian and William were not saluting the flag was simple enough. They meant no disrespect to Old Glory. They admired the Stars and Stripes when they saw it fluttering in the breeze above the schoolhouse. It was just that they had been taught in their church and in their home that saluting the flag was a violation of their religion.

For the family of Walter Gobitis belonged to the Jehovah's Witnesses faith and they took seriously as well as literally the Bible's Ten Commandments. In the Old Testament they found clear instructions on what to do about saluting the flag. There it was written out for all to see in the Book of Exodus, Chapter 20, verses 3 through 5:

3. Thou shalt have no other gods before me.

4. Thou shalt not make unto thee any graven image, or any likeness of any thing that is in heaven above, or that is in the earth beneath, or that is in the water under the earth:

5. Thou shalt not bow down thyself to them, nor serve them. . . .

How could it be plainer than that? When you saluted the flag, you were bowing down before a graven image and that was prohibited by the Word of God, as expressed in the Holy Writ, as long ago as the delivery of the Ten Commandments to Moses on Mount Sinai. And so the mother and father of Lillian and William Gobitis told their children not to join the teachers and the other children in the morning patriotic exercises at school.

Here was head-on conflict between the individual citizen and the government—at the level nearest the citizen, his local school board.

The Minersville Board of Education consisted of a broad range of the community's leaders, including business and professional men, from the offices and stores and industries. Dr. T. J. McGurl and Dr. E. A. Valibus took precious time and went to monthly meetings. So did David I. Jones, Claude L. Price, Thomas B. Evans, and William Zapf. The Superintendent of Public Schools was Charles E. Roudabush and he too was a solid and respected citizen.

These men had acted in good faith when they placed the pledge of allegiance and the flag salute in the daily public school program. They believed that the ceremony of the salute would promote patriotism and good citizenship. But the family of Walter Gobitis was acting in equally good faith. The family also was patriotic, although it believed that patriotic citizens were first of all religious citizens who obeyed the commands of God. It asked not that the ceremony be abolished for all, but that conscientious objectors be excused from participating in a rite offensive to their cherished beliefs.

The members of the Minersville Board of Education talked the question over, up one side and down the other. In the end they just could not see how it would hurt any American child to salute the national flag. So they declined to make an exception for the Gobitis children. The board members directed Superintendent of Schools Roudabush to expel the children, which he did.

When you really believe that an act is a deadly sin, forbidden by the Ten Commandments, you do not give in easily. Walter Gobitis did not yield an inch. He and his wife took Lillian and William out of public school. But the family circumstances were modest and the costs of a private school became a matter of economic concern.

Gobitis discussed the situation with fellow members of his church. He got some legal advice and some help. He discovered that beyond Minersville, in Philadelphia, in New York, and elsewhere, there were people and organizations interested in questions like the one he had raised. Since the early 1920s the American Civil Liberties Union had as its major purpose the provision of legal help in such situations.

The head of the house of Gobitis thought about it a lot before he did anything, for he wanted to do only what was right. Then, regretfully but resolutely, he filed a suit in court on behalf of his children, and on his own behalf, to be relieved of the financial burden of the additional educational costs. He also sued to prevent the Board of Education from continuing to require the flag salute as a condition to his children's attendance at the Minersville school. He pointed to the fact that the laws of Pennsylvania made attendance at school compulsory and yet his children were not allowed to attend free public school because of the regulation of the Minersville Board of Education.

The case was heard in federal district court in Philadelphia by Judge Albert B. Maris, who had been appointed to the federal bench in 1936 by President Franklin D. Roosevelt. Judge Maris granted "relief" to the Gobitis father and children. He did so, the United States Supreme Court said later, "on the basis of a thoughtful opinion, at a preliminary stage." The Minersville Board of Education appealed to the United States Circuit Court of Appeals for the Third Circuit at Philadelphia. After further proceedings, the court of appeals upheld the decree of Judge Maris.

Legally, what happened was that the courts had denied a motion of the Minersville Board of Education to dismiss the bill of complaint which sought to enjoin the school authorities from continuing to require the flag salute as a condition for attending school.

Walter Gobitis had now carried the day at the first and second levels of the federal judiciary. There remained the third and highest level in Washington, and to the Supreme Court of the United States the Minersville school board took its appeal of the case against Lillian and William Gobitis and their father. The year was 1940.

Three times before the question of a compulsory flag salute had been appealed to the Supreme Court. Three times the Supreme Court had disposed of it briefly in an unsigned *per curiam* opinion, declaring that no substantial federal question was involved. It was a local or at most a state matter. The first flag-salute regulation appeared in Kansas in 1907, and three decades later it had been taken up in only eighteen states. One hundred and twenty children were known to have refused for religious reasons to comply. As recently as April 1939, the Supreme Court had unanimously denied an appeal from the supreme court of California which had upheld the requirement of a flag salute.

This time, however, the appeal situation was different. Instead of upholding the flag-salute requirement, the lower courts had granted relief to a father and his children who opposed the rite as part of a school program. Furthermore, Europe had gone to war. People all over the United States were wondering how long their country could stay out of the bitter conflict. As the danger increased, there was more and more in the way of patriotic ceremony and exercise, not less.

And so the Supreme Court of the United States put its precedent rulings to one side and agreed to listen to arguments in the case of *Minersville School District* v. *Gobitis.* It did so, the Supreme Court said, "to give the matter full consideration."

Things were going from bad to worse in Europe when Case No. 690 of the October 1939 term was argued on April 25, 1940. Sitting on the highest tribunal that uneasy spring day were a Wilson appointee, Justice James Clark McReynolds of Tennessee, a Coolidge appointee, Justice Harlan F. Stone of New York, two Hoover appointees, Chief Justice Charles Evans Hughes of New York and Justice Owen J. Roberts of Pennsylvania, and five who held their commissions from President Roosevelt. The New Deal quintet were Justices Hugo L. Black of Alabama, Stanley F. Reed of Kentucky, Felix Frankfurter of Massachusetts, William O. Douglas of Connecticut, and Frank Murphy of Michigan. It was a Supreme Court with a lot of fresh blood and the newcomers had markedly lowered the average age.

Word went around Washington that the arguments would be something to hear. The case had not drawn as counsel a Daniel Webster or a Joseph H. Choate or a John W. Davis, but even so it would be worth anybody's time. Joseph W. Henderson of the Philadelphia bar spoke up for the Minersville Board of Education. He presented three major contentions:

1. The expulsion of the Gobitis children did not violate their rights under the Constitution of the United States.

2. The expulsion did not violate their rights under the Constitution of the Commonwealth of Pennsylvania.

3. The refusal of the Gobitis children to salute the flag at school exercises because they believed to do so would violate the law of Almighty God, as contained in the Bible, was not founded on a religious belief.

George K. Gardner of Boston, a professor at the Harvard Law School, carried the burden of the argument for the Gobitis children and their father, who appeared in the title of the case as "their next friend." He and his associates made two main points. The first was that "The creature man shall be free to exercise his conscientious belief in God and his obedience to the law of Almighty God, the Creator, and may not be compelled to obey the law or the rule of the state, which law, as he conscientiously believes, is in direct conflict with the law of Almighty God." The second was that "the rule made and enforced by [the Minersville Board of Education] compelling children and teachers to indulge in a ceremony of saluting the flag is violative of the Fourteenth Amendment of the Constitution of the United States of America."

The Gobitis family could not have been other than surprised at the array of legal talent from all over the country that came to sit, figuratively at least, on its side of the counsel table. For in addition to the professor from the Harvard Law School, there were the others who joined in the friends-of-the-court brief of the American Civil Liberties Union—Arthur Garfield Hays, Osmond K. Fraenkel, William G. Fennell, and Jerome M. Britchey of New York and Alexander H. Frey of Philadelphia. Among these distinguished members of the bar were veteran fighters for freedom in the United States for more than a quarter century.

Between the expulsion of the Gobitis children and the appeal of their case to the Supreme Court, a remarkable thing had happened. Alarmed by the rash of so-called loyalty statutes of the early 1930s, teachers' oath laws, and other infringements on individual freedom, one of the bar's most eminent members, Grenville Clark of New York, had persuaded the American Bar Association to set up a committee on the Bill of Rights to investigate "seeming substantial violations of constitutional liberties" in the country. The committee was created in 1938 and its authority to enter into litigation defined in January 1940. Almost at once the chairman, Grenville Clark, and one of the committee members, Zechariah Chafee, Jr., professor of law at Harvard and an authority on civil liberty, went to work on a brief supporting the stand taken by the Gobitis family. When their brief was submitted to the Supreme Court, it bore the names of some of the most eminent members of the legal profession in the country. They included Charles P. Taft of Ohio, Lloyd K. Garrison of Wisconsin, Douglas Arant of Alabama, George I. Haight of Illinois, Monte M. Lemann of Louisiana, and Ross L. Malone of New Mexico.

Their brief was bold and challenging. "So far as the respondent children are concerned, the salute must be regarded as a religious ritual," it declared. "We suggest that no American court should presume to tell any person that he is wrong in his opinion as to how he may best serve the God in which he believes." Its second major point was that "There is no such public need for the compulsory flag salute as to justify the overriding of the religious scruples of the children." Here the committee struck doubly hard. It contended not only that the "alleged public need [was] not sufficiently urgent," but that "even if the challenged legislation be deemed to serve a public need, there are other reasonable ways of accomplishing the purpose without infringing the religious convictions of children."

The American Bar Association's committee saw still other objections to the demand of the Minersville Board of Education. "Even if the salute be considered incapable of any religious meaning, compulsory salute legislation is void as an unjustifiable infringement of the liberty of the individual." Furthermore, "the compulsory flag salute cannot be sustained on the ground that public school education is granted as a matter of grace so that the requirement, even though arbitrary and capricious, can be enforced by expulsion from public school."

A brief so courageous deserved a courageous conclusion. Here was the high note struck on its final page:

The philosophy of free institutions is now being subjected to the most severe test it has ever undergone. Advocates of totalitarian government point to the speed and efficiency with which such systems are administered, and assert that democracy can offer nothing to outweigh these advantages. The answer is to be found in the value of certain basic individual rights and the assurance afforded by free institutions that these shall not be required to yield to majority pressure no matter how overwhelming.

The worth of our system must ultimately be judged in terms of the importance of those values and the care with which they are safeguarded. We consider them immeasurably important. We believe that the letter and spirit of our Constitution demand vindication of the individual liberties which are abridged by the challenged regulation.

Now the case of Lillian and William Gobitis and their father had gone all the way. Starting in their hometown in 1936, it had completed the three levels of the courts of the United States in four years. It had been argued with dignity and earnestness and conviction on both sides at the apex of the judiciary and then taken for decision.

Alas, the impressive arguments, oral and written, and the briefs of the American Civil Liberties Union and the American Bar Association committee were almost completely unavailing so far as the *Gobitis* decision went. By a vote of 8 to 1, the justices reversed the lower court decision.

Chief Justice Hughes assigned the writing of the majority opinion to Justice Felix Frankfurter, who had arrived on the bench barely a year earlier. Frankfurter was a 1906 graduate of the Harvard Law School, a classmate of Grenville Clark and Monte M. Lemann of the American Bar Association's committee. Latterly, Justice Frankfurter had been a colleague of Professor Zechariah Chafee and George K. Gardner on the Harvard Law faculty. But these old associations counted for little if anything. Something that might have mattered, although of course nothing was said about it, was the fact that Justice Frankfurter was the only member of the Supreme Court who was not native born. It is more than possible that Hughes had this in mind when he placed the Court's opinion in Frankfurter's talented hands. The chief justice knew that an opinion by Frankfurter on the side of the Minersville school district would not only be eloquent, but would also appeal to the nation's spirit of patriotism in an increasingly trying time of international danger.

And so Felix Frankfurter, emigrant from Austria at the age of eleven, went to work on an opinion concerning the Stars and Stripes that he expected would be supported by all of his black-robed brothers. But Justice Stone had met the Jehovah's Witnesses in earlier Supreme Court tests. "All human experience teaches us that a moral issue cannot be suppressed or settled by making its supporters martyrs," he had written. Even while the Gobitis case was under deliberation, Justice Stone addressed to the famous international lawyer John Bassett Moore words that recalled Justice Oliver Wendell Holmes's historic dissent in the Rosika Schwimmer citizenship case. "I suppose there are limits," wrote Stone, "beyond which personally offensive free speech cannot be pressed, but there would not be much necessity for free-speech protection if it extended only to those things we would like to hear."

Without saying much about it, Justice Stone had made up his mind to dissent in behalf of the rights of the Gobitis family. This impending stand by a senior member of the Court disturbed Justice Frankfurter to such an extent that just a week before the decision was to be handed down, he wrote his older colleague a five-page letter in an attempt to convince him that the *Gobitis* opinion was really only an application of principles which Justice Stone himself had asserted in other important cases.

The compulsory-flag-salute question was, Justice Frankfurter wrote, a "tragic issue," and all the more sensitive for him because it presented a "clash of rights, not the clash of wrongs" and "for resolving such a clash we have no calculus." Stone's feelings had made him reexamine his own views, Frankfurter went on, for he had always opposed "foolish and harsh manifestations of coercion" and favored "the amplest expression of dissident views, however absurd or offensive." But the school authorities certainly could establish "flag-saluting exercises." Since they felt that exempting the Gobitis children would disrupt the ceremony, "it seems to me that we do not trench upon an undebatable territory of libertarian immunity" by allowing them to make the children conform.

After recalling "many talks with Holmes about his espionage opinions,"[1] which he regarded as providing a guideline for the flag-salute case, Justice Frankfurter explained his opinion would be "a vehicle for preaching the true democratic faith of not relying on the Court for the impossible task of assuring a vigorous, mature, self-protecting and tolerant democracy." This task was the responsibility of "the people and their representatives."

Bear in mind how very little this case authorizes and how wholly free it leaves us for the future [he continued]. . . . It is not a case where conformity is exacted for something that you and I regard as foolish—namely a gesture of respect for the symbol of our national being—even though we deem it foolish to exact it from Jehovah's Witnesses. . . . It is not a case where the slightest restriction is involved against the fullest opportunity to disavow —either on the part of the children or their parents—the meaning that ordinary people attach to the gesture of respect. . . . We ought to let the legislative judgment stand and put the responsibility where it belongs.[2]

Justice Stone replied in an undated, pencil-written note. He distinguished between a "vulgar intrusion of law" in the domain of conscience and in legislation dealing with the control of property. The Court's responsibility is the larger, he wrote, in the domain of conscience. Then he said: "I am truly sorry not to go along with you. The case is peculiarly one of the relative weight of imponderables

[1] *Schenck* v. *United States* (1919) and *Abrams* v. *United States* (1919). In the Schenck case, the Supreme Court upheld the conviction for conspiracy under the Espionage Act of the general secretary of the Socialist party who had sent out 15,000 leaflets urging conscripted men to oppose the World War I draft law. In the unanimous opinion, Justice Holmes asserted his famous doctrine that what must be determined is whether the words are used in circumstances that would "create a clear and present danger" such as Congress has a right to prevent. In the Abrams case, five Russians were found guilty of violating the Espionage Act by publishing two leaflets that denounced "capitalist nations" for "interfering" with the Russian Revolution. The leaflets urged workers in munitions factories in the United States not to "betray" their "Russian comrades." The Supreme Court upheld the convictions, 7–2, Justices Holmes and Brandeis dissenting.

[2] This intimate and revealing letter from Justice Frankfurter to his senior colleague is little known. The only place where it appears in full in print, so far as the author knows, is as an appendix to A. T. Mason, *Security Through Freedom: American Political Thought and Practice* (Cornell, 1955). It is extensively quoted in Mason's monumental biography, *Harlan Fiske Stone: Pillar of the Law* (Viking Press, 1953, 1956).

and I cannot overcome the feeling that the Constitution tips the scales in favor of religion."

The much awaited decision came down on June 3, 1940, almost as if an observance by the Supreme Court of Flag Day that year. By then Hitler's armored might had run through the Netherlands, Belgium, and Luxembourg. The heroic withdrawal from Dunkirk had been written imperishably in the annals of free men. It was a time for heroic thinking as well. Partly under the prodding of his law clerk, Allison Dunham, who very strongly opposed the compulsory flag salute, Justice Stone drafted his dissent. But he waited so long that by the time it could be circulated to the other justices, support for the Frankfurter opinion was general. Justices Black, Douglas, and Murphy were not very happy about it and devoted their efforts to bringing about certain modifications in the Frankfurter opinion on the side of freedom of conscience. Had Justice Stone prepared his dissent earlier he might well have had company in his disagreement.

Justice Frankfurter's opinion faced the dilemma of the liberals squarely in the first paragraph. "A grave responsibility confronts this Court whenever in the course of litigation it must reconcile the conflicting claims of liberty and authority." The pursuit of one's convictions "about the ultimate mystery of the universe and man's relation to it" was clearly beyond the reach of law, but at the same time, the community as a whole had rights that must also be respected. "The mere possession of religious convictions which contradict the relevant concerns of a political society does not relieve the citizen from the discharge of political responsibilities."

"The ultimate foundation of a free society is the binding tie of cohesive sentiment," Frankfurter declared. The flag is "the symbol of our national unity . . . the emblem of freedom in its truest, best sense." To argue that a law requiring schoolchildren to salute the flag violated the constitutional guarantees of freedom of conscience would be to exceed the limits of judicial "competence." He continued:

The influences which help toward a common feeling for the common country are manifold. Some may seem harsh and others no doubt are foolish. Surely, however, the end is legitimate. And the effective means for its attainment are still so uncertain and so unauthenticated by science as to preclude us from putting the widely prevalent belief in flag-saluting beyond the pale of legislative power. It mocks reason and denies our whole history to find in the allowance of a requirement to salute our flag on fitting occasions the seeds of sanction for obeisance to a leader.

Why might the school board members insist on the authority to expel Lillian and William Gobitis rather than allow them to be excused from the morning flag ceremony? Justice Frankfurter answered this way:

What the school authorities are really asserting is the right to awaken in the child's mind considerations as to the significance of the flag contrary to those implanted by the parent. In such an attempt the state is normally at a disadvantage in competing with the parent's authority, so long—and this is the vital aspect of religious toleration—as parents are unmolested in their right to counteract by their own persuasiveness the wisdom and rightness of those loyalties which the state's educational system is seeking to promote. . . . That the flag-salute is an allowable portion of a school program for those who do not invoke conscientious scruples is surely not debatable. But for us to insist that, though the ceremony may be required, exceptional immunity must be given to dissidents, is to maintain that there is no basis for a legislative judgment that such an exemption might introduce elements of discipline, might cast doubts in the minds of the other children which would themselves weaken the effect of the exercise.

Although Frankfurter had been expected to read his opinion before the assembled Court, he merely announced the result, allowing interested persons to follow his reasoning in the printed record. Justice Stone, however, was so stirred by the case that he read his dissent in full. Moving forward in his chair, he spoke with deep emotion in a raised voice.

After paying tribute to the good citizenship of the Gobitis children and their father, he hit hard at the regulation of the Minersville Board of Education, which, he said, "does more than suppress freedom of speech and more than prohibit the free exercise of religion. . . . For by this law the state seeks to coerce these children to express a sentiment which, as they interpret it, they do not entertain, and which violates their deepest religious convictions."

Justice Stone conceded that the government may "make war and raise armies" and that to do so it may subject citizens to military training despite their religious objections. "But it is a long step and

one I am unable to take to the position that government may, as a
supposed educational measure and as a means of disciplining the
young, compel public affirmations which violate their religious conscience." There were better ways of inculcating patriotism in a
child, he insisted, than forcing him "to affirm that which he does not
believe." It is one thing to "elicit" expressions of loyalty, another
to "command" them.

The Constitution expresses more than the conviction of the people that
democratic processes must be preserved at all costs [Justice Stone con-
cluded]. It is also an expression of faith and a command that freedom of
mind and spirit must be preserved, which *government* must obey, if it is to
adhere to that justice and moderation without which no free government
can exist. . . . I cannot say that the inconveniences which may attend some
sensible adjustment of school discipline in order that these children may
be spared, presents a problem so momentous or pressing as to outweigh
the freedom from compulsory violation of religious faith which has been
thought worthy of constitutional protection.

There it was: 8 to 1. The lower courts had been reversed, the
Minersville school district upheld. Walter Gobitis and his children,
Lillian and William, had lost. Yet the country remained to be heard
from, and a large part of the reaction, which came quickly, was on
the dissenting side. More than 170 leading newspapers condemned
the decision while only a few supported it. "We think this decision
of the United States Supreme Court is dead wrong," the St. Louis
Post-Dispatch said.

We think its decision is a violation of American principle. We think it is
a surrender to popular hysteria. If patriotism depends upon such things as
this—upon violation of a fundamental right of religious freedom, then it
becomes not a noble emotion of love for country, but something to be
rammed down our throats by the law.

Some of Justice Frankfurter's closest friends were dismayed. The
British political scientist Harold J. Laski wrote from London to
Justice Stone: "I want to tell you how right I think you are in that
educational case from Pennsylvania and, to my deep regret, how
wrong I think Felix is." The New Deal lawyer Benjamin V. Cohen
said: "When a liberal judge holds out alone against his liberal brethren, I think he ought to know when he has spoken not for himself
alone, but has superbly articulated the thoughts of his contemporar-

ies who believe with him in an effective but tolerant democracy."
John Bassett Moore made this comment: "I am sorry to see Frankfurter acting as the mouthpiece of such measures which are likely
to create disloyalty more than to promote loyalty."

On the heels of the decision came a wave of fanatical patriotism,
with violence heaped on the Jehovah's Witnesses in many places. A
meeting hall was burned in Kennebunkport, Maine. A Bible meeting
was attacked in Rockville, Maryland. A lawyer who attempted to
represent embattled Jehovah's Witnesses at Connersville, Indiana,
was beaten and driven from the town. Veterans organizations participated in the bitter reaction in many communities. In Jackson,
Mississippi, the Witnesses were banned. Arkansas, California,
Texas, and Wyoming were among the other states which saw instances of violent reaction attributable at least in part to the flag-
salute decision. In several states children in Jehovah's Witnesses
families who continued to refuse to salute the flag in school exercises were declared delinquents by the courts and committed to
reformatories.

After a caravan of Witnesses' automobiles was overturned in
Litchfield, Illinois, the St. Louis *Post-Dispatch* took an overall look at
the lamentable situation:

> It would be a mistake to attribute these outbreaks of violence against
> religious minorities solely to the United States Supreme Court's opinion
> upholding the compulsory flag salute in public schools. . . . Yet there can
> be little doubt that that most unfortunate decision will be an encourage-
> ment for self-appointed guardians of patriotism and the national moralists
> to take the law into their own hands.

Two facts about the decision reassured Justice Frankfurter. One
was the overwhelming vote of eight to one. The other was the
presence of Chief Justice Hughes among the eight, for Hughes,
more than any other member of the court, had spoken up in the past
for the liberties protected by the Bill of Rights. In cases involving
freedom of the press, freedom of speech, and freedom of association the elderly, bewhiskered chief justice had written some of the
strongest decisions in Supreme Court history.

But change was overtaking the Supreme Bench, and with it would
come a new point of view. In less than a year the ultraconservative
Justice McReynolds stepped down and Senator James F. Byrnes of

South Carolina was appointed to his seat. Shortly thereafter, Chief Justice Hughes retired. The following October, President Roosevelt elevated Justice Stone to the chief justiceship and nominated Attorney General Robert H. Jackson of New York to the vacancy created by the advancement of Stone.

Meantime, a new Jehovah's Witnesses case—or rather set of cases —was on the way to the Supreme Court. All grew out of tests of the constitutionality of municipal ordinances under which members of that faith were convicted for not paying license taxes on the religious publications which they sold on street corners and from door to door. Roscoe Jones ran afoul of such an ordinance in Opelika, Alabama; Lois Bowden and Zada Sanders in Fort Smith, Arkansas; and Charles Jobin in Casa Grande, Arizona. Meantime also, Justices Black, Douglas, and Murphy were growing increasingly concerned about their support of the *Gobitis* decision. For added to the editorial reaction and the violence which came in the wake of the decision was the almost uniformly adverse judgment of the law reviews and journals.

And so Justices Black, Douglas, and Murphy resolved to get themselves separated from the *Gobitis* decision at their earliest opportunity. They found it in *Jones* v. *Opelika,* as the new cases were called. They left the Frankfurter standard en masse and joined Stone. In addition to supporting the dissent of the chief justice, the three added a separate statement of their own, doubtless unique in Supreme Court history:

The opinion of the Court sanctions a device which in our opinion suppresses or tends to suppress the free exercise of a religion practiced by a minority group. This is but another step in the direction which *Minersville School District* v. *Gobitis* took against the same religious minority and is a logical extension of the principles upon which that decision rested. Since we joined in the opinion in the *Gobitis Case,* we think this is an appropriate occasion to state that we now believe that it was also wrongly decided. Certainly our democratic form of government functioning under the historic Bill of Rights has a high responsibility to accommodate itself to the religious views of minorities however unpopular and unorthodox those views may be. The First Amendment does not put the right freely to exercise religion in a subordinate position. We fear, however, that the opinions in these and the *Gobitis Case* do exactly that.

The disavowal of *Gobitis* by three of its adherents made the decision in *Jones* v. *Opelika* 5 to 4. Supporting Justice Reed's majority opinion upholding the license tax ordinances were Justices Roberts and Frankfurter from *Gobitis* and the new justices, Byrnes and Jackson. But this was only a transitional step, although a most significant one. Outright reversal of *Gobitis* was on the way. Justice Byrnes resigned from the Court in a year to become war mobilization director. To his place President Roosevelt appointed court of appeals judge Wiley B. Rutledge of Iowa. Justice Rutledge, a former law school dean, was a staunch libertarian and his views on freedom of religion were well established.

The compulsory-flag-salute issue quickly came up again in several states. In West Virginia the legal basis of the salute requirement was much broader than the authority of the Minersville school district. Now it was an order of the West Virginia State Board of Education, based on an act of the West Virginia Legislature, duly signed by the governor. That the *Gobitis* decision prompted this action cannot be doubted. For West Virginia amended its laws in 1941 so as to require all schools, public, parochial, and private, to prescribe courses "for the purpose of teaching, fostering and perpetuating the ideals, principles and spirit of Americanism, and increasing the knowledge of the organization and machinery of the government."

Implementing this statute, the state board of education, on January 9, 1942, approved a resolution that drew heavily on Justice Frankfurter's *Gobitis* opinion. It ordered school authorities in each community to make the flag salute "a regular part of the program of activities." This directive commanded that all teachers and pupils "shall be required to participate in the salute honoring the Nation represented by the flag." It also provided that "refusal to salute the flag be regarded as an act of insubordination, and shall be dealt with accordingly." The penalty was expulsion with readmission denied until compliance was agreed to. Moreover, an expelled child, not in school, was "unlawfully absent" and subject to proceedings as a "delinquent." Parents or guardians were liable to fines and jail terms.

As a result of the decree a number of the children of Jehovah's Witnesses were expelled from West Virginia schools and threatened with incarceration in reformatories for criminally inclined juveniles. Fathers and mothers were prosecuted. A group of these parents challenged the law and the implementing regulations as an invasion of individual rights. Walter Barnette, Paul Stull, and Lucy McClure sued in federal district court in Charleston for an injunction to stop enforcement of the compulsory aspects against Jehovah's Witnesses.

The positions taken by the contending sides amounted to a rematching of the adversaries in the Gobitis case. The parents, speaking for their children, objected to "an unconstitutional denial of religious freedom and free speech." The state board of education asserted its authority, cited *Gobitis,* and asked that the complaint be dismissed as without merit. Because of the importance of the controversy the federal district court set up a special bench of three judges to hear the case and called in a jurist from the federal court of appeals at Richmond, Virginia, Judge John J. Parker of North Carolina, as one of the three. The spin of the wheel of fate that brought Judge Parker into the case was curious, since the scholarly North Carolinian had reason to believe that adherence to precedents had been a leading factor in preventing his confirmation by the Senate when he was appointed to the Supreme Court in 1930 by President Herbert Hoover.

Be that as it may, Judge Parker and his colleagues on the special bench did not follow the *Gobitis* precedent. Pointing out that at least four justices were now opposed to *Gobitis* and that the majority in *Jones* v. *Opelika* distinguished *Gobitis* instead of relying upon it, the three judges issued a decree against enforcement of the compulsory flag salute in schools. Speaking through Judge Parker, they said:

> Under such circumstances, and believing as we do that the flag salute here required is violative of religious liberty when required of persons holding the religious views of plaintiffs, we feel that we would be recreant to our duty as judges if through a blind following of a decision which the Supreme Court itself has thus impaired as authority, we should deny protection to rights which we regard as among the most sacred of those protected by constitutional guaranties.

Thereupon the West Virginia State Board of Education appealed directly to the Supreme Court, as the law provided it might do. The case was heard in Washington on March 11, 1943. The West Virginia State Board of Education was represented before the highest tribunal by W. Holt Wooddell, state assistant attorney general, and from Indianapolis came a friend-of-the-court brief on behalf of the American Legion, which was beating the drums for the compulsory flag salute. The protesting West Virginians relied on counsel Hayden C. Covington of Philadelphia, who had assisted the Gobitis family three years earlier. The American Civil Liberties Union again presented a strong brief for individual liberty and so did the Committee on the Bill of Rights of the American Bar Association. Changes in the bar committee's personnel brought the names of Basil O'Connor and Abe Fortas, among others, to the side of the Jehovah's Witnesses.

When the Supreme Court handed down its second flag-salute decision in 1943, it truly was a Flag Day observance for the date actually was June 14. The *Gobitis* precedent was not ignored or bypassed. It was squarely and completely overruled, with direct reference to its wrongness. Chief Justice Stone, who had been joined by Justices Black, Douglas, and Murphy in the *Opelika* tax case, now had the further support of Justices Jackson and Rutledge. The 8 to 1 in *Gobitis* had become 6 to 3 the opposite way. In *West Virginia State Board of Education* v. *Barnette* only Justices Roberts and Reed were on the side of the Frankfurter dissent and they did not join in that opinion, but merely noted that they adhered to the views expressed in *Gobitis* and so believed that the judgment in the West Virginia case should be reversed.

The majority opinion of Justice Jackson and the dissent of Justice Frankfurter were two of the strongest opinions in Supreme Court history. Each was clear, direct, eloquent, and fraught with a sense of urgency, making the most convincing argument its author could marshal. A few sentences from the pros and cons will suggest what awaits the reader who goes to the full opinions. Justice Jackson stated:

A person gets from a symbol the meaning he puts into it, and what is one man's comfort and inspiration is another man's jest and scorn. . . .

To sustain the compulsory flag salute we are required to say that a Bill of Rights which guards the individual's right to speak his mind, left it open to public authorities to compel him to utter what is not in his mind. . . .

Those who begin coercive elimination of dissent soon find themselves exterminating dissenters. Compulsory unification of opinion achieves only the unanimity of the graveyard. . . . It seems trite but necessary to say that the First Amendment was designed to avoid these ends by avoiding these beginnings.

In conclusion Jackson struck off one of the golden paragraphs in the literature of the Supreme Court:

If there is any fixed star in our constitutional constellation, it is that no official, high or petty, can prescribe what shall be orthodox in politics, nationalism, religion, or other matters of opinion or force citizens to confess by word or act their faith therein. If there are any circumstances which permit an exception, they do not now occur to us.

On that high note, the new majority declared the action compelling the flag salute and pledge to be an unconstitutional invasion of "the sphere of intellect and spirit."

Justice Frankfurter began his dissent with what must be the most personal and poignant sentence ever written in a Supreme Court opinion. "One who belongs to the most vilified and persecuted minority in history," he said, "is not likely to be insensible to the freedoms guaranteed by our Constitution." After this arresting reference to himself, he continued:

Were my purely personal attitude relevant I should wholeheartedly associate myself with the general libertarian views in the Court's opinion, representing as they do the thought and action of a lifetime. But as judges we are neither Jew nor Gentile, neither Catholic nor agnostic. We owe equal attachment to the Constitution and are equally bound by our judicial obligations whether we derive our citizenship from the earliest or the latest immigrants to these shores. As a member of this Court I am not justified in writing my private notions of policy into the Constitution, no matter how deeply I may cherish them or how mischievous I may deem their disregard.

Justice Frankfurter then proceeded to reply to the majority with his own epigrammatic thrusts:

In the light of all the circumstances . . . it would require more daring than I possess to deny that reasonable legislators could have taken the action which is before us for review.

The constitutional protection of religious freedom terminated disabilities, it did not create new privileges. It gave religious equality, not civil immunity.

Law is concerned with external behavior and not with the inner life of man. . . . One may have the right to practice one's religion and at the same time owe the duty of formal obedience to laws that run counter to one's beliefs.

And so, three years almost to the day after the delivery of the *Gobitis* decision, that ruling was most impressively reversed. Seldom has the Court experienced so complete a change of heart in so short a time. As Justices Black and Douglas wrote in their concurring opinion in the *Barnette* case, the principle of *Gobitis* (that state legislatures must be allowed much freedom of action in dealing with local problems) was sound, but "its application in the particular case was wrong." And they added: "Words uttered under coercion are proof of loyalty to nothing but self-interest. Love of country must spring from willing hearts and free minds."

Chief Justice Stone, the lone dissenter in 1940, expressed his personal appreciation to Justice Black in a letter: "The sincerity and the good sense of what you have said will, I believe, make a very deep impression on the public conscience. It also states in simple and perfectly understandable form good constitutional law as I understand it." A venerated friend wrote him a congratulatory note, and the head of the Court replied: "All's well that ends well, but I should like to have seen the case end well in the first place without following such a devious route to the desired end."

In the next two decades many cases involving the constitutional separation of church and state would reach the same august bench. These tests would concern transportation of parochial school pupils, "released time" and "dismissed time" programs of sectarian devotions in public schools, the use of the mails for highly dubious appeals in the name of religion, and conscientious objection to arms-bearing as a bar to the practice of law and admission to citizenship. Still other legal controversies would swirl around censorship of motion pictures on grounds of immorality and sacrilege, Bible reading and recitation of officially approved prayers in public school rooms, and the requirement of a declaration of belief in the existence of God as a condition to holding public office.

Popular views about these and other issues concerning man's religion—or lack of it—would differ widely. But the compulsory-flag-salute cases were in a class by themselves. For they wrote a unique chapter in the history of the Supreme Court and its changing personnel in the midst of the worst war of all time. They would remain the most fascinating of all these cases for they dealt with little children and their parents, with intensely held faith in the Ten Commandments, and with the red, white, and blue symbol of the American nation under which some citizens would serve by withholding obeisance while others offered their lives.

The School Desegregation Case

BY ALFRED H. KELLY

(Brown v. Board of Education of the City of Topeka, 347 U.S. 483)

"Brown versus Board of Education" is probably the best-known and most important case in the modern history of the Supreme Court. The contrast it presents with the Court's early days, when John Marshall decided the fate of William Marbury, is startling. Then the nation was small, the Court's authority uncertain, the general view of the power of the federal government (indeed of all government) limited. The effectiveness of the Constitution was untested. In 1954 the United States was the most powerful nation on earth, the Court a tribunal of acknowledged might, the government's right to act with immense force in order to advance the general welfare unquestioned.

The meaning of the Constitution, however, remained subject to debate, and as individuals quarreled over its cryptic phraseology, the Supreme Court continued to interpret it, thus maintaining its vitality and securing the stability of the American political system.

More and more, what is and is not constitutional has come to depend on the general wisdom of the justices. But as this essay by the late Alfred H. Kelly makes clear, the justices must still depend on the actions of citizens intent upon their own ends who have brought their quarrels before it for settlement. Their strengths and weaknesses, their prejudices, canniness, determination, and intelligence inevitably influence the decisions of the Court. And these shape the future of all the people.

Kelly, an authority on constitutional history, played an important behind-the-scenes role in the drama he describes on the following pages.

On a certain warm and humid day in May 1896, when the Supreme Court of the United States delivered its opinion in the Louisiana "Jim Crow" car case, entitled *Plessy* v. *Ferguson*, [1] American

[1] See Chapter X.

THURGOOD MARSHALL WITH LITTLE ROCK
HIGH SCHOOL STUDENTS, 1958.

blacks stood at a kind of new nadir in their long struggle for decency and humanity. An overwhelming number of white Americans both North and South, the idealism of the Radical Republicans of a generation earlier now conveniently forgotten, rested secure in the comfortable assumption of the biological, cultural, and social superiority of the white race.

The "separate but equal doctrine" which incorporated this racial myth into law and upon which Justice Henry Billings Brown rested his decision, was almost a half-century old in 1896, having first been formulated in 1850 by a distinguished Massachusetts Supreme Court jurist, Lemuel Shaw, in a now famous school segregation case, *Roberts* v. *the City of Boston.* As of 1868, when the Fourteenth Amendment with its "equal protection clause" went onto the books, virtually all the states outside New England had some form of legalized racial segregation, most frequently in their public school laws.

Adoption of the Fourteenth Amendment had made no practical difference whatever in the status of such legislation, for one state supreme court after another had ruled that laws of this kind did not come within the purview of the new constitutional guarantee of "equal protection." Even as Brown spoke in 1896, nearly thirty states of the Union, including the entire South, the border states, New York, Indiana, Kansas, and most of the West including California, had "separate but equal" school laws on their books. At law there was a close parallel between Jim Crow car acts and Jim Crow school statutes, and Justice Brown brought them all together with a stroke of the judicial pen.

Constitutional purists frequently observe that Brown's remarks on segregated schools were mere *obiter dicta,* that is, side remarks not essential to the settlement of the case at hand, and under the rule of *stare decisis* therefore not legally binding on the Court in subsequent school cases. They observe, also, that the Court for some thirty years after the Plessy decision managed to avoid, seemingly with almost meticulous care, any specific decision that the *Plessy* rule applied to segregated state public schools and that state laws providing for such were compatible with the "equal protection" clause.

Not until *Gong Lum* v. *Lee,* in 1927, did the Supreme Court at last face the segregated school question squarely. Then Chief Justice

William Howard Taft declared that the matter of the constitutionality of segregated state public schools was one "which has many
times been decided [by the Supreme Court] to be within the power
of the state legislatures to settle without the intervention of the
federal courts under the federal constitution." Technically, Taft was
wrong and the constitutional purists are right—it had not been
formally "so decided" at all, let alone many times. But practically
Taft was right: there had been no serious disposition on the part of
the courts of the previous generation to challenge the "separate but
equal" rule, embodiment as it was of the overwhelmingly prevalent
myth of black inferiority.

It was to be a long road from *Plessy* and *Gong Lum* to that day in
May 1954 when Chief Justice Earl Warren, speaking for a unanimous Supreme Court, tossed the "separate but equal" rule into the
rubbish heap of outworn constitutional doctrine. But just as in
1896, when Brown had spoken for a segregated America, the Supreme Court in 1954 was still adhering to its own larger rule: it was
again "following the election returns." For in between *Plessy* and
Brown v. *the Board of Education of the City of Topeka* there ensued a vast
sociopolitical revolution in the status of American blacks.

Seen in historical perspective, it is now apparent that this twentieth-century "revolution" was to be no less far-reaching in its social
and political consequences than that earlier revolution in the status
of blacks precipitated by the Civil War and Radical Republican
Reconstruction. The "first revolution," 1861–68, freed the slaves
and endowed them with nominal citizenship and legal equality.
Once the revolutionary tide had subsided, however, it left them
stranded in what amounted, throughout most of the Republic, to an
inferior status reminiscent of that of the Helots of ancient Sparta or
the Untouchables of modern India. The "second revolution" in
status, which today is far from complete, was to inaugurate the
progressive destruction of the racial caste system in the United
States and to commence at the same time the genuine integration
of blacks into the social, economic, and political fabric of American
life.

The rise and progress of this vast new twentieth-century revolution in status makes up too complex a story to be told in great detail
here, but there can be no real grasp of the meaning of *Brown* v. *Board*
without some understanding of it. Perhaps it is no great oversim-

plification to assert that it had its beginnings in the rise of numerically important and hence politically significant black communities in the many large and middle-sized cities of the American North, resulting in turn from successive waves of migration from the states of the old Confederacy. Between 1910 and 1940, the black population of New York City rose from 60,000 to 450,000. That of Detroit increased from 4,000 to about 100,000 in these years, while Philadelphia's black population grew from 60,000 to 250,000 and Chicago's from 30,000 to 277,000. Lesser cities, such as Akron, Canton, Gary, and Rockford, experienced similar growth. By 1940 twenty-six Northern cities had black populations of 10,000 or more.

The small black elites in these cities, composed of lawyers, doctors, schoolteachers, social workers, ministers, and the like, exercised a political influence all out of proportion to their numbers. They represented a community which even in the North was frightfully ghettoized and discriminated against economically, but which nonetheless had one all-important instrument of political power denied them in the South—the vote. Black leaders used the votes they controlled to make alliances with local urban political machines, and so to win concessions for the black community. In Chicago, for example, blacks were an important element in the political machine put together in the 1920s by William Hale Thompson and his henchmen. Blacks traded votes with Thompson for jobs on the city police force and the city hall bureaucracy, assurances of fair play in the courts, access to a "fair share" of the city's bathing beaches, a lax attitude toward rent evictions, and so on. Similar alliances in the 1920s came into existence between the black community and the Vare machine in Philadelphia and the Tammany Hall organization in New York.

Political power of this kind in the 1920s was still essentially localized and without much influence on national political parties or national policy. However, the Great Depression and the New Deal nationalized the blacks' political significance in the great cities of the North by incorporating black voters as an essential ingredient in the new political machine which Franklin Roosevelt put together after 1933. Blacks suffered severely in the depression, and came into the Roosevelt political combine with a new awareness of their significance and a powerful determination to make the most of it. For the first time since Reconstruction, they had a recognized position in a winning political combination of national scope.

The blacks' new political power revived almost immediately an old, old dream—that of "first-class citizenship" in an integrated America. For two reasons, however, this dream found no very important political expression in the immediate postdepression period. First, the early New Deal had an overwhelming preoccupation with problems concerned with economic rehabilitation, a preoccupation which blacks fully shared. In some cities of the North, for example, both direct relief and such agencies as WPA and PWA amounted almost to black rescue operations.

Equally important in inhibiting any powerful New Deal drive for desegregation was the fact that Roosevelt's political combination rested upon a delicate balance between two exceedingly disparate parts: Northern urban political machines and Southern white Democratic conservatives of the type represented by Senators Joe Robinson of Arkansas, Tom Connally of Texas, and Pat Harrison of Mississippi. To these men any desegregation drive would have been anathema, and thus would have threatened party unity.

However, the World War II crisis worked another substantial acceleration in the growth of black political power and influence. First, it created an unprecedentedly large demand for labor in the great cities of the North. This not only produced a new wave of migration from the South, which increased the voting power of the Northern black community, it also forced blacks into jobs, pay ratings, union memberships, and the like never open before. The wartime Detroit story of the black laborer who upon drawing his first defense-job paycheck cried out in jubiliation, "Thank God for Hitler," is not without its point.

Second, the equalitarian ideology of American war propaganda, which presented the United States as a champion of democracy engaged in a death struggle with the German racists, created in the minds and hearts of most white people a new and intense awareness of the shocking contrast between the country's too comfortable image of itself and the cold realities of American racial segregation. Both pragmatic propaganda interests and the new idealism demanded further integration, both in society and in the war effort.

Some of this crisis-imposed, wartime integration took place on an official level: in a series of executive orders, the Roosevelt administration expanded the employment of blacks in the federal bureaucracy, wrote "no discrimination" clauses into war contracts, established in 1941 the Fair Employment Practices Commission, and even took a few hesitant steps toward racial integration in the armed forces. Meantime, in 1939, Attorney General Frank Murphy, already something of a radical idealist on the integration and civil rights questions, had established the Civil Rights Division in the Department of Justice, which in turn undertook what was to prove to be a generation-long legal quest for new federal guarantees against lynching and new safeguards for black voting rights. Congress also bestirred itself. The Soldiers Vote Act of 1942 abolished the poll tax as a prerequisite for voting by members of the armed services, while the so-called La Follette Civil Liberties Committee began its own investigation into the lynching problem.

It was inevitable that the new political power of blacks enhanced their economic position, and the vast improvement in ideological climate in the country presently would spill over into the courts. The dynamics of this process are hardly mysterious. Several of the Roosevelt appointees to the Court after 1937 were practical politicians whom the exigencies of the New Deal had made intensely aware of the "political power shift" implicit in the blacks' new party role. Hugo Black, Robert Jackson, Frank Murphy, and Wiley Rutledge all fell into this category. Or, like Felix Frankfurter and William O. Douglas, the new appointees were legal academicians who reflected the equalitarian idealism of the liberal university communities of the North.

James Byrnes, to be sure, was a thoroughgoing conservative on the race question who later would mobilize his state in an all-out defense of the Southern segregation citadel, but he did not remain on the Court very long. And against him one could balance Harlan Fiske Stone, whom Roosevelt rewarded for his imaginative treatment of New Deal legislation with promotion to chief justice in 1941 upon the retirement of Charles Evans Hughes.

It needs only to be added here that the succession of justices appointed to the Court after the war—Fred M. Vinson, Harold Burton, Sherman Minton, and Tom Clark—while they tended generally to be more conservative than New Deal era justices, nonetheless had been trained in the hard practical school of politics and shared to the full an awareness of the altered position of blacks in

American society. Earl Warren, the mild-mannered middle-of-the-road Republican who came to the chief justiceship in 1953, epitomized as no one else could have this new politico-judicial understanding.

It is hardly open to question, then, that this flow of Democratic and Republican appointees to the High Court after 1937 would in no great length of time have produced something of a constitutional revolution in the status of blacks. But this process, inevitable as it may well have been, was vastly accelerated by the legal assault on segregation first launched in the late 1930s by the National Association for the Advancement of Colored People. The desegregation campaign commenced about 1935 by the NAACP got under way very slowly, but it continued without interruption and with growing success for the next generation. It was a campaign which would make the NAACP the "cutting edge" of all the complex social and political forces that were at work to produce a desegregated America.

The NAACP, organized back in 1909 as an offshoot of the so-called Niagara Movement after a series of infamous Illinois race riots, had speedily become one of the two or three most influential black pressure groups in the country. Under the leadership of board chairman Joel R. Spingarn, a Columbia University English professor, the Association by 1922 had attained a membership of some 100,000 and had about four hundred active chapters scattered across the country.

During the 1920s, however, the NAACP was as yet not devoted very clearly to any broad integrationist program, although on occasion its leaders gave expression to the old dream of first-class citizenship. Walter White, the exceedingly competent executive secretary who took over principal direction of the organization in the mid-1920s, devoted most of his energies to activities that promised more immediate returns: campaigns against lynching, interventions to secure fair trials in criminal cases which had racist overtones (as in the notorious 1922 Sweet murder trial in Detroit, where the Association enlisted the services of Clarence Darrow in a successful defense of a black who had fired into a crowd attacking his home), and so on. In 1930 the Association succeeded in blocking the nomination of John J. Parker as a Supreme Court justice. So far from any clear desegregationist objective was the NAACP in this era that W.

E. B. Du Bois, the distinguished historian who edited the Association's principal journal, *The Crisis,* consistently preached a kind of extreme militant black segregationism, then in harmony with the professed objectives of the Communist party.

However, the nationalization of black political power in the New Deal era produced a radical new shift in NAACP objectives. It was now possible for blacks once more to take up seriously the old dream, all but abandoned after Reconstruction, of total integration. Walter White, who now envisioned the Association as the principal instrument for accomplishing this objective, soon broke with Du Bois, who in 1934 severed his connection with the organization. White's call for a desegregation campaign soon justified itself completely. It brought a great leap forward in Association membership, which by 1945 was to total more than 300,000 in some sixteen hundred active chapters. Significantly, much of this new activity centered in the South, where White's militancy evoked startling expressions of a new black spirit.

Along with new objectives came a fresh crop of leaders. White, who realized early that one of the most promising "fronts" in the campaign was destined to be the courts, deliberately attracted into the Association a number of brilliant young black lawyers, who were to become the Association's principal reservoir of brains and legal skill in its generation-long campaign for legal desegregation in America.

The Association's early desegregation cases were under the general direction of Charles Houston, an Amherst Phi Beta Kappa, Harvard Law School graduate, and dean of the Howard University Law School, whom William Hastie was later to describe as "the Moses" who "led us through the wilderness of second-class citizenship toward the dimly perceived promised land of legal equality." Houston's ability and dedication also attracted lawyers to the Association cause. Among them were Hastie himself, one day to become a judge of the United States court of appeals; James Nabrit, who presently succeeded Houston as dean of the Howard Law School; Ralph Bunche, who after 1945 would acquire world fame as a delegate to the United Nations; and William R. Ming, successively a professor of law at Howard and the University of Chicago and a highly successful practicing attorney in Chicago. Others included Loren Moore, a Chicago lawyer and officer of the National Bar

Association; Spottswood Robinson III, a Richmond lawyer who would one day assume a prominent role in the Brown case; Loren Miller of Los Angeles, and George Vaughn of St. Louis.

Destined to become by far the greatest legal asset of the Association, however, was Thurgood Marshall, a native of Baltimore, graduate of Lincoln University in Pennsylvania, and a product of Houston's training at the Howard Law School. Marshall, who joined the NAACP legal staff in the mid-1930s, brought to the Association a wonderfully keen and incisive mind, a sharp sense of legal strategy and political realities, and an ebullient spirit tempered both by a mordant sense of humor and a deep dedication to the cause. In 1939, he became general counsel of the newly created NAACP Legal Defense and Education Fund, a unit technically divorced from the Association's propaganda and legislative activities. By 1950, Marshall, through the Legal Defense Fund, was directing the expenditure of some $150,000 annually in the prosecution of various desegregation cases throughout the country. So great was his success that the black community had come to know him as "Mr. Civil Rights."

There were a number of "fronts" in the Association's early legal campaign against segregation of which the attack on Jim Crow schools was only one. Others included suits against so-called white primaries, against restrictive covenants in housing, and against Jim Crow transportation. The attack on white primaries, after some reverses, met with success in 1944 when the Supreme Court ruled that such elections violated the Fifteenth Amendment. Prosecution directed against segregation in transportation was also successful. Milestones came in *Mitchell* v. *United States* (1941), where the Supreme Court in effect ordered the desegregation of Pullman facilities; in *Morgan* v. *Virginia* (1945), in which the Court struck down state laws imposing racial segregation in interstate transportation facilities; and in *Henderson* v. *United States* (1950), in which the Court knocked out dining car segregation. (This series of decisions was capped in 1955 by an Interstate Commerce Commission order directing the complete desegregation of all interstate transportation facilities in the country.)

Of more ultimate significance for the *Brown* case was the Association's campaign to destroy restrictive racial covenants, in the course of which the NAACP developed a series of techniques which were to prove of great value in the campaign against school segregation. Of great importance was the resort to a series of regional and national lawyers' planning conferences, in which Marshall's New York office became a kind of "general staff headquarters," coordinating policy and strategy with the local attorneys handling such cases. The Association also engaged in extensive consultation with academic experts in economics, sociology, housing, and public administration, another technique which would prove to be of great value in fighting school segregation. It was also able to bring about publication of numerous sympathetic articles in legal journals propounding the Association's point of view toward restrictive convenants. Finally, Marshall and his colleagues expended much time and money on careful staff planning, both in New York and in "the field." The climax of this carefully staged and well-coordinated campaign came in 1948, when the Supreme Court, in *Shelley* v. *Kraemer,* ruled that neighborhood racial covenants, while not in themselves unlawful, nonetheless could not be enforced in state courts, since such enforcement constituted state action in support of discrimination and hence violated the Fourteenth Amendment.

The Association's attack on segregated schools began in the mid-1930s, but for some years it yielded decidedly meager results. For a time, Houston and White toyed with the notion of flooding the Southern states with a massive series of taxpayers' suits against elementary and secondary school segregation, which they hoped, somewhat optimistically, would force the Southern states to abandon dual school systems as impossibly expensive.

However, Houston sooned junked this idea as impracticable. Instead, he and his lieutenants hit upon the stratagem of an "indirect attack" on the "segregation fortress"—a series of suits to force the admission of blacks to Southern graduate professional schools, above all state university law schools. Several major considerations led NAACP officials to adopt this scheme. First, most Southern states did not even attempt to maintain a facade of equality in professional educational facilities, so that their classic "separate but equal" defense, the Association hoped, would prove to be inapplicable. Second, NAACP lawyers believed that if the Southern states countered this strategy by trying to provide genuinely equal facilities in graduate education, the effort would prove to be both awesomely expensive and impossible to achieve. In any event, since the education of only a few graduate students would be at issue, the Association hoped that the Southern states, confronted with a long and difficult legal battle, might "break down" and admit qualified blacks to white professional schools.

The NAACP lawyers were also deliberately exploiting a peculiarity of Southern racial sentiment. The South, Houston and his colleagues knew, somehow regarded racial mixing in graduate and professional education as far less invidious than in primary and secondary schools or even in collegiate education. As a consequence, they hoped, Southern officials might be expected to resist graduate school integration with less emotional conviction than would be the case for lower-level schools. As Marshall, with characteristic humor, later put the matter:

Those racial supremacy boys somehow think that little kids of six or seven are going to get funny ideas about sex and marriage just from going to school together, but for some equally funny reason youngsters in law school aren't supposed to feel that way. We didn't get it but we decided that if that was what the South believed, then the best thing for the moment was to go along.

This "beachhead" strategy in the attack on school segregation started slowly enough, although it eventually yielded spectacular results. The first important victory came in 1938, when the Supreme Court ruled, in *Missouri ex rel Gaines* v. *Canada,* that refusal of a state university to admit a black to its law school, there being no comparable "separate but equal" institution available, constituted a violation of the "equal protection" clause. Missouri, following a custom then common among Southern states, had offered to pay the prospective student's expenses to an unsegregated school in the North. But the Court refused to accept this device any longer. By Missouri's laws, Chief Justice Hughes's opinion pointed out, "a privilege has been created for white law students which is denied to Negroes." Sending the student to school in another state could not "remove the discrimination," which violated the Fourteenth Amendment.

The Gaines decision constituted, after all, only a very small breach in the wall of Southern segregation, and for some time no further advances occurred. War conditions and—as Marshall admitted later—a general lack of interest on the part of potential black graduate and professional students prevented the Association from following up its victory for the next several years. Ironically, even Gaines failed to take advantage of the educational opportunity won for him and instead mysteriously disappeared.

Then at length, in 1948, in *Sipuel* v. *Board of Regents,* the Association's lawyers scored again, as the Supreme Court unanimously struck down an Oklahoma attempt to deny a black admission to the state university law school. Superficially, the decision resembled that in the *Gaines* case, but its significance became apparent when the Oklahoma Board of Regents soon thereafter voted, seven to one, to admit blacks to any course of study not provided by the State College for Negroes. In short, Oklahoma now recognized that duplication of facilities for professional education was impossible. "You can't build a cyclotron for one student," Oklahoma University President George L. Cross was said to have remarked at the time.

Two years later, in 1950, came Marshall's far more dramatic victory in *Sweatt* v. *Painter,* in which the Supreme Court spoiled a spectacular Texas attempt to turn the equal protection question aside by setting up overnight a separate law school for blacks. The plaintiff, a Houston mail carrier, had pressed an Association-backed suit in the state courts for admission to the law school of the University of Texas. But the state supreme court, instead of granting the request, had merely ordered the university to furnish Sweatt with "substantially equal" facilities for a legal education. Thereupon the university, in an atmosphere of intense controversy highlighted by faculty and student mass meetings on both sides of the question, "fitted out" a special law school and invited Sweatt to attend.

Sweatt, backed by Marshall and his colleagues, of course refused to oblige, and instead sued once more in the state courts. Marshall now deliberately drew heavily upon the techniques which the Association had matured in the covenant cases. A parade of legal and academic experts came to the stand, all of them carefully calculated to furnish testimony which would overwhelm the state's argument that the fly-by-night law school in question could in any real sense constitute substantial equality. Professor Malcolm Sharp of the University of Chicago Law School and Dean Charles Thompson of the Howard University Law School both testified to the hopeless inadequacy of the school when measured against its white counterpart.

Marshall's *pièce de résistance* was the testimony of Robert Redfield, a distinguished University of Chicago anthropologist. Very carefully Marshall led Redfield through testimony calculated to show that contemporary anthropology had virtually discarded the notion that there were any inherent differences between whites and blacks. Thus, quite deliberately and without fanfare, Marshall opened his attack upon the social theory lying behind the "separate but equal" dictum, even though this strategy was not immediately relevant to settlement of the *Sweatt* case itself. The Texas supreme court, setting testimony of this sort to one side, again ruled against Sweatt.

However, the Supreme Court of the United States on appeal ordered Sweatt's admission to the university's white law school. Chief Justice Vinson's opinion ridiculed the Texan claim that the state had managed to establish facilities for legal education that had any substantial equality, in faculty, library, or prestige. "It is difficult to believe," Vinson said, "that one who had a free choice between these law schools would consider the question close."

Once admitted, Sweatt promptly flunked out. But this unhappy denouement hardly damaged the case's legal significance: the attempt to provide overnight "separate but equal" facilities could not stand up in court.

McLaurin v. *Oklahoma Regents,* another Supreme Court decision handed down the same day as the Sweatt case, constituted an almost equally significant Association victory. Here the University of Oklahoma, compelled by suit to admit a black to its School of Education, had attempted to maintain segregation within the university itself by compelling the student to sit in a roped-off class section marked "reserved for colored," to use like reserved sections in the library and dining room, and so on. Unhesitatingly, the Court struck this practice down. Restrictions of this sort, Vinson's opinion said sternly, inevitably "handicapped" the student in his pursuit of "effective graduate instruction" and so violated the Fourteenth Amendment.

It was obvious to Marshall and his lieutenants that the *Sweatt* and *McLaurin* cases were of great significance, for they could be used to destroy racial segregation in graduate education virtually everywhere in the South. On the other hand, technically the Court had done nothing whatever to undermine the old *Plessy* "separate but equal rule." On the contrary, in one sense, at least, it had strengthened it, since in both cases it had held that the facilities in question were inadequate solely because they failed to meet the standard that the "separate but equal" rule required. Although equality in segregated facilities might well be impossible to achieve at the graduate level, there seemed to be no reason why the South at large, given a little time and the willingness to spend a goodly amount of money, might not achieve such equality for its black primary and secondary schools. Indeed, all over the South, white boards of education, reading this implication into the *Sweatt* and *McLaurin* decisions, began crash programs of school building, calculated, as Governor Byrnes of South Carolina presently frankly confessed, "to remedy a hundred years of neglect" of black education, lest the Supreme Court "take matters out of the state's hands."

Marshall later admitted that the NAACP was at this point at a kind of crossroads. The legal gap between the *Sweatt* and *McLaurin* cases on the one hand and an outright destruction of the *Plessy* precedent appeared to be appallingly wide, and he and his colleagues were not at all sure they could cross it. Might it not be well to "go along" with the Southern procedure, at least in part? At this stage of the game, Marshall later told the author, if the school boards in key Southern states had shown a general disposition to accept any kind of gradualist program combining more adequate schools with some primary and secondary desegregation, the Association might well have agreed to cooperate, at least for a time.

Instead, school boards in South Carolina and in Virginia's Prince Edward County, both critical areas in the Association's planning, rejected outright all overtures for a gradualist program. "Sometimes history takes things into its own hands," Marshall said later, indicating that in his opinion Southern intransigence literally drove the NAACP to wage all-out war in the courts on segregated schools at every level.

Following a national conference on strategy in New York in September 1950, Marshall and his staff commenced the prosecution of five segregation suits, at carefully selected points around the country. In Topeka, Kansas; in Clarendon County, South Carolina; and in Prince Edward County, Virginia, the Association filed suits in equity in federal district courts, in the name of local black schoolchildren, demanding their admission to white schools. These suits charged not only that local schools for blacks were inferior to their white counterparts, but also that the "separate but equal" rule itself violated the equal protection clause of the Fourteenth Amendment. Another suit commenced in the chancery court of the state of Delaware made substantially the same demands. A fifth action, begun in the District of Columbia, charged that segregation in the nation's capital violated the due process clause of the Fifth Amendment, the same constitutional provision which Chief Justice Taney, nearly a hundred years earlier, had drawn on in the *Dred Scott* case to rule that slavery could not be barred from any federal territory.

As Marshall had calculated, these cases at the outset encountered substantial failure. In the *Topeka* case, which presently would lend its name to the celebrated 1954 decision, the three-man federal court ruled not only that *Plessy* v. *Ferguson* was still the law of the land, but also that local black and white schools were substantially comparable in quality. The three-man federal court in South Carolina conceded that the facilities were indeed unequal, but it merely ordered the Clarendon school board to initiate measures calculated to raise black schools to a level comparable to that of the white schools. And like the court in Kansas, it also ruled that *Plessy* was still good law, although one member of the court dissented at length, arguing that school segregation violated the Fourteenth Amendment on its face.

In the Virginia suit, Spottswood Robinson and his associate Oliver Hill used the now familiar technique, borrowed originally from the covenant cases, of introducing extensive testimony from social scientists, including the distinguished black psychologist Kenneth Clark of New York University. These experts testified at length both as to the marked inferiority of local black schools and the damaging effects of segregation generally upon both black and white children. But the court, sweeping all this testimony aside, refused to grant the plaintiffs any relief whatever. Conceding that the black schools were indeed "substantially inferior," the court held that the school board was now moving rapidly to construct new ones, so that "an injunction could accomplish nothing more." Meanwhile, in the District of Columbia case, Marshall's carefully drawn brief encountered a similar fate, the court refusing to overturn adverse precedents of earlier years.

Only in Delaware, where Marshall's assistant Jack Greenberg and the quiet, Harvard-trained Louis Redding argued the Association's cause, did an initial suit score even a partial victory. Here the chancery court granted an injunction ordering the children in question forthwith admitted to white schools on the ground that the schools involved were indeed "substantially unequal." On appeal, the Delaware supreme court upheld this finding. Even here, however, the court refused to overturn the *Plessy* rule itself, implying instead that a more adequate school program might sometime in the future make racial segregation lawful.

All this, of course, amounted to little more than preliminary legal sparring. During the course of 1952, the Supreme Court granted reviews in all five of the foregoing cases, and in December the Court heard arguments from both sides. Marshall, Nabrit, Redding, Greenberg, and the other NAACP lawyers involved contended that *Plessy* v. *Ferguson* had been erroneously decided and was in any event obsolete, while Edward T. McGranahan, President Truman's attorney general, also filed a brief as *amicus curiae* asking the Court to declare school segregation invalid under the equal protection clause. In addition, in an appendix to the Association's brief, thirty social scientists of national reputation, among them R. M. McIver, Floyd Allport, Robert Redfield, Alfred McClung Lee, and Kenneth Clark, not only attacked school segregation as possible in fact "only insofar as it is combined with discrimination" against black children, but also argued at length that segregation did vast psychic damage to all children. In turn, John W. Davis, constitutional lawyer and former Democratic presidential candidate of 1924, presented a "powerful and effective" argument in defense of segregation for the school boards.

In June 1953, after a six-month silence, the Supreme Court spoke. Instead of handing down a simple "yes" or "no" decision, however, the justices set the case for reargument, and asked counsel to prepare answers to a series of historical questions the justices now propounded, most of them having to do with the original intent of the framers of the Fourteenth Amendment with respect to school segregation.

"What evidence is there," the Court now asked, "that the Congress which submitted and the state legislatures that ratified the Fourteenth Amendment . . . understood that it would abolish segregation in the public schools?" Assuming that Congress and the states had made no such assumption, the Court continued, was there nevertheless any evidence that the framers of the amendment had understood that Congress might legislate in pursuance of it to abolish school segregation or that the federal courts might properly construe the amendment as "abolishing such segregation of its own force"? And was it, in any event, within the Court's judicial power to order the abolition of segregated schools, even if the framers' original intent remained unclear? Finally, and very significantly, the Court asked counsel whether, if the justices were to declare school segregation unconstitutional, it would thereby necessarily follow that the Court must forthwith admit black children to the "white schools of their choice," or whether it might, in the exercise of its equity powers, "permit an effective gradual adjustment" from existing segregated school systems "to a system not based on color distinctions."

The very nature of these queries made it evident that the NAACP already had scored a significant victory. In a sense, the Court already had "taken sides," in that it had at long last consented to reexamine the question of the Fourteenth Amendment's "original" meaning. The implication in the very raising of such a question was obvious enough. The Court intended to destroy the "separate but equal" rule if it could discover a plausible rationale for doing so. The justices, in fact, seemed virtually to be saying something like the following to the NAACP lawyers: "Provide us, if you can, with some plausible historical argument which will relieve us of undue embarrassment and we will only too gladly set the 'separate but equal' rule aside."

Here was opportunity—magnificent opportunity, as Marshall and his fellows recognized—but opportunity hedged about with evident danger. The Association lawyers were not historians, and they had no idea of what a careful examination of the evidence might reveal. The debates in the *Congressional Globe* for 1866 might not reveal the framers' intent with respect to school segregation. Worse yet, investigation of the historical record might even provide the proponents of segregation with historical arguments so decisive that the Court would feel itself obliged to confirm the *Plessy* rule. As Marshall put it later, what looked like a "golden gate" might "turn out to be a booby trap with a bomb in it."

Confronted with this touchy problem, Marshall decided to turn once more to the academic world for assistance—a step he would later characterize as "the smartest move I ever made in my life." He called an NAACP conference to meet in New York in late September, and issued invitations to some 130 social scientists, most of them American historians and constitutional experts. At the same time, he sought out and commissioned several historians to prepare research papers on various aspects of the questions the Court had posed. Howard J. Graham of Los Angeles and the present author, both constitutional historians, prepared monographs on the passage and ratification of the Fourteenth Amendment by Congress and the states, while the historians C. Vann Woodward and John Hope Franklin prepared monographs on the role of segregation in Southern Reconstruction. Horace Bond, then president of Lincoln University in Pennsylvania, prepared a monograph on state public schools in the Reconstruction Era.

All this activity promised to be exceedingly expensive, and in late June Marshall announced that the Association had raised a special fund of $32,700 for legal research, conferences, and other expenses in connection with the forthcoming presentation to the Supreme Court. The CIO presently donated $2,500 to the Legal Defense Fund for this purpose, while the *Pittsburgh Courier,* a leading black newspaper, also raised several thousand dollars to help pay the expenses of the September conference. Other gifts, both large and small, poured in over the next few months from a variety of sources. One morning in November, for example, Marshall found fifteen shares of a valuable oil stock in his mail, together with a simple penciled notation—"Use for school cases." All this was dramatic evidence of the new position of blacks in American society. No longer were they helpless pawns whose fate rested in the hands of contending white factions. Instead, their economic power and political prestige enabled the Association's lawyers to raise the funds necessary to fight this last critical school segregation battle.

The strategy conference convened on September 23, with headquarters at the Press Club and the Algonquin Hotel. Some forty historians and constitutional experts had answered the Association's call. Present were all the authors of the various monographs Marshall had commissioned, with the exception of Howard Graham, while Marshall had also recruited constitutional experts Robert K. Carr of Dartmouth; Robert Cushman, Jr., and Milton Konvitz of Cornell; Walter Gellhorn of the Columbia Law School; and John

Frank of the Yale Law School. In addition, the NAACP staff lawyers were in attendance; these included, beside Marshall himself, Robert Carter (who had argued the Kansas case in the lower courts), Jack Greenberg, and Constance Motley. Present also were the various lawyers from "the field" who had worked on one or another phase of the several cases, among them Robinson, Redding, Ming, and Nabrit.

The conference, which organized itself into a series of small seminars broken by periodic general sessions, concerned itself mainly with the evidence which the historians had turned up in their various research papers and the way this material ought to be incorporated in the forthcoming brief. The evidence involved was both good and bad. The most serious difficulty which emerged was clear enough: the Civil Rights Act of 1866, quite generally regarded by historians as the immediate progenitor of the Fourteenth Amendment, had been amended in the House specifically to eliminate any prohibition of state racial segregation laws. This had been done at the insistence of John A. Bingham of Ohio, who shortly became one of the authors of the amendment itself. At first blush, this looked very bad for the Association's cause.

Fortunately, however, there was a good deal more to the historical record. Bingham himself, in arguing for the critical amendment to the Civil Rights Bill, had asserted that his objections rested solely upon a want of congressional power, and that the proper way to achieve the desegregation objective was by constitutional amendment. This was conceivably a reference to the Fourteenth Amendment itself, presently reported to the floor of Congress by the Committee of Fifteen, of which Bingham was a member.

An examination of the debates on the amendment itself added strength to this supposition. In the Senate, Jacob Howard of Michigan had asserted categorically in presenting the amendment that the proposal "abolishes all class legislation in the states" and "would do away with the injustice of subjecting one class of persons to a code not applicable to another."

In both Houses, proponents of the amendment had talked grandly of equalitarian purposes far broader than the relatively narrow guarantees of the recent Civil Rights Act. Senator Poland of Vermont, for example, described the amendment as one which would "uproot and destroy" all discriminatory legislation which "violates the spirit of the Declaration of Independence," and he went on to point out that such an amendment was deemed necessary because "persons entitled to high consideration" (i.e., Bingham) had raised objections to doing so by legislation alone. In short, it appeared that the amendment, when carefully considered, could be conceived as having purposes broad enough to encompass the destruction of segregation either by statute or Court decision.

The historians, in short, had succeeded in demonstrating that the NAACP had something of a case with respect to congressional intent to destroy state segregation laws generally. But it was by no means an open-and-shut case. It rested upon the demonstration of a certain "general atmosphere" of broad purpose in the Thirty-ninth Congress rather than upon any specific showing of formally announced purpose.

The problem of strategy for the Association's lawyers therefore remained very serious. At the conference, William Ming argued forcibly that the evidence from the actual congressional debates was too scanty to build a convincing case on specific intent and that the Association's lawyers therefore ought to fall back upon a demonstration of the very broad equalitarian purposes of the antislavery crusaders and Republican Radicals before and during the Civil War. The historians present contended, on the contrary, that there appeared to be enough specific evidence to provide the Court with at least a plausible series of favorable answers to the questions it had asked. The September conference ended with this question of fundamental strategy unresolved.

In mid-October, Marshall called Ming and the present author back to New York. He asked the former to essay the drafting of a brief, with the constitutional historian sitting at his shoulder to advise him upon what he could or could not legitimately say without exceeding the bounds of historical accuracy. Three or four days of sharp interchange and argument produced a draft which Ming thought satisfactory.

However, after a series of conferences with the various staff and field lawyers, Marshall decided that this draft, while valuable, needed drastic revision. For the Ming brief failed to come to grips directly with the questions which the Court had posed, resorting instead to a very generalized exposition. Marshall feared that the justices, particularly Frankfurter and Douglas, the academicians on the Court, would resent this tactic as sophistic, devious, and even dishonest. "I gotta argue these cases," Marshall presently explained, "and if I try this approach those fellows will shoot me down in flames."

Accordingly, in early November, Marshall staged a new series of small conferences at the Legal Defense Fund offices in New York. Over a period of several days, Marshall, John Frank of the Yale Law School, and the present author reworked the Ming draft very carefully, this time coming to grips directly with the historical queries the Court had posed. The new line of argument emphasized the distinction between the narrow scope of the Civil Rights Act of 1866 and the much broader purposes of the Fourteenth Amendment itself. It came down hard on Senator Howard's sweeping language in presenting the amendment to the floor of the Senate, and it dwelt at some length on the broad equalitarian objectives which Bingham, Poland, Thaddeus Stevens, and other members of Congress had expounded in the course of the subsequent debate. So modified and rewritten, the brief was then polished and perfected in numerous long and exhausting sessions participated in both by interested social scientists and by the various lawyers involved. By mid-November, the brief was ready.

The brief's argument was, of course, not history in any professional sense; rather it was legal advocacy. That is, it sought to place the most favorable gloss upon the critical historical evidence that the Association's staff and advisers could develop without going beyond the facts. This process was later attacked by Southern segregationists, who argued that the NAACP, with the unscrupulous help of social scientists, somehow succeeded in deceiving the Court into making a wholly unjustified decision.

Such criticism, however, ignores the whole Anglo-American system of advocacy, which demanded that Marshall and his colleagues —and the other side as well—present the Court with the best case they could muster. Inherent in this system is the assumption that the court will itself be able to reach a balanced and intelligent conclusion after weighing the arguments presented by both sides. That the Court, in any event, was deceived either by Marshall's brief or the equally biased and lopsided prosegregationist brief of John W. Davis is unlikely in the extreme. The Court unquestionably was looking for a way out. Repeatedly, during the planning of the NAACP case, Marshall had told his advisers that they did not need to *win* the historical argument. All that was required was a face-saving draw. "A nothin'-to-nothin' score," he said with typical directness, "means we win the ball game." Actually, in *Brown* v. *Board* the justices put aside the historical evidence and based their decision upon "sociological" grounds. In short no deceit was intended, and none occurred.

On November 15, the Association filed with the Court its formal brief in *Brown* v. *Board of Education of the City of Topeka.* "The evidence makes clear," this document proclaimed, "that it was the intent of the proponents of the Fourteenth Amendment that it could, of its own force, prohibit all state action based upon race or color" and "all segregation in public education." The "separate but equal" rule of *Plessy* v. *Ferguson,* the brief added, had been "conceived in error" and should be reversed forthwith. Moreover, any delay in executing the judgment of the Court would involve "insurmountable difficulties," so that the plaintiff children in question should be admitted at once, "without distinctions of race or color," to the schools of their choice.

A few days later, Attorney General Herbert Brownell, acting technically as "a friend of the Court," filed the long-awaited brief of the Department of Justice. The stand the Eisenhower administration would take on school segregation had been the subject of considerable political speculation, for it involved a critical matter of Republican party strategy: whether the administration should continue its courtship of Southern Democrats or recognize frankly the political importance of the powerful Northern black vote. This dilemma, which was further sharpened by the decisive stand in favor of desegregation which the Truman administration had assumed a year earlier, had lately been the subject of repeated conferences between Brownell and the President.

Brownell's brief cut through the Republicans' dilemma very nicely by declaring in favor of desegregation but expressing the hope that the Court would order a transition period before desegregation became fully effective. The brief conceded that the historical evidence as to the intent of the amendment's authors was "not conclusive," but emphasized nonetheless the amendment's broad equalitarian purpose—"to secure for Negroes full and complete equality before the law and to abolish all legal distinctions based upon race." Hence, the brief concluded, the Court now could properly construe the amendment to prohibit segregated schools, but it would do well to order a one-year transition period in the South, because of the complex social and educational problems involved.

This analysis produced an outburst of anger and disappointment in the South. Representative E. C. Gathings of Arkansas accused the attorney general of "trying to subvert the will of the people," while Governor Tallmadge of Georgia attacked the brief as "wholly political." "Radical elements are vying with each other to see who can plunge the dagger deepest into the heart of the South," Tallmadge proclaimed.

The briefs for the various "respondent" school boards, filed over a period of several days in late November, contained hardly any surprises. The Delaware brief, for example, emphasized the significance of the fact that Reconstruction Congresses had repeatedly voted funds for segregated schools in the District of Columbia, clear evidence, it contended, that the authors of the Fourteenth Amendment had not intended to strike at segregated schools. South Carolina's brief, while reinforcing this historical argument, argued that the fundamental issue was one of states' rights—"whether the people of South Carolina may, on the exercise of their judgment, based on a first-hand knowledge of local conditions, decide that the state objective of free public education is best served by a system consisting of separate schools for white and colored children." Virginia asserted on its part that a reversal of the "separate but equal" rule would "overthrow the established meaning of the Fourteenth Amendment." The city of Topeka already had notified the Court that it was voluntarily desegregating its school system, but Kansas nonetheless filed a brief arguing that "federal interference" in the state's schools "is neither necessary nor justified." The District of Columbia's brief, evading higher argument, merely pointed out that the Fourteenth Amendment did "not apply" to it.

On December 8, a Supreme Court chamber filled to overflowing heard Marshall and Spottswood Robinson argue that the framers of the Fourteenth Amendment had intended to ban segregation "as a last vestige of slavery." John W. Davis, presenting oral arguments for the respondents, asserted in reply with equal confidence and force that "it is not within the judicial power" for the Court to set aside, merely "on a sociological basis," a school system that "has stood for three-quarters of a century."

The justices themselves interrupted from time to time to ask an occasional searching question. Frankfurter rather pointedly inquired of Marshall whether, if the Southern states now were to agree to spend money for "more and better schools for Negroes," he would still insist that segregation was unconstitutional. Needless to say, the justice got a strongly affirmative answer. And Douglas asked Solicitor General J. Lee Rankin, who presented the government's brief, whether the Court properly could decide the present cases "either way." No, Rankin insisted, the Court "properly could find only one answer."

The Court's decision, handed down on May 17, 1954, after another long silence, could hardly have occasioned any great surprise either to the proponents or enemies of segregated schools. Chief Justice Warren's opinion for a unanimous Court was remarkable both for its simplicity and for the extraordinary fashion in which it avoided all legal and historical complexities. The historical question of intent which had occasioned both sides so much anxiety he pushed aside almost impatiently as impossible of resolution. But in the light of conditions in the twentieth century, he said, it was obvious that enforced segregation generated "a feeling of inferiority" in children which might well inflict such grave damage to their minds and hearts that it could never be undone. Public school segregation by state law, therefore, violated the equal protection clause of the Fourteenth Amendment; the old *Plessy* "separate but equal" rule, he added, was herewith formally overruled.

Thus the NAACP came to its greatest triumph—a landmark decision destroying completely the constitutional foundations upon which legalized segregation in the South rested.

It was the end of a long road, yet in another sense only a beginning. For the justices did not order immediate desegregation of Southern schools in the 1954 opinion; instead, in a subsidiary decision a year later, the Court invoked a principle from equity law to order desegregation carried out under local federal court direction "with all deliberate speed."

Thus the justices carefully separated the delineation of the principle of integration from the actual implementation thereof. At the same time they avoided very nicely the crisis they would have produced had they ordered *immediate* desegregation. And one can speculate that this very careful separation of principle from implementation was one reason the Court was able to present a united front to the world in its 1954 decision.

Yet for all its cautious self-limitation, the Court's decision in *Brown* v. *Board* remains one of the great landmarks in the history of American liberty. In a sense, the Court was "legislating," for, sweeping aside state decisions and decisions based on mere law and precedent, it vested its opinion on broad considerations of national welfare. Thus the decision was indeed "political" in the deepest sense of the word, as the Court's enemies charged. Yet the fact is that the Court's greatest decisions have always been political, for unless we subscribe to the notion of a completely static Constitution and a "slot machine" theory of constitutional law, the Court must perforce decide questions of the kind it faced in *Brown* in a "political" fashion.

In this connection it is interesting to compare the Court's decision in *Brown* v. *Board* with another piece of judicial "legislation" on the race question—that involved in the Court's decision in *Dred Scott* v. *Sandford,* almost a hundred years earlier. In both cases, the Court used its extraordinary powers to "legislate," in bold and powerful strokes, upon the role and future of black people. In the *Dred Scott* case, the Court not only spoke for slavery and against the development of liberty in the American social order, it also flouted in flagrant fashion the wishes and aspirations of a large majority of the American people. In so doing it helped plunge the American Republic into a terrible Civil War.

But in *Brown* v. *Board* the Court not only spoke for liberty, thereby giving expression to the deepest and most profound ethical aspirations of a great majority of Americans, it also reflected quite accurately certain new power realities in the evolving political structure and in the social order. For these reasons, despite the fact that *Brown* v. *Board* precipitated a protracted political and social conflict in the South over desegregation, the court's decision will in all probability endure for many years as one of the great foundations of a stable and ordered constitutional system, and one possessing epoch-making significance in the evolution of constitutional democracy.

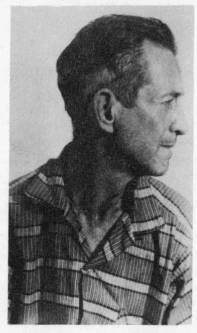

CLARENCE GIDEON.

The Case of the Florida Drifter

BY ANTHONY LEWIS

(*Gideon* v. *Wainwright*, 372 U.S. 335)

The controversy described in this chapter, like all the others here considered, illustrates what the author, Anthony Lewis, calls "the extraordinary role of law and the courts in the United States." Lewis adds that the controversy also illustrates "something astonishing and uniquely American" about the nation's legal system. An oft-convicted felon, languishing in a Florida prison, dispatched a crude, handwritten letter to the Supreme Court of the United States. By so doing he set in motion events that changed the meaning of the part of the Sixth Amendment that guarantees an accused person's right to "the assistance of counsel," thus affecting the fate of thousands of poor people accused of crimes. As a result of his interest in this case, Lewis, a New York Times correspondent, wrote Gideon's Trumpet, *a book on which this account is based.*

       A shabby setting in a rundown corner of the Florida panhandle: the Bay Harbor Poolroom, Panama City. In the early hours of June 3, 1961, someone broke in, took a few bottles of beer and wine from the bar, and forced the jukebox and the cigarette machine for the coins. It was a petty crime in an obscure place. But in a manner of speaking it led to a change in the meaning of the Constitution.

    The police in Panama City quickly found a suspect, a fifty-one-year-old white man named Clarence Earl Gideon. He was charged with "feloniously" breaking and entering the poolroom "with intent to commit a misdemeanor, to-wit, petit larceny." On August 4 he was tried and convicted by a jury. The judge gave him the maximum possible sentence, five years in prison, because Gideon had been convicted of felonies four times before, in various jurisdictions.

Gideon looked the part of a loser. His face was prematurely wrinkled, his hair white; his voice and his hands trembled. He was a drifter who had made his way by gambling and occasional thefts. But a flame still burned in Clarence Gideon. He had a passion for justice, and in particular an obsessive feeling that he had been denied justice in this case.

The injustice, as Gideon saw it, was that he had been tried without a lawyer. He could not afford to hire one, and he believed that the Constitution of the United States entitled a poor man charged with crime to have a lawyer provided for his defense. That belief came out at the start of his trial.

The Court [*Hon. Robert L. McCrary, Jr.*]: The next case on the docket is the case of the State of Florida, Plaintiff, versus Clarence Earl Gideon, Defendant. What says the State, are you ready to go to trial in this case?

Mr. Harris [*William E. Harris, Assistant State Attorney*]: The State is ready, your Honor.

The Court: What says the Defendant? Are you ready to go to trial?

The Defendant: I am not ready, your Honor.

The Court: Did you plead not guilty to this charge by reason of insanity?

The Defendant: No sir.

The Court: Why aren't you ready?

The Defendant: I have no counsel.

The Court: Why do you not have counsel? Did you not know that your case was set for trial today?

The Defendant: Yes sir, I knew that it was set for trial today.

The Court: Why, then, did you not secure counsel and be prepared to go to trial? . . .

The Defendant: Your Honor, I request this Court to appoint counsel to represent me in this trial.

The Court: Mr. Gideon, I am sorry, but I cannot appoint counsel to represent you in this case. Under the laws of the State of Florida, the only time the court can appoint counsel to represent a Defendant is when that person is charged with a capital offense. I am sorry, but I will have to deny your request to appoint counsel to defend you in this case.

The Defendant: The United States Supreme Court says I am entitled to be represented by counsel.

Gideon was wrong. The Supreme Court had not said, then, that any poor person facing state criminal charges was entitled to a free lawyer. Rather, it had held that the Constitution required provision of a lawyer only when a poor defendant labored under some special disability, such as mental backwardness, or when, as under the Florida rule stated by Judge McCrary, he or she faced a possible death sentence.

In fact, without knowing it, Gideon had touched on issues that had divided the Supreme Court for decades. One was the extent of the right to counsel mentioned in the Constitution. That in turn touched the profound question of the nature of American federalism: To what degree the states are affected by federal power and federally guaranteed rights.

It is the Sixth Amendment to the Constitution that explicitly mentions the right to counsel. The Amendment provides, among other things: "In all criminal prosecutions, the accused shall enjoy the right . . . to have the Assistance of Counsel for his defence." Before the clause could apply to Gideon's case, it would have to be interpreted in two ways: (1) to cover state as well as federal criminal prosecutions, and (2) to guarantee lawyers for poor defendants as well as those able to hire them. Both those interpretations were far from self-evident then.

At the time of their adoption, it was generally agreed that the first eight amendments limited only the *federal* government's power and procedures. Fear of power invested in the new national government had led to demands for a Bill of Rights in the first place. The understanding that the Bill of Rights applied only to federal actions was written into law in 1833 when Chief Justice John Marshall, in the case of *Barron* v. *Baltimore,* held that it did not cover the states.

The Civil War brought about fundamental changes in the constitutional balance, enlarging federal power over that of the states. The Fourteenth Amendment, adopted in 1868, said: "No State shall . . . deprive any person of life, liberty, or property, without due process of law; nor deny to any person within its jurisdiction the equal protection of the laws." In those clauses judges have found reason to hold unconstitutional an infinite variety of state actions.

Some believe that those who wrote the Fourteenth Amendment intended with its grand and general language to incorporate all the provisions of the Bill of Rights and apply them to the states. This theory of incorporation, as it is called, has been advanced many times in the Supreme Court. In 1947, in the case of *Adamson* v. *California,* four justices endorsed it in dissent. But it has never commanded a majority.

Instead, over the years the Supreme Court has selectively applied one or another clause of the first eight amendments to the states by reading those clauses into the general language of the Fourteenth Amendment. This has been done by finding that certain rights are so "fundamental" that a state's violation of them amounts to a denial of "due process of law." This approach was notably articulated by Justice Benjamin N. Cardozo. In the 1937 case of *Palko* v. *Connecticut* he wrote that rights "implicit in the concept of ordered liberty" had been taken into the Fourteenth Amendment by a "process of absorption."

What rights, then, were to be considered fundamental? The first time the Supreme Court so identified one was in 1925, when it said that the First Amendment guarantee of freedom of speech applied to the states through the Fourteenth Amendment. But for years afterward the Court was reluctant to do the same with the guarantees of fair criminal procedure in the Bill of Rights: the Fourth Amendment's provisions on search and seizure, for example; the Fifth Amendment's double-jeopardy clause; and the Sixth Amendment's many protections for the accused, including the right to counsel.

Those who wrote the right-to-counsel clause of the Sixth Amendment were concerned with making sure that United States courts did not follow the common-law rules of the English courts. Amazingly, from our current standpoint, felony defendants in England were not allowed to be represented by lawyers. Not until 1836 did Parliament pass a law abrogating that judge-made rule and letting the accused hire counsel.

Thus originally the Sixth Amendment was almost certainly not designed to reach the problem of a person too poor to retain a lawyer. But by the twentieth century that *was* the problem. A very large proportion of those charged with crime in America could not afford lawyers. And slowly, case by case, the Supreme Court dealt in constitutional terms with that reality.

Early in the Great Depression seven young black men were arrested in Scottsboro, Alabama, and charged with raping two white women aboard a freight train on which all of them were traveling. Six days later, under guard of the state militia because of threats of violence, the men went to trial—without counsel. Juries convicted them in a day and sentenced all to death.

The *Scottsboro* case went to the Supreme Court as *Powell* v. *Alabama.* The Court's opinion, handed down in 1932, was written by one of the conservative justices of the day, George Sutherland. But it was a ground-breaking opinion, asserting liberal values in language that has lost none of its power.

"The defendants," Justice Sutherland wrote, "young, ignorant, illiterate, surrounded by hostile sentiment, haled back and forth under guard of soldiers, charged with an atrocious crime regarded with especial horror in the community where they were to be tried, were thus put in peril. . . . Even the intelligent and educated layman . . . lacks both the skill and knowledge adequately to prepare his defense, even though he have a perfect one. He requires the guiding hand of counsel at every step in the proceedings against him. Without it, though he be not guilty, he faces the danger of conviction because he does not know how to establish his innocence. If that be true of men of intelligence, how much more true is it of the ignorant and illiterate?"

The Court concluded that the Scottsboro Boys, as they came to be known, had been denied the due process of law guaranteed by the Fourteenth Amendment when Alabama tried them without appointing counsel for their defense. It was the first time that the Supreme Court had set aside a state criminal conviction on any constitutional ground.

In his moving discussion of the need for counsel, Justice Sutherland did not rely on the Sixth Amendment. The Supreme Court addressed that question six years later in *Johnson* v. *Zerbst,* a federal prosecution for counterfeiting. A new justice, Hugo L. Black, in his first term on the Supreme Court, wrote the opinion. It held that in federal trials every defendant was entitled to a lawyer—a free lawyer if he or she could not afford to pay for one. The English historical background to the Sixth Amendment was no longer relevant. The

Sixth Amendment, Justice Black said, "withholds from Federal courts . . . the power and authority to deprive an accused of his life or liberty unless he has or waives the assistance of counsel."

Many thought that the Supreme Court was bound to extend the newly defined counsel requirement of the Sixth Amendment to the states. But that expectation was confounded in 1942, in what one dissenter later called the "ill-starred decision" in *Betts* v. *Brady*.

Smith Betts was a Maryland farmhand accused of robbery. Just as Clarence Earl Gideon was to do in Florida twenty years later, Betts asked the court to give him a lawyer. The judge refused. By a vote of 6–3, the Supreme Court held that Betts did not have a constitutional right to a free lawyer just because he was poor. It was not a capital case, like *Powell* v. *Alabama,* and Betts was not illiterate or overborne by community hostility. He was able "to take care of his interests," Justice Owen J. Roberts said. Moreover, there was an important consideration of federalism: "The states should not be straitjacketed." And the states took diverse views of the need for counsel. Justice Black spoke for the dissenters. No accused, he said, should be "deprived of counsel merely because of his poverty."

The decision in *Betts* v. *Brady* came under heavy criticism from the moment it was announced. Distinguished lawyers as well as ordinary citizens rejected the premise that different constitutional rules should govern the requirement for counsel in federal and state criminal trials. Moreover, the rule of *Betts* v. *Brady* was extremely difficult to apply in practice. It required free counsel only when a poor defendant faced "special circumstances"—a capital charge, his own backwardness or youth, a complicated legal situation. And how was any trial judge to know whether higher courts would find such circumstances in a particular case?

Certainly for years there was no consistency in the way the Supreme Court itself applied the *Betts* rule. In case after case state convicts claimed that they should have had lawyers at their trials. The Court looked at the facts and found sometimes that there had, sometimes that there had not been "special circumstances" requiring a lawyer. Scholars trying to make sense of the distinctions could not.

Then during the 1950s the Supreme Court, without directly questioning the rule of *Betts* v. *Brady,* took to reversing conviction after conviction in which states had tried poor defendants without counsel. And in 1961 the Court signaled a change in its attitude toward federalism. In the case of *Mapp* v. *Ohio* it applied to the states for the first time the Fourth Amendment's prohibition on unreasonable police searches and the rule that matter seized in illegal searches must be excluded from evidence.

Clarence Earl Gideon, in short, was riding a new legal tide when he claimed an absolute constitutional right to counsel. And defeat did not discourage him in making the claim. When he lost in the Florida courts, he wrote to the Supreme Court of the United States from the state prison in Raiford—on lined prison paper, in pencil. He said: "When at the time of the petitioners trial he ask the lower court for the aid of counsel, the court refused this aid. Petitioner told the court that this Court made decision to the effect that all citizens tried for a felony crime should have aid of counsel. The lower court ignored this plea."

Gideon asked the Supreme Court to review his case. Nine judges in a country of more than 200 million people cannot possibly decide every case that disappointed litigants would push upon them. So Congress, in laws defining the Court's jurisdiction, has largely let the Court itself choose which cases it will hear. Its first duty, that is, is to decide what it will decide.

On June 4, 1962, the Supreme Court issued an order in the Gideon case. It granted Gideon's petition for review. And it said it wanted to hear argument on this question: "Should this Court's holding in *Betts* v. *Brady,* 316 U.S. 455, be reconsidered?"

Something astonishing and uniquely American had happened. A person on the fringe of society, a man utterly without power, had succeeded in bringing to the point of decision a legal issue that could affect millions of people. But now that the Supreme Court had agreed to consider Gideon's claim, who would take up the question posed by the Court and urge it to overrule *Betts* v. *Brady*? In a local court in Florida Gideon had had to fend for himself. But in the Supreme Court of the United States he would certainly have counsel —eminent counsel. For the Court's tradition is to appoint an outstanding lawyer to argue the case of any poor person whose petition for review it has granted.

To represent Gideon the Supreme Court named Abe Fortas, a leading Washington lawyer, later named to the Court himself by President Johnson. The choice of Fortas assured the justices that they would have a foundation of thorough research if they decided to overrule *Betts* v. *Brady*. With the resources of a large law firm, and with the special responsibility of someone chosen by the Supreme Court to speak for an indigent in a potentially historic case, Fortas would certainly prepare a brief that examined every aspect of the right-to-counsel issue: the arguments of history, of federalism, of practicality, of justice.

But first Fortas had to make what he called a moral choice: Should he find out more about Clarence Earl Gideon? The fact that the Supreme Court had asked the question of whether to reconsider the *Betts* decision indicated it was ready to do so. But a lawyer in the Anglo-American tradition does not represent abstract principles, such as the right to counsel; he represents clients. Fortas's client was Gideon, and it could be that Gideon could win his case without having to persuade the Supreme Court to take the rare step of changing its mind. The record of the trial might show that Gideon suffered from some special disability and hence should have had a lawyer even under the *Betts* rule. Fortas sent for a transcript of the trial.

The transcript showed that it was the simplest of cases. The main witness for the prosecution was one Henry Cook, who said he was outside the Bay Harbor Poolroom at 5:30 that morning and saw Gideon inside; then Gideon came out with a pint of wine in his hand, and Cook went in and saw the broken cigarette machine. Gideon, told he could cross-examine, asked Cook if he had been convicted of a felony; he said no. The few witnesses Gideon called had nothing helpful to say.

It was, indeed, a classic case to test what Justice Roberts had said in *Betts* v. *Brady:* that an ordinary person accused of crime could "take care of his interests" without a lawyer. Gideon was not mentally defective. The case was not complicated, and Gideon had not been menaced by bias in the courtroom. But it was obvious at once to Abe Fortas that a lawyer would have made a world of difference. Gideon had not made a single objection to the prosecution's evidence. He had not asked the judge to explain the necessary standard of proof to the jury. He had said nothing before his sentencing.

The printed brief that Fortas submitted to the Supreme Court built on the facts of Gideon's trial to argue that "the aid of counsel is indispensable to a fair hearing" in any criminal case. The brief said the *Betts* rule did not serve the interests of federalism: It led the Supreme Court and other federal courts to reexamine the facts of state trials case by case to see whether a lawyer had been necessary, a much more intrusive federal intervention in state matters than a flat rule requiring counsel would be.

Justice Felix Frankfurter, a leading supporter of the *Betts* rule, had said in 1947 that an "abrupt" change in it "would furnish opportunities hitherto uncontemplated for opening wide the prison doors of the land." That is, state prisoners convicted without lawyers at their trials would demand to be released. Fortas's brief dealt unflinchingly with that concern, saying that the trend of Supreme Court decisions had given the states ample warning by now that counsel might be required.

Another point of concern was how far a universal requirement for lawyers would extend. To all criminal cases, however petty? To traffic offenses? Fortas said there would be time enough later to explore the limits. Gideon had been convicted of a felony and given a five-year sentence, surely a serious enough case to require a lawyer's help.

Now came a marvellous irony. In a local court in Florida, Clarence Gideon had stood alone against the power of the state. In the proceedings before the Supreme Court of the United States, he had one of Washington's shrewdest and most experienced lawyers on his side. And the state was represented by an assistant attorney general who had never set foot in the Supreme Court before. He was Bruce R. Jacob, twenty-six years old, a bright recent law school graduate who found himself confronting, alone, the movement of legal history and the resources of Abe Fortas.

Jacob's brief made the arguments of history and federalism against forcing the states to provide lawyers for poor criminal defendants. It urged the practical concern that the line could not be drawn at felonies—that misdemeanor defendants would have to be included too, and the result would be "an enormous burden on members of the bar." It said a survey of the Florida prisons showed that 5,093 of the 7,836 then in custody had been tried without counsel, so that in Florida alone "as many as 5,093 hardened criminals may be eligible to be released in one mass exodus" if *Betts* v. *Brady* were overruled.

The case was significant enough that several outside interests filed briefs as friends of the court. One of these was highly unusual. Bruce Jacob had written to the attorneys general of the other forty-nine states asking them to submit friend-of-the-court briefs on Florida's side. Two, Alabama and North Carolina, did join in such a brief, urging the Supreme Court to stick to the *Betts* rule. But the attorney general of Minnesota, Walter F. Mondale (later senator and vice president), reacted differently when he got Jacob's letter. He replied that Minnesota required provision of counsel for all poor felony defendants, it worked well, and he would "welcome" it as a national requirement. A brief that took Gideon's side was drafted in the office of the Massachusetts attorney general, and in the end twenty-three states signed it: a rare, perhaps unprecedented instance of states asking the Supreme Court to impose a constitutional requirement on them.

The brief of the twenty-three states showed how far the country had moved since *Betts* v. *Brady*. Whatever the view had been in 1942, the right to counsel could now fairly be described as "implicit in the concept of ordered liberty"—Justice Cardozo's phrase for provisions of the original Bill of Rights so fundamental that they had become absorbed into the American view of due process of law and hence bound the states as well as the federal government.

Abe Fortas hoped that all nine justices of the Supreme Court could be persuaded to that conclusion. Unanimity was highly desirable, he thought, if the Court were to overrule a decision as hotly attacked and defended as *Betts* had been. But if a majority seemed ready to abandon the *Betts* rule, a unanimous Court seemed unlikely. Justice Frankfurter, the most passionate defender of the rule, had just retired. But another influential figure on the Court, Justice John Marshall Harlan, believed deeply in the values of federalism and of adherence to precedent.

The Supreme Court heard argument in the Gideon case on January 15, 1963. Fortas had not been on his feet long, opening the argument, when Justice Harlan intervened. Fortas was saying that the transcript of this trial showed the impossibility of any accused conducting "his own defense adequately."

"That's not the point, is it, Mr. Fortas?" Justice Harlan asked. "*Betts* didn't go on the assumption that a man can do as well without an attorney as he can with one, did it? Everyone knows that isn't so."

In fact, Justice Roberts's opinion in *Betts* v. *Brady* had suggested that in a simple case there was little for a lawyer to do. But Fortas did not argue the point. Instead, he took Justice Harlan's observation as an implicit concession and built on it. "I entirely agree, Mr. Justice Harlan, with the point you are making" he said. "Namely, that of course a man cannot have a fair trial without a lawyer. . . . I was reminded the other night, as I was pondering this case, of Clarence Darrow when he was prosecuted for trying to fix a jury. The first thing he realized was that he needed a lawyer—he, one of the country's great criminal lawyers. . . . And so the real basis of Betts against Brady must be the understanding sensitivity of this Court to the pull of federalism."

For some reason the last phrase seemed to anger Justice Harlan. He reddened, leaned forward on the high bench, and said sharply, "Really, Mr. Fortas, 'understanding sensitivity' seems to me a most unfortunate term to describe one of the fundamental principles of our constitutional system."

"Mr. Justice Harlan," Fortas replied calmly, "I believe in federalism. It is a fundamental principle for which I personally have the highest regard and concern, and which I feel must be reconciled with the result I advocate. But I believe that Betts against Brady does not incorporate a proper regard for federalism. It requires a case-by-case supervision by this Court of state criminal proceedings, and that cannot be wholesome. . . . Intervention should be in the least abrasive, the least corrosive way possible."

Fortas had used Justice Harlan's intervention as the occasion to make what he considered his central argument: that a universal requirement of counsel would be less offensive to the rights and sensitivities of the states than the uncertainties of the *Betts* rule.

Bruce Jacob had a difficult case to argue, and he knew it. He emphasized the need and the desire of individual states to experiment—in criminal procedures as in other matters. In constitutional cases, he said, "history argues against the drawing of inflexible lines. . . . By imposing an inflexible rule, we feel this Court would be intruding into an area historically reserved to the states. It would stifle state experimentation. For example, a state might eliminate prosecutors as well as defense counsel and leave the whole trial to the judge." "Don't go too far now," Justice Harlan interjected. Justice Potter Stewart observed that "Gideon would not be allowed to represent others in court." Jacob responded: "If a defendant asked for him, I'm sure the judge wouldn't object." Justice Black: "The local bar association might!"

Jacob spoke of one of the consequences of overruling *Betts*, the potential release of those 5,093 Florida inmates who had been tried without lawyers. Chief Justice Earl Warren asked whether some of them were illiterate. His point was plain: an illiterate defendant was entitled to counsel even under the *Betts* rule. Jacob conceded that some of the 5,093 were illiterate. So they had been tried unconstitutionally, and they had failed to win redress in the courts only because they lacked Clarence Gideon's determination or luck.

At the end Fortas had a short rebuttal. "I think Betts and Brady was wrong when it was decided," he said. "I think time has made that clear. And I think time has now made it possible for the correct rule, the civilized rule, the rule of American constitutionalism, the rule of due process to be stated by this Court with limited disturbance to the states."

Justice Harlan had the last word. Had Fortas in his research, he asked, found any errors in the history of the right to counsel as stated by Justice Roberts in *Betts* v. *Brady*? That would make it easier for Justice Harlan to reconsider the decision, but Fortas could give him no comfort. "I don't say that the historical technique of constitutional interpretation will reach my result," he said. Justice Harlan commented finally: "What one is left with is getting one's hands on something that has happened in the last twenty years."

On March 18 the Supreme Court decided the case of *Gideon* v. *Wainwright*. Chief Justice Warren, with an appropriate sense of history, had assigned the opinion of the Court to Justice Black. "When *Betts* v. *Brady* was decided," Black later told a friend, "I never thought I'd live to see it overruled." But it was, that day.

Justice Black's opinion began by stating the facts of Gideon's case and noting that they strikingly resembled those in the trial of Smith Betts. Accordingly, Gideon's claim of a constitutional right to counsel would have to be rejected if *Betts* v. *Brady* were "left standing." But that decision had been wrong from the start, Justice Black said. It had turned away from the teaching of the *Scottsboro* case and others, making "an abrupt break" with precedent.

Not only these precedents but also reason and reflection require us to recognize that in our adversary system of criminal justice, any person haled into court, who is too poor to hire a lawyer, cannot be assured a fair trial unless counsel is provided for him. . . . That government hires lawyers to prosecute and defendants who have the money hire lawyers to defend are the strongest indications of the widespread belief that lawyers in criminal courts are necessities, not luxuries. The right of one charged with crime to counsel may not be deemed fundamental in some countries, but it is in ours.

"Fundamental," Justice Black said—and thus the right-to-counsel clause of the Sixth Amendment was absorbed into the Fourteenth Amendment and now bound the states. There the opinion left it, giving no guidance on subsidiary questions such as whether the new rule applied to less serious criminal cases, or whether all those in prison who had not had lawyers were now entitled to new trials.

The Court was unanimous on the result. But Justice Harlan spoke for himself, not joining the Black opinion. "I agree that *Betts* v. *Brady* should be overruled, but consider it entitled to a more respectful burial," he said. He did not think the *Betts* decision had been a break from precedent when it was decided. But its special-circumstances doctrine had had "a troubled journey," continuing to exist in form "while its substance has been substantially and steadily eroded. . . . To continue a rule which is honored by this Court only with lip service is not a healthy thing and in the long run will do disservice to the federal system."

That was the end of the Gideon case in the Supreme Court. But it was only a stage in the long process of ensuring that all defendants in American courts receive the effective assistance of counsel. The declaration of a constitutional right could not guarantee that a poor person in Panama City or New York would have a *competent* lawyer to defend him against a criminal charge.

But *Gideon* v. *Wainwright* did have immediate effects. At the time it was decided, thirteen of the fifty states had no laws or court rules providing for appointment of counsel in criminal cases; those states quickly established systems. Florida's legislature enacted a public-defender law barely two months after the decision. Governor Farris Bryant said: "In this era of social consciousness it is unthinkable that an innocent man may be condemned to penal servitude because he is unfamiliar with the intricacies of criminal procedure."

Other Florida prisoners petitioned for their release, as Bruce Jacob had predicted. At the beginning of its next term, in October 1963, the Supreme Court dealt with ten of those petitions, asking the Florida courts to reconsider the cases "in light of *Gideon* v. *Wainwright.*" The Florida authorities decided to release many prisoners who had been tried without counsel, forgoing the attempt to convict them again in new trials with counsel because the evidence was so stale. A year after the *Gideon* decision, about a thousand Florida prisoners had been discharged.

What of Gideon himself? While his case was awaiting argument in the Supreme Court, he wrote a long letter to Abe Fortas about his life and thoughts. The spelling was a bit eccentric; the story a sad one of a boy whose father had died and who turned rebellious in resentment, as he said, of a stepfather. "I am not proud of this biography," he wrote. "I have no illusions about law and courts or the people who are involved in them. I have read the complete history of law ever since the Romans first started writing them down and before of the law of religions. I believe that each era finds a improvement in law each year brings something new for the benefit of mankind. Maybe this will be one of those small steps forward."

But Gideon's victory in the Supreme Court did not mean immediate freedom for him. He was entitled only to a new trial, with a lawyer, and the state of Florida did not forgo the opportunity to retry him. On August 5, 1963, in the same courtroom in Panama City, Judge McCrary called the case of "State of Florida versus Clarence Earl Gideon." This time, when he asked whether the defendant was ready for trial, the answer was yes—and it came from a lawyer. At Gideon's request, Judge McCrary had appointed a local lawyer, Fred Turner, to represent him. Once again the main prosecution witness was Henry Cook. But Fred Turner did some effective cross-examination. He asked suggestively why Cook was outside the Bay Harbor Poolroom at 5:30 in the morning. He brought out that Cook, despite his denial at the first trial, had a criminal record. He produced a witness who said that later in the morning Cook had spoken of being picked up himself by the police for questioning about the poolroom break-in. In his address to the jury Turner scornfully accused Cook and his friends of committing the crime. The jury was out for an hour. Its verdict was not guilty.

A lawyer had made a difference—the difference between conviction and acquittal. The principle established in the abstract in the Supreme Court of the United States, the one for which Justice Black had labored for twenty years, had worked in the concrete circumstances of the circuit court, Bay County, Florida.

The Gideon case demonstrated the extraordinary role of law and the courts in the United States. It showed that the least influential of beings can set in motion a reexamination of the premises of justice. It showed how our written Constitution is reinterpreted in the light of changed understanding. It showed that courts respond to the grievances of society. And that is no small thing when so many feel defeated by the system.

It is a romantic story, with poetic justice at the end. But of course most of real life is not romance. Abe Fortas defended Gideon without compensation, considering it an honor to perform such a service at the behest of the Supreme Court. Twenty years after the *Gideon* decision a handful of poorly paid, overworked lawyers struggled to handle the urgent cases of more than two hundred prisoners in Florida's death row. And everywhere it remained the reality that poor defendants were likely to have lawyers with less experience, less time, and fewer resources for investigation than those retained by better-off defendants.

But for Gideon himself the story did not turn sour. He was in trouble with the law only once more, and trivially. After a losing day at the Kentucky Derby he was charged with vagrancy. He showed the judge a book about his case. The judge said he was impressed to meet the subject of so famous a decision. Perhaps, he said, Gideon would like to try extending the right to counsel to petty offenses, like vagrancy. He had planned just to let Gideon go, the judge said, but instead he could impose a six-month sentence so that Gideon could appeal on up to the Supreme Court again. Gideon said he would just as soon go. (In *Argersinger* v. *Hamlin*, 407 U.S. 25 [1972], the Supreme Court extended the counsel rule to all cases where any prison term is imposed.)

Gideon died on January 18, 1972, in Fort Lauderdale, Florida. His mother brought the body home to Hannibal, Missouri. When someone who had met him during his Supreme Court case telephoned, she said, "He could have been most anything if he'd gone to school as he ought to, and behaved himself." She did not understand that, for all his mistakes and his wrongs, he was something.

Because his family was not proud of him, Gideon was buried in a grave without a marker. Twelve years later the American Civil Liberties Union decided to do something about that. It arranged for a gravestone to commemorate a man who proved that in this vast country one person can still make a difference. Somewhat to the surprise of the ACLU, various dignitaries of Hannibal and the state of Missouri attended the dedication ceremony. The mayor, John Lyng, said that Hannibal had had many cranky citizens, including Mark Twain. Gideon, he said, was "the kind of character we value in Hannibal. At one point in his life he decided to take a stand. We should all continue to have that kind of courage."

The gravestone has on it words from Clarence Earl Gideon's letter to Abe Fortas: "I believe that each era finds improvement in law. Maybe this will be one of those small steps forward."

The Abortion Case

BY ROSALIND ROSENBERG

(*Roe* et al. v. *Wade, District Attorney of Dallas County,* 410 U.S. 113)

The authors of these essays have demonstrated that controversies between individuals and between citizens and their government have repeatedly caused changes in the meaning of the Constitution. Another way of making this point is to say that the justices of the Supreme Court have time and again not merely interpreted existing law but have in effect made new law, made it as much as any Congress or state legislature. In most instances the decisions of the Court in such matters have been accepted by most people without further argument; the fact that someone *must have the final say is at least tacitly accepted by nearly everyone.*

There have been, however, exceptions. The Dred Scott *decision was resented by thousands of Northerners, and the school desegregation decision encountered bitter resistance, especially in the South, for many years. Many people have also refused to be reconciled to the Court's decision in the case that is the subject of our final chapter, which involves the abortion controversy. It is the work of Rosalind Rosenberg of Barnard College, an authority on both constitutional history and the history of women. Professor Rosenberg is the author of* Beyond Separate Spheres: Intellectual Roots of Modern Feminism.

Norma McCorvey was not out to change the Constitution; all she wanted was to have an abortion in Texas within the bounds of the law. An "army brat" with only a ninth-grade education, twenty-five years old, divorced, "down on her luck," she was—as she later reported—"trying to make ends meet" by working as a ticket seller in a traveling carnival. One hot night in August 1969 she and two other young women from the carnival were walking back to their motel in Augusta, Georgia, when they suddenly realized they were being followed by three men.

NORMA McCORVEY.

"You want to divide them up or take on all of them?" a male voice asked.

"Hell, I can handle as many as there are."

"Well, let's see if you can act as big as you can talk."

Frightened, the women kept on walking as the three men overtook them. One was white, one black, and one appeared part black and part Mexican. All were drunk. Norma McCorvey spoke crudely to the men, hoping that they would leave, but the man next to her put his hand on her breast. Furious and terrified, she slapped his face as hard as she could.

After that, she said, she could remember only fragments. The man threw her down on the gravel road with such force that he knocked the wind out of her. She struggled to get up, but he was on top of her, slamming her head back against the ground. He jammed his tongue in her mouth, ripped off her pants, and raped her. When he had finished, the other two took their turn.

After they had left, she lay on the ground for a long time, not sure what to do. The other women had fled. She was too sore to move. Finally, she passed out. When she came to, it was light. Struggling to her feet, she panicked as she heard someone come up behind her. "The postman was delivering his rounds," she later recalled. "He took off his jacket or his shirt, or something, I don't really remember, and gave it to me so that I could cover myself."

The postman took her back to her room, and from there she went to the police. "One of the officers said that he remembered me, that I was one of the girls that worked in the sideshow, so I knew right then and there that I didn't have a prayer. I just went back to my room and had a good cry." Back in the motel she discovered that her two roommates had left. Stunned, she decided to return home to Texas. She went to the carnival, picked up her pay, and bought a bus ticket. Forty-one hours later she was in the Dallas bus station, calling a girlfriend to pick her up.

Home had little to offer. Her childhood had been marred by the dislocations of army life, a drunken father, and an embittered mother who found fault in all that she did. Desperate to get away from home, she dropped out of school at sixteen, married an aspiring rock musician, and became pregnant. Unfortunately, her new husband wanted nothing of fatherhood. She returned home, delivered her baby girl, then went to work in a bar while her mother cared for her child. But the old pattern of recriminations soon recurred. Her mother condemned her as unfit to have a child, forced her to sign some papers she did not understand, and took her baby away. Crushed and alone, McCorvey joined the carnival.

The friend who picked her up at the Dallas bus station offered to let her stay in her trailer. McCorvey got back her job in the bar and started to feel better. But several weeks later she began waking up nauseous every morning. She was pregnant. At first she didn't know what to do. "This can't be. I can't have this child. I don't even have a goddamned place to lie my head down." She went to the doctor who had delivered her daughter and asked for an abortion, but he informed her that it was a crime to perform an abortion in Texas except to save the life of the mother. She would have to fly to California if she wanted one.

"I told the doctor, 'I don't want to have the baby. I can't afford to go to California. I can't even afford to eat.' " She said she would have the baby, "but I won't keep it. I would hate it." Her doctor referred her to an attorney who handled adoptions, but when she went to see him, he asked her a number of insinuating questions about the rape. She left his office in disgust, and decided to look for a doctor who would perform an abortion. At last she found one, but he told her the price would be $650. When she said she did not have that much money, he said he could not help her.

Disillusioned by the callous condescension of everyone to whom she turned and defeated by the relentless passage of time, McCorvey resigned herself to going through with her pregnancy. "It seemed that everybody I went to for help didn't have the time. . . . I felt that life had dealt me a dirty deal. I wasn't getting any aces."

But then her luck began to change. Her original doctor referred her to Linda Coffee, a young attorney who favored legalizing abortions. "I went to meet her and I liked her right away," McCorvey later recalled. Coffee was the first person to show sympathy for her plight, to take the time to talk to her. McCorvey described the rape, her dismay at discovering she was pregnant, and her effort to find a doctor who would perform an abortion she could afford. The young lawyer asked her if she would be willing to be a plaintiff in a suit attacking the Texas abortion law, and McCorvey replied, "Yes, absolutely."

Coffee then introduced McCorvey to two other lawyers. One was Henry McCloskey, Jr., who specialized in arranging adoptions; the other was Sarah Weddington, a friend of Coffee's from law school who also wanted to fight the Texas abortion law. Like Coffee, Weddington was sympathetic. "I remember going to [her] apartment," McCorvey recalled. "She had on pedal pushers and a white blouse. . . . I sat right down on the floor and she listened to me. You can talk to some people easier than you can talk to other people who don't listen. . . . She's always had time for me."

Weddington questioned McCorvey closely. Was she sure that she would be willing to go all the way with a suit? Even to the Supreme Court? McCorvey was not certain what Weddington meant by the Supreme Court. She thought she was probably referring to the Federal Building in Dallas. But she replied that the two women could count on her.

Coffee and Weddington promised that McCorvey would be known merely as Jane Roe and that she would not have to appear in court. McCorvey was grateful for the guarantee of anonymity, not only for herself but for her daughter, who was still living with her mother. "My child was very young at the time, and I didn't want her to be subject to public ridicule." And so this young woman, poor, ill-educated, and forced by circumstances beyond her control to have a baby she did not want became the plaintiff in a case that changed the Constitution.

Linda Coffee and Sarah Weddington had been two of only five women to graduate from the University of Texas Law School in 1967. As Coffee recalls, "It was an oddity for a woman to go to law school and have a career. For a long time I thought there was something wrong with me. . . . It was only when I really began to talk to other women and found out that many of them thought the way I did that I realized I was not so different. I had been afraid to say anything to anyone before."

For young professional women like Coffee and Weddington, abortion was an especially important issue. The right to have one was the ultimate guarantee that they could control their lives and that an unplanned pregnancy could not sabotage their careers. More broadly, they believed that all the other rights for which women were fighting in the late 1960s and early 1970s—the right

to equal education, the right to equal job opportunities, the right
to equal pay, and the right to equal political power—depended on
securing this right to control their own bodies.

Before 1821, no statutes governed abortion in America. The only
legal inhibition, inherited from the English common-law tradition,
was that abortion before "quickening" was, at worst, a misdemeanor. "Quickening" referred to that time in pregnancy when a
woman could first feel fetal movement, usually between the fourth
and the sixth month. So for the first trimester of pregnancy (and for
much of the second, given the difficulty of determining whether a
woman was pregnant) abortion went essentially unregulated. In
1821 Connecticut enacted a law that followed the common-law rule,
and in the decades that followed most states did the same. But these
statutes were introduced as part of a general trend toward the
codification of state laws, not because of any campaign to stop
abortions. If a woman wanted to terminate a pregnancy, the law
rarely stood in her way.

Nevertheless, before about 1840 abortion was generally, regarded as the last recourse of the desperate, especially of the unmarried woman fearful of bearing an illegitimate child. Thereafter,
however, a rapidly increasing proportion of the women who sought
abortions were married, native-born, Protestant women, frequently
of the middle or upper classes. As urbanization put pressure on
families to have fewer children, as increased educational opportunities for women gave them a greater awareness of the possibility of
controlling their own bodies, and in the absence of effective birth
control, abortion became a regularly sought means of limiting fertility.

For women who had access to newspapers and who did not live
in isolated rural areas, procuring an abortion was not difficult. Many
advertisements lauded "clinics for ladies" where menstrual ir-
regularities "from whatever cause" could be corrected and where
confidentiality was assured. Over the course of the nineteenth century the birth rate in America fell from seven children per family to
3.5. No one knows how important abortion was to this decline, but
estimates from varying sources suggest that by the middle of the
nineteenth century approximately 20 percent of all pregnancies
were being aborted.

The relatively open and accepting attitude toward abortion changed sharply in the 1850s, and by 1900 every state in America had enacted a law making abortion a crime at *any stage* of pregnancy. Anyone who performed an abortion was guilty of a felony, and in many states the woman also faced the possibility of criminal indictment, something women had not had to fear before. The change came to Texas in 1854, when the legislature enacted a law making it a crime to perform an abortion unless the purpose was "saving the life of the mother."

Historians once assumed that religious groups, especially the Roman Catholic church, led the campaign against abortion. But the Catholic church, though opposed to abortion, lacked sufficient political power to achieve the legislative change that took place. And Protestant denominations, though politically powerful, took no stand on abortion in those years. The leadership of the antiabortion campaign came instead from the medical profession, which was spurred to action by a combination of new scientific knowledge and concern over the absence of standards in the medical practice of the day. In 1827 the existence of the human egg was established, and most well-trained doctors came to believe that life began at conception, not quickening. If abortion after quickening was immoral, and most people believed it was, then given the new knowledge, abortion before quickening must be so too.

Not all doctors shared this knowledge, however. In fact, early in the century democratic currents had washed away most of the restrictions on medical practice that had existed in the colonial period, and by mid-century regularly trained physicians found themselves in competition with a proliferation of "healers," whose medical preparation varied widely. Concerned by the absence of medical standards, "regular" physicians founded the American Medical Association in 1847. The AMA was deeply divided on many issues, but it was able to reach a consensus on one: abortion by the unskilled was dangerous and by anyone was immoral. Regular physicians contended that women should be protected from unskilled practitioners and taught that they had been misled by the stress on quickening to think that the fetus was not alive until quickening occurred.

Doctors' concern over professional standards and medical ethics was real enough, but the campaign against abortion might not have become the special vehicle for expressing that concern had it not been for two other interrelated social issues that worried both doctors and the wider public. First, the rising rate of abortions among married, middle-class women seemed to pose a threat to the traditional role of women in the family. And second, the declining fertility of the native-born middle class alarmed those who saw in the high fertility of newly arrived immigrants a potential political threat. Ironically, Protestants' fears about not keeping up with the reproductive rates of Catholic immigrants played a greater role in the drive for antiabortion laws in nineteenth-century America than Catholic opposition to abortion did. Building on these fears, doctors persuaded the great majority of the public that abortion at any time of pregnancy was murder.

For all their talk about murder, however, doctors did not insist on laws that barred abortions completely. Restrictive legislation always included a provision permitting abortions that were necessary "to save the life of the mother." This deliberately ambiguous phrase guaranteed that physicians would exercise ultimate authority over the abortion issue. All doctors might agree to perform an abortion only to protect the life of the mother, but some interpreted protecting life broadly to mean protecting the quality of life, while others interpreted it to mean only in cases where the woman faced imminent death. As a consequence of the "save the life" loophole, women's experiences with abortion varied dramatically. Depending on where she lived, what her social and economic circumstances were, and who her doctor was, a woman might find securing an abortion relatively easy or virtually impossible.

The demand for abortions was much greater than the legal supply. Whereas roughly one out of five pregnancies was interrupted by abortion before restrictive laws were passed, in the 1930s the most liberal hospital in the country, Bellevue Hospital in New York, performed only one abortion for every seventy-six live births. No doubt many abortions were done by physicians in their offices or in their patients' homes. But the great majority were probably done by unlicensed abortionists. The best data on induced abortion for the twentieth century, found in the Kinsey Report, reveal that between one in four and one in five women who had ever been married had aborted a pregnancy and that 90 percent of premarital pregnancies were ended by abortions, most of them illegal. Restrictive laws did not prevent abortions, but they left women subject to the vagaries of medical judgment and they forced most women who sought abortions to have them in secret, often performed by unscrupulous and unskilled practitioners.

For decades, despite the misery that attended the abortion experiences of so many women, the medical monopoly of the issue blocked any challenge to state laws. But beginning in the 1950s, the very profession that had sought to restrict abortion took steps to liberalize its position. Their professional respectability long since secured, physicians began to wrestle with some of the unanticipated consequences of their predecessors' reforming zeal. As medical practice moved increasingly into hospitals, doctors found it difficult to overlook the markedly different ways in which they were interpreting state laws. Many began to worry that local authorities might disagree with their medical judgment and subject them to criminal prosecution. A growing number called for the reform of abortion laws in order to clarify the circumstances under which abortion was permissible.

In 1959, responding to the demands of physicians, the American Law Institute drafted a "model" abortion law. The proposed statute legalized abortions when necessary to protect the life or health (including the mental health) of the mother, in cases of rape and incest, and in cases where there was a probability of defects appearing in the embryo. In other words, the statute provided legal sanction for the kinds of abortions that many physicians were in fact performing.

Those most active in the campaign to reform abortion policies were an elite group of doctors and lawyers, but by the 1960s other factors were contributing to the pressure for change. First, a growing concern about the dangers of overpopulation had replaced the nineteenth-century fear of population decline. Birth control, long a taboo subject in polite society, was openly discussed in the decades after World War II as a legitimate means of combatting overpopulation. By the 1960s many Americans were prepared to accept the idea that abortion offered another weapon in the anti-overpopulation arsenal. Second, medical progress led to new questions regarding quality of life. Drugs like thalidomide and illnesses like German measles were shown to cause massive birth defects, and many women faced with the prospect of a deformed infant sought abortions instead. Abortion no longer seemed to involve a choice between absolutes—life and death—but rather a choice about what kind of life was worth living. Third, the political, economic, and educational achievements won by women over the century since the antiabortion campaign made women much more assertive about their individuality and their right to control their own fates than their grandmothers had been. And finally, medical progress had greatly reduced the danger once associated with abortions: the nineteenth-century argument that abortions should be barred because of the health risk they posed to mothers no longer made sense. All these factors added force to the doctors' call for legislative reform.

When Norma McCorvey sought an abortion in 1969, the Texas abortion law of 1854 was still on the books but about a third of the states had liberalized their laws to some extent. Georgia, for instance, permitted abortion if a committee of doctors, having examined the woman, agreed in writing that an abortion was necessary. Georgia also permitted abortion in the case of rape, but the law would not have helped McCorvey, even if she had stayed in Georgia.

Augusta police had turned their backs on her when she had sought their assistance. Moreover, the solicitor general had to provide the court with a certified statement that the rape had occurred.

Such "liberal" laws greatly eased the plight of well-educated, middle-class women who had the knowledge and the money to run the procedural maze that stood in the way of getting abortions. But poor, ill-educated women like Norma McCorvey were scarcely better off than they were under the conservative regime in Texas.

The country's least restrictive laws were those enacted in California in 1967 and New York in 1970. These allowed abortions if a doctor believed it necessary to protect the mental or physical health of the mother. Between 1967 and 1971 the number of legal abortions sought and performed in California increased twentyfold. Of all the women who applied for abortions, 99.2 percent were able to have one. Indeed, one out of every three California pregnancies ended in abortion. Yet even in California women still needed the approval of a doctor. Abortion was not their right.

With the rise of the women's movement in the late 1960s, growing numbers began to argue that the abortion reform being advocated by doctors and lawyers served doctors' needs far better than women's. As long as doctors controlled access to abortion, women would be dependent on the personal views of physicians. Increasingly, they began to insist that only outright repeal of abortion statutes would guarantee women what they began to call "the right to control their own bodies."

Yet there was a danger inherent in asserting this right. So long as doctors had control of the abortion issue, disagreements over what conditions justified an abortion could generally be confined to doctors' offices. To claim that abortion was a woman's right was to risk a resurgence of the countervailing claim that society and the fetus had rights as well.

When Sarah Weddington and Linda Coffee decided in 1970 to attack the Texas abortion statute, they had little to guide them. Attorneys around the country were just beginning to use the courts to challenge state abortion laws. As yet no consensus on how to proceed had emerged. Weddington and Coffee wanted the court to strike down the Texas statute in its entirety, so they did not base the case on McCorvey's report that she had been raped. The rape would be difficult to prove, given the absence of a police report. Moreover, if they emphasized rape, the most they could hope for would be a decision that would extend the right of abortion to women who had been raped.

They also decided against basing the case solely on the ground that the law was so vague that people to whom it might apply could not be sure which of their actions might violate the law. The problem of vagueness was important to doctors like Dr. James Hallford, who had been indicted for performing abortions and whom the Texas district court allowed to join in the case. But for pregnant women, the problem was not the statute's lack of clarity. Indeed, if by judicial construction the Texas law were made clearer, it would restrict women's ability to obtain abortions in an even greater number of instances.

Weddington and Coffee decided to bring a class action suit on behalf of Jane Roe and all other women "similarly situated" (that is, pregnant and seeking an abortion), and to challenge the Texas law's constitutionality on the broadest possible grounds. The suit became *Jane Roe* et al. v. *Wade, District Attorney of Dallas County.* Believing that the court might find it easier to decide a case involving a married couple than one involving an unmarried woman, the lawyers also filed a second case on behalf of a couple who came to be known as John and Mary Doe. Both cases charged that by denying women the right to decide whether to bear a child and by interfering with the privacy of the doctor-patient relationship the law violated the First, Fourth, Fifth, Ninth, and Fourteenth Amendments of the United States Constitution.

The clearest precedent for the abortion case was *Griswold* v. *Connecticut* (1965). That case had grown out of a challenge to Connecticut's anticontraception law by Estelle T. Griswold, executive director of the Connecticut Planned Parenthood League. For decades Planned Parenthood had tried without success to change the Connecticut law barring the use of contraceptives, but the Catholic-dominated legislature blocked all reform efforts. Griswold therefore turned to the courts. She set up a birth control clinic in New Haven and dared the police to arrest her. The police obliged; Griswold was convicted; she appealed; and her case made its way to the Supreme Court.

On June 7, 1965, Supreme Court Justice William O. Douglas handed down the Court's 7–2 opinion striking down the Connecticut law. Conceding that the Supreme Court does "not sit as a super-legislature," Douglas declared that married couples could not be prohibited from using contraceptives. They had a right to privacy, not mentioned in the Constitution, but nevertheless protected by it. That right, said Douglas, could be found in the "penumbras" and "emanations" of the Bill of Rights, whose guarantees applied to the states through the due process clause of the Fourteenth Amendment.

Justices Arthur Goldberg and John Harlan joined in the Court's judgment but offered different reasons for doing so. Goldberg proposed that the Ninth Amendment offered a more persuasive basis for invalidating the Connecticut statute than the specific guarantees of the first eight amendments, none of which concerned marital privacy. "The Ninth Amendment," Goldberg wrote, "shows a belief of the Constitution's authors that fundamental rights exist that are not expressly enumerated in the first eight amendments." The "traditions . . . of our people" reveal, he continued, that the right to marital privacy was as "fundamental" a right as any other mentioned in the Bill of Rights. It thus deserved recognition as one of those unenumerated rights that were "retained by the people" and protected from the interference of state governments by the Fourteenth Amendment.

Justice Harlan argued that the "liberty" protected by the due process clause of the Fourteenth Amendment provided a more obvious basis for invalidating the Connecticut law than any of the first nine amendments. Due process generally meant that a person could not be convicted of a crime or denied rights without a fair hearing. But it could also mean that a state had to be more than merely fair or reasonable, it had to show a compelling need before it could infringe certain fundamental rights.

A few cases going back to the 1920s had protected rights under the Fourteenth Amendment that related in important ways to the contraception issue. In *Meyer* v. *Nebraska* (1923) and again in *Pierce* v. *Society of Sisters* (1925), Justice James C. McReynolds argued that the Fourteenth Amendment's protection of "liberty" included the right of people to marry and to raise their children as they thought best and, more generally, the right "to enjoy those privileges long recognized at common law as essential to the orderly pursuit of happiness by free men."

This broad reading of the due process clause, known as "substantive" due process, had come into bad repute in recent decades, however, because in the past it had served as the principal vehicle by which the Supreme Court had protected the economic liberty of employers. From *Lochner* v. *New York* (1905) through *Tipaldo* v. *New York* (1936)[1] the Court had routinely struck down state laws that infringed what it regarded as the fundamental economic liberty of employers to contract freely with their employees. To revive the idea of substantive due process might invite a return to the glorification of economic liberty that had once made reform in America so difficult. Harlan was of course aware of this history, but he insisted that the due process clause, however it had been misused in the past, remained the most convincing basis for invalidating the Connecticut ban on contraception.

Justices Potter Stewart and Hugo Black disagreed with the Court's judgment and with the reasons marshaled in its defense. Stewart called the Connecticut law "uncommonly silly." Black de-

[1]See Chapter XVI, "The Case of the Wenatchee Chambermaid."

clared it to be "every bit as offensive to me as it is to my Brethren." But neither justice could find a right to privacy either in the Bill of Rights, the Ninth Amendment, or the Fourteenth Amendment that could justify the Court's striking down the offending statute.

Stewart's and Black's dissents notwithstanding, Weddington and Coffee looked to *Griswold* in preparing their brief for the district court. Douglas's concern with the "privacy" of the marital bedroom did not, however, seem directly pertinent to their needs. And Harlan's attempt to resurrect substantive due process appeared too dangerous. They settled instead on Goldberg's theory that there were certain personal rights retained by the people through the Ninth Amendment. Was not abortion sufficiently like contraception to be subject to the same protection?

As the young lawyers approached the U.S. district court in Dallas, they felt confident. All three judges were known to be liberal. One was a woman, and another had just imposed a busing system on the local schools. The lawyers' optimism proved well founded.

The right to choose whether to have children is a right secured by the Ninth Amendment, the court declared in June 1970. That right was not absolute, but it was sufficiently fundamental that "the burden is on the defendant to demonstrate to the satisfaction of the Court that [the infringement of that right] is necessary to support a compelling state interest." The state had a legitimate interest in seeing that abortions were performed by competent persons, and it might also have an interest in protecting the "quickened" fetus. But it could not justify a statute that prohibited *all* abortions except those to save the life of the mother or that was so vague that doctors might be unsure whether they were breaking the law in performing abortions. District Attorney Wade having failed to demonstrate that the abortion law represented a compelling state interest, the Texas abortion law was unconstitutional.

The same month that the district court struck down the Texas abortion law, Norma McCorvey gave birth to a daughter. She had agreed to surrender the baby for adoption, but a nurse made a mistake and brought the baby to her. Then another nurse came in to take the baby away. "I just got out of that bed like you wouldn't believe," McCorvey later explained, "and I grabbed her and I said 'Hey, wait a minute, that's my kid.' " She was sedated and never saw the child again. For a while she worried about whether she had done the right thing in bringing suit. She wondered if perhaps people who spoke of abortion as the killing of babies were right. But in the end she concluded that abortion was needed to prevent the tragedy she had so often witnessed of unwanted children growing up hungry, dirty, neglected, and abused.

The state of Texas appealed *Roe* v. *Wade* directly to the Supreme Court, as was its right in a case decided by a three-judge federal court. Coffee was not able to take the time to work on the case after it was decided in the district court, but *Roe* v. *Wade* had attracted national attention, and a number of lawyers came to Weddington's aid in preparing the case for the Supreme Court. Most helpful were lawyers from Planned Parenthood, who regarded *Roe* as the appropriate sequel to *Griswold*.

On December 13, 1971, Sarah Weddington, just four years out of law school, stood before the justices of the Supreme Court for the first time. Waiting his turn to defend Texas's abortion statute was Jay Floyd, an assistant attorney general. Weddington told the Court that "pregnancy to a woman can completely disrupt her life." Many schools in Texas required that a teacher resign if she became pregnant. Employers often forced women to leave their jobs early in pregnancy, and the state provided no unemployment compensation or welfare for them. "So a pregnancy to a woman is perhaps one of the most determinative aspects of her life . . . [and] is a matter which is of such fundamental and basic concern to the woman involved, that she should be allowed to make the choice as to whether to continue or to terminate her pregnancy," Weddington continued.

On what provision of the Constitution, Justice Stewart wanted to know, was she relying in asserting this fundamental right? "We originally brought this suit," Weddington replied, "alleging both the due process clause, equal protection clause, the Ninth Amendment, and a variety of others. . . ."

"And anything else that might have been appropriate," interjected Justic Byron White sarcastically. Weddington laughed, but White had made his point. The Court was always reluctant to endorse that kind of broad constitutional claim.

"Well, do you or don't you say that the constitutional right [to have an abortion] . . . reaches up until the time of birth, or what?" White asked.

"The Constitution, as I see it, gives protection to people after birth," she answered.

Jay Floyd began his defense of the Texas law by arguing that the case was moot (no longer a controversy) because Jane Roe was no longer pregnant. One of the justices reminded him that this was a class action suit: "Surely you would, I suppose we could almost take judicial notice of the fact that there are, at any given time, unmarried pregnant females in the state of Texas." The audience erupted in laughter.

Floyd then moved on to his central argument. He asserted that the state of Texas had an interest in protecting fetal life. As for Weddington's argument that women should have control over their bodies, "Freedom over one's body . . . is not absolute," he stated. Many laws, such as those prohibiting the use of certain drugs, restricted one's personal freedom. Floyd concluded that the regulation of abortion was a matter of public policy that ought to be left to state legislatures.

Justice Thurgood Marshall was not satisfied. When, he asked, does a fetus come to have full constitutional rights?

"At any time, Mr. Justice; we make no distinction," Floyd answered. "There is life from the moment of impregnation."

"And do you have any scientific data to support that?" Marshall asked.

"Well, we begin, Mr. Justice, in our brief, with the development of the human embryo, carrying it through to the development of the fetus, from about seven to nine days after conception," Floyd answered.

"Well, what about six days?" Marshall asked, eliciting a chuckle from the audience.

"We don't know," Floyd answered.

"But this statute clearly goes back to one hour," Marshall said. Floyd was in trouble. Marshall saw no basis for the claim that a fetus had full constitutional rights, and he had doubts about a law that cast its protective net so broadly as to include a life that might not even exist.

The Court next turned to a related case from Georgia, *Doe* v.

Dalton, which the Court had decided to consider along with *Roe* v. *Wade.* After attorney Margie Pitt Hames summarized her client's case against the Georgia law that required abortions to be approved by two doctors and a hospital committee, Justice Harry Blackmun took up the questioning. He asked Hames about the widespread practice of requiring that medical panels—not simply one doctor—approve certain types of abortion, thus making them difficult to obtain.

Blackmun's three daughters and his wife had made him particularly aware of the abortion issue. Moreover, as a former lawyer for the Mayo Clinic in Minnesota he tended to sympathize with doctors, and he disapproved of excessive government interference with medicine practice. On the other hand, he generally held to the view expressed in *Munn* v. *Illinois*[2] that the states had broad power to decide what kind of legislation should be enacted to protect the health and welfare of the public.

At their first conference after the oral argument, the justices discussed their reactions. Since two new justices, Lewis Powell and William Rehnquist, had not yet been sworn in, the cases would be decided by a seven-man Court. Chief Justice Warren Burger seemed to favor upholding the laws and Byron White clearly wished to uphold them. William Douglas, William Brennan, and Thurgood Marshall strongly favored invalidating them. Potter Stewart and Harry Blackmun believed that at least some portions of the laws should be invalidated because they interfered unduly with the professional discretion of physicians. In short, at least five of the seven justices voted to disapprove some, if not all, of the abortion statutes.

Justice Douglas was elated. He had long hoped that the Supreme Court would deal with the abortion issue, but he had not expected that a majority of his colleagues would join him in striking down antiabortion statutes. His elation turned to indignation, however, when, the following afternoon, Burger assigned to Blackmun the task of writing the Court's opinion in *Roe* v. *Wade*. The Chief Justice had the right to assign the writing of opinions for cases in which he was a member of the majority, but in the abortion cases Douglas was sure Burger was not. Therefore he, as the senior member of the majority, should decide who would write the opinion.

[2]See Chapter VIII, "The Case of the Unscrupulous Warehouseman."

This was not a procedural quibble. It was an election year, and Douglas believed that Burger had a political motive. President Richard Nixon, who had appointed him, favored restrictive abortion laws. Faced with the likelihood that the Court was going to strike them down, Burger had decided to stall until after the election by assigning the case to Blackmun, the Court's slowest writer and the justice least likely to write a strong majority opinion. Douglas protested, but Burger held firm. Blackmun was to write the opinion.

Blackmun was both pleased and concerned by the assignment. Public support for abortion had grown steadily. But as support had grown, so too had opposition. No matter what Blackmun wrote, he would anger many people. However, he agreed that Burger could only have assigned the case to him. Douglas was far too liberal. Brennan was a Catholic and should not be subjected to the attacks of antiabortion groups. Marshall should not be made to appear to be writing an opinion of special benefit to blacks. Stewart was the only other possible choice, but he did not have Blackmun's medical background. Douglas was being terribly unfair in assuming that he could not act independently in this matter, Blackmun believed. It was true that he had known Burger from his childhood in St. Paul, but he was no "Minnesota Twin."

When Blackmun began to work on his opinion, he concluded that the problem posed by the abortion cases was in essence medical. When a state licensed doctors, it was entrusting them with the power to make medical decisions. State laws restricting abortions interfered with that power. Abortions were no more dangerous than minor surgery. To bar them completely or to require complicated review boards to monitor doctors' decisions was unjustifiable. As counsel to the Mayo clinic Blackmun had advised the staff on the legality of the abortions the hospital had performed, and many of his recommendations would not have satisfied the Georgia and Texas laws.

That winter Blackmun secluded himself for hours in the justices' library, poring over histories of English and American law on abortion, studying the medical evidence on the safety of abortions and the scientific evidence on fetal development. In May 1972, only weeks before the end of the term, he finished a rough draft and circulated it among the justices. Everyone saw problems in the draft.

It concluded that abortion was permissible early in pregnancy but not later, that abortion laws infringed doctors' professional judgment, and that the Texas law was vague and thus unconstitutional. But the bases for these conclusions were not clear. Nevertheless, Stewart, Douglas, Brennan, and Marshall agreed to go along with Blackmun's opinion. As Douglas put it, Blackmun had come a long way. Only White dissented, but he did so in strong terms at the next conference. Striking down the Texas law for vagueness was simply stupid. The statute might have serious defects, but vagueness was not one of them—it could not be more specific in delineating the circumstances when abortion was permitted.

Blackmun was deeply disturbed by White's attack, and as he reviewed his draft he decided to work on it further. Once again, Douglas seethed. He was sure that this was another trick concocted by Burger to delay the opinion until after the election. But in conference a majority of the justices decided to put the case over. In the new term two new justices would join the bench. Nine justices would speak more authoritatively than seven.

Over the summer Blackmun returned to Rochester, Minnesota, to redraft his opinion. Each day he spoke with his clerk in Washington, who incorporated changes into the text. The right to an abortion, Blackmun now concluded, was rooted in the right to privacy, identified in *Griswold.* It was not absolute, being limited by the state's interest in protecting the pregnant woman's health and the potential life of the fetus. The crucial question was, When did the interest in protecting the life of the fetus outweigh the woman's right to privacy? The Constitution offered no answer. But Blackmun believed that medicine did. Doctors typically divided pregnancy into three stages. Abortions were generally safe in the first trimester and, under proper conditions, could be performed safely in the second trimester. But after six months the fetus became viable, that is, able to live on its own. At that point the state's interest in protecting the health of the mother and the potential life of the fetus seemed to converge. Blackmun's new draft emerged as a strong prohibition against the state regulation of abortions before the third trimester.

After the Court reconvened, a second round of oral argument took place on October 11, 1972. The justices met in conference the next day. Blackmun made an impassioned argument for striking down the abortion laws. He persuaded five of his eight colleagues to join him. The new justices split, Powell joining the majority and Rehnquist the dissenters. Burger was still undecided.

But Blackmun's revised draft raised new questions in the minds of the other majority justices. Brennan had several concerns. By tying the state's interest in fetal life to viability, the Court risked the possibility that medical advances would push viability into ever-earlier stages of pregnancy. In addition, Blackmun treated the state's interest in the fetus and in maternal health as closely related, but they were not. They should be treated separately. Finally, the draft focused on the rights of doctors and the state. It did not say enough about the most important party, the pregnant woman. Blackmun had alluded to the right of privacy established by *Griswold*, but he had not explained the relationship between the right to use contraceptives and the right to have an abortion.

During the previous term, Brennan had attempted to build a bridge between contraception and abortion. While Blackmun had been working on his first draft, Brennan had written the majority opinion in *Eisenstadt* v. *Baird,* which overturned the conviction of a man charged with distributing birth control devices without a license. This opinion concluded: "If the right to privacy means anything, it is the right of the individual, married or single, to be free from unwarranted governmental intrusion into matters so fundamentally affecting a person as the decision to bear or beget a child." The case dealt only with contraception, the decision not to beget a child, but Brennan had added the reference to the decision to "bear" a child with abortion in mind. Brennan gave Blackmun a forty-eight-page summary of his thoughts and suggestions.

Blackmun thought he saw a way to satisfy one of Brennan's concerns and at the same time win the vote of Burger, who refused to join the majority so long as the opinion permitted unrestricted abortions up to viability. Instead of one dividing point, viability, Blackmun would create two. Early abortions would be unrestricted, but the state could intervene after the first trimester to regulate abortions to protect the health of the mother, and after the second to protect the potential life of the fetus.

Eliminating a single dividing line mollified Burger, but now Marshall objected. He thought the new arrangement worked to the disadvantage of poor and ill-educated women who might not get to a doctor until after the first trimester. Marshall preferred Blackmun's original linkage to viability. If viability were the cutoff point, it would better protect the rural poor. Someday viability might be reduced to a few weeks in fancy hospitals in Boston, but that was not likely to happen in rural Alabama. Poor women needed to be allowed more time.

Blackmun compromised. He kept the first dividing line, but, respecting Marshall's understanding of social problems, he made "viability" the second dividing line. States could regulate the Conditions under which abortions were performed after the first trimester to protect women's health, but they could not *prohibit* abortions until after viability. As a practical matter the rural poor would be able to get abortions up until the final weeks of pregnancy.

With the problem of dividing lines resolved, Stewart mentioned two further changes that he thought ought to be made. He wanted a specific statement that a fetus is not a person within the meaning of the Fourteenth Amendment. No decision had ever held that it was, but Stewart believed that the Court would be better off with only one set of rights to defend, those of women. Blackmun thought that the point was implicit in the opinion, but he agreed to include it.

Stewart was also bothered by the continuing weakness of the constitutional basis of the right to an abortion. Although he had dissented in *Griswold,* he believed in following precedent and had accepted the Court's judgment that a state could not ban the use of contraceptives. But he still did not like Douglas's zones of privacy. The protection in the Bill of Rights against the snooping of the state had little to do with contraception and even less to do with abortion. Following Harlan's concurrence in *Griswold,* Stewart had come to believe that the right to an abortion, much like the right to use contraceptives, was a matter of personal liberty, protected by the due process clause of the Fourteenth Amendment. He urged Blackmun to adopt this view. Again Blackmun compromised. Without abandoning Douglas's "penumbras," he added a statement saying that privacy was also protected by the concept of liberty guaranteed by the Fourteenth Amendment.

Curiously, no justice endorsed the district court's reliance on the Ninth Amendment, though it offered an even greater open-endedness than the due process clause without any of the latter's unfortu-

QUARRELS THAT HAVE SHAPED THE CONSTITUTION

nate historical baggage. The silence of nearly two hundred years, however, discouraged most judges from seeking a basis there for establishing fundamental rights. Justice Goldberg had relied on it in *Griswold,* but only in a concurrence and he was no longer on the Court. None of those deciding *Roe* found sufficient basis in the Ninth Amendment to rest his opinion on it.

The justices' clerks found the open brokering among their bosses hard to swallow. Justices often wrote concurrences if they wished to join the majority in a particular decision but disagreed with the reasons given for that decision in the majority opinion. Rarely, however, did justices intervene so directly in the writing of the opinion itself. In the clerks' view the pulling and hauling over the opinion in *Roe* made the justices look like politicians, not judges.

The atmosphere that so unsettled the clerks could hardly have been avoided, however, unless the justices had turned a deaf ear to the social revolution taking place outside their chambers. Women were questioning the roles they had traditionally played in American society, and the practical effects of this questioning were already apparent. In March 1972 Congress had passed the Equal Rights Amendment and sent it to the states for possible ratification. A year earlier the Court had overturned an Idaho law that gave men preference over women as administrators of estates. And listed on the Court's docket for the 1972–73 term was a case that challenged the army's policy of denying to women officers benefits routinely given to men. *Frontiero* v. *Richardson,* as the case was called, raised the boldest constitutional claim yet made on behalf of women: that the Court should apply to sex the same "strict scrutiny" it had long given race in reviewing laws that limited women's rights.

The justices were being forced by both the women's movement and the cases confronting them to think about equality and liberty in new ways. In the long months since Sarah Weddington had first stood before them, a solid majority of the justices had come to the conclusion that the right to have an abortion was fundamental. The Constitution and its history offered scant guidance as to how that conclusion could be justified, but the social changes taking place prompted nearly all of the justices to search for a larger meaning within the constitutional provisions safeguarding equality and liberty than previous decisions had identified. In the end, only White and Rehnquist dissented. Rehnquist believed that the case was moot, and both thought that the states, not the Supreme Court, should decide when abortions were permissible.

No one knew what Burger planned to do until January 12, 1973, when he announced at a conference that he was going to join the majority, but needed a week to write a concurring opinion. Brennan and Stewart were convinced that he was stalling again. He would be administering the oath to Richard Nixon at his second inauguration on January 20. They believed that he wanted to avoid the embarrassment of swearing in the man who had appointed him just after having agreed to a politically explosive decision that repudiated the President's views on the subject. Though disgruntled by the further loss of time, the justices agreed to a ten-day delay.

On January 22, 1973, Blackmun announced the Court's long-awaited ruling in the case of *Roe* v. *Wade.* The decision began with a frank acknowledgment of the "sensitive and emotional nature of the abortion controversy, of the vigorous opposing views, even among physicians, and of the deep and seemingly absolute convictions that the subject inspires." Blackmun recalled the dissenting words of Justice Oliver Wendell Holmes, Jr., in *Lochner* v. *New York:* "[The Constitution] is made for people of fundamentally differing views, and the accident of our finding certain opinions natural and familiar or novel and even shocking ought not to conclude our judgment upon the question whether statutes embodying them conflict with the Constitution of the United States."

The case was not moot, Blackmun continued. "The normal 266-day human gestation period is so short that the pregnancy will come to term before the usual appellate process is complete. If that termination makes a case moot, pregnancy litigation seldom will survive much beyond the trial state, and appellate review will be effectively denied."

Blackmun next reviewed the ways that abortion was treated in philosophy, law, and medicine, stressing the recent vintage of restrictive laws and the fact that abortions, once so dangerous, could now be performed with less risk than childbirth entailed. To the extent that the laws passed a century before were premised on a desire to protect women from the danger of having an abortion, these laws could no longer be justified. Medical progress had rendered them irrelevant because abortions had become relatively simple and safe procedures, especially in the first trimester.

More important, Blackmun continued, the Constitution guaranteed citizens a right to privacy broad enough to include the right to have an abortion. Though the Constitution does not explicitly mention a right to privacy, that right could be found in the "penumbras" of the Bill of Rights, as they apply to the states through the Fourteenth Amendment. Almost in passing he added that the right of privacy could also be found in the concept of liberty guaranteed by the Fourteenth Amendment. Although the right to have an abortion was not absolute, it was not offset by the existence of the fetus, for the fetus was not a person within the meaning of the Fourteenth Amendment. An abortion could not be performed without the concurrence of a responsible physician, however, and after the first trimester, abortions could be subject to state regulation aimed at protecting the health of the mother.

Finally, Blackmun addressed the troubling issue of the states' interest in protecting the unborn fetus. Texas, he observed, asserted that life begins at conception. "We need not resolve the difficult question of when life begins," he responded, in order to say that "we do not agree that, by adopting one theory of life, Texas may override the rights of the pregnant woman that are at stake." Blackmun concluded that the state's interest in protecting potential life did not become "compelling" until viability. After that point states could prohibit abortion, except under circumstances in which the life or health of the mother was in danger.

Justices Stewart, Douglas, and Burger issued concurring opinions that reflected the special concerns they had voiced throughout the abortion debate. Stewart wrote that whatever the Court may have said, its decisions in both *Griswold* and *Roe* could be rationally understood only as holding that the contraception and abortion statutes under review "substantively invaded the 'liberty' that is protected by the Due Process Clause of the Fourteenth Amendment." Burger, troubled by the potential sweep of the Court's holding, added that "the Court today rejects any claim that the Constitution requires abortions on demand." And Douglas reiterated his conviction that, "with all respect" to Stewart, neither *Griswold* nor *Roe* had anything to do with substantive due process.

Justices White and Rehnquist dissented. Neither could find anything in the language or history of the Constitution to support the Court's judgment, and both concluded therefore that the abortions issue ought to be "left with the people" and to their elected representatives. "As an exercise of raw judicial power," White declared, "the Court perhaps has authority to do what it does today; but in my view its judgment is an improvident and extravagant exercise of the power of judicial review that the Constitution extends to this Court."

Despite its importance, the decision of *Roe* v. *Wade* did not attract as much immediate attention as had been anticipated. Former President Lyndon Baines Johnson died the same day, and the news so dominated the media that the abortion decision got relatively little newspaper or television coverage. Blackmun was understandably disappointed.

Norma McCorvey first learned of the Court's decision from her roommate, who saw the story in a newspaper. When McCorvey began to cry, her roommate looked at the paper and said, "Don't tell me you knew LBJ?" McCorvey had never mentioned her role in the case. "I'm Jane Roe," she replied.

Two days later Sarah Weddington called. "How does it make you feel to know that women are going to be able to go to a clinic and get a legal abortion?"

"It makes me feel like I'm on the top of Mount Everest," McCorvey answered.

Reactions to the decision were just as intense among others who had followed the case closely. Women's rights groups and members of birth control organizations were jubilant, though many lamented the power still accorded physicians over abortion decisions. On the other hand, Catholic organizations and Protestant fundamentalists condemned the Court's judgment. As the years passed, *Roe* v. *Wade* came to figure in American political debates as had no other decision since the school desegregation case, *Brown* v. *Board of Education* (1954).[3] Antiabortionists decried the destruction of fetal life and deplored the threat to motherhood they believed the legalization of abortion entailed. They sought a constitutional amendment that would grant full rights to fetuses from the moment of conception. They also persuaded Congress not to fund abortions for poor women. Yet polls showed that public support for the right of women

[3]See Chapter XVIII, "The School Desegregation Case."

to choose whether or not to bear a child continued to grow. However passionate the opposition to *Roe,* a substantial majority of the population came to believe, as one poll found, "that abortion is sometimes the best thing in a bad situation."

The popular acceptance of abortion, at least in "bad situations," stands in sharp contrast, however, to scholarly opinion of the Court's abortion decision. Few opinions in the Court's history have drawn as much criticism as *Roe* v. *Wade.* The dissents have nothing to do with abortion. Rather, the dispute is about the legitimate extent of judicial review.

Over the past thirty years the Court has often been criticized for its judicial activism. *Brown* was condemned for going beyond the original meaning of the equal protection clause. The criminal procedure cases of the 1960s, of which *Miranda* v. *Arizona* (1965) is the most famous, were denounced for extending the protection of certain procedural guarantees beyond what the framers could have intended. Yet these cases were linked to specific provisions of the Constitution. *Roe* was not.

Blackmun quoted Justice Holmes's dissent in *Lochner,* but many legal authorities claimed that, like the majority in that case, he had created a fundamental right for which the Constitution provided inadequate grounding. Even those who believed that the Court was justified in identifying a right to abortion lamented Blackmun's failure to link that right to any body of law or inherited tradition. In particular, Blackmun had failed to explain why the abortion right should be considered more worthy of constitutional protection than other rights that the Constitution does not guarantee, such as the right to contract to work sixteen hours a day, or the right to refuse medical treatment. Why should the Court protect the right to abortion and not protect the economic freedom that the *Lochner* case had endorsed? Or the right to die?

The scholarly reaction against *Roe* raises serious questions about how the decision has shaped the Constitution. The justices thought they were taking the next logical step along a course of liberal jurisprudence that had been charted years before: mediating between the conflicting claims of private right and public good. The critics have seen it as a radical leap beyond the bounds of the Constitution, a return to *Lochner.*

Some scholars have argued that with the *Roe* decision the Court took a dangerously antidemocratic turn. It became, they charge, a superguardian, imposing its values on legislatures, rather than limiting itself to the resolution of those issues that the Constitution had given it the authority to decide. Despite having conceded that there was wide disagreement over the question of when life begins, for instance, the Court decided to override state laws rather than defer to them. It identified no authority for doing so. When a legislature decides that life begins at a certain point, it can claim that its choice represents, in an imperfect way, the will of the people. But no appointed court can rest its strength on an appeal to the democratic principle when it invokes the doctrine of judicial review. In the case of the Supreme Court, only the provisions of the Constitution and the values inferable from them stand between it and the charge of arbitrary decision making based upon naked political preferences. Many who hold this opinion favor the right to have an abortion and yet have trouble finding a basis in the Constitution for striking down state restrictive laws. To them *Roe* serves as an example of unrestrained judicial power.

Others maintain, however, that the lesson of *Roe* is very different, that the decision revealed the inadequacy of a jurisprudence confined too rigidly by the explicit language of the Constitution. According to this view, the Court did not exceed its authority in identifying a fundamental right not explicitly spelled out in the Constitution. But embarrassing memories of *Lochner* v. *New York* kept it from properly justifying what it had done. The Court had identified a right grounded in the "liberty" guaranteed by the Fourteenth Amendment without clearly saying so and without explaining why that right should be accorded more importance than the competing state interest of protecting fetal life.

Many issues of personal liberty raised in post–New Deal constitutional history could have been treated more coherently, these critics argue, if the Supreme Court had never abandoned the substantive due process argument. If it had conceded the importance of economic liberty but had concluded that in a modern economy labor legislation serves a public purpose that outweighs that private right, substantive due process could have continued to serve as a license for articulating fundamental values without jeopardizing the New Deal reforms. The Court would have found it easier to decide *Griswold,* for instance, if it could have treated the use of contraceptives as an aspect of personal liberty, rather than straining to connect it to free speech and the freedom from search and seizure. In short, if the Court had not abandoned substantive due process, it could have faced earlier the problem it has had to face since *Roe*—justifying more convincingly its choice of certain rights as fundamental, and of determining what public interests are sufficiently compelling to outweigh them.

The debate concerns the most basic problem of our political system: how to resolve the tension inherent in our Constitution between a respect for majority rule and a commitment to individual liberty. Whenever the Court attempts to mediate between a claim of liberty denied (such as that made by Jane Roe) and a conflicting public interest (such as Texas's desire to protect potential life), the Court poses a threat to majority rule and risks losing the popular respect on which its power ultimately rests. Whenever it abjures that mediating function, however, it risks sacrificing the individual liberty without which democracy cannot survive.

For Harry Blackmun the controversy that surrounded his opinion in *Roe* v. *Wade* proved painful. Thousands of letters poured into the Court, damning him for the decision. Gradually, the attacks wore him down. At breakfast with his clerks, when the discussion turned to *Roe,* Blackmun would pick up his water glass reflectively, turn it slightly on edge, and stare into it in silence.

A few months after handing down the opinion, however, Blackmun had an experience that cheered him. He gave a speech at Emory Law School in Atlanta. Afterwards, as he chatted with students and faculty, a young woman ran up the steps to the stage. She squeezed through the group, threw her arms around Blackmun, and burst into tears, saying, "I'll never be able to thank you for what you have done." She then turned and ran from the room.

Blackmun was startled. He suspected that the woman was probably someone who had been able to obtain an abortion after the Court's decision. But he was wrong. "Mary Doe," the married woman who had joined Norma McCorvey in filing the suit against the Texas abortion law, had just embraced him.

*   *   *

Epilogue: After the abortion decision Norma McCorvey continued to live in relative obscurity in Dallas, fearing that she would become the target of antiabortionists. By the mid-1980s, however, she had become active in the abortion rights movement. She worked with feminist groups, appeared at rallies, and in the summer of 1987 agreed to appear in a television documentary about *Roe* v. *Wade*, to be aired as part of the bicentennial celebration of the Constitution. In that documentary she made a startling revelation—she had never been raped! Indeed, she had never left Dallas. She became pregnant, she told interviewer Carl T. Rowan, "through what I thought was love," but decided to seek an abortion "because of economic reasons." The rape story evolved out of her desire to win sympathy and, she hoped, exemption from the tough Texas antiabortion statute.

Norma McCorvey's recantation has no legal significance, for never in the lengthy process of litigation did her lawyers ever mention the word rape. Her admission does, however, have important historical meaning. When she became pregnant in 1969, society scorned unwed mothers, Texas prohibited abortion, and poverty stood in the way of seeking help elsewhere. That she claimed to have been raped underscores how little liberty there was for one who was poor, unmarried, and pregnant in the years before *Roe* v. *Wade*.

Index

(Page numbers in **boldface** indicate illustrations)